D1566245

Transmission Analysis in Communication Systems
Volume 2

ELECTRICAL ENGINEERING, COMMUNICATIONS, AND SIGNAL PROCESSING

ISSN 0888-2134
Raymond L. Pickholtz, Series Editor
William W Wu, Series Editor

OTHER WORKS OF INTEREST

*These previously published books are in the *Electrical Engineering, Communications, and Signal Processing* series but they are not numbered within the volume itself. All future volumes in this series will be numbered.

Transmission Analysis in Communication Systems
Volume 2

Osamu Shimbo
International Telecommunications
Satellite Organization (INTELSAT)

COMPUTER SCIENCE PRESS

Computer Science Press
1803 Research Boulevard
Rockville, Maryland 20850

1 2 3 4 5 6 Printing   Year   93 92 91 90 89 88

Shimbo, Osamu, 1931-
Transmission analysis in communication systems / Osamu Shimbo.
p. cm.—(Electrical engineering communications and signal
processing series; 11)
Bibliography: p.
Includes index.

ISBN 7167-8151-4
1. Modulation theory. I. Title. II. Series.

TK5102.5S475 1988
621.38'043—dc19

                                                            87-34199
                                                            CIP

CONTENTS

PREFACE

The author experienced several revolutionary changes in communication transmission systems during his contributions of over thirty years to the industry. Initially, the terrestrial microwave FDM/FM (TV/FM) and coaxial cable FDM systems were introduced to overcome the fading problems of the H.F. radio transmission systems. These new transmission systems helped increase the channel capacities of telephone and data channel tremendously. After these systems were developed, research for operational applicability was done on milimeter transmission systems to obtain more channel capacity. But it was found that this system was not suitable because of the insufficient performance of the circular wave guides. Then, PCM systems using terrestrial cables and PSK/PCM microwave terrestrial systems began to be successfully applied in operations around 1960. Also starting from around 1965, satellite communications systems were successfully introduced by INTELSAT, and they became one of the most important international communications systems which made the transmission of live TV pictures possible for the first time. Finally, optical fibre communication systems were introduced in operations around 1975 and are still being developed.

While there are many books on communication theory applications, the author tried to write a book based on his industrial experiences of more than thirty years in these areas, which would be of a high theoretical level and very practical for the analysis of communication transmission systems. The material in this book, mostly computerized and utilized in operational systems, is of a high theoretical level, although it cannot be exactly called academic because it comes entirely from industrial experiences. The author believes that this book is a very useful tool to educate graduate students because it can be immediately applied to operational systems and because it improves the knowledge of professional engineers in this area. The author also hopes that his book can be used as an important reference in the field of transmission analysis.

Chapter 1

INTRODUCTION

Transmission Analysis in Communication Systems is written for undergraduate and graduate students, system engineers, and professionals in communications engineering to help them understand and develop the theoretical analysis of modulation, demodulation, and transmission systems in depth. This book is also intended to be a textbook in undergraduate and graduate schools for a communications engineering curriculum. Therefore, it is written in a self-contained manner so that readers can follow the development of material without referring to other references or books.

However, some elementary knowledge of theories of random processes and special functions is required. These topics are usually taught in undergraduate or graduate school courses.

Transmission Analysis in Communication Systems is based on the author's thirty years of experience in communication engineering industries. Most materials in this book have been applied and computerized for the analysis and design of real communication systems in which the author worked or is now working. Those industries include OKI in Japan, Hirst Research Centre of General Electric Company in England, Bell Northern in Canada, COMSAT Laboratories, American Satellite, Computer Science, Satellite Business Systems and currently INTELSAT in the U.S.A.

Some analytical techniques (e.g., intermodulation, modulation transfer, and transmission optimization techniques based on theories described in this book) have been computerized and are still being used throughout the world by INTELSAT member countries.

Volume I of *Transmission Analysis in Communication Systems* is a preparation for reading the second volume. Thus, Volume I concentrates on providing fundamental information regarding baseband modulation and carrier modulation. In addition, the mathematics used in Volumes I and II and power spectrum analysis are described.

In Volume II, single carrier and multi-carrier transmission problems related to thermal noise, filtering, nonlinear devices, and interferences are analyzed in depth. The analyses in Volume II are advanced and highly theoretical and are therefore recommended mainly for graduate students and professional engineers in this field. On the other hand, Volume I is recommended for senior undergraduate and graduate students who have no extensive knowledge in this area.

Chapter 2 of Volume I presents the mathematics required to understand the analysis of this book. It is recommended that readers pursue this chapter before they start the following chapters, or, when they encounter mathematical difficulties, they should come back to this chapter. The mathematical formulae are explained in as physical terms as possible in connection with engineering problems. In this chapter, Q-functions, Gaussian functions, error probabilities, Hermite functions, δ functions and modified δ functions, Fourier series, power series, Fourier transforms, Hankel and Hilbert transforms, autocorrelation functions, characteristics functions, theory of nonlinear devices, etc., are described.

In Chapter 3 of Volume I, most important practical problems in the area of baseband modulation and transmission are analyzed. The term "modulation" here means that the information to be transmitted is converted to a signal form, which is more suitable for transmission through such transmission media as microwave, satellites, or cables. In the case of baseband transmission, the high frequency carrier (a sine wave) is not used, i.e., the spectrum of this signal is centered around a low frequency, which is not suitable for transmission through the air but possible through cables. In Chapter 4 of Volume I, cases where the carrier is used for this conversion so that the signal may be transmitted through the air are analyzed. Analog and digital baseband modulations are analyzed separately and timing and framing synchronizations are explained, which are required for digital baseband transmission.

Chapter 4 of Volume I also explains the carrier modulation and demodulation of many signals. The carrier here refers to that high frequency sinusoidal wave whose amplitude, phase, or frequency is modulated by an information waveform to be transmitted or a baseband modulated signal. The latter modulation is naturally a double modulation (baseband modulation first and carrier modulation second). Thus, there are amplitude, phase and frequency (frequency is the derivation of phase), and hybrid modulations.

In amplitude modulation, there are cases with and without residual carrier power (after modulation) and cases with and without double sidebands. In frequency modulation, there are SCPC/FM, FDM/FM, TV/FM (analog modulations), and FSK (digital modulation). In phase modulation, there are M-ary PSK, staggered PSK, and MSK, which are all in the digital modulation category. There are analog phase modulation techniques, but they are not described in this book, since this type of modulation is not common in practice and it is actually a modification of an FM signal (an integral of FM). There are also hybrid modulations. Finally, carrier and bit timing recovery is analyzed. The former is required in both analog and digital modulations and the latter is required only in digital modulation.

Signals in this chapter are all represented in ideal forms; i.e., there is no distortion due to filters or nonlinear devices and no interference is added except the thermal noise. Note that some distortions are analyzed in Chapter 3. The distortions and interference of modulated carriers are analyzed in Volume II, Chapters 2, 3, and 5, respectively.

In Chapter 5 of Volume I, the power spectra of modulated carriers are analyzed in theoretical detail, i.e., those of FM and PM signals. The power spectra of carrier modulated signals are an important tool in deciding the signal transmission bandwidth and in the analysis of interference.

For FM modulations, FDM/FM, SCPC/FM, TV/FM (analog), and FSK (digital) and energy dispersal cases are analyzed. In FSK both the phase continuous and discontinuous cases are analyzed, which are very different in power spectrum distribution. In phase modulations, the M-ary PSK and MSK are analyzed and correlated random variable cases are also treated.

Chapter 2 of Volume II discusses single carrier transmission and Chapter 3 of Volume II multi-carrier transmission.

Chapter 2 of Volume II analyzes the effects of filters, thermal noise, and nonlinear devices on FM and PSK signals. Linear and nonlinear interactions of various signals are analyzed separately in Volume II, in Chapters 3 and 5.

Chapter 3 in Volume II analyzes the intermodulation products (and related problems) and modulation transfer due to AM/AM and AM/PM characteristics of nonlinear devices when a plural number of modulated carriers are amplified through a common nonlinear device.

Chapter 4 in Volume II explains the concept of multiple access techniques (time division, frequency division, and coded division multiple access) and reports on overall transmission optimization under these multiple access transmission systems. A thorough understanding of this multiple access technique is important only for those readers who wish to master the content of this book; it is not required for the average reader. A detailed analysis of transmission system optimization is not included since this area is not yet fully developed. However, an understanding of the other chapters in this book will enable the reader to appreciate the detailed mathematical presentations of this chapter.

In Chapter 5 of Volume II, the interference between various signals such as FDM/FM, TV/FM, SCPC/FM, SCPC/PSK, continuous mode PSK, and TDMA/PSK (there are 36 combinations in all) signals is described separately. Interference between a particular set of signals will have special properties. This is the reason why each of the 36 combinations is analyzed separately. The analysis of this chapter is dependent for the most part on the results of Chapter 5 in Volume I, but in some cases time-domain analysis is needed because of filter transients. It is the author's intention to write additional volumes on Transmission Analysis in Communication Systems covering new developments in the field.

Chapter 2

TRANSMISSION IMPAIRMENTS: SINGLE CARRIER TRANSMISSION ANALYSIS

2.0 INTRODUCTION

Chapter 2 discusses single carrier transmission where no interaction with other carriers is assumed except for thermal noise; the distortions of a single modulated carrier due to filters and nonlinear devices with thermal noise are analyzed first. For FM cases, the filter distortions (and echo distortions), and the nonlinear effects are first analyzed. Then, the effects of the thermal noise above, at and below threshold are discussed in detail. The effects of pre-emphasis, of the mechanism of the threshold extension method, and the FSK signal transmission are also explained. For digital phase modulations, the effects of filters (inter-symbol interferences), thermal noise, and nonlinear devices are analyzed. The signals of these cases are PSK, MSK, DPSK, TDMA/PSK, etc. Finally, Chapter 2 covers the transmission problems of analog and digital amplitude and phase modulation (APM).

When a single signal is transmitted from a terminal to another terminal through a channel, the signal will be distorted by filters and nonlinear devices such as TWTA or SSPA, even though no other signal is interfering with it. This is called signal distortion in single carrier transmission cases. In this chapter, the signal transmission channel is modeled as shown in Figure 2.1. The type of signals which can be used at this time and most likely in the future is as follows:

FM signals (FDM/FM, SCPC/FM)
PSK signals (continuous PSK signals, TDMA PSK signals)
SCPC/PSK signals
TV/FM signals
SSB signals
AP analog modulated signals
AP digital modulated signals.

In the following Sections, for each signal listed above, the signal distortions produced by the channel model shown in Figure 6.1, when there is no interaction

4

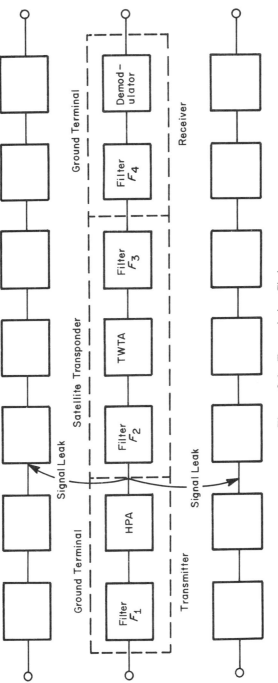

Although the transmission chain shown below is for satellite communications, the other cases are small modifications of this case.

Figure 2.1 Transmission Chains

with other signals (single carrier transmission), will be analyzed. Accordingly, cochannel interferences, adjacent channel interferences, intermodulation products, modulation transfers which are produced by interactions with other signals, are not considered in Chapter 2. These are discussed in Chapters 3 and 5.

2.1   FM TRANSMISSION

In general, an FM signal can be represented as

$$e_i(t) = A \cos(\omega_0 t + \phi(t) + \theta) \qquad (2.1.1)$$

where A, $\phi(t)$, θ and ω_0 represent respectively the amplitude, modulating phase, phase constant and angular carrier frequency. In FM modulation, $(2\pi)^{-1}\phi(t)'$ is the baseband signal. More particularly, this baseband signal consists of the frequency division multiplexed (FDM) voice channels described in Section 3.1.4 of Volume 1 in the FDM/FM signals case. In the SCPC/FM signals, it represents a single voice. In this book, the following complex form will be used for the function $e_i(t)$ defined in Equation 2.1.1 because of mathematical convenience

$$e_i(t) = A \exp[j\omega_0 t + \phi(t) + \theta]. \qquad (2.1.2)$$

The instantaneous frequency of Equations 2.1.1 and 2.1.2 is given by

$$f_0 + \frac{1}{2\pi} \frac{d}{dt} \phi(t) \qquad (2.1.3)$$

where

$$f_0 = \frac{\omega_0}{2\pi}. \qquad (2.1.4)$$

For the FDM/FM signals with more than 60 active channels, $\phi(t)$ (or $\phi'(t)$) can be assumed to be a Gaussian process as explained in Section 3.1.4 of Volume 1.

In cases where the number of active channels of FDM/FM signal is fewer than 60, or in SCPC/FM cases, $\phi(t)$ (or $\phi'(t)$) is a complicated non-stationary random process. Therefore, these cases are much harder to analyze.

In this Section, the thermal noise effects on FM signals and the analysis of FM distortions due to filters are first shown. The combined effect of this distortion with nonlinear devices (HPA and TWTA or SSPA), as shown in Figure 2.1, is then analyzed.

2.1.1   Filter Distortions of FM Signals

The following approaches to calculate the FM distortions due to filters have been commonly used:

(i) Power series expansion of transfer function of filters.
(ii) Fourier series expansion of transfer function of filters.

(iii) Assuming the distortion is much smaller than the signal, expanding it in power series (in time domain) without using any approximation for the filter transfer function of the filter.
(iv) Assuming the modulation index is small, the second order, third order and fifth order distortions are only considered (or second and third order only).

Before describing the details of these applications, a general analysis to obtain the FM distortion is given.

Assume that the FM signal represented by Equation 2.1.2 is passed through a bandpass filter whose transfer function is given by

$$Y_c(f) = Y_{c+}(f-f_0) + Y_{c-}(f+f_0). \qquad (2.1.1.1)$$

$Y_{c+}(f-f_0)$ and $Y_{c-}(f+f_0)$ represent respectively the positive and negative frequency portions of the transfer function. It is assumed here that the bandpass filter is narrow enough so that $Y_{c+}(f-f_0)$ and $Y_{c-}(f+f_0)$ do not overlap.

In order for the impulse response of $Y_c(f)$ to be a real function, the following relation between Y_{c+} and Y_{c-} (Volume I, Section 2.8) must be satisfied:

$$Y_{c+}(f) = Y_{c-}(-f)^* \qquad (2.1.1.2)$$

where * denotes "complex conjugate of." Then the low-pass analog of the bandpass impulse response of $Y(f)$ is given by

$$h(t) = \int_{-\infty}^{\infty} Y_{c+}(f) \, e^{j2\pi ft} \, df. \qquad (2.1.1.3)$$

Using $h(t)$, the output of the filter $Y_c(t)$ when the input is $e_i(t)$, is given by

$$e_0(t) = A \, e^{j\omega_0 t + j\theta} \int_{-\infty}^{\infty} e^{j\phi(x)} \, h(t-x) \, dx \qquad (2.1.1.4)$$

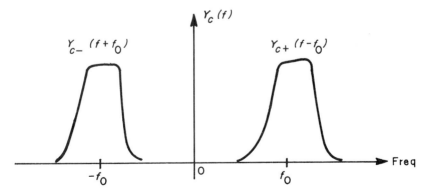

Figure 2.1.1.1 Transfer Function of Bandpass Filter Used for FM Filter Distortion Model

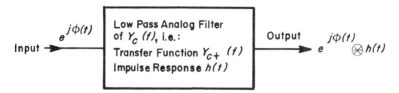

Figure 2.1.1.2 Low Pass Analog Model for FM Distortions

where the physical output of the filter, is $\mathrm{Re}\{e_0(t)\}$ ($\mathrm{Re}\{\ \}$ represents "real part of"). Rewrite $e_0(t)$ as

$$e_0(t) = B\{1 + \epsilon(t - t_0)\} \exp[j\omega_0(t - t_0) + j\phi(t - t_0) + j\,d(t - t_0)] \quad (2.1.1.5)$$

where ϵ and d are respectively the amplitude and phase distortions. B is the new amplitude of the signal modified by the filter and t_0 represents the time delay of the signal which takes normally the group delay value of the flat passband of the filter. However, to be more precise, t_0 should be chosen so that the power of $d(t)$ (or $\epsilon(t)$ in some cases) may be minimized. This makes the approximation of computation easier. In the FDM/FM cases, $d(t)$ contains some pure signal components because of a multiplexed channel structure, as explained in another Section later. In simple FM signal transmission where no nonlinearity is involved, the effect of the hardlimiter in the receiver eliminates the amplitude fluctuation due to $\epsilon(t)$ and the phase distortion $d(t)$ can be obtained by

$$d(t - t_0) = \mathrm{Im}\log\{e_0(t)/e_i(t - t_0)] \quad (2.1.1.6)$$

where Im denotes "Imaginary part of."

This form can be modified and approximated as follows:

$$d(t - t_0) = \mathrm{Im}\log\left[1 + \frac{e_0 - e_i}{e_i}\right] \simeq \mathrm{Im}\left\{\frac{e_0 - e_i}{e_i}\right\}$$

$$= \mathrm{Im}\left\{\frac{e_0}{e_i}\right\} \quad (2.1.1.7)$$

where it is assumed that

$$\left|\frac{e_0 - e_i}{e_i}\right| = \left|\frac{e_0 - e_i}{A}\right|,$$

$$\underset{\phi}{E}\left\{\left|\frac{e_0 - e_i}{e_i}\right|^2\right\} = \underset{\phi}{E}\left\{\left|\frac{(e_0 - e_i)}{A}\right|^2\right\} \quad (2.1.1.8)$$

is small enough to satisfy this approximation. Note here that $|e_i| = A$ because of the complex form for e_i defined by Equation 2.1.2. In most practical cases, the above approximation is valid. Thus,

$$d(t - t_0) \simeq \operatorname{Im}\{e^{-j\phi(t-t_0)} \int_{-\infty}^{\infty} e^{j\phi(x)} h(t - x) \, dx\}. \qquad (2.1.1.9)$$

In general, it is not easy to find t_0 minimizing $d(t)$ but t_0 can be good enough to be chosen as the group delay of the flat passband (usually the group delay value of $f = f_0$) so that the approximation of Equation 2.1.1.7 may be valid. Therefore, in the following, it is assumed that the value of the group delay of $Y_{c+}(f - f_0)$ in the passband (specifically that of $f = f_0$) is used for t_0. Another requirement to make $|e_0 - e_i/e_0|$ small enough so that the approximation of Equation 2.1.1.7 may be satisfied is that the gain of $Y_{c+}(f)$ (or $Y_c(f)$) must be unity (0 dB) in the flat passband area where the main signal spectrum passes through. Therefore, it is also assumed in the following that the gain (or loss) of the filter at the flat passband (more specifically $f = f_0$) is unity (0 dB).

As shown later, the distortion $d(t)$ contains components which are the pure signals for the individual channels of FDM/FM signal, although these must be considered as distortions for SCPC/FM and TV/FM signals.

2.1.1.1 Power Series Expansion of Filter Transfer Function

This approach has been used for many practical cases. However, it is only valid when the frequency deviation is small compared with the filter bandwidth (i.e., when there is no overdeviated case). Assume that $Y_{c+}(f)$ is expanded by a power series of frequency f as

$$Y_{c+}(f) = \sum_{k=0}^{\infty} a_k f^k \qquad (2.1.1.1.1)$$

where a_k is a complex number. Then, $h(t)$ defined by Equation 2.8.40 of Volume I (or 2.1.1.3 of Volume II) becomes

$$h(t) = \sum_{k=0}^{\infty} a_k \frac{1}{(2\pi j)^k} \delta^{(k)}(t) \qquad (2.1.1.1.2)$$

where $\delta^{(k)}(t)$ is the k-th derivation of δ-function.

Note here that, for a general function $g(t)$ whose k-th derivative exists,

$$\int_{-\infty}^{\infty} g(t) \, \delta^{(k)}(t) \, dt = (-1)^k \, g^{(k)}(0) \qquad (2.1.1.1.3)$$

where $g^{(k)}(t)$ is the k-th derivative of $g(t)$. Substituting $h(t)$ of Equation 2.1.1.1.2 into Equation 2.1.1.6, $e_0(t)$ becomes

$$e_0(t) = A \, e^{j\omega_0 t} \sum_{k=0}^{\infty} \left(\frac{1}{j2\pi}\right)^k a_k \int_{-\infty}^{\infty} e^{j\phi(t-x)} \delta^{(k)}(x) \, dx \qquad (2.1.1.1.4)$$

where applying Equation 2.1.1.1.3 into this result

$$\int_{-\infty}^{\infty} e^{j\phi(t-x)}\, \delta^{(k)}(x)\, dx \;=\; \frac{d^k}{dt^k}\{e^{j\phi(t)}\}. \qquad (2.1.1.1.5)$$

Thus, we have

$$e_0(t) \;=\; A\, e^{j\omega_0 t} \sum_{k=0}^{\infty} \left(\frac{1}{j2\pi}\right)^k a_k \frac{d^k}{dt^k}\{e^{j\phi(t)}\}. \qquad (2.1.1.1.6)$$

For example,

$$\frac{d}{dt}\, e^{j\phi(t)} \;=\; j\phi(t)'\, e^{j\phi(t)},$$

$$\frac{d^2}{dt^2}\, e^{j\phi(t)} \;=\; \{-\,[\phi(t)']^2 + j\phi(t)''\}e^{j\phi(t)},$$

$$\frac{d^3}{dt^3}\, e^{j\phi(t)} \;=\; \{j[-(\phi')^3 + \phi'''] - 3\phi'\phi''\}e^{j\phi}. \qquad (2.1.1.1.7)$$

In a case where the frequency deviation is not small compared with the filter bandwidth, many terms are required so as to obtain an accurate result, which is impractical. Assuming the normalizations on filter gain and group delay in passband are done, the distortion $d(t)$ is given by

$$d(t) \;\simeq\; \mathrm{Im}\left\{ \sum_{k=0}^{\infty} \frac{a_k}{(j2\pi)^k}\, e^{-j\phi(t)} \frac{d^k}{dt^k}[e^{j\phi(t)}] \right\}. \qquad (2.1.1.1.8)$$

If we use up to four terms ($k = 0, 1, 2, 3$) then,

$$d(t) \;=\; \mathrm{Im}\left\{ a_0 + \frac{a_1}{2\pi}\,\phi' - j\frac{a_2}{(2\pi)^2}\,\phi'' - \frac{a_3}{(2\pi)^3}\,\phi''' \right\}$$
$$+\; \mathrm{Im}\left\{ \frac{a_2}{(2\pi)^2}(\phi')^2 + \frac{a_3}{(2\pi)^3}[(\phi')^3 - j3\phi'\phi''] \right\}. \qquad (2.1.1.1.9)$$

Since $d(t)$ is the phase distortion, the demodulated distortion of the FM signal is given by

$$(2\pi)^{-1}\, d(t)' \;=\; \mathrm{Im}\left\{ \frac{a_1}{(2\pi)^2}\,\phi'' - j\frac{a_2}{(2\pi)^3}\,\phi''' - \frac{a_3}{(2\pi)^4}\,\phi'''' \right\}$$
$$+\; \mathrm{Im}\left\{ \frac{a_2}{(2\pi)^3}\,2\phi'\phi'' + \frac{a_3}{(2\pi)^4}\,[3\phi''(\phi')^2 \right.$$
$$\left. -\, j\,3(\phi'')^2 - j3\phi'\phi'''] \right\}$$
$$=\; \frac{1}{2\pi}\frac{d}{dt}\, d_1(t) + \frac{1}{2\pi}\frac{d}{dt}\, d_2(t). \qquad (2.1.1.1.10)$$

In TV/FM and SCPC/FM, the first term of Equation 2.1.1.1.10, $1/2\pi \, d_1'$ (linear components of $\phi^{(k)}$) and second term $1/2\pi \, d_2(t)'$ are considered to be the distortion, since the whole $\phi(t)$ itself is required to give an information (i.e., a picture or a voice), which is undesirable.

However, in a FDM/FM signal case, the $1/2\pi \, d_1$ component in $1/2\pi \, d(t)'$ should not be considered as a distortion component, since $\phi''(t)$, $\phi'''(t)$ and $\phi''''(t)$ are not distortions in this case. The proof of this fact is given as follows.

Represent the spectrum of $1/j2\pi \, \phi'$ as $Y_{\phi'}(f)$ (for a certain finite time period). Then the spectra of $\phi''/(j2\pi)^2$, $\phi'''/(j2\pi)^3$, and $\phi''''/(j2\pi)^4$ are respectively given by $fY_{\phi'}(f), f^2Y_{\phi'}(f), f^3Y_{\phi'}(f)$.

The change of these spectra in one channel is very small. ($Y_{\phi'}(f)$ of the FDM signal is limited between approximately 12 KHz and 4 MHz in satellite communications). Note here that the bandwidth of one channel is about 3.1 KHz. Thus, the level of each channel is slightly changed by the effect of $1/2\pi \, d_1(t)'$, since $1/2\pi \, d_1(t)'$ is usually small compared with the signal (each channel itself receives almost no distortion by $1/2\pi \, d_1(t)'$), while $1/2\pi \, d_2(t)'$ consists of the cross terms between channels in the FDM/FM baseband signal. For example, $\phi''(\phi')^2$ consists of a mixture of all the channels. Thus, we can say here for the evaluation of the FM distortions due to filters that:

(a) The averge power of $1/2\pi \, d/dt \, (d_1 + d_2)$ during a certain period of time should be evaluated for SCPC/FM and TV/FM cases, where $\phi'(t)$ is a video signal for TV/FM and a voice signal SCPC/FM.
(b) For the FDM/FM signal, the power spectrum of $1/2\pi \, d/dt \, d_2(t)$ must be evaluated, since each individual channel must be evaluated for the distortion, where

$$\frac{1}{2\pi}\frac{d}{dt}d_2(t) = \text{Im}\left\{\frac{a_2}{(2\pi)^3}2\phi'\phi'' + \frac{a_3}{(2\pi)^4}[3\phi''(\phi')^2 - j3(\phi'')^2 - j3\phi'\phi''']\right\} \quad (2.1.1.1.11)$$

Since $1/2\pi \, \phi'$ can be assumed as a Gaussian process (if there are more than 60 channels) by the Holbrook and Dixon's investigation (see Section 3.1.4 of Volume I.), it is possible to evaluate the power spectrum of Equation 2.1.1.1.11. However, this form makes the analysis complicated. Therefore, a different approach will be shown later.

2.1.1.2 *Fourier Series Expansion of Filter Transfer Functions*

This approach is useful for cases where the filter transfer function can be well approximated by a Fourier series or where the Fourier series expansion of the filter transfer function is analytically known, as in an ideal cut-off filter case. Expand the low pass analog of the bandpass filter $Y_{c+}(f)$ by

$$Y_{c+}(f) = \sum_{k=-\infty}^{\infty} a_k \, e^{-j\frac{2\pi}{F_0} kf} \tag{2.1.1.2.1}$$

In this case, the impulse response of the low pass analog is given by

$$h(t) = \sum_{k=-\infty}^{\infty} a_k \int_{-\infty}^{\infty} e^{j2\pi\left(t - \frac{k}{F_0}\right)f} df$$

$$= \sum_{k=-\infty}^{\infty} a_k \, \delta\left(t - \frac{k}{F_0}\right) \tag{2.1.1.2.2}$$

In order for this approach to work, $Y_{c+}(f)$ must be well approximated by a Fourier series in the frequency band beyond which the spectrum of the FM signal $e_i(t)$ seldom goes. This is an important point of this approximation. Thus, the phase distortion of the FM signal $d(t)$ is given by

$$d(t) = \text{Im}\left\{ \sum_{k=-\infty}^{\infty} a_k \, e^{j\phi\left(t - \frac{k}{F_0}\right) - j\phi(t)} \right\}. \tag{2.1.1.2.3}$$

Similarly, as mentioned in the power series expansion case, the average power (or magnitude) of $d(t)$ should be evaluated for the SCPC/FM and TV/FM cases. For the FDM/FM case, the form of Equation 2.1.1.2.3 is not a convenient one and therefore in the following, the power spectrum of the crosstalk (i.e., $d_2(t)$ in the previous Section) will be analyzed for this case.

The approach by Fourier series described here is very convenient when the a_k's are analytically known, as in the ideal cut-off filter case, which will be explained later. An important point here is that the value of F_0 must be large enough so that the spectrum of the FM signal is within the value of $f_0 \pm F_0/2$. Usually, the larger the value of F_0, the more terms in Equation 2.1.1.2.3 must be added to obtain an accurate result.

In order to separate the signal components and crosstalks and to evaluate the power spectrum of the crosstalk component in the FDM/FM case, (which is required for the noise power evaluation due to filter distortion of the FDM/FM signal), the autocorrelation function of $d(t)$ given by Equation 2.1.1.2.3 will be shown here. The autocorrelation function of $d(t)$ is

$$E_\phi\{d(t)\, d(t+\tau)\} = E_\phi\left[\text{Im}\left\{ \sum_{k=-\infty}^{\infty} a_k \, e^{j\phi\left(t - \frac{k}{F_0}\right) - j\phi(t)} \right\} \right.$$

$$\left. \cdot \text{Im}\left\{ \sum_{k=-\infty}^{\infty} a_k \, e^{j\phi\left(t + \tau - \frac{k}{F_0}\right) - j\phi(t+\tau)} \right\} \right]. \tag{2.1.1.2.4}$$

Using a simple formula,

$$\text{Im}(\alpha)\ \text{Im}(\beta)\ =\ \frac{1}{2}\ \text{Re}\{\alpha\beta^* - \alpha\beta\} \tag{2.1.1.2.5}$$

for any complex number α and β. The autocorrelation function of Equation 2.1.1.2.4 is given by

$$R_d(\tau) = \frac{1}{2}\ \text{Re}\left\{ \sum_{k_1=-\infty}^{\infty} \sum_{k_2=-\infty}^{\infty} a_{k_1}\ a_{k_2}^*\ \underset{\phi}{E} \right.$$

$$\cdot \left[e^{j\phi\left(t - \frac{k_1}{F_0}\right) - j\phi(t) - j\phi\left(t + \tau - \frac{k_2}{F_0}\right) + j\phi(t+\tau)} \right]$$

$$- \sum_{k_1=-\infty}^{\infty} \sum_{k_2=-\infty}^{\infty} a_{k_1}\ a_{k_2}\ \underset{\phi}{E}$$

$$\left. \cdot \left[e^{j\phi\left(t - \frac{k_1}{F_0}\right) - j\phi(t)\ j\phi\left(t + \tau - \frac{k_2}{F_0}\right) - j\phi(t+\tau)} \right] \right\}. \tag{2.1.1.2.6}$$

Since $\phi(t)$ can be assumed as a Gaussian process in FDM signal cases (when there are more than 60 channels), the averages in Equation 2.1.1.2.6 can be obtained as follows:

$$\underset{\lambda}{E}\ \{e^{ju\lambda(t)}\} = e^{-\frac{u^2}{2}\sigma_\lambda^2} \tag{2.1.1.2.7}$$

where

$$\underset{\lambda}{E}\ \{\lambda\} = 0$$

$$\underset{\lambda}{E}\ \{\lambda^2\} = \sigma_\lambda^2 \tag{2.1.1.2.8}$$

where λ is a zero mean Gaussian process. Then,

$$\underset{\phi}{E}\ \left\{ \exp\left[j\phi\left(t - \frac{k_1}{F_0}\right) - j\phi(t) \pm \phi\left(t + \tau - \frac{k_2}{F_0}\right) \mp \right.\right.$$

$$\left.\left. j\phi(t+\tau) \right\} = \exp\left[-2R_\phi(0) + R_\phi\left(\frac{k_1}{F_0}\right) + R_\phi\left(\frac{k_2}{F_0}\right) \right.$$

$$\mp R_\phi(\tau) \mp R_\phi\left(\tau + \frac{k_1}{F_0} - \frac{k_2}{F_0}\right) \pm R_\phi\left(\tau + \frac{k_1}{F_0}\right)$$

$$\pm R_\phi\left(\tau - \frac{k_2}{F_0}\right) \Big]. \tag{1.1.1.2.9}$$

Using this result in Equation 2.1.1.2.6,

$$R_d(\tau) = \frac{1}{2} \text{Re}\left\{ \sum_{k_1=-\infty}^{\infty} \sum_{k_2=-\infty}^{\infty} \exp\left[-2R_\phi(0) + R_\phi\left(\frac{k_1}{F_0}\right) + R_\phi\left(\frac{k_2}{F_0}\right) \right] \right.$$

$$\left. \cdot \left[a_{k_1} a_{k_2}^* \, e^{R_\nu(\tau, k_1, k_2)} - a_{k_1} a_{k_2} \, e^{-R_\nu(\tau, k_1, k_2)} \right] \right\} \qquad (2.1.1.2.10)$$

where $R\phi(\tau)$ is the autocorrelation function of $\phi(t)$ and

$$R_\nu(\tau) = R_\phi(\tau) + R_\phi\left(\tau + \frac{k_1}{F_0} - \frac{k_2}{F_0} \right)$$

$$- R_\phi\left(\tau + \frac{k_1}{F_0} \right) - R_\phi\left(\tau - \frac{k_2}{F_0} \right). \qquad (2.1.1.2.11)$$

As mentioned before, $R_d(\tau)$ contains the direct current component and signal component for the FDM signal.

The direct current component, as is well known, is given by

$$\text{Lim}_{\tau \to \infty} R_d(\tau) = R_d^{(\infty)}$$

$$= \frac{1}{2} \text{Re}\left\{ \sum_{k_1=-\infty}^{\infty} \sum_{k_2=-\infty}^{\infty} \exp\left[-2R_\phi(0) + R_\phi\left(\frac{k_1}{F_0}\right) \right. \right.$$

$$\left. \left. + R_\phi\left(\frac{k_2}{F_0}\right) \right] [a_{k_1} a_{k_2}^* - a_{k_1} a_{k_2}] \right\}. \qquad (2.1.1.2.12)$$

This is equal to

$$\sum_{k_1=-\infty}^{\infty} \sum_{k_2=-\infty}^{\infty} \exp\left[-2R_\phi(0) + R_\phi\left(\frac{k_1}{F_0}\right) + R_\phi\left(\frac{k_2}{F_0}\right) \right] \text{Im}(a_{k_1}) \, \text{Im}(a_{k_2})$$

$$= \left[\sum_{k=-\infty}^{\infty} \text{Im}(a_k) \exp\left\{ -R_\phi(0) + R_\phi\left(\frac{k}{F_0}\right) \right\} \right]^2. \qquad (2.1.1.2.13)$$

The signal component in Equation 2.1.1.2.10 is given by expanding $e^{\pm R_\nu}$ by a power series of R_ν and taking only the linear terms of R_ν, i.e.,

$$R_d^{(s)}(\tau) = \sum_{k_1=-\infty}^{\infty} \sum_{k_2=-\infty}^{\infty} \text{Re}(a_{k_1})$$

$$\cdot \text{Re}(a_{k_2}) \exp\left[-2R_\phi(0) + R_\phi\left(\frac{k_1}{F_0}\right) + R_\phi\left(\frac{k_2}{F_0}\right) \right] R_\nu(\tau; k_1, k_2) \qquad (2.1.1.2.14)$$

where the formula

$$\text{Re}(\alpha)\, \text{Re}(\beta) = \frac{1}{2} \text{Re}\{\alpha\beta^* + \alpha\beta\} \qquad (2.1.1.2.15)$$

is used above. The power spectrum of the signal component of Equation 2.1.1.2.14 is given by Fourier-transforming Equation 2.1.1.2.14 with respect to τ.

Before the final result is shown, represent the power spectrum of $\phi(t)$ by $W_\phi(f)$, then

$$W_\phi(f)e^{j2\pi fa} = \int_{-\infty}^{\infty} R_\phi(\tau + a)e^{-j2\pi f\tau}\, d\tau. \qquad (2.1.1.2.16)$$

Using this result, the power spectrum corresponding to Equation 2.1.1.2.14 is given by

$$W_d^{(s)}(f) = \sum_{k_1 = -\infty}^{\infty} \sum_{k_2 = -\infty}^{\infty} \mathrm{Re}(a_{k_1})\, \mathrm{Re}(a_{k_2})$$

$$\cdot \exp\left[-2R_\phi(0) + R_\phi\left(\frac{k_1}{F_0}\right) + R_\phi\left(\frac{k_2}{F_0}\right) \right]$$

$$\cdot \left[W_\phi(f) + W_\phi(f)\, e^{j2\pi \frac{(k_1 - k_2)}{F_0}f} \right.$$

$$\left. - W_\phi(f)e^{j\frac{2\pi}{F_0}k_1 f} - W_\phi(f)e^{-j\frac{2\pi}{F_0}k_2 f} \right]$$

$$= W_\phi(f) \left| \sum_{k = -\infty}^{\infty} \mathrm{Re}(a_k)e^{-R_\phi(0) + R_\phi\left(\frac{k}{F_0}\right)} \left(1 - e^{j2\pi\frac{k}{F_0}f}\right) \right|^2$$

$$= 4\, W_\phi(f) \left| \sum_{k = -\infty}^{\infty} \mathrm{Re}(a_k)e^{-R_\phi(0) + R_\phi\left(\frac{k}{F_0}\right)} \right.$$

$$\left. \cdot \sin\left(\frac{\pi k}{F_0}f\right) e^{j\pi\frac{k}{F_0}f} \right|^2$$

$$= G(f)\, W_\phi(f) \qquad (2.1.1.2.17)$$

where

$$G(f) = 4 \left| \sum_{k = -\infty}^{\infty} \mathrm{Re}(a_k)e^{-R_\phi(0) + R_\phi\left(\frac{k}{F_0}\right)} \right.$$

$$\left. \cdot \sin\left(\frac{\pi k}{F_0}f\right) e^{j\pi\frac{k}{F_0}f} \right|^2. \qquad (2.1.1.2.18)$$

Although $G(f)$ is a function of f, the change of $G(f)$ within a channel whose bandwidth is only 3.1 KHz, is very small and therefore, the effect of $G(f)$ on each individual channel can be ignored, and the component whose power spectrum is $G(f)\, W_\phi(f)$ can be considered as a signal (and not as a distortion). In order to obtain the power spectrum of the distortion (crosstalk) component which is required to obtain the S/D ratio of each channel, the direct current component and the signal component must be subtracted and the Fourier transformation must be applied to it. Represent the power spectrum of this component by $W_d^{(c)}(f)$, then

$$W_d^{(c)}(f) = \int_{-\infty}^{\infty} R_d^{(c)}(\tau) e^{j2\pi f \tau} \, d\tau \qquad (2.1.1.2.19)$$

where

$$
R_d^{(c)}(\tau) = \frac{1}{2} \text{Re} \left\{ \sum_{k_1=-\infty}^{\infty} \sum_{k_2=-\infty}^{\infty} \exp \left[-2R_\phi(0) \right. \right.
$$

$$
\left. + R_\phi\left(\frac{k_1}{F_0}\right) + R_\phi\left(\frac{k_2}{F_0}\right) \right]
$$

$$
\cdot \left[a_{k_1} a_{k_2}^* \, e^{R_v(\tau, k_1, k_2)} - a_{k_1} a_{k_2} \, e^{-R_v(\tau, k_1, k_2)} \right.
$$

$$
- \left(a_{k_1} a_{k_2}^* - a_{k_1} a_{k_2} \right)
$$

$$
\left. - \left(a_{k_1} a_{k_2}^* + a_{k_1} a_{k_2} \right) R_v(\tau) \right].
$$

$$(2.1.1.2.20)$$

This result is very useful to calculate the power spectrum of the distortion especially when the Fourier coefficients a_k are analytically known as in the ideal cut-off filter cases. For the ideal cut-off filter,

$$
a_k = \frac{1}{F_0} \int_{-\infty}^{\infty} Y_{c+}(f) e^{j\frac{2\pi}{F_0} kf}
$$

$$
df = \left[\frac{\sin\left(\pi \frac{B}{F_0} k\right)}{\left(\pi \frac{B}{F_0} k\right)} \right] \left(\frac{B}{F_0}\right) \qquad (2.1.1.2.21)
$$

where

$$
Y_{c+}(f) = 1 \qquad |f| \le \frac{B}{2}
$$

$$
= 0 \qquad |f| > \frac{B}{2}. \qquad (2.1.1.2.22)
$$

The result of Equation 2.1.1.2.19 is only analytically available at this time to calculate the filter distortion of the FDM/FM signal when the frequency deviation is large compared with the filter bandwidth (overdeviated case).

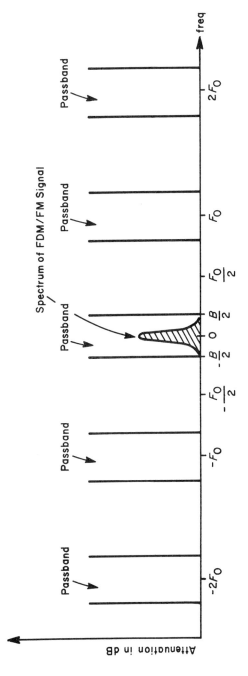

Figure 2.1.1.2.1 Periodic Filter of Equation 2.1.1.2.1

If there is no pre-emphasis applied to the FDM baseband signal, the function $R_\phi(\tau)$ of Equation 2.1.1.2.20 is simply given by (for the noise loading case)

$$
\begin{aligned}
R_\phi(\tau) &= \int_{f_l}^{f_h} \frac{\sigma^2}{(f_h - f_l)} \frac{1}{f^2} \cos(2\pi f\tau) df \\[2mm]
&= \frac{\sigma^2}{(f_h - f_l)} \left[-\frac{\cos(2\pi f_h \tau)}{f_h} + \frac{\cos(2\pi f_l \tau)}{f_l} \right] \\[2mm]
&\quad - \frac{\sigma^2}{(f_h - f_l)} 2\pi\tau \left[\mathrm{Si}(2\pi f_h \tau) - \mathrm{Si}(2\pi f_l \tau) \right] \quad (2.1.1.2.23)
\end{aligned}
$$

where

$$
\begin{aligned}
W_\phi(f) &= \frac{1}{f^2} \frac{\sigma^2}{(f_h - f_l)}, f_l \le f \le f_h \\[2mm]
&= 0, \text{ Elsewhere } (0 \le f < \infty). \quad (2.1.1.2.24)
\end{aligned}
$$

f_h, f_l and σ are respectively the highest channel frequency, the lowest channel frequency and the r.m.s. frequency deviation.

In case there is a pre-emphasis application, $R_\phi(\tau)$ must be obtained numerically by computer Fourier transform subroutine or by an approximation, i.e.

$$
R_\phi(\tau) = \int_{f_h}^{f_l} \frac{\sigma^2}{(f_h - f_l)} \frac{1}{f^2} G_p(f) \cos(2\pi f\tau) df \quad (2.1.1.2.25)
$$

where $G_p(f)$ is the pre-emphasis function. When the transfer function of the filter $h(t)$ is analytically known, the coefficients a_k can be well approximated for F_0 whose value must be chosen large enough, i.e.,

$$
\begin{aligned}
a_k &= \frac{1}{F_0} \int_{-\frac{F_0}{2}}^{\frac{F_0}{2}} Y_{c+}(f) e^{j2\pi \frac{k}{F_0} f} df \\[2mm]
&\simeq \frac{1}{F_0} \int_{-\infty}^{\infty} Y_{c+}(f) e^{j2\pi \frac{k}{F_0} f} df = \frac{1}{F_0} h\left(\frac{k}{F_0}\right) \cdot \quad (2.1.1.2.26)
\end{aligned}
$$

For example, in a single time filter case,

$$
Y_{c+}(f) = \frac{\exp\left[j\dfrac{f}{f_e}\right]}{1 + j\left(\dfrac{f}{f_e}\right)} \quad (2.1.1.2.27)
$$

where f_e is the 3 dB half bandwidth and the factor e^{jf/f_e} is attached to give the group delay at the center a frequency ($f = 0$) zero, as mentioned before. In this case,

$$a_k \simeq 2\pi \left(\frac{f_e}{F_0}\right) \exp\left[-\frac{2\pi f_e k}{F_0} - 1 \right]$$

$$k + 2\pi \frac{F_0}{f_e} > 0$$

$$a_k \simeq 0$$

$$k + 2\pi \frac{F_0}{f_e} < 0. \qquad (2.1.1.2.28)$$

Some calculated results for these cases are shown in Figure 2.1.1.2.2. For a more detailed discussion of these applications, see Reference [28].

2.1.1.3   *General Approach Without Approximation of* $h(t)$

This approach still uses the first order approximation and Equation 2.1.1.7, i.e.,

$$d(t) = \operatorname{Im}\left\{ e^{-j\phi(t)} \int_{-\infty}^{\infty} e^{j\phi(t-x)} h(x)\, dx \right\} .$$

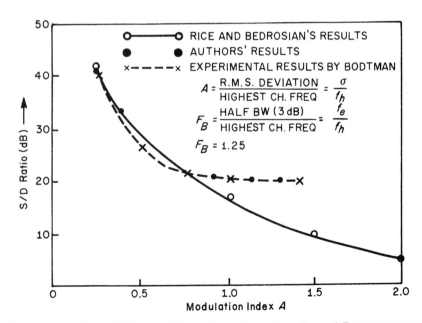

Figure 2.1.1.2.2(a)   S/D Ratio of Single Pole Filter at Top Channel Frequency versus Modulation Index A

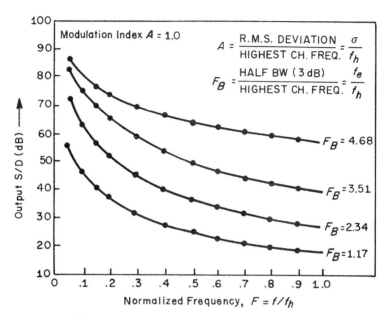

Figure 2.1.1.2.2(b)   Distortion Due to Ideal Filter

Following a similar approach used in Section 2.1.1.2,

$$R_d(\tau) = \frac{1}{2} \text{Re} \left\{ \int_{-\infty}^{\infty} \int_{-\infty}^{\infty} h(x)h(y)^* \right.$$

$$\cdot \underset{\phi}{E} \left[\exp\{ j\phi(t-x) - j\phi(t) + j\phi(t+\tau-y) - j\phi(t+\tau) \} \right] dx \, dy$$

$$- \int_{-\infty}^{\infty} \int_{-\infty}^{\infty} h(x)h(y) \underset{\phi}{E} [\exp\{ j\phi(t-x) - j\phi(t)$$

$$\left. - j\phi(t+\tau-y) + j\phi(t+\tau) \}] \, dx \, dy \right\} . \tag{2.1.1.3.1}$$

After taking the average on ϕ in a way similar to Section 2.1.1.2,

$$R_d(\tau) = \frac{1}{2} \text{Re} \left\{ \int_{-\infty}^{\infty} \int_{-\infty}^{\infty} [h(x)h(y)^* \, e^{R_v(\tau,x,y)} \right.$$

$$\left. - h(x)h(y) \, e^{-R_v(\tau,x,y)}] \, e^{-2R_\phi(0) + R_\phi(x) + R_\phi(y)} \, dx \, dy \right\} \tag{2.1.1.3.2}$$

where $\phi(t)$ is assumed to be a Gaussian process for the FMD/FM case in the calculation of the above average.

$$R_v(\tau,x,y) = R_\phi(\tau) - R_\phi(\tau+x)$$

$$- R_\phi(\tau - y) + R_\phi(\tau + x - y). \qquad (2.1.1.3.3)$$

In a way similar to Section 2.1.1.2, the direct current component in Equation 2.1.1.3.2 is given by

$$R_d^{(\infty)} = \left[\int_{-\infty}^{\infty} e^{-R_\phi(0) + R_\phi(x)} \, \text{Im}\{h(x)\} dx \right]^2. \qquad (2.1.1.3.4)$$

The unsymmetric part of the filter only contributes to this component, i.e.,

$$\frac{Y_{c+}(f) - Y_{c+}(-f)}{2}. \qquad (2.1.1.3.5)$$

The power spectrum of the signal component in Equation 2.1.1.3.2 is given, in a way similar to Section 2.1.1.2, by:

$$R_d^{(s)}(\tau) = 4W_\phi(f) \left| \int_{-\infty}^{\infty} e^{-R_\phi(0) + R_\phi(x)} \right.$$

$$\left. \cdot \text{Re}\{h(x)\} \, e^{j\pi fx} \, \sin(\pi fx) dx \right|^2$$

$$= G(f) W_\phi(f) \qquad (2.1.1.3.6)$$

where

$$G(f) = 4 \left| \int_{-\infty}^{\infty} e^{-R_\phi(0) + R_\phi(x)} \, \text{Re}\{h(x)\} e^{j\pi fx} \, \sin(\pi fx) dx \right|^2. \qquad (2.1.1.3.7)$$

The physical meaning of $G(f)$ is the same as that of Equation 2.1.1.2.18 (for FDM/FM cases). Then, the power spectrum of the (channel) cross component, which results from subtracting the D.C. component and signal component from Equation 2.1.1.3.2, and from Fourier transforming it, is given by

$$W_d^{(c)}(f) = \int_{-\infty}^{\infty} R_d^{(c)}(\tau) \, \cos(2\pi f\tau) \, d\tau$$

$$= \frac{1}{2} \text{Re} \left\{ \int_{-\infty}^{\infty} \int_{-\infty}^{\infty} \int_{-\infty}^{\infty} [h(x)h(y)* \{e^{R_v(\tau,x,y)}} \right.$$

$$- 1 - R_v(\tau,x,y)\} - h(x)h(y) \{e^{-R_v(\tau,x,y)}}$$

$$- 1 + R_v(\tau,x,y)\}] \, e^{-2R_\phi(0) + R_\phi(x) + R_\phi(y)}$$

$$\left. \cdot \cos(2\pi f\tau) d\tau \, dx \, dy \right\}. \qquad (2.1.1.3.8)$$

If the filter is symmetric around the FM carrier frequency, then $h(x)$ becomes a real function and then $W_d^{(c)}(f)$ can be represented by

$$W_d^{(c)}(f) = \frac{1}{2} \int_{-\infty}^{\infty} \int_{-\infty}^{\infty} \int_{-\infty}^{\infty} h(x)h(y)$$

$$\cdot \, [e^{R_v(\tau,x,y)} - e^{-R_v(\tau,x,y)} - 2R_v(\tau,x,y)]$$

$$\cdot \, e^{-2R_\phi(0) + R_\phi(x) + R_\phi(y)} \cos(2\pi f\tau) dx \, dy \, d\tau. \quad (2.1.1.3.9)$$

The signal-to-noise-channel ratio at channel frequency f is

$$\text{N.P.R.} = \frac{f^2 W_\phi(f)}{f^2 W_d^{(c)}(f) G_p(f)}$$

$$= \frac{W_\phi(f)}{W_d^{(c)}(f) G_p(f)} \quad (2.1.1.3.10)$$

where the power spectrum of the baseband signal (i.e., P.S. of $1/2\pi \, \phi'(t)$) is $f^2 W_\phi(f)$ and the power spectrum of the crosstalk is $f^2 W_d^{(c)}(f) G_p(f)$ represents the pre-emphasis effect. In the noise loading test case, the N.P.R. value is given by

$$\text{N.P.R.} = \frac{\dfrac{\sigma^2}{M\Delta f}}{f^2 G_p(f) W_d^{(c)}(f)} \quad (2.1.1.3.11)$$

where $W_\phi(f)$ is given by Equation 2.1.1.2.24 and $\Delta f = 4$ kHz (without any pre-emphasis).

In a case where the frequency deviation is small enough compared with the filter bandwidth, it is usually sufficient to calculate the second and third order distortion only, and the higher order distortions can be ignored. If we expand $e^{\pm R_v(\tau,x,y)}$ by a power series of $R_v(\tau,x,y)$ as

$$e^{\pm R_v} = \sum_{k=0}^{\infty} \frac{(\pm 1)^k}{k!} [R_v(\tau)]^k, \quad (2.1.1.3.12)$$

the k-th order distortion is the term due to $[Rv]^k$.

While, in order to include the higher order distortions, the approach of Equation 2.1.1.3.12 is very complicated and the triple integral of Equation 2.1.1.3.8 must be evaluated, this approach can give us a good physical insight while still of an analyzable complexity. Thus, the second order distortion is given by

$$W_{d_2}^{(c)}(f) = \frac{1}{2} \int_{-\infty}^{\infty} \int_{-\infty}^{\infty} \int_{-\infty}^{\infty} \text{Im}[h(x)] \, \text{Im}[h(y)]$$

$$\cdot \, [R_v(\tau,x,y)]^2 \, e^{-2R_\phi(0) + R_\phi(x) + R_\phi(y)}$$

$$\cdot \cos(2\pi f\tau) d\tau \, dx \, dy. \quad (2.1.1.3.13)$$

When $Y_{c+}(f)$ is approximated by a power series of f, then substituting $h(t)$ of Equation 2.1.1.1.2 into Equation 2.1.1.3.13, $W_{d_2}^{(c)}(f)$ is given by

$$W_{d_2}^{(c)}(f) = \frac{1}{2} \sum_{k_1=0}^{\infty} \sum_{k_2=0}^{\infty} \text{Im}\left\{\frac{a_{k_1}}{(2\pi j)k_1}\right\}$$

$$\cdot \text{Im}\left\{\frac{a_{k_2}}{(j2\pi)k_2}\right\} (-1)^{k_1+k_2} e^{-2R\phi(0)}$$

$$\cdot \int_{-\infty}^{\infty} \left[\frac{\partial^{k_1+k_2}}{\partial x^{k_1} \partial y^{k_2}} \left\{[R_v(\tau,x,y)]^2 e^{R\phi(x)+R\phi(y)}\right\}\right]_{\substack{x=0 \\ y=0}}$$

$$\cdot \cos(2\pi f\tau) d\tau \tag{2.1.1.3.14}$$

and $W_{d_3}^{(c)}(f)$ is given by

$$W_{d_3}^{(c)}(f) = \frac{1}{6} \sum_{k_1=0}^{\infty} \sum_{k_2=0}^{\infty} \text{Re}\left\{\frac{a_{k_1}}{(2\pi j)^{k_1}}\right\} \text{Re}\left\{\frac{a_{k_2}}{(2\pi j)^{k_2}}\right\}$$

$$\cdot (-1)^{k_1+k_2} e^{-2R\phi(0)} \int_{-\infty}^{\infty} \left[\frac{\partial^{k_1+k_2}}{\partial x^{k_1} \partial y^{k_2}} \left\{[R_v(\tau,x,y)]^3\right.\right.$$

$$\left.\left.\cdot e^{R\phi(x)+R\phi(y)}\right\}\right]_{\substack{x=0 \\ y=0}} \cos(2\pi f\tau) d\tau. \tag{2.1.1.3.15}$$

Using the relations

$$R_\phi^{(2k+1)}(0) = 0 \qquad \text{and}$$

$$\int_{-\infty}^{\infty} R_\phi^{(k)}(\tau) e^{j2\pi f\tau} d\tau = (-j2\pi f)^k W_\phi(f), \tag{2.1.1.3.16}$$

the above second and third order distortions can be evaluated. The author stops here expecting the readers to do them themselves. For the detailed results which are directly usable for practical cases, see Reference [28]. If the Fourier series expansion is applied for $Y_{c+}(f)$ as in Equation 2.1.1.2.1, substituting $h(t)$ of Equation 2.1.1.2.2 for Equation 2.1.1.3.8 and completing the integrals with respect to x and y, Equation 2.1.1.3.8 becomes the same as Equation 2.1.1.2.20.

2.1.1.4 Approach Considering Higher Order Terms of Equation 2.1.1.7

The three approaches described above use the first term of the following expansion only (Equation 2.1.1.7)

$$d(t) = \text{Im}\left\{\sum_{k=1}^{\infty} \frac{(-1)^{k-1}}{k} \left(\frac{e_0}{e_i} - 1\right)^k\right\} \cdot \tag{2.1.1.4.1}$$

If we use more terms in the approximation of $d(t)$, more accurate results can be obtained. For example, the sum is done up to $k = 2$.

$$d(t) \simeq \text{Im}\left(\frac{e_0}{e_i}\right) - \frac{1}{2}\text{Im}\left[\left(\frac{e_0}{e_i}\right)^2 - 2\left(\frac{e_0}{e_i}\right)\right]$$

$$= 2\,\text{Im}\left(\frac{e_0}{e_i}\right) - \frac{1}{2}\text{Im}\left\{\left(\frac{e_0}{e_i}\right)^2\right\} \qquad (2.1.1.4.2)$$

where

$$e_0/e_i = \int_{-\infty}^{\infty} e^{j\phi(x)-j\phi(t)}\,h(t-x)\,dx \qquad (2.1.1.4.3)$$

$$\left(\frac{e_0}{e_i}\right)^2 = \int_{-\infty}^{\infty}\int_{-\infty}^{\infty} e^{j\phi(x)+j\phi(y)-2j\phi(t)}\,dx\,dy. \qquad (2.1.1.4.4)$$

We can develop a similar but more complicated result using the approaches shown in the previous sections.

2.1.2 Echo Distortions

Section 2.1.2 analyses the distortions of a carrier modulated signal produced when it goes through two or more transmission paths and when all these signals are superposed at the receiver. A typical example of this case is a microwave terrestrial FM signal which has two passes in the propagation as shown in Figure 2.1.2.2.

Suppose that e_i is a carrier modulated signal (e.g., a FDM/FM signal). Then, e_{0k} ($1 \leqq k \leqq n$) is given by

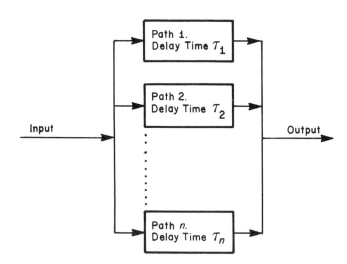

Figure 2.1.2.1   Diagram of General Echo Distortion

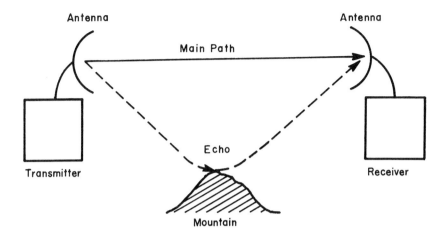

Figure 2.1.2.2 Echo Distortions Due to Two Paths

$$e_{0k}(t) = g_k \, e_i(t - \tau_k). \qquad (2.1.2.1)$$

This is equivalent to the extent that the signal e_i went through the following linear circuit whose impulse response is

$$h_k(t) = g_k \, \delta(A - \tau_k). \qquad (2.1.2.2)$$

Therefore, the transfer function is

$$Y_k(f) = \int_{-\infty}^{\infty} g_k \, \delta(t - \tau_k) \, e^{-j2\pi f t} \, dt = g_k \, e^{-j2\pi \tau_k f}. \qquad (2.1.2.3)$$

Thus, the equivalent transfer function of the linear circuit for Figure 2.1.2.1 is given by

$$Y(f) = \sum_{k=1}^{n} g_k \, e^{-j2\pi \tau_k f}. \qquad (2.1.2.4)$$

As seen from this result, the amplitude and phase (or group delay) characteristics of this linear circuit is a sum of sinusoidal functions whose periods are $(\tau_k)^{-1}$ $(k = 1, 2, \ldots, n)$.

To see the physical insight, take the case of $n = 2$, i.e.,

$$Y(f) = g_1 \, e^{-j2\pi \tau_1 f} + g_2 \, e^{-j2\pi \tau_2 f}. \qquad (2.1.2.5)$$

Then, the amplitude characteristic of this circuit is given by

$$|Y(f)|^2 = |g_1|^2 + |g_2|^2 + 2\mathrm{Re}\{g_1 g_2 \, e^{-j2\pi f(\tau_1 - \tau_2)}\}. \qquad (2.1.2.6)$$

The phase characteristic is

$$
\angle g_1 - j2\pi f \tau_1 + \tan^{-1} \left[\frac{ \operatorname{Im}\left\{ \dfrac{g_2}{g_1} e^{j2\pi(\tau_1 - \tau_2)f} \right\} }{ 1 + \operatorname{Re}\left\{ \dfrac{g_2}{g_1} e^{j2\pi(\tau_1 - \tau_2)f} \right\} } \right] . \tag{2.1.2.7}
$$

One can see from this result that both characteristics are periodic functions of $(\tau_1 - \tau_2)^{-1}$. Note here that the term $\angle g_1 - j2\pi\,\tau_1 f$ only gives the phase change and signal time delay of τ_1 which is unimportant from the distortion point of view.

Thus, the analytical approaches shown in Section 2.1.1 are applicable to the FM signal distortions produced by this circuit. Note here that the transfer function of Equation 2.1.2.4 (or Equation 2.1.2.5) must be approximated only in the frequency range where the FM signal power spectrum cannot be ignored (i.e., the approximation for the frequency range where the FM power spectrum is very small can be arbitrary, since it does not effect the analytical result).

2.1.3   Combined Effects of Filters and Nonlinear Devices

As shown in Figure 2.1, the real signal transmission system consists of filters and nonlinear devices.

The analysis of the FM filter distortion shown in Section 2.1.1 must be modified because of the existence of nonlinear devices in the transmission chain. In the following, the nonlinear devices are assumed to be memoriless.

Assume that the input signal to a nonlinear device (no other signal co-exists with this signal through the nonlinear device) is represented by

$$
e_i(t) = A e^{j\omega_0 t + j\theta}, \tag{2.1.3.1}
$$

i.e., e_i is an unmodulated single tone (C.W.). Then, the output signal can be represented by

$$
e_0(t) = g(A)\, e^{j\omega_0 t + j\theta + jf(A)}
$$

$$
= \frac{g(A)}{A}\, e^{jf(A)}\, e_i(t) \tag{2.1.3.2}
$$

where $g(A)$ and $f(A)$ are respectively the amplitude (AM/AM) and phase (AM/PM) characteristics measured by a single tone as defined by Equation 2.1.3.1. If the nonlinear device is memoriless, $g(A)$ and $f(A)$ do not change with ω_0. More precisely, even if A and θ are functions of t, the output can still be represented by Equation 2.1.3.2 under the memoriless condition. This approximation is valid for the present FM signal bandwidth and nonlinear devices (traveling wave tubes and solid state power amplifiers, etc.).

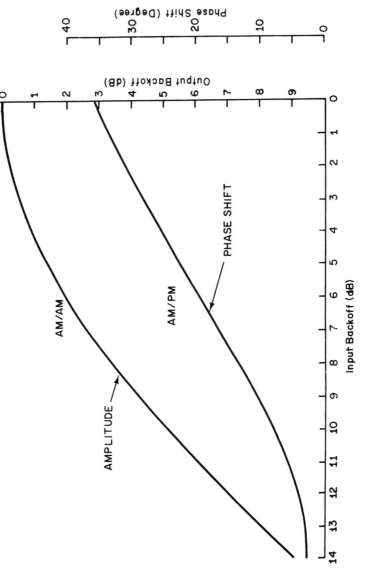

Figure 2.1.3.1 Single Carrier Amplitude and Phase Characteristics of Typical INTELSAT V TWTA

The AM/AM and AM/PM characteristics $g(A)$ and $f(A)$ for a single tone test are only available from laboratory measurements. Therefore, the characteristics of multi-carriers with modulations must be derived from the single carrier $g(A)$ and $f(A)$. Normally, in laboratories, instead of $g(A)$ and $f(A)$, dB/dB and degree/dB are respectively measured. A typical measure data is shown in Figure 2.1.3.1

The input and output powers are usually normalized by the power saturating points, in which case 0 dB, in the input power means that the output power saturates at this input power, and 0 dB output power means the saturated output power. The relationship betwen $g(A)$, $f(A)$ and their dB corresponding value is given as follows:

$$x_A = 10 \log_{10} \left(\frac{A^2}{2} \right)$$

$$y_A = 10 \log_{10} \left[\frac{\{g(A)\}^2}{2} \right] \tag{2.1.3.3}$$

$$A = \sqrt{2}\ 10^{\frac{x_A}{20}}$$

$$g(A) = \sqrt{2}\ 10^{\frac{y_A}{20}} \tag{2.1.3.4}$$

$$G(x_A)'\ (\text{dB/dB}) = A\ \frac{g(A)'}{g(A)}$$

$$F(x_A)'\ (\text{degree/dB}) = \left(\frac{\ln(10)}{20} \right) \left(\frac{180}{\pi} \right) A f(A)' \tag{2.1.3.5}$$

where $G(X_A)$ represents the output power versus input power (dB/dB) and $F(X_A)$ represents the outphase change versus input power (degree/dB). As shown later, most of the analytical results can be nicely represented by $G(X_A)'$ and $F(X_A)'$. Returning to our problem, the output signal of the pre-HPA filter F_1 in Figure 2.1 (when the input signal is an ideal FM signal as in Equation 2.1.1) can be represented by

$$e_0^{(1)}(t) = A_1 [1 + \epsilon^{(1)}(t)]\ e^{j d^{(1)}(t)}\ e^{j \omega_0 t + j \phi(t) + j \theta}$$

$$= \left(\frac{A_1}{A} \right) (1 + \epsilon^{(1)})\ e^{j d^{(1)}}\ e_i(t) \tag{2.1.3.6}$$

where the amplitude and group delay of the filter F_1 are normalized so that the amplitude distortion $\epsilon^{(1)}(t)$ and phase distortion $d^{(1)}(t)$ may be small and therefore, the first order approximation, as in Equation 2.1.1.7, can be applied (see Section 2.1.1). Thus, under the condition of the first order approximation,

$$\epsilon_{(t)}^{(1)} = \text{Re}\left\{ e^{-j\phi(t)} \int_{-\infty}^{\infty} e^{j\phi(x)} h_1(t-x)\,dx - 1 \right\}$$

$$d^{(1)}(t) = \text{Im}\left\{ e^{-j\phi(t)} \int_{-\infty}^{\infty} e^{j\phi(x)} h_1(t-x)\,dx \right\} \qquad (2.1.3.7)$$

where $h_1(t)$ is the low pass analog impulse response of the filter F_1, A_1/A is the gain or loss of F_1 and the signal path. Now, the output of HPA becomes

$$e_0^{(2)}(t) = g_H(A_1(1 + \epsilon^{(1)})) \, e^{jf_H(A_1(1+\epsilon^{(1)}))}$$

$$\cdot e^{j\omega_0 t + j\phi(t) + j\theta + jd^{(1)}(t)}. \qquad (2.1.3.8)$$

Since $\epsilon^{(1)}$ and $d^{(1)}$ are small (Taylor series expansion),

$$g_H(A(1 + \epsilon^{(1)})) \simeq g_H(A_1) + g_H(A_1)' A_1 \epsilon^{(1)}$$

$$= g_H(A_1)\left[1 + A_1 \frac{g_H(A_1)'}{g_H(A_1)} \epsilon^{(1)} \right]$$

$$= g_H(A_1)\,[1 + G_H(x_{A_1})'\,\epsilon^{(1)}]$$

$$= A_2[1 + \epsilon^{(2)}],$$

$$f_H(A_1(1 + \epsilon^{(1)})) = f_H(A_1) + f_H(A_1)' A_1 \epsilon^{(1)}$$

$$= f_H(A_1) + \frac{20}{\ln(10)}\left(\frac{\pi}{180} \right) F_H(x_{A_1})'\,\epsilon^{(1)}$$

$$= f_H(A_1) + \beta F_H(x_{A_1})'\,\epsilon^{(1)}$$

$$= f_H(A_1) + d^{(2)} \qquad (2.1.3.9)$$

where $G_H(X_A)'$ is defined by Equation 2.1.3.5 and by the slope dB/dB at the X_A dB input backoff. $F(X_A)$ is also defined by Equation 2.1.3.5 and by the slope of the nonlinear phase characteristic degree/dB. $\pi/180$ in Equation 2.1.3.9 is the conversion factor from degree to radian.

$$A_2 = g_H(A_1), \quad \epsilon^{(2)} = G_H(x_{A_1})'\,\epsilon^{(1)},$$

$$\beta = \frac{20}{\ln(10)}\frac{\pi}{180} \simeq 0.151, \quad d^{(2)} = \beta F_H(x_{A_1})'\,\epsilon^{(1)}.$$

Now, the input to the satellite input filter F_2 is given by

$$e_i^{(1)}(t) = A_2(1 + \epsilon^{(2)}) e^{jd^{(2)} + jd^{(1)}}\, e^{j\omega_0 t + j\phi + j\theta + jf_H(A_1)}. \qquad (2.1.3.10)$$

Then, the output of F_2 can be represented by

$$e_0^{(3)}(t) \simeq A_2(1 + \epsilon^{(2)} + \epsilon^{(3)}) e^{jd^{(1)} + jd^{(2)} + jd^{(3)}}\, e^{j\omega_0 t + j\phi + j\theta + jf_H(A_1)} \qquad (2.1.3.11)$$

where $\epsilon^{(3)}$ and $d^{(3)}$ are respectively the amplitude and phase distortions due to F_2 when the input signal is the ideal FM signal of Equation 2.1.1. The reason why the approximation of Equation 2.1.3.11 is possible is that the cross terms can be ignored because the distortions due to F_1 and F_2 are small and therefore the superposition theory can be applied, i.e.,

$$\epsilon^{(3)}(t) = \mathrm{Re}\left\{ e^{-j\phi(t)} \int_{-\infty}^{\infty} e^{j\phi(x)} h_2(t-x)\, dx - 1 \right\}$$

$$d^{(3)}(t) = \mathrm{Im}\left\{ e^{-j\phi(t)} \int_{-\infty}^{\infty} e^{j\phi(x)} h_2(t-x)\, dx \right\} \qquad (2.1.3.12)$$

where $h_2(t)$ is the low pass analog impulse response of F_2. Now, the output of the TWTA can be given by

$$
\begin{aligned}
e_0^{(4)}(t) &= g_T(A_2(1+\epsilon^{(2)}+\epsilon^{(3)}))\, e^{jf_T(A_2(1+\epsilon^{(2)}+\epsilon^{(3)}))} \\
&\quad \cdot e^{jd^{(1)}+jd^{(2)}+jd^{(3)}}\, e^{j\omega_0 t + j\phi + j\theta + jf_H(A_1)} \\
&\simeq g_T(A_2)[1 + G_T(x_{A_2})'(\epsilon^{(2)}+\epsilon^{(3)})] \\
&\quad \cdot e^{jf_T(A_2)+j\beta F_T(x_{A_2})'(\epsilon^{(2)}+\epsilon^{(3)})}\, e^{jd^{(1)}+jd^{(2)}+jd^{(3)}} \\
&\quad \cdot e^{j\omega_0 t + j\phi + j\theta + jf_H(A_1)} \qquad (2.1.3.13)
\end{aligned}
$$

where $G_T(X_{A_2})'$ is the slope dB/dB of the TWTA at the input backoff X_{A_2} and $F_T(X_{A_2})'$ is the phase slope of the TWTA at the same backoff (degree/dB).

Define the new notations as

$$A_4 = g_T(A_2),\ \epsilon^{(4)} = G_T(X_{A_2})'(\epsilon^{(2)}+\epsilon^{(3)}),$$

$$d^{(4)} = \beta F_T(X_{A_2})'(\epsilon^{(2)}+\epsilon^{(3)}). \qquad (2.1.3.14)$$

Then, $e_0^{(4)}(t)$ can be rewritten

$$
\begin{aligned}
e_0^{(4)} &= A_4(1+\epsilon^{(4)})\, e^{jd^{(1)}+jd^{(2)}+jd^{(3)}+jd^{(4)}} \\
&\quad \cdot e^{j\omega_0 t + j\phi + j\theta + jf_H(A_1) + jf_T(A_2)}. \qquad (2.1.3.15)
\end{aligned}
$$

Finally, the output of the filters F_3 and F_4 (in Figure 2.1)

$$
\begin{aligned}
e_0^{(5)}(t) &\simeq A_4(1+\epsilon^{(4)}+\epsilon^{(5)})\, e^{jd^{(1)}+jd^{(2)}+jd^{(3)}+jd^{(4)}+jd^{(5)}} \\
&\quad \cdot e^{j\omega_0 t + j\phi + jf_H(A_1) + jf_T(A_2)} \qquad (2.1.3.16)
\end{aligned}
$$

where $\epsilon^{(5)}$ and $d^{(5)}$ are the amplitude and phase distortions due to the filters F_3 and F_4 respectively, when the input is the ideal FM signal of Equation 2.1.1.

$$\epsilon^{(5)}(t) = \text{Re}\left\{e^{-j\phi(t)}\int_{-\infty}^{\infty} e^{j\phi(x)}h_3(t-x)dx - 1\right\}$$

$$d^{(5)} = \text{Im}\left\{e^{-j\phi(t)}\int_{-\infty}^{\infty} e^{j\phi(x)}h_3(t-x)dx\right\} \qquad (2.1.3.17)^\dagger$$

where

$d^{(1)}$ = Phase distortion due to F_1 when the input is the ideal FM signal of Equation 2.1.1.

$d^{(2)}$ = $\beta F_H(X_{A_1})' \epsilon^{(1)}$. Where $\epsilon^{(1)}$ = Amplitude distortion due to F_1 when the input is the ideal FM signal. $F_H(X_{A_1})$ = Slope of the phase characteristic of HPA at the operating input backoff (X_{A_1}). β is given by Equation 2.1.3.9.

$d^{(3)}$ = Phase distortion due to F_2 when the input is the ideal FM signal.

$d^{(4)}$ = $\beta F_T(X_{A_2})'(\epsilon^{(2)} + \epsilon^{(3)})$,

where

$\epsilon^{(2)}$ = $G_H(X_{A_1})' \epsilon^{(1)}$.

$\epsilon^{(3)}$ = Amplitude distortion due to F_2 when the input is the ideal FM. $F_T(X_{A_2})'$ is the phase slope of the TWTA at the operating backoff (X_{A_2}) (degree/dB). $G_H(X_{A_1})'$ is the gain slope of the HPA at the operating backoff (X_{A_1}) (dB/dB).

$d^{(5)}$ = Phase distortion due to $F_3 + F_4$ when the input is the ideal FM signal.

Thus, the total distortion is given by

$$d = d_1 + \beta F_H' \epsilon^{(1)} + d^{(3)}$$
$$+ \beta F_T' G_H' \epsilon^{(1)} + \beta F_T' \epsilon^{(3)} + d^{(5)}$$
$$= [d_1 + \beta(F_H' + F_T' G_H')\epsilon^{(1)}]$$
$$+ [d^{(3)} + \beta F_T' \epsilon^{(3)}] + d^{(5)}. \qquad (2.1.3.18)$$

The physical meaning of each component of Equation 2.1.3.18 is as follows. $d^{(1)}$, $d^{(3)}$, and $d^{(5)}$ are the phase distortion due respectively to filters F_1, F_2 and $F_3 + F_4$. If there is no nonlinear device, only the sum of these phase distortions

---

$^\dagger h_3(t)$ is the low pass analog impulse response of the filters F_3 and F_4.

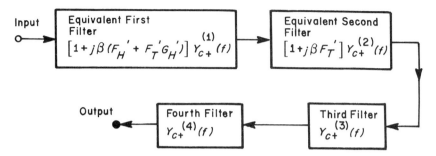

Figure 2.1.3.2   Equivalent Linear Filters for Satellite Nonlinear Channel of Figure 2.1
for FM Signals

should be taken into consideration after the chain of the filters. $\beta F'_H \epsilon^{(1)}$ is the
component produced by the amplitude fluctuation (distortion) of $e_i(t)$ after F_1
which is transferred into the phase of the signal after HPA, due to the AM/PM
nonlinearities of HPA. $\beta F'_T G'_H \epsilon^{(1)}$ is the component produced by the amplitude
fluctuation due to F_1 which is modified by AM/AM of HPA by the factor G'_H
and transferred into the phase of the signal by AM/PM of TWTA (by the factor
$\beta F'_T$).

In a linear system with no nonlinear devices (HPA and TWTA), the combined
transfer function of $F_1 + F_2 + F_3 + F_4$ can be equalized to reduce the filter
distortion. However, in our present case, the effects due to terms $\epsilon^{(1)}$ and $\epsilon^{(3)}$
must be considered in the equalization.

As can be easily proved, the result of Equation 2.1.3.18 is the same as the
phase distortion produced by the following single filter.

$$Y(f) = [1 + j\beta(F'_H + F'_T G'_H)] \, Y^{(1)}_{c+}(f)$$

$$+ \, [1 + j\beta F'_T] \, Y^{(2)}_{c+}(f) + Y^{(3)}_{c+}(f) + Y^{(4)}_{c+}(f) \quad (2.1.3.19)$$

where $Y^{(1)}_{c+}(f)$, $Y^{(2)}_{c+}(f)$, $Y^{(3)}_{c+}(t)$ and $Y^{(4)}_{c+}(f)$ are respectively the transfer functions of F_1, F_2, F_3 and F_4. Note here that, since $Y(f)$ is not normalized in the
passband of the signal spectrum, in order to make the approximation of Equation
2.1.1.7 possible, Equation 2.1.1.7 must be modified as follows. Represent $Y(0)$
as

$$Y(0) = 4 + j\beta(F'_H + F'_1 G'_H + F'_1) \quad (2.1.3.20)$$

assuming $Y^{(1)}_{c+}$, $Y^{(2)}_{c+}$, $Y^{(3)}_{c+}$ and $Y^{(4)}_{c+}$ are normalized as

$$Y^{(1)}_{c+}(0) = Y^{(2)}_{c+}(0) = Y^{(3)}_{c+}(0) = Y^{(4)}_{c+}(0) = 1$$

$$d(t) = \mathrm{Im} \log \left[1 + \frac{c_0}{c_i} \frac{Y(0)c_i}{Y(0)} \right] \quad (2.1.3.21)$$

$$\simeq \text{Im}\left\{\frac{e_0}{e_i Y(0)} - 1\right\} = \text{Im}\left\{\frac{e_0}{e_i Y(0)}\right\}. \qquad (2.1.3.22)^{\dagger}$$

In order to equalize the transmission chain in Figure 2.1 for the filter distortions, $Y_{c+}^{(1)}(f)$ and/or $Y_{c+}^{(4)}(f)$ must be adjusted so that the group delay and amplitude characteristics of $Y(f)$ may be as flat as possible in the signal passband, since the other two filters are in satellite and are not adjustable.

2.1.4 Effects of Pre-Emphasis

As explained in Sections 4.1 of Volume I, 2.1.1, and 2.1.5 of Volume 2, the demodulated FM signal disturbances are the derivatives of the phase disturbances (produced by filter distortions or thermal noise) in time domain. This means that the power spectrum of a demodulated FM disturbance is that of the phase disturbance multiplied by $(2\pi f)^2$. Since the power spectrum of the phase demodulated disturbance is very roughly similar to that of the r.f. noise spectrum (in thermal noise cases) or that of the baseband signal (in FM distortions), the power spectrum of the FM demodulated disturbances has a triangular shape (i.e., proportional to $(2\pi f)^2$). Thus, the higher frequency components of the baseband signal receive more disturbances than those of the lower frequency components.

The transmission qualitites of the baseband signals are determined by the worst frequency components of the disturbances and, therefore, this triangle disturbance power spectrum is not convenient from the transmission point of view. An idea for improving on this problem is to emphasize the higher frequency components of the baseband signal at the transmitter side and de-emphasize the higher frequency components in the same amount at the receiving side, so that the received signal does not receive any distortions because of the pre-emphasis circuit.

If the demodulated disturbances are independent from the baseband signal (approximately in FM signal cases), the pre-emphasis gain at each frequency component f is given by the frequency characteristics of the pre-emphasis circuit. The signal-to-noise ratio at each frequency in this case is

$$(S/N)(f) = \frac{G_s(f)}{G_D(f)/G_{\text{pre}}(f)} = \frac{G_s(f)\, G_{\text{pre}}(f)}{G_D(f)} \qquad (2.1.4.1)$$

where $G_s(f)$, $G_{\text{pre}}(f)$ and $G_D(f)$ are respectively the signal power spectrum, pre-emphasis gain and disturbance power spectrum. In a case where the disturbances are dependent on the baseband signal, the formula of Equation 2.1.4.1 is unusable. However, there are some good pre-emphasis gains in such cases, although the analysis is more complicated (e.g., the FM distribution due to filters).

---

†In this analysis, it is assumed that the linear superposition of the distortions is approximately valid, since the distortions are all small and the cross terms are even smaller.

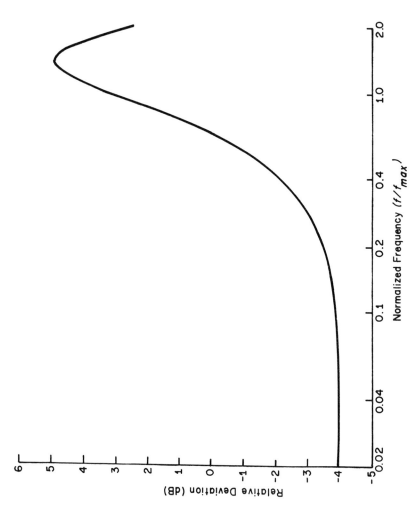

Figure 2.1.4.1   Pre-emphasis Characteristic for Telephone

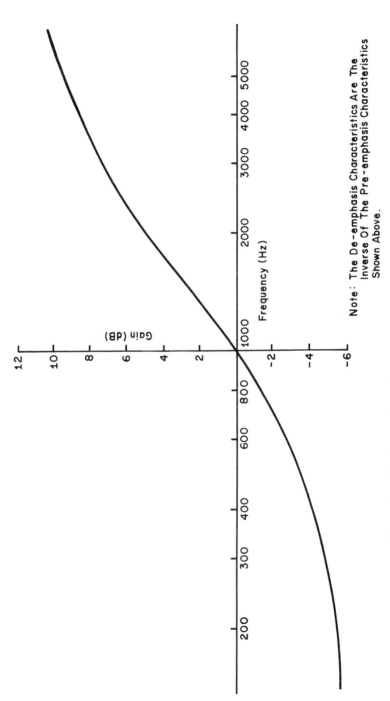

Figure 2.1.4.2 Pre-emphasis Characteristics for Companded SCPC/FM

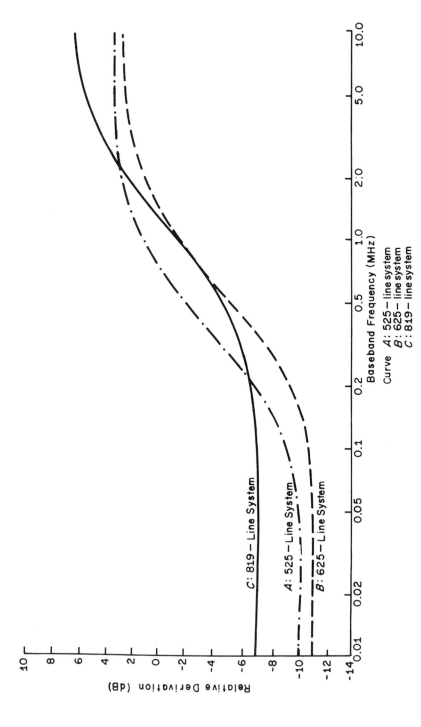

Figure 2.1.4.3 Pre-emphasis Characteristic for Television on 525-, 625-, and 819-line Systems

Based on analyses and experiments, for the FDM-FM signal transmission, the gain difference of the pre-emphasis between the highest and lowest frequency channels is normally 8 dB. Figure 2.1.4.1 shows the characteristics of the pre-emphasis gain v.s. channel frequency recommended by CCIR for a FDM/FM signal. Similarly, Figure 2.1.4.2 shows the pre-emphasis characteristic of companded SCPC/FM. For TV/FM cases, the characteristics of the pre-emphasis gains are shown in Figure 2.1.4.3.

As seen from these curves, the higher frequency area characteristics are proportional to f^2, but the characteristics are flattened in the lower frequency areas considering other types of noises (other than those produced by transmission channel, e.g., equipment noise) which are most likely to come up in a flat power spectrum.

2.1.5   Effects of Thermal Noise on FM Signals

Let us represent an FM signal with thermal noise as

$$e(t) = A e^{j2\pi f_0 t + j\phi(t)} + N(t) e^{j2\pi f_0 t} \qquad (2.1.5.1)$$

where $(2\pi)^{-1} \phi(t)'$ is the baseband signal and,

$$N(t) = N_c(t) + j N_s(t) \qquad (2.1.5.2)$$

where N_c and N_s are respectively the inphase and quadrature components of the narrow r.f. thermal noise as explained in Section 2.1 of Volume 1. Let us rewrite Equation 2.1.5.1 as

$$e(t) = B(t) e^{j2\pi f_0 t + j\phi(t) + j\theta(t)} \qquad (2.1.5.3)$$

where $B(t)$ is a positive real function and $\theta(t)$ is the phase change due to the thermal noise, i.e.,

$$\ln e(t) = \ln B(t) + j2\pi f_0 t + j\phi(t) + j\theta(t). \qquad (2.1.5.4)$$

It is obvious from Equation 2.1.5.1 that

$$\theta(t) = \text{Im} \ln \left\{ 1 + \frac{N(t)}{A} e^{-j\phi(t)} \right\}. \qquad (2.1.5.5)$$

Therefore, as explained in Section 4.1 of Volume 1,

$$\frac{1}{2\pi} \frac{d}{dt} \theta(t) = \frac{1}{2\pi} \frac{d}{dt} \text{Im} \ln \left\{ 1 + \frac{N(t)}{A} e^{-j\phi(t)} \right\} \qquad (2.1.5.6)$$

is the demodulated output of the FM demodulation due to thermal noise.

The important practical problem is to know the power spectrum of this demodulated FM thermal noise as a function of the carrier-power-to-noise-power ratio, i.e.,

$$\frac{C}{E\left\{\frac{1}{2}|N(t)|^2\right\}} = \frac{C}{E\{N_c^2\}} = \left(\frac{C}{N}\right). \qquad (2.1.5.7)$$

Although this is confusing because of the notation N, it is represented as (C/N).
   This power spectrum of $1/2\pi \, d/dt \, \theta(t)$, $W_\theta'(f)$ has three phases as a function
of (C/N), i.e.,

(i)   Above threshold (normally $(C/N) > 10$ dB, approximately) where $W_\theta'(f)$
      is proportional to $(C/N)^{-1}$.
(ii) At threshold where $W_\theta'(f)$ becomes nonlinear with respect to $(C/N)^{-1}$.
(iii) Below threshold, where $W_\theta'(f)$ is a very nonlinear function of $(C/N)^{-1}$ and
      $W_\theta'(f)$ increases at a much faster rate than that above threshold.

   The area A corresponds to that of (i), B, to that of (ii) and C, to that of (iii).
In area A if the (C/N) value changes to x dB, W_θ' also changes x dB (linearly).

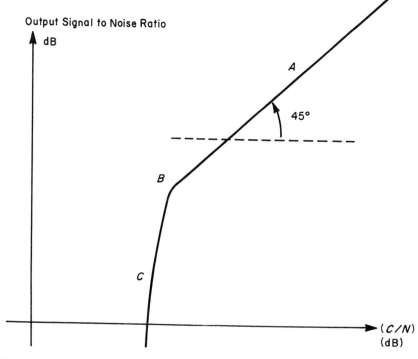

Figure 2.1.5.1   Demodulated FM Signal to Noise Characteristic Ratio versus Input
                     C/N

Above Threshold

In this area, the demodulated noise of Equation 2.1.5.6 can be approximated as:

$$\frac{1}{2\pi} \frac{d}{dt} \text{Im} \ln \left\{ 1 + \frac{N(t)}{A} e^{-j\phi(t)} \right\}$$

$$\approx \frac{1}{2\pi} \frac{d}{dt} \text{Im} \left\{ \frac{N(t)}{A} e^{-j\phi(t)} \right\} . \qquad (2.1.5.8)$$

As seen from this result, the demodulated noise power is proportional to that of $N(t)$.

In this case, the demodulated noise power spectrum is that of

$$\text{Im} \left\{ \frac{N(t)}{A} e^{-j\phi(t)} \right\} \qquad (2.1.5.9)$$

multiplied by f^2.

Using

$$\text{Im} \left\{ \frac{N(t)}{A} e^{-j\phi(t)} \right\} = \frac{1}{2j} \left[\frac{N(t)}{A} e^{-j\phi(t)} - \frac{N(t)^*}{A} e^{j\phi(t)} \right], \qquad (2.1.5.10)$$

the autocorrelation function of this noise is given by

$$\frac{1}{2} \text{Re} \left\{ \frac{N(t) \, N(t+\tau)^*}{A^2} e^{-j\phi(t)+j\phi(t+\tau)} \right.$$

$$\left. - \frac{N(t) \, N(t+\tau)}{A^2} e^{-j\phi(t)-j\phi(t+\tau)} \right\} . \qquad (2.1.5.11)$$

From the result of Section 2.1 in Volume 1,

$$E\{N(t) \, N(t+\tau)\} = 0. \qquad (2.1.5.12)$$

Assuming that $N(t)$ and $\phi(t)$ are statistically independent, Equation 2.1.5.11 is reduced to

$$\frac{1}{2} \text{Re} \, \frac{1}{A^2} E\{N(t) \, N(t+\tau)^*\} \, E\{e^{-j\phi(t)+j\phi(t+\tau)}\}. \qquad (2.1.5.13)$$

As seen from the result of Section 5.1 in Volume 1,

$$E\{e^{-j\phi(t)+j\phi(t+\tau)}\} \qquad (2.1.5.14)$$

is equal to the Fourier transform of

$$W_c(f)/C \qquad (2.1.5.15)^\dagger$$

where

$$C = \frac{A^2}{2}. \qquad (2.1.5.16)$$

Note that the center of $W_c(f)$ is zero frequency.

On the other hand, from the result of Section 2.1 in Volume 1,

$$E\{N(t)\, N(t+\tau)^*\} = 2E\{N_c(t)\, N_c(t+\tau)\} = 2\, R_N(\tau) \qquad (2.1.5.17)$$

where $R_N(\tau)$ is the autocorrelation function of the r.f. noise whose center frequency is shifted to zero.

Thus, the demodulated noise spectrum is the Fourier-transform of Equation 2.1.5.13, i.e.,

$$\left[\frac{1}{2C^2} \, W_N(f) \circledast W_c(f) \right] f^2 \; (-\infty < f < \infty) \qquad (2.1.5.18)$$

where $W_N(f)$ and $W_c(f)$ are respectively the power spectra of the r.f. noise and FM signal whose centers are shifted to zero frequency. Obviously, the demodulated signal is

$$\frac{1}{2\pi} \, \phi(t)'. \qquad (2.1.5.19)$$

Represent the power spectrum of this baseband signal by $W\phi'(f)$. Then the output power spectrum of the FM demodulator becomes

$$W\phi'(f) + \frac{1}{2C^2} \, [W_N(f) \circledast W_c(t)] \, f^2 \; (-\infty < f < \infty). \qquad (2.1.5.20)$$

For example, in FDM-FM signal and flat spectrum thermal noise cases, $W_N(f)$ is flat within the r.f. signal bandwidth (because of the receiver bandwidth filter) and $W_c(f)$ is distributed much more narrowly within the noise band as seen from Figure 2.1.5.2.

Therefore, $W_N(f) \circledast W_c(f)$ is approximated as

$$W_c(f) \circledast W_N(f) \simeq C\, N_0 \qquad (2.1.5.21)$$

within the baseband signal bandwidth, i.e., in

$$-f_h < f < f_h \qquad (2.1.5.22)$$

$^\dagger W_c(f)$ is the power spectrum of the FM signal of Equation 2.1.5.1 whose center frequency is shifted to zero. Note that $W_c(f)$ defined by Equation 5.1.4 in Volume I is different from this $W_c(f)$ through factor C.

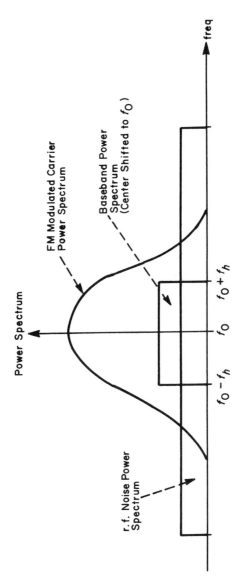

Figure 2.1.5.2 Power Spectra of Baseband Modulated FM Carrier and r.f. Noise

where f_h is the highest channel frequency.

Thus, the second term of Equation 2.1.5.20 is given by

$$\frac{1}{2C^2} \times C\,N_0 f^2 = \frac{N_0}{2C} f^2\;(-f_h \le f \le f_h). \qquad (2.1.5.23)$$

On the other hand,

$$W_{\phi'}(f) = \frac{\sigma^2}{2f_h}\;(-f_h \le f \le f_h) \qquad (2.1.5.24)$$

where σ^2 is the power of the baseband signal.

Therefore, considering only the positive frequencies (positive and negative frequency components are symmetric), the signal-to-noise-power ratio at each channel (called NPR - noise power ratio) is given by

$$(S/N) \simeq \frac{\dfrac{\sigma^2}{f_h}\,\Delta f\,G_{pv}(f)}{\dfrac{N_0}{C} f^2\,\Delta f} = \left(\frac{C}{N_0}\right)\frac{\sigma^2}{f_h\,f^2}\,G_{pr}(f) \qquad (2.1.5.25)$$

where Δf is the voice channel bandwidth and $G_{pr}(f)$ is the pre-emphasis gain. Note here that within $f + \Delta f$, the above functions are almost constant.

For general interference cases, where the power spectrum is not necessarily flat, the analysis is a little more complicated but can be done in a way similar to that shown in Chapter 5 (FM Section).

For example, the following analyses the effects of the up- and downlink noise on FM signals in satellite communications, where nonlinear effects exist, in order to show how the transponder nonlinearities affect the FM demodulation scheme.

Present the input to the satellite by

$$e_{S+N}(t) = A\,e^{j\omega_0 t + j\phi(t) + j\theta} + N_u(t)\,e^{j\omega_0 t} \qquad (2.1.5.26)$$

where

$$N_u(t) = N_{uc}(t) + j\,N_{us}(t). \qquad (2.1.5.27)$$

N_{uc} and N_{us} are inphase and quadrature components of the narrow band noise (i.e., the bandwidth of the noise is much smaller than the center frequency f_0).

Then,

$$e_{S+N} = |B(t)|\,e^{j\omega_0 t + j\angle B(t)} \qquad (2.1.5.28)$$

and $\angle$ denotes "the angle of" and

$$B(t) = A\,e^{j\phi + j\theta} + N_u. \qquad (2.1.5.29)$$

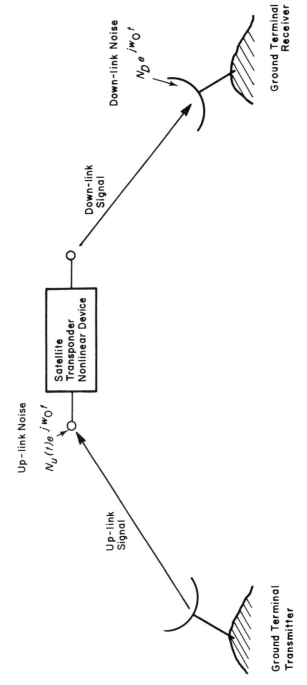

Figure 2.1.5.3 Effects of Uplink and Downlink Noises

The output of the TWTA is given by

$$e_{S+N}^{(0)} = \frac{g(|B|)}{|B|} e^{jf(|B|)} e_{S+N}. \qquad (2.1.5.30)$$

Expanding $g(|B|)/|B|\ e^{jf(|B|)}$ using the Taylor series expansion on N_{cu} and N_{su}, we have

$$e_{S+N}^{(0)} \simeq g(A) e^{j\omega_0 t + j\phi(t) + j\theta + jf(A)}$$

$$+ [j\ \mathrm{Im}\{N_u e^{-j\phi - j\theta}\} + \{G(x_A)' + j^{\beta F(x_A)'}\}$$

$$\cdot \mathrm{Re}\{N_u e^{-j\phi - j\theta}\}] \frac{g(A)}{A} e^{jf(A)} e^{j\omega_0 t + j\phi + j\theta}$$

$$= A e^{j\omega_0 t + j\phi + j\theta}$$

$$\cdot \left[1 + \frac{j}{A} \mathrm{Im}\left\{ N_u e^{-j\phi - j\theta} \right\} \right.$$

$$+ \frac{1}{A} \left\{ G(x_A)' + j\beta F(x_A)' \right\}$$

$$\left. \cdot \mathrm{Re}\left\{ N_u e^{-j\phi - j\theta} \right\} \right] \frac{g(A)}{A} e^{jf(A)}. \qquad (2.1.5.31)$$

If the TWTA is linear ($G(x_A)' = 1$ and $F(x_A)' = 0$), the above becomes

$$e_{S+N}^{(0)} = g_0 A e^{j\omega_0 t + j\phi + j\theta}$$

$$\cdot \left[1 + \frac{1}{A} N_u\ e^{-j\phi - j\theta} \right] \qquad (2.1.5.32)$$

where $g(A)/A = g_0$ and $f(A) = 0$. This result is linear to the input as is expected. In case of the ideal hardlimiter, $G(x_A)' = 0$ and $F(x_A)' = 0$, then

$$e_{S+N}^{(0)} = g_h e^{j\omega_0 t + j\phi + j\theta}$$

$$+ \frac{g_h}{A} j\ \mathrm{Im}\{N_u e^{-j\phi - j\theta}\} e^{j\omega_0 t + j\phi + j\theta} \quad (g(A) = g_h). \qquad (2.1.5.33)$$

The noise is perpendicular to the signal in this case, as is expected. The factor $g(A)/A\ e^{jf(A)}$ is irrelevant in the analysis,[†] since it is common both in noise and signal, and $e_{S+N}^{(0)}$ can be represented as

---

[†] Assuming that the FM signal is the ideal one, i.e., that there is no amplitude fluctuation (A is a time invariant constant).

$$e_{S+N}^{(0)} \simeq A e^{j\omega_0 t + j\phi + j\theta}$$

$$+ \, [j \, \mathrm{Im}(N_u e^{-j\phi - j\theta}) + (G(x_A)' + j\beta F(x_A)')$$

$$\cdot \, \mathrm{Re}(N_u e^{-j\phi - j\theta})] \, e^{j\omega_0 t + j\phi + j\theta}. \tag{2.1.5.34}$$

Rewrite $e_{S+N}^{(0)}$ of this result as

$$e_{S+N}^{(0)} = A e^{j\omega_0 t + j\phi + j\theta} + \eta(t) e^{j\omega_0 t + j\phi + j\theta} \tag{2.1.5.35}$$

where

$$\eta(t) = j \, \mathrm{Im}\{N_u e^{-j\phi - j\theta}\} + (G(x_A)' + j\beta F(x_A)')$$

$$\cdot \, \mathrm{Re}\{N_u e^{-j\phi - j\theta}\}. \tag{2.1.5.36}$$

As seen from the above results, while in the linear case the inphase and quadrative components are independent from each other, and the average power of these two components is equal, this is no longer true as seen from the hardlimiter case of Equation 2.1.5.33 where only the perpendicular component to the signal vector exists. In addition to the uplink noise of Equation 2.1.5.26, the downlink noise must be added before the FM receiver, i.e.,

$$e_{S+N}^{(i)} = A e^{j\omega_0 t + j\phi + j\theta} + \eta(t) e^{j\omega_0 t + j\phi + j\theta} + N_D e^{j\omega_0 t} \tag{2.1.5.37}$$

where

$$N_D = N_{DC} + j N_{DS} \tag{2.1.5.38}$$

where N_{CD} and N_{SD} are respectively the inphase and quadrature components of the downlink noise

$$e_{S+N}^{(i)} = A e^{j\omega_0 t + j\phi + j\theta} + N(t) e^{j\omega_0 t + j\phi + j\theta} \tag{2.1.5.39}$$

$$N(t) = \eta(t) + N_D(t) e^{-j\phi - j\theta}. \tag{2.1.5.40}$$

To obtain the demodulated output of the FM receiver at ground station, rewrite Equation 2.1.5.40 as

$$e_{S+N} = A e^{j\omega_0 t + j\phi + j\theta} \left[1 + \frac{N}{A} \right]$$

$$= A \left| 1 + \frac{N}{A} \right| e^{j\omega_0 t + j\phi + j\theta} \exp\left[j \, \mathrm{Im}\left\{ \log\left(1 + \frac{N}{A} \right) \right\} \right]. \tag{2.1.5.41}$$

Thus, the demodulated output by the FM demodulator is given by

$$\frac{1}{2\pi} \frac{d}{dt} \phi(t) + \frac{1}{2\pi} \frac{d}{dt} \mathrm{Im}\left\{ \log\left(1 + \frac{N}{A} \right) \right\}. \tag{2.1.5.42}$$

Above the FM threshold, the second term of this result which is the demodulated noise, is approximated by

$$(2\pi)^{-1} \frac{d}{dt} \operatorname{Im}\left\{\frac{N}{A}\right\} = (2\pi)^{-1} \frac{d}{dt} \operatorname{Im}\left\{\frac{(N_u + N_D)}{A} e^{-j\phi - j\theta}\right\}$$

$$+ (2\pi)^{-1} \frac{d}{dt} A^{-1} \beta F(x_A)' \operatorname{Re}\{N_u e^{-j\phi - j\theta}\}$$

(2.1.5.43)

since the average $\{|N/A|^2\} \ll 1$ holds. The power spectrum of Equation 2.1.5.43 is that of

$$\operatorname{Im}\left\{\frac{N}{A}\right\}$$

(2.1.5.44)

multiplied by f^2 as explained before. The autocorrelation function of Equation 2.1.5.44 is

$$\frac{1}{2}\frac{1}{A^2} \operatorname{Re}\{E[N(t) N(t+\tau)^*] - E[N(t) N(t+\tau)]\}$$

$$= \frac{1}{A^2} [R_{Nu}(\tau)\{1 + (\beta F(x_A)')^2\} + R_{ND}(\tau)] e^{-R_\phi(0) + R_\phi(\tau)}$$

$$= \frac{R_N(\tau)}{A^2} e^{-R_\phi(0) + R_\phi(\tau)}$$

(2.1.5.45)

where $R_N(\tau)$ is the autocorrelation function of

$$N_{us}[1 + (\beta F(x_A)')^2]^{1/2} + N_{DS}$$

and $\exp[-R_\phi(0) + R_\phi(\tau)] \cos(\omega_0 \tau)$ is the autocorrelation function of the FM signal whose power is unity.

In deriving Equation 2.1.5.45, N_u and $N_D(t)$ are independent and therefore all the cross correlation functions are zero. Further

$$E\{N_u(t) N_u(t+\tau)\} = E\{N_D(t)$$

$$N_D(t+\tau)\} = 0$$

and

$$E\{N_u(t) N_u(t+\tau)^*\} = 2 R_{Nu}(\tau)$$

$$E\{N_D(t) N_D(t+\tau)^*\} = 2 R_{ND}(\tau)$$

(2.1.5.46)

where

$$R_{Nu}(\tau) = E\{N_{uc}(t) N_{uc}(t+\tau)\}$$

$$= E\{N_{us}(t) N_{us}(t+\tau)\}$$

$$R_{ND}(\tau) = E\{N_{DC}(t) N_{DC}(t+\tau)\}$$

$$= E\{N_{DS}(t) N_{DS}(t+\tau)\}. \qquad (2.1.5.47)$$

The autocorrelation function of the r.f. up- and downlink noise,

$$N_{uc}(t) \cos \omega_0 t - N_{us}(t) \sin \omega_0 t \quad \text{and}$$

$$N_{Nu}(t) \cos \omega_0 t - N_{ND}(t) \sin \omega_0 t \qquad (2.1.5.48)$$

are respectively given by

$$R_{UN}(\tau) \cos (\omega_0 \tau) \text{ and } R_{DN}(\tau) \cos (\omega_0 \tau).$$

In practical cases (even at the saturating power of TWTA), $(\beta F(XA))')^2 \ll 1$ and it can be ignored (this means that the nonlinear effects on the uplink noise is negligible and can be treated linearly). The power spectrum for Equation 2.1.5.45 (Fourier-transform of Equation 2.1.5.45) is given by

$$\frac{1}{2C} \int_{-\infty}^{\infty} W_N(x) W_C(f-x) dx = \frac{1}{2C} I_N(f) \ (-\infty < f < \infty) \quad (2.1.5.49)$$

where $W_N(f)$ is the power spectrum of the noise (Fourier transform of $R_N(\tau)$) and $W_C(f)$ is that of the FM signal of unit power (Fourier-transform of $\exp[-R_\phi(0) + R_\phi(\tau)]$). C is the FM carrier power.

Thus, the power spectrum of the demodulated noise is given by

$$\frac{f^2}{2C} I_N(f), \quad -\infty < f < \infty. \qquad (2.1.5.50)$$

Using this result, the N.P.R. value at channel frequency f is

$$\text{N.P.R.} = \frac{\dfrac{\sigma^2}{(f_h - f_l)} \Delta f}{2 \dfrac{f^2}{2C} I_N(f) G_{pr}(f)^{-1} \Delta f}$$

$$= \frac{C}{I_N(f)} \frac{\sigma^2}{f^2} \frac{1}{(f_h - f_l)} \frac{1}{G_{pr}(f)^{-1}} . \qquad (2.1.5.51)$$

In practical cases, the thermal noise has a flat spectrum of a frequency range much wider than the power spectrum of the FM signal ($W_c(f)$) and baseband spectrum and therefore

$$I_N(f) = N_0 \qquad (2.1.5.52)$$

where N_0 is the power spectrum density of the r.f. noise. Thus, the N.P.R. (in the noise loading test) of Equation 2.1.5.51 becomes

$$\text{N.P.R.} = \frac{C}{N_0} \frac{\sigma^2}{f^2} \frac{1}{(f_h - f_l)} \frac{1}{G_{pr}(f)^{-1}} .$$ (2.1.5.53)

This result is very well known for FM engineers. In case of a signal interference instead of the thermal noise, $I_N(f)$ assumes more complicated forms which will be analyzed in Chapter 5.

Threshold and Below Threshold

The following analyses the areas of threshold and below threshold. In order to explain how the phenomenon at threshold and below threshold physically occurs, separate Equation 2.1.5.1 into the inphase and quadrature components

$$I = A \cos \phi(t) + N_c \text{ (imphase component)}.$$

$$Q = A \sin \phi(t) + N_s \text{ (quadrature component)}.$$ (2.1.5.54)

Two cases cause the threshold phenomenon.

(i) Let us use a $PR - UV$ axis instead of the IQ axis in Figure 2.1.5.4. While the PR axis component of the vector OP_1 stays in the negative side (i.e., on the OR line), the UV component of the same vector crosses the origin (0). In the area of C/N at around 10 dB, this happens very quickly in time, since the point P_1 cannot stay in the negative side of the PR axis for a long time because of the small noise power (compared with the carrier power $A^2/2$). Therefore, the phase of the FM signal plus noise (e) changes $2\pi(360°)$ very quickly like a step function.

Thus, the FM demodulator has an impulse at this moment, since it is the derivative of the phase. Representing the components of $N(t)$ on the PR and UV axes by N_R and N_v, the probability of this occurence is

$$A + N_R < 0$$ (2.1.5.55)

and N_v crosses zero at the same time. If N_v crosses zero from the U side to the V side, the positive impulse occurs and, if it occurs from the V side to the U side, the negative impulse occurs. In this case, the integral of $\theta(t)$ at this moment is approximately 2π. Therefore, the power spectrum due to these impulses has approximately a same density in the low frequency area, where it is almost flat because of the impulse noise.

(ii) When point P in Figure 2.1.5.4 leaves the region P, cuts across the segment OP close to O, and then returns to P, θ changes rapidly by nearly $\pm \pi$ during the sweep past O. However, the resulting pulse in θ' has little low-frequency content since the integral of θ taken over such an excursion is nearly zero. Hence, the output of the low-pass filter is much smaller than that for an excursion in which θ changes $\pm 2\pi$.

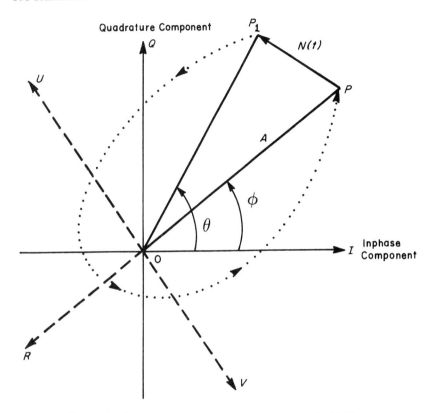

Figure 2.1.5.4 Click Noise Occurrence Diagram of FM Signal

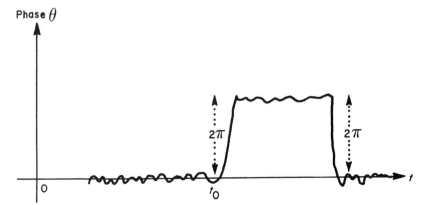

Figure 2.1.5.5 Phase Change Due to Click Noise

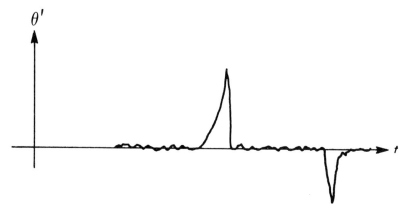

Figure 2.1.5.6 Impulse Noise at FM Demodulator Output

Based on the physical insight explained above, the power spectrum of these impulses at FM threshold has been approximately analyzed [37]. The result of this analysis concurs with that of the exact analytical result using the precise autocorrelation function of the output noise, in which the case of an unmodulated carrier plus noise is exactly analyzed. Although the above heuristic approach to obtain the threshold characteristic in [37] is a good model for unmodulated carrier plus noise cases, it cannot be applied to the case where the carrier is modulated rapidly in relation to the instantaneous change of the thermal noise, since the above approach in [37] is fixing the angle φ first and obtaining the threshold characteristic heuristically, and then taking the average of the noise power thus obtained (the average with respect to φ). This method is only applicable when φ does not change much faster than $N(t)$.

Therefore, in order to obtain the exact characteristics at and below threshold, an exact analysis must be done [34].

Since the exact solution for the unmodulated carrier plus noise in [89] does not show separately the terms which give the characteristics above, at and below threshold, in the following, three terms respectively above, at, and below threshold are obtained.

Although the modulated carrier case has been exactly solved in [90], (modulated by a Gaussian or sine wave baseband signal), it is not shown here, since it is beyond the scope of this book.

The analysis starts from Equation 2.1.5.6 putting φ(t) = 0, i.e.,

$$\theta'(t) = \operatorname{Im} \frac{d}{dt} \ln\left\{1 + \frac{N(t)}{A}\right\} = \operatorname{Im}\left\{\frac{\left(\frac{N(t)'}{A}\right)}{1 + \left(\frac{N(t)}{A}\right)}\right\}$$

$$= \frac{1}{2j} \frac{N(t)'}{1 + \dfrac{N(t)}{A}} - \frac{1}{2j} \frac{N(t)'^*}{1 + \dfrac{N(t)^*}{A}} \qquad (2.1.5.56)$$

Therefore, assuming $A = 1$,[†]

$$\theta(t)' \theta(t + \tau)' = \frac{1}{2} \operatorname{Re} \left\{ \frac{N(t)' \, N(t + \tau)'^*}{[1 + N(t)][1 + N(t + \tau)]^*} \right.$$

$$\left. - \frac{N(t)' \, N(t + \tau)'}{[1 + N(t)][1 + N(t + \tau)]} \right\} . \qquad (2.1.5.57)$$

The eight variables' average on $N_c(t)$, $N_s(t)$, $N_c(t + \tau)$, $N_s(t + \tau)$, $N_c'(t)$, $N_s'(t)$, $N_c'(t + \tau)$ and $N_s'(t + \tau)$ is required to obtain the autocorrelation function of $\theta'(t)$. Represent these variables by

$$z_1 = N_s(t), \ z_2 = N_c(t), \ z_3 = N_s(t)', \ z_4 = N_c(t)',$$

$$z_5 = N_s(t + \tau), \ z_6 = N_c(t + \tau), \ z_7 = N_s(t + \tau)', \ z_8 = N_c(t + \tau)'. \qquad (2.1.5.58)$$

Then, the autocorrelation function of $\theta'(t)$ is given by

$$R_{\theta'}(\tau) = \int_{-\infty}^{\infty} \int_{-\infty}^{\infty} \cdots \int_{-\infty}^{\infty} \theta(t)' \, \theta(t + \tau)' \, p(z_1, z_2, \ldots, z_8) \, dz_1 \, dz_2 \cdots dz_8 .$$

$$(2.1.5.59)$$

From the analysis of Section 2.12 and 2.1 of Volume 1, the characteristic function of $p(z_1, \ldots, z_8)$ is

$$c(t_1, t_2, \ldots, t_8) = \exp \left[- \frac{W}{2} (t_1^2 + t_2^2 + t_5^2 + t_6^2) \right.$$

$$- \frac{V}{2} (t_3^2 + t_4^2 + t_7^2 + t_8^2) - (t_1 t_5 + t_2 t_6) U(\tau)$$

$$- (t_1 t_7 + t_2 t_8 - t_3 t_5 - t_4 t_6) U(\tau)'$$

$$\left. + (t_3 t_7 + t_4 t_8) U(\tau)'' \right] \qquad (2.1.5.60)$$

where

$$E\{z_1 \, z_1\} = E\{z_2 \, z_2\} = E\{z_5 \, z_5\} = E\{z_6 \, z_6\} = W \qquad \text{(a)}$$

$$E\{z_3 \, z_3\} = E\{z_4 \, z_4\} = E\{z_7 \, z_7\} = E\{z_8 \, z_8\} = V \qquad \text{(b)}$$

$$E\{z_1 \, z_2\} = E\{z_1 \, z_3\} = 0 \qquad \text{(c)}$$

[†] This does not affect the general rule, since the signal and noise power are relatively important.

$$E\{z_2\, z_4\} = 0 \tag{d}$$

$$E\{z_3\, z_4\} = 0 \tag{e}$$

$$E\{z_5\, z_7\} = E\{z_5\, z_6\} = 0 \tag{f}$$

$$E\{z_6\, z_8\} = 0 \tag{g}$$

$$E\{z_1\, z_4\} = E\{z_1\, z_6\} = E\{z_1\, z_8\} = 0 \tag{h}$$

$$E\{z_2\, z_3\} = E\{z_2\, z_5\} = E\{z_2\, z_7\} = 0 \tag{i}$$

$$E\{z_3\, z_6\} = E\{z_3\, z_8\} = 0 \tag{j}$$

$$E\{z_4\, z_5\} = E\{z_4\, z_7\} = 0 \tag{k}$$

$$E\{z_5\, z_8\} = 0 \tag{l}$$

$$E\{z_6\, z_7\} = 0 \tag{m}$$

$$E\{z_1\, z_5\} = E\{z_2\, z_6\} = U(\tau) \tag{n}$$

$$E\{z_1\, z_7\} = E\{z_2\, z_8\} = -E\{z_3\, z_5\} = -E\{z_4\, z_6\} = U(\tau)' \tag{o}$$

$$E\{z_3\, z_7\} = E\{z_4\, z_8\} = -U(\tau)'' \tag{p}$$

$$\tag{2.1.5.61}$$

where W is the total power of the r.f. noise, i.e.,

$$W = \int_{-\infty}^{\infty} W_N(f)\, df. \tag{2.1.5.62}$$

Note that $W_N(f)$ is the r.f. noise power spectrum whose center is shifted to zero frequency. V is the total power of $N_c'(t)$ (or $N_s'(t)$), i.e.,

$$V = \int_{-\infty}^{\infty} 4\pi^2 f^2\, W_N(f)\, df (= -U(0)''). \tag{2.1.5.63}$$

$U(\tau)$ is the autocorrelation function of $N_c(t)$ or $N_s(t)$, i.e.,

$$U(\tau) = \int_{-\infty}^{\infty} W_N(f)\, e^{j2\pi f\tau}\, df. \tag{2.1.5.64}$$

$U'(\tau)$ is the derivative of $U(\tau)$, i.e.,

$$U(\tau)' = \int_{-\infty}^{\infty} (j2\pi f)\, W_N(f)\, e^{j2\pi f\tau}\, df \tag{2.1.5.65}$$

$$-U(\tau)'' = \int_{-\infty}^{\infty} (2\pi f)^2\, W_N(f)\, e^{j2\pi f\tau}\, df. \tag{2.1.5.66}$$

The relation of (c), (d), (e), (f), (g) in Equation 2.1.5.61 comes from the statistical independency of $z_1, \ldots, z_8$ and that of (h), (i), (j), (k), (l), (m) comes from the symmetry of the r.f. noise spectrum around the carrier frequency.

All these results of Equation 2.1.5.61 can be easily proved by the analysis shown in Sections 2.1 and 2.11 of Volume 1 where the noise is represented by a sum of sine waves. Using these results, Equation 2.1.5.59 becomes, since the Fourier-transform of $C(t_1, t_2, \ldots, t_8)$ is $P(z_1, z_2, \ldots, z_8)$,

$$
(2\pi)^{-8} \int_{-\infty}^{\infty} \cdots \int_{-\infty}^{\infty} \exp[j\{t_1 z_1 + t_2 z_2 + \cdots + t_8 z_8\}] \, \theta(t)' \theta(t+\tau)'
$$

$$
\cdot \exp\left[-\frac{W}{2}(t_1^2 + t_2^2 + t_5^2 + t_6^2) - \frac{V}{2}(t_3^2 + t_4^2 + t_7^2 + t_8^2) \right.
$$

$$
- U(\tau)(t_1 t_5 + t_2 t_6) - U(\tau)'(t_1 t_7 + t_2 t_8 - t_3 t_5 - t_4 t_6)
$$

$$
\left. + U(\tau)''(t_3 t_7 + t_4 t_7) \right] dz_1 dz_2 \cdots dz_8 \cdot dt_1 dt_2 \cdots dt_8.
$$

$$(2.1.5.67)$$

In order to finish the integrals of $z_1, z_2, \ldots, z_8$, in Equation 2.1.5.67, let us evaluate the following integral:[†]

$$
\int_{-\infty}^{\infty} \int_{-\infty}^{\infty} \int_{-\infty}^{\infty} \int_{-\infty}^{\infty} \frac{z_4(1+z_2)}{(1+z_2)^2 + z_1^2} \, e^{jt_1 z_1 + jt_2 z_2 + jt_3 z_3 + jt_4 z_4} \, dz_1 \, dz_2 \, dz_3 \, dz_4.
$$

$$(2.1.5.68)$$

Using the formula for the δ-functions in Section 2.4 of Volume 1, this becomes

$$
-j(2\pi)^2 \delta(t_3) \delta(t_4)' \int_{-\infty}^{\infty} \int_{-\infty}^{\infty} \frac{(1+z_2)}{(1+z_2)^2 + z_1^2}
$$

$$
\cdot e^{jt_2 z_2 + jt_1 z_1} \, dz_1 \, dz_2.
$$

$$(2.1.5.69)$$

The integrals with respect to z_1 and z_2 are done by transforming z_1 and z_2 into the polar coordinate transform,

$$
1 + z_2 = r \cos \theta
$$

$$
z_1 = r \sin \theta
$$

$$(2.1.5.70)$$

$$
-j(2\pi)^2 \delta(t_3) \delta(t_4)' \, e^{-jt_2} \int_0^{2\pi} \int_0^{\infty} \frac{r \cos \theta}{r^2}
$$

$$
\cdot e^{j(t_2 \cos \theta + t_1 \sin \theta)r} \, r \, dr \, d\theta
$$

$$(2.1.5.71)$$

[†]The integrals for the other z's can be done in a way similar to this case and are therefore not shown here.

where

$$\cos\theta\; e^{j(t_2\cos\theta + t_1\sin\theta)r} = \left(\frac{e^{j\theta} + e^{-j\theta}}{2}\right) e^{jr\sqrt{t_1^2 + t_2^2}\,\sin\left(\theta + \tan^{-1}\frac{t_2}{t_1}\right)}$$

$$= \left(\frac{e^{j\theta} + e^{-j\theta}}{2}\right) \sum_{k=-\infty}^{\infty} J_k\left(\sqrt{t_1^2 + t_2^2}\,r\right)$$

$$\cdot \exp\left[jk\left(\theta + \tan^{-1}\frac{t_2}{t_1}\right)\right]. \qquad (2.1.5.72)$$

See Section 2.3 of Volume 1 for this expansion.
Using the relation

$$\int_0^{2\pi} e^{jk\theta}\, d\theta = 0 \qquad (k \neq 0)$$

$$= 2\pi \qquad (k = 0), \qquad (2.1.5.73)$$

the integral of Equation 2.1.5.72 with respect to θ is

$$\pi J_{-1}\left(\sqrt{t_1^2 + t_2^2}\,r\right) e^{-j\tan^{-1}\frac{t_2}{t_1}} + \pi J_1\left(\sqrt{t_1^2 + t_2^2}\,r\right) e^{j\tan^{-1}\frac{t_2}{t_1}}$$

$$= (j2\pi) J_1\left(\sqrt{t_1^2 + t_2^2}\,r\right) \frac{t_2}{\sqrt{t_1^2 + t_2^2}} \cdot \qquad (2.1.5.74)$$

Now, the integral of Equation 2.1.5.74 with respect to r is given by

$$\int_0^{\infty} J_1\left(\sqrt{t_1^2 + t_2^2}\,r\right) dv = \left[\frac{-J_0\left(\sqrt{t_1^2 + t_2^2}\,r\right)}{\sqrt{t_1^2 + t_2^2}}\right]_{r=0}^{r=\infty}$$

$$= \frac{1}{\sqrt{t_1^2 + t_2^2}} \cdot \qquad (2.1.5.75)$$

Therefore, Equation 2.1.5.71 becomes

$$(2\pi)^3\, \delta(t_3)\, \delta(t_4)'\, e^{-jt_2}\, \frac{t_2}{(t_1^2 + t_2^2)} \cdot \qquad (2.1.5.76)$$

Thus, the integrals with respect to t_3, t_4, t_7 and t_8 can be easily done by using the integral formulae of $\delta(t)$ and $\delta'(t)$ in Section 2.4[†] of Volume I. Equation 2.1.5.67 now becomes

---

[†]The δ-functions of t_7 and t_8 can be obtained when the variables of the z's other than z_1, z_2, and z_4 are eliminated in a way similar to the case of Equation 2.1.5.68.

$$\frac{1}{2}(2\pi)^{-2}\,\mathrm{Re}\int_{-\infty}^{\infty}\int_{-\infty}^{\infty}\exp\left[-\frac{W}{2}(t_1^2+t_2^2+t_5^2+t_6^2)-U(\tau)\right.$$

$$(t_1t_5+t_2t_6)\Bigg]\left\{\frac{(t_1+jt_2)(t_5-jt_6)}{(t_1^2+t_2^2)(t_5^2+t_6^2)}\left[2U(\tau)''-U'(\tau)^2(t_1+jt_2)\right.\right.$$

$$(t_5-jt_6)]+\frac{(t_1+jt_2)(t_5+jt_6)}{(t_1^2+t_2^2)(t_5^2+t_6^2)}\,U'(\tau)^2(t_1-jt_2)(t_5-jt_6)\Bigg\}$$

$$e^{-jt_2-jt_6}\,dt_1\,dt_2\,dt_5\,dt_6. \tag{2.1.5.77}$$

Transforming (t_1, t_2) and (t_5, t_6) to polar coordinates, using the same expansion formula as in Equation 2.1.5.72, and using Equation 2.1.5.73, Equation 2.1.5.77 becomes

$$\left[-U(\tau)''+\frac{U'(\tau)^2}{U(\tau)}\right]\int_0^\infty\int_0^\infty I_1(Uxy)\,J_0(x)\,J_0(y)$$

$$\cdot\exp\left[-\frac{W^2}{2}(x^2+y^2)\right]dx\,dy$$

$$-2U''(\tau)\int_0^\infty\int_0^\infty\sum_{n=1}^\infty I_n(Uxy)'\,J_n(x)\,J_n(y)\,e^{-\frac{W}{2}(x^2+y^2)}\,dx\,dy$$

$$-2U'(\tau)^2\int_0^\infty\int_0^\infty\sum_{n=1}^\infty I_n(Uxy)''\,J_n(x)\,J_n(y)\,e^{-\frac{W}{2}(x^2+y^2)}\,xy\,dx\,dy$$

$$+2U'(\tau)^2\int_0^\infty\int_0^\infty\sum_{n=1}^\infty I_n(Uxy)\,J_n(x)\,J_n(y)\,e^{-\frac{W}{2}(x^2+y^2)}\,xy\,dx\,dy.$$

$$\tag{2.1.5.78}$$

The second and third terms can be rewritten as

$$-\frac{d^2}{d\tau^2}\,2\int_0^\infty\int_0^\infty\left\{\sum_{n=1}^\infty I_n(Uxy)J_n(x)\,J_n(y)\right\}\frac{1}{xy}\,e^{-\frac{W}{2}(x^2+y^2)}\,dx\,dy. \tag{2.1.5.79}$$

This double integral is a function of $U(\tau)$ and the Fourier-transform of it (excluding the double differentiation) gives a flat power spectrum in low frequency areas (baseband frequency areas).

Therefore, the Fourier-transform of Equation 2.1.5.79 (the power spectrum of this component) is approximately proportional to f^2 because of the double differentiation with respect to τ (in the baseband frequency area).

In the above threshold area (C/N) > 10 dB, the following approximation holds

$$\sum_{n=1}^{\infty} I_n(Uxy)J_n(x) J_n(y) \simeq \frac{1}{2} U(\tau) \, xy \, J_1(x) J_1(y) \qquad (2.1.5.80)$$

where this approximation was done by expanding the function of $U(\tau)$ to the power series and by taking only the term of $U(\tau)$ (ignoring the higher power of U).

Then, Equation 2.1.5.79 is approximated as

$$\left[\int_0^{\infty} J_1(x) \, e^{-\frac{W}{2} x^2} dx \right]^2 \left[-\frac{d^2}{d\tau^2} U(\tau) \right] = (1 - e^{-\frac{1}{2W}})^2$$

$$\left(-\frac{d^2}{d\tau^2} U(\tau) \right) \simeq -\frac{d^2}{d\tau^2} U(\tau). \qquad (2.1.5.81)$$

This result is equal to that of Equation 2.1.5.18, considering that it is assumed here that

(a) there is no modulation, i.e.,

$$\frac{1}{c} W_c(f) = \delta(f) \qquad (2.1.5.82)$$

and,

(b)

$$A = 1, \text{ i.e.,}$$
$$2C = 2A^2/2 = 1. \qquad (2.1.5.83)$$

Note that, in this case,

$$R_N(\tau) = U(\tau) \qquad (2.1.5.84)$$

since both are the autocorrelation function of $N_c(t)$ (or $N_S(t)$).
The Fourier-transform of Equation 2.1.5.81 is

$$(2\pi f)^2 \, W_N(f). \qquad (2.1.5.85)$$

Therefore, the demodulated noise power spectrum is given by

$$W_N(f)f^2 \, (-\infty < f < \infty). \qquad (2.1.5.86)$$

This is equal to Equation 2.1.5.18 under the above simplifications.
Let us take the fourth term of Equation 2.1.5.78, i.e.,

$$2\rho'(\tau)^2 \sum_{n=1}^{\infty} \int_0^{\infty} \int_0^{\infty} I_n(\rho xy) \, J_n\left(\frac{x}{\sqrt{W}}\right) J_n\left(\frac{y}{\sqrt{W}}\right) xy \, e^{-\frac{1}{2}(x^2 + y^2)} \, dx \, dy$$

(2.1.5.87)

where

$$\rho(\tau) = U(\tau)/W.$$

(2.1.5.88)

Using Equation 2.1.51 of Volume 1 twice for x and y, this becomes

$$\frac{2\rho'(\tau)^2}{(1-\rho^2)} e^{-\frac{1}{2W}\frac{2}{(1-\rho^2)}} \sum_{n=1}^{\infty} I_n\left(\frac{\rho}{(1-\rho^2)W}\right).$$

(2.1.5.89)

From Equation 2.3.32 in Volume 1,

$$\sum_{n=1}^{\infty} I_n\left(\frac{\rho}{(1-\rho^2)W}\right) = \frac{1}{2}\left[e^{\frac{\rho}{W(1-\rho^2)}} - I_0\left(\frac{\rho}{W(1-\rho^2)}\right)\right].$$

(2.1.5.90)

Thus, Equation 2.1.5.89 becomes

$$\frac{\rho'(\tau)^2}{(1-\rho^2)} e^{-\frac{1}{2W}\frac{2}{(1+\rho)}}\left[1 - e^{-\frac{2\rho}{2W(1-\rho^2)}} I_0\left(\frac{2\rho}{2W(1-\rho^2)}\right)\right].$$

(2.1.5.91)

As shown in [88], this term gives the threshold characteristic whose power spectrum is flat around zero frequency (around the baseband frequency).

As shown also in [88], this flat power spectrum around zero frequency can be approximated by the Fourier integral at $f = 0$ with the approximation

$$\rho(\tau) \doteq 1 + \frac{\rho''(0)}{2}\tau^2$$

(2.1.5.92)

and

$$1 - e^{-\frac{2\rho}{2W(1-\rho^2)}} I_0\left(\frac{2\rho}{2W(1-\rho^2)}\right) \doteq 1 - \frac{1}{\sqrt{2\pi}}\sqrt{\frac{2W(1-\rho^2)}{2\rho}}$$

$$\doteq 1.$$

(2.1.5.93)

Namely, this flat threshold power spectrum becomes approximately[†]

[†]Since the power spectrum of this noise is much more spread than that of the r.f. noise bandwidth, the Fourier-Transform of this autocorrelation function around $f = 0$ is determined by the approximation of Equation 2.1.5.92 as shown in the following.

$$\int_{-\infty}^{\infty} \frac{\rho'(\tau)^2}{1-\rho^2(\tau)} e^{-\frac{2}{2W(1+\rho)}} d\tau \simeq \frac{(\rho''(0)\tau)^2}{2(-\frac{1}{2}\rho''(0)\tau^2)} \int_{-\infty}^{\infty} e^{-\frac{2(1-\rho)}{2W(1+\rho)} - \frac{2\rho}{2W(1+\rho)}} d\tau$$

$$\simeq (-\rho''(0)) e^{-\frac{1}{2W}} \int_{-\infty}^{\infty} e^{\frac{1}{2}\frac{\rho''(0)}{2W}\tau^2} d\tau$$

$$= \sqrt{2W} \sqrt{-\rho''(0)} \sqrt{2\pi} e^{-\frac{1}{2W}} (-\infty < f < \infty)$$

(2.1.5.94)

where

$$-\rho''(0) = \frac{V}{W}.$$

(2.1.5.95)

Then, Equation 2.1.5.94 becomes

$$2\sqrt{2V}\sqrt{2\pi} e^{-\frac{1}{2W}} \quad (0 \le f)$$

(2.1.5.96)

where it should be noted that

$$C/N = \frac{1}{2W}.$$

(2.1.5.97)

The result of Equation 2.1.5.96 is equal to that obtained in [37] and [88].

The first term of Equation 2.1.5.78 is important for the below threshold area, which can be rewritten as

$$-\frac{1}{2}\left[\frac{\rho''}{\rho} - \frac{\rho'^2}{\rho^2}\right] 2\rho \int_0^{\infty} \int_0^{\infty} I_1(\rho xy) J_0\left(\frac{x}{\sqrt{W}}\right) J_0\left(\frac{y}{\sqrt{W}}\right) e^{-\frac{(x^2+y^2)}{2}} dx\, dy.$$

(2.1.5.98)

In the limit $W \to \infty$, Equation 2.1.5.98 corresponds to the case where there is no signal carrier and only noise. Thus, the autocorrelation function of the FM demodulator output when the input is only the thermal noise is given by

$$-\frac{1}{2}\left[\frac{\rho''}{\rho} - \frac{\rho'^2}{\rho^2}\right] 2\rho \int_0^{\infty} \int_0^{\infty} I_1(\rho xy) e^{-\frac{x^2+y^2}{2}} dx\, dy \quad (2.1.5.99)$$

where

$$\lim_{W \to \infty} J_0\left(\frac{x}{\sqrt{W}}\right) = 1$$

(2.1.5.100)

and

$$2\rho \int_{-\infty}^{\infty} \int_{-\infty}^{\infty} I_1(\rho xy) \, e^{-\frac{(x^2+y^2)}{2}} \, dx \, dy = -\ln(1-\rho^2). \quad (2.1.5.101)$$

Therefore, Equation 2.1.5.99 becomes

$$\frac{1}{2}\left[\frac{\rho''}{\rho} - \frac{\rho'^2}{\rho^2}\right] \ln(1-\rho^2). \quad (2.1.5.102)$$

This result is the same as that of [35].

As shown in [35], this function has ∞ value when $\tau \to 0$, which means that the output of the ideal discriminator has infinite power when the input consists of thermal noise only. This term is only important below threshold and, since the signal is operating normally close to or above threshold, the demodulated noise spectrum at threshold or above, which is that of Equations 2.1.5.96 and 2.1.5.86, is shown in the following.

Assume for the sake of simplicity that the r.f. thermal noise is flat in the r.f. band, i.e.,

$$W_N(f) = N_0 = \frac{W}{B}, \quad |f| \le \frac{B}{2}$$
$$= 0, \quad |f| > \frac{B}{2}$$
$$(2.1.9.103)$$

where B is the r.f. noise bandwidth. In this case, V of Equation 2.1.5.66, i.e., Equation 2.1.5.63 is given by

$$V = \int_{-\frac{B}{2}}^{\frac{B}{2}} 4\pi^2 f^2 \frac{W}{B} \, df = 4\pi^2 \frac{W}{B} 2 \frac{1}{3} \left(\frac{B}{2}\right)^3$$

$$= (\pi^2/3) W B^2. \quad (2.1.5.104)$$

The power spectrum of the demodulated noise at and above threshold is

$$\frac{W_N(f)}{c} f^2 + \frac{1}{\sqrt{6\pi}} \sqrt{2W} \, B \, e^{-\frac{1}{2W}}$$

$$= \frac{W_N(f)}{c} f^2 + \frac{1}{\sqrt{6\pi}} B \left(\frac{C}{N}\right)^{-\frac{1}{2}} e^{-\left(\frac{C}{N}\right)} \quad (0 < f). \quad (2.1.5.105)$$

Note here that

$$\left(\frac{1}{2}A^2\right)W^{-1} = \frac{1}{2W} = \left(\frac{C}{N}\right)$$

in this case.

The first term of Equation 2.1.5.105 gives the triangle noise above threshold, and the second term gives the output noise around threshold.

2.1.6 FSK Signal Transmission

Let us analyze the case of Figure 2.1.5 from Volume 1. Ideally, the input to this receiver of a FSK signal is given by

$$e_i(t) = \sum_{n=-\infty}^{\infty} A \sin\{2\pi(f_0 + a_n\Delta f)t + \theta_n\} s(t - nT) \qquad (2.1.6.1)$$

where a_n takes ± 1 independently with the equal probability $\frac{1}{2}$. Also, for simplicity's sake, let us assume that a_n and $a_m(n \neq m)$ are independent. $s(t)$ is defined by Equation 4.3.3 from Volume 1, i.e.,

$$s(t) = 1 , \quad |t| < \frac{T}{2}$$

$$= 0 , \quad |t| \geq \frac{T}{2} . \qquad (2.1.6.2)$$

f_1 and f_2 of Figure 2.1.5 from Volume 1 are

$$f_1 = f_0 + \Delta f$$

$$f_2 = f_0 - \Delta f. \qquad (2.1.6.3)$$

Equation 2.1.6.1 means that $e_i(t)$ takes the frequency f_1 or f_2 in each symbol interval, $(nT - T/2, nT + T/2)$ $(n = 0, \pm 1, \ldots)$.

$e_i(t)$ of Equation 2.1.6.1 can be divided into two portions:

$$e_{i1}(t) = \left[\sum_{n=-\infty}^{\infty} \left(\frac{1 + b_n}{2}\right) s(t - nT)\right] \sin\{2\pi(f_0 + \Delta f)t + \theta_{1n}\}$$

$$+ \left[\sum_{n=-\infty}^{\infty} \left(\frac{1 + c_n}{2}\right) s(t - nT)\right] \sin\{2\pi(f_0 - \Delta f)t + \theta_{2n}\}.$$

$$(2.1.6.4)$$

where b_n can take ± 1 independently with equal probability $\frac{1}{2}$. c_n takes also ± 1 randomly but it always has to satisfy

$$b_n + c_n = 0. \qquad (2.1.6.5)$$

As seen from the analysis of Section 5.6.1 in Volume I, the power spectrum of

$$\sum_{n=-\infty}^{\infty} \left(\frac{1 + b_n}{2}\right) s(t - nT) \quad \text{or}$$

$$\sum_{n=-\infty}^{\infty} \left(\frac{1 + c_n}{2}\right) s(t - nT) \tag{2.1.6.6}$$

has the shape of Figure 2.1.6.1.

Therefore, the power spectrum of the first term of Equation 2.1.6.4 is given by Figure 2.1.6.2.

The power spectrum of the second term of Equation 2.1.6.4 is that of Figure 2.1.6.2 whose $f_0 + \Delta f$ is replaced by $f_0 - \Delta f$. However, from Section 5.6.4 of Volume 1, the power spectrum of $e_i(t)$ is given by Figure 2.1.6.3.

In the above power spectrum example, the phase discontinuous case of the FSK signal is assumed (see Section 5.6.4 of Volume 1).

Suppose, in this case, that the signal $f_0 + \Delta f = f_1$ is sent in the k-th time interval $(kT - T/2, kT + T/2)$.

Then, the output of Filter II whose centre frequency is $f_0 - \Delta f$ should only be the thermal noise but, in reality, there is a signal output due to some leakage from the spectrum of the signal f_1 which is sent. Also, the output of Filter I fluctuates because of the intersymbol interference effects which can be analyzed in a way similar to the cases of Section 3.2.1 of Volume 1 and 2.3.2 of Volume 2.

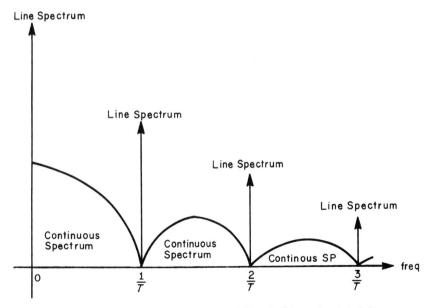

Figure 2.1.6.1   Power Spectrum of Signal of Equation 2.1.6.6

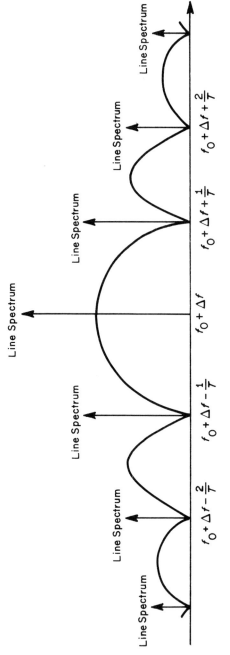

Figure 2.1.6.2 Power Spectrum of Signal of First Term of Equation 2.1.6.4

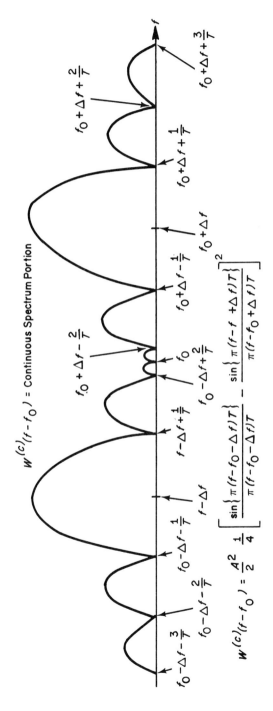

Figure 2.1.6.3(a) Continuous Power Spectrum Portion of Phase Discontinuous FSK Signal

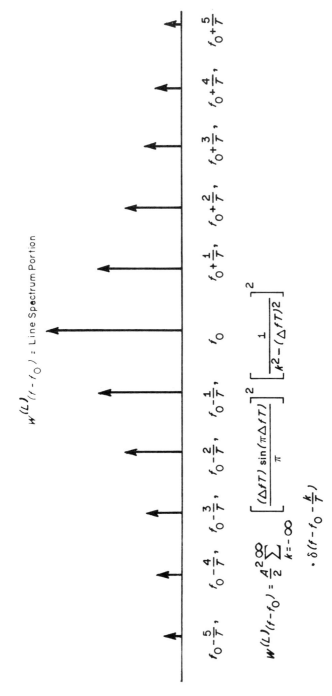

$$W^{(L)}(f-f_0) = \frac{A^2}{2} \sum_{k=-\infty}^{\infty} \left[\frac{(\Delta fT) \sin(\pi \Delta fT)}{\pi} \right]^2 \left[\frac{1}{k^2 - (\Delta fT)^2} \right]^2$$

$$\cdot \, \delta(f - f_0 - \tfrac{k}{T})$$

$W^{(L)}(f - f_0) = $ Line Spectrum Portion

$f_0 - \frac{5}{T}$, $f_0 - \frac{4}{T}$, $f_0 - \frac{3}{T}$, $f_0 - \frac{2}{T}$, $f_0 - \frac{1}{T}$, f_0, $f_0 + \frac{1}{T}$, $f_0 + \frac{2}{T}$, $f_0 + \frac{3}{T}$, $f_0 + \frac{4}{T}$, $f_0 + \frac{5}{T}$

Figure 2.1.6.3(b) Line Power Spectrum Portion of Phase Discontinuous FSK Signal

Thus, the outputs of Filters I and II, in Figure 2.1.5 of Volume 1 fluctuate due to these effects. Also, the noise power of Filters I and II cannot be exactly equal.

Therefore, the probability of error for this FSK signal receiver, when the f_1 signal is sent, is given by (see Equation 2.1.82) of Volume I).

$$P_e = \frac{-\sigma_1^2}{\sigma_1^2 + \sigma_2^2} \exp\left[-\frac{\alpha^2}{2}\frac{\sigma_1^2}{\sigma_1^2 + \sigma_2^2} - \frac{\beta^2}{2}\frac{\sigma_2^2}{\sigma_1^2 + \sigma_2^2}\right]$$

$$\cdot I_0\left(\frac{\sigma_1\sigma_2}{\sigma_1^2 + \sigma_2^2}\alpha\beta\right) + Q\left(\frac{\sigma_2\beta}{\sqrt{\sigma_1^2 + \sigma_2^2}}, \frac{\sigma_1\alpha}{\sqrt{\sigma_1^2 + \sigma_2^2}}\right) \quad (2.1.6.7)$$

where

$$\alpha = \frac{A_1}{\sigma_1}, \quad \beta = \frac{A_2}{\sigma_2}. \quad (2.1.6.8)$$

σ_1^2 and σ_2^2 are respectively the output noise power of Filters I and II. In this case,

$$A_1 = A + \Delta A_1$$

$$A_2 = \Delta A_2 \quad (2.1.6.9)$$

where ΔA_1 is the fluctuation due to intersymbol interferences and ΔA_2 is the spectrum leakage from the f_1 signal, sent as explained above, and due to intersymbol interferences from its own signal.

Although the result of Equation 2.1.6.7 is accurate, in order to see the physical insight, let us see what happens to this P_e in the ideal case where no such disturbance occurs, i.e.,

$$A_1 = A$$

$$A_2 = 0 \quad (2.1.6.10)$$

$$P_e \simeq \frac{1}{2}\exp\left[-\frac{1}{2}\frac{A^2}{2\sigma_1^2}\right] \quad (2.1.6.11)$$

assuming that

$$\sigma_1 = \sigma_2 \quad (2.1.6.12)$$

which is approximately true in most practical cases.

2.1.7 FM Click Noise Due to Overdeviation (and Filter Distortions)[†]

If the FM signal modulation is overdeviated against filters, not only do phase distortions occur but also amplitude distortions (amplitude fluctuations) are pro-

---

[†]The analysis of this section is done by Dr. N. Mathews.

duced. Then, because of an instantaneous FM amplitude reduction, the amount of FM click noise (threshold noise) is increased. The analysis for this case is as follows. The probability density function of the envelope of the filter output $e_0(t)$ (see Equation 2.1.1.4) is first calculated and then, the number of clicks per second will finally be evaluated. Now, the instantaneous peak power of the distorted FM signal is given by

$$\rho = |e_0(t)|^2 = A^2 \left| \int_{-\infty}^{\infty} e^{j\phi(t-x)} h(x)\,dx \right|^2 . \qquad (2.1.7.1)$$

The cumulative probability distribution function of ρ is given by

$$D(\rho_0) = \text{Pro}\{\rho \leq \rho_0\}$$

$$= \int_{-\infty}^{\infty} u(\rho_0 - \rho) P(\rho)\,d\rho \qquad (2.1.7.2)\dagger$$

where Pro means "probability of" and u is the unit step function, i.e.,

$$u(x) = 1 \quad x \geq 0$$

$$= 0 \quad x < 0. \qquad (2.1.7.3)$$

The evaluation of Equation 2.1.7.2 is fairly difficult but it can be obtained for some special cases. Expand $\phi(t-x)$ by a Taylor series of x as

$$\phi(t-x) = \phi(t) - \phi(x)'x + \frac{1}{2!}\phi''(x)\,x^2 - \frac{\phi(t)'''}{3!}x^3 + \cdots . \qquad (2.1.7.4)$$

Take only the first two terms of this result as

$$\phi(t-x) \simeq \phi(t) - \phi(t)'x \qquad (2.1.7.5)$$

and substitute this into Equation 2.1.7.1. Then, the function ρ of Equation 2.1.7.1 is obtained by

$$\rho \simeq A^2 \left| \int_{-\infty}^{\infty} e^{j\phi(t) - j\phi(t)'x} h(x)\,dx \right|^2$$

$$= A^2 \left| Y_{c+} \left(\frac{\phi'}{2\pi} \right) \right|^2 . \qquad (2.1.7.6)$$

Since $1/2\pi\ \phi'$ is the instantaneous frequency, in this equation, $|Y_{c+}(\phi'/2\pi)|^2$ is the factor which shows the attenuation of the filter at the instantaneous frequency $1/2\pi\ \phi'(t)$. Thus, in this case, $D(\rho_0)$ of Equation 2.1.7.2 means the cumulation probability with which the filter attenuation at the instantaneous frequency becomes higher than a certain level. Namely, the approximation of

---

$\dagger P(\rho)$ is the probability density function of ρ.

Equation 2.1.7.5 is valid when the baseband signal $1/2\pi \; \phi'(t)$ is slow, i.e., the stationary analysis can be applied under the assumption of Equation 2.1.7.5. However, the approximation of Equation 2.1.7.5 is not valid for a general case. Accordingly, more terms must be used in the expansion of Equation 2.1.7.4. It has been found that it is enough to consider the terms up to $\phi'''(t)$, i.e.,

$$\phi(t-x) \simeq \phi(t) - \phi(t)'x + \frac{1}{2!}\phi(t)''x^2 - \frac{1}{3!}\phi(t)'''x^3$$

$$= \phi(t) - ux + vx^2 - wx^3 \tag{2.1.7.7}$$

$$u = \phi(t)', \; v = \frac{1}{2!}\phi(t)'', \; w = \frac{1}{3!}\phi(t)'''. \tag{2.1.7.8}$$

Then,

$$\rho \simeq A^2 \left| \int_{-\infty}^{\infty} e^{-jux+jvx^2-jwx^3} \right|^2$$

$$= \rho(u, v, w) \tag{2.1.7.9}$$

$$D(\rho_0) = \int_{-\infty}^{\infty} u(\rho_0 - \rho) \, P(\rho)d\rho$$

$$\simeq \int_{-\infty}^{\infty} \int_{-\infty}^{\infty} \int_{-\infty}^{\infty} u(\rho_0 - \rho) \, P(u, v, w)du \; dv \; dw. \tag{2.1.7.10}^{\dagger}$$

The Equation 2.1.7.10 can be evaluated only for special cases, e.g., when $\phi'(t)$ is a Gaussian process. Some investigation showed that $\phi'(t)$ for FDM/FM signals is a Gaussian process (see Section 3.1.4 of Volume 1).

Under this Gaussian process assumption, Equation 2.1.7.10 can be evaluated. In this case,

$$\alpha_1^2 = E\{u^2\} = (2\pi)^2 \int_{-\infty}^{\infty} W_{\phi'}(f)df$$

$$\alpha_2^2 = E\{v^2\} = \frac{(2\pi)^4}{4} \int_{-\infty}^{\infty} f^2 \, W_{\phi'}(f)df$$

$$\alpha_3^2 = E\{w^2\} = \frac{(2\pi)^6}{36} \int_{-\infty}^{\infty} f^4 W_{\phi'}(f)df$$

$$E\{uv\} = E\{vw\} = 0$$

$$-\alpha_c^2 = E\{u \cdot w\} = -\frac{2}{3}\alpha_2^2 \tag{2.1.7.11}$$

$^{\dagger}P(u, v, w)$ is the probability density function of u, v and w.

where $W_{\phi'}(f)$ is the power spectrum of the baseband signal $(2\pi)^{-1}\phi'(t)$. Therefore, the covariance matrix of u, v and w is given by

$$K = \begin{bmatrix} \alpha_1^2 & 0 & -\alpha_c^2 \\ 0 & \alpha_2^2 & 0 \\ -\alpha_c^2 & 0 & \alpha_3^2 \end{bmatrix} \qquad (2.1.7.12)$$

The probability density function of u, v, and w is given by

$$P(u, v, w) = \frac{e^{-\frac{v^2}{2\alpha_2^2}}}{\sqrt{2\pi}\,\alpha_2} \frac{e^{-\frac{\alpha_3^2 u^2 + \alpha_1^2 w^2 + 2\alpha_c^2 wu}{2(\alpha_1^2\alpha_3^2 - \alpha_c^4)}}}{(\sqrt{2\pi})^2\,\sqrt{\alpha_1^2\alpha_3^2 - \alpha_c^4}}. \qquad (2.1.7.13)$$

Using this result and Equation 2.1.7.10, the cumulative probability function $D(\rho_0)$ is given in Figure 2.1.7.1 as an example, where curve 1 considers only u, curve 2 considers only u and v, and curve 3 considers all u, v and w. As seen from this example, curves 2 and 3 are fairly close and this shows that the convergence increasing the number of terms is very quick. The convergence of this calculation can be proved in a general way, although it is beyond the scope of this book. The number of clicks/second is a function of σ_N^2 and ρ (instantaneous envelope)[†] assuming the change of ρ is not as fast as that of the thermal noise (this can be shown in [34]) and can be represented by $M_c(\sigma_N, \rho_0)$.

Thus, the average number of clicks considering the fluctuation of ρ, is given by

$$M_{cT} = \int_0^\infty M_c(\sigma_N, \rho_0)\,dD(\rho_0) = \int_0^\infty M_c(\sigma_N, \rho_0)D(\rho_0)'\,d\rho_0. \qquad (2.1.7.14)$$

Once the result of Figure 2.1.7.1 is known, the evaluation of M_{cT} is done simply, since the function M_c is experimentally or theoretically known [37].

2.1.8 Extension of Threshold of FM Signal Demodulation

As analyzed in Section 2.1.5, the demodulated signal-to-noise-power ratio (S/N) is a function of (C/N) (carrier-to-noise-power ratio) at or below threshold. Therefore, if the r.f. noise power N (of C/N) is reduced, the extension of the threshold point becomes possible. The reduction of the r.f. noise power at the FM demodulator input becomes possible, if the r.f. noise bandwidth is significantly reduced without distorting the signal.

As explained in Section 2.1.7, if the FM receiver bandwidth becomes smaller (than Carson's bandwidth), the FM signal bandwidth fluctuates and the click

---

[†] σ_N^2 is the thermal noise power added to this signal.

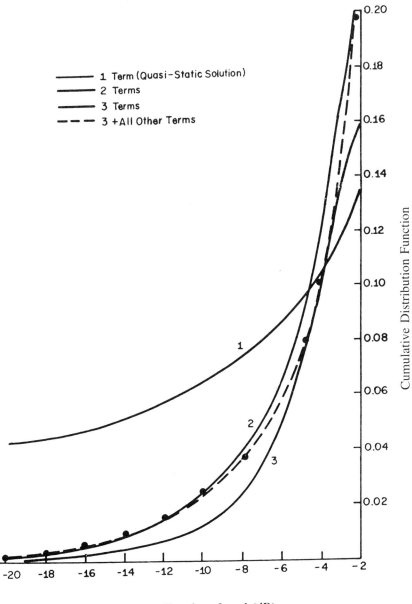

1 Term (Quasi-Static Solution)
2 Terms
3 Terms
3 +All Other Terms

Envelope Level (dB)

Figure 2.1.7.1 Cumulative Distribution Function of Distorted FM Envelope (Nyquist Filter—0.3 Roll Off)

Cumulative Distribution Function

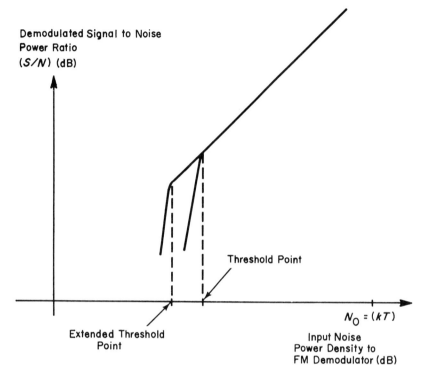

Figure 2.1.8.1   Extension of Threshold Characteristics

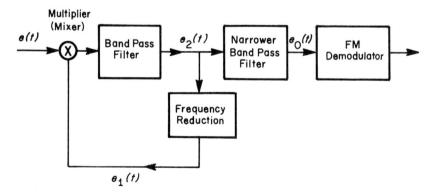

Figure 2.1.8.2   Simplified FM Feedback Circuit for Threshold Extension (Theoretical Model)

noise is increased, which deteriorates threshold characteristics. Also, filter distortion is increased (see Section 2.1.1). There are two approaches to achieve noise bandwidth reduction without distorting the signal.

(i) Feedback systems. The input $e(t)$ after the receiver (Carson's bandwidth) filter is represented as

$$e(t) = A \sin\{\omega_0 t + \phi(t) + \theta\} \qquad (2.1.8.1)$$

where $(2\pi)^{-1}\phi(t)'$ is the FM baseband signal and θ is an arbitrary carrier phase. Represent the output of the bandpass filter and input of the narrower filter as

$$e_2(t) = B \sin\{\omega_1 t + L\phi(t) + \lambda\} \qquad (2.1.8.2)$$

where λ is an arbitrary phase. Represent the output of the frequency reduction circuit (instantaneous FM frequency divider) as

$$e_1(t) = C \sin\left\{\frac{\omega_1}{M} t + \frac{L}{M} \phi(t) + \frac{\lambda}{M}\right\}. \qquad (2.1.8.3)$$

Then,

$$e(t)e_1(t) = \frac{AC}{2} \cos\left\{\left(\omega_0 - \frac{\omega_1}{M}\right)t + \left(1 - \frac{L}{M}\right)\phi(t) + \theta - \lambda\right\}$$
$$+ \frac{AC}{2} \cos\left\{\left(\omega_0 + \frac{\omega_1}{M}\right)t + \left(1 + \frac{L}{M}\right)\phi(t) + \theta + \lambda\right\}. \qquad (2.1.8.4)$$

Then, the bandpass filter output is

$$e_2(t) = \frac{AC}{2} \cos\left\{\left(\omega_0 - \frac{\omega_1}{M}\right)t + \left(1 - \frac{L}{M}\right)\phi(t) + \theta - \lambda\right\}. \qquad (2.1.8.5)$$

Comparing this result with that of Equation 2.1.8.2,

$$\left(1 - \frac{L}{M}\right)\phi(t) = L\phi(t)$$

$$\left(\omega_0 - \frac{\omega_1}{M}\right)t = \omega_1 t$$

$$\frac{AC}{2} = B$$

$$\theta - \frac{\lambda}{M} = \lambda. \qquad (2.1.8.6)$$

Thus,

$$L = \frac{1}{\left(1 + \dfrac{1}{M}\right)}$$

$$\omega_1 = \frac{\omega_0}{\left(1 + \dfrac{1}{M}\right)} \,. \tag{2.1.8.7}$$

Therefore, the frequency deviation of $e_2(t)$ can be smaller than that of $e(t)$ and therefore the narrower filter of Figure 2.1.8.2 reduces the power of the noise without distorting the signal. Although the model of Figure 2.1.8.2 is too simple to obtain more precise results, the author thinks that giving a heuristic explanation to the readers is enough. At all events, note that the exact solution of this feedback system is almost impossible to achieve.

(ii) Instantaneous frequency tracking. The r.f. receiving signal is represented by Equation 2.1.8.1. The instantaneous frequency of this signal is given by

$$f_0 + (2\pi)^{-1} \phi(t)'. \tag{2.1.8.8}$$

If the local oscillator (or phase lock loop) (see Figure 2.1.8.3) tracks this instantaneous frequency roughly,

$$e_1(t) = B \sin(\omega_1 t + \beta\phi(t) + \lambda). \tag{2.1.8.9}$$

Thus, the output of the mixer can be

$$e_2(t) = \frac{AB}{2} \cos\{(\omega_0 - \omega_1)t + (1 - \beta)\phi(t) + \theta - \lambda\}$$

$$+ \frac{AB}{2} \cos\{(\omega_0 + \omega_1)t + (1 + \beta)\phi(t) + \theta + \lambda\} \tag{2.1.8.10}$$

$$(1 - \beta < 1).$$

Therefore, the zonal filter to pick up the $(\omega_0 - \omega_1)$ component in Equation 2.1.8.10 can be narrower than that of the Carson one in the bandwidth. Thus, the noise power of the FM demodulator and C can be smaller (at threshold point). The word "roughly" mentioned just before Equation 2.1.8.9 means that the frequency deviation of $e_1(t)$ does not have to be the same (it can be smaller) but it must follow the time change, ϕ'. In this case, the frequency tracking circuit can be an instantaneous frequency divider as that of case (i) described above,

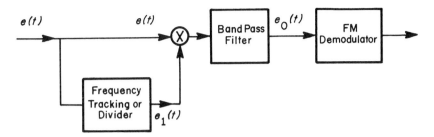

Figure 2.1.8.3 Frequency Tracking Circuit for Threshold Extension

where

$$\beta = \frac{1}{M}$$

$$\omega_1 = \frac{\omega_0}{M} \cdot \tag{2.1.8.11}$$

Then,

$$e_0(t) = \frac{AB}{2} \cos\{(\omega_0 - \omega_1)t + (1 - \beta)\phi(t) + \theta - \lambda\}$$

or

$$e_0(t) = \frac{AB}{2} \cos\left\{\left(1 - \frac{1}{M}\right)\omega_0 t + \left(1 - \frac{1}{M}\right)\phi(t) + \theta\left(1 - \frac{1}{M}\right)\right\} \cdot \tag{2.1.8.12}$$

2.2 SINGLE SIDEBAND SIGNAL (SSB) TRANSMISSION

As explained in a simple way in Section 4.2.4 of Volume I, the SSB signal is one of the sidebands of an amplitude modulated signal in which the baseband signal (modulating signal) is normally a voice signal.

Represent an amplitude modulated signal (by a voice) by

$$e(t) = A[1 + \phi(t)] \cos(\omega_0 t + \theta) \tag{2.2.1}$$

where A, ϕ, ω_0 and θ are respectively amplitude, baseband (a voice), angular carrier frequency and arbitrary phase of the AM signal.

Our ears can only distinguish the power of each frequency component of the voice signal, i.e., $|Y_\phi(f)|^2$ is only important for our ears, where $Y_\phi(f)$ is the spectrum of $\phi(t)$,

$$Y_\phi(f) = \int_{-\infty}^{\infty} \phi(t) e^{-j2\pi ft} \, dt. \tag{2.2.2}$$

In other terms, our ears are insensitive to the phase of $Y_\phi(f)$. Therefore, the transmission problems can be analyzed by power spectrum approach.

The autocorrelation function of $e(t)$ is given by

Average $\{A[1 + \phi(t)] \, A[1 + \phi(t + \tau)] \ \cos\{\omega_0 t + \theta\} \cos\{\omega_0(t + \tau) + \theta\}\}$

$$= (A^2/2) \, [1 + E\{\phi(t) \, \phi(t + \tau)\}] \cos(\omega_0 t)$$

$$= (A^2/2) \, [1 + R_\phi(\tau)] \cos(\omega_0 \tau) \tag{2.2.3}$$

where

$$E\{\phi(t)\} \ = \ E\{\phi(t + \tau)\} \ = \ 0 \tag{2.2.4}$$

and $R_\phi(\tau)$ is the autocorrelation function of $\phi(t)$.

Fourier-transforming the result of Equation 2.2.3, the power spectrum of $e(t)$ is given by

$$\frac{A^2}{2} \left[\frac{1}{2} \delta(f - f_0) + \frac{1}{2} \delta(f + f_0) \right]$$

$$+ \frac{A^2}{2} \left[\frac{1}{2} W_\phi(f - f_0) + \frac{1}{2} W_\phi(f + f_0) \right] (-\infty < f < \infty) \tag{2.2.5}$$

where $W_\phi(f)$ is the power spectrum of $\phi(t)$ $(-\infty < f < \infty)$.

As seen from Figure 2.2.1, the AM signal power spectrum consists of three components, a line spectrum (residual carrier power) and the power spectra of the upper sideband and of the lower sideband. The upper sideband power spectrum is the same as that of the baseband signal except for the fact that all the frequency components are shifted by f_0. The power spectrum of the lower sideband is symmetric to that of the upper sideband around f_0.

In the SSB systems, only the upper sideband is transmitted and the other two components are not transmitted (or vice versa).

At the receiver, the frequency components of this upper sideband are shifted down by f_0, which obviously becomes the transmitted voice signal. If this f_0 is not the same as the transmitted f_0, the received signal becomes distorted. Therefore, the receiver must generate a sine wave whose frequency is very close to the transmitted f_0 (e.g., within ± 5 Hz) or the transmitter must transmit a pilot from which the receiver generates the precise f_0 component.

Although this transmission system is convenient because

1. The transmission bandwidth is the same as that of the baseband signal (voice bandwidth), and
2. The modulators and demodulators are very simple.

there are two main disadvantages, i.e.,

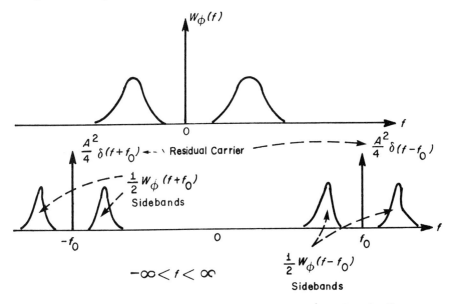

Figure 2.2.1(a)   Power Spectrum for Single Sideband Signals in Complex Representation

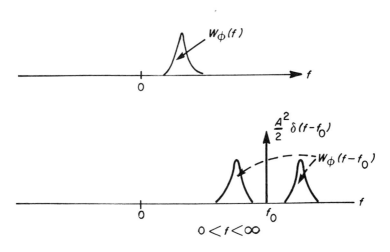

Figure 2.2.1(b)   Power Spectrum for Single Sideband Signals Real Representation

(a) there is no modulation gain compared with other systems. Thus, more transmitting power is required. For example, in FM systems, the demodulated signal-to-noise-power ratio is better than the r.f. signal-to-noise-power ratio ((C/N)). But, in this system, the noise power ratio of the demodulated signals is equal to (C/N).

(b) The SSB signal is very weak for intelligible crosstalks (understandable voice or tonal interferences). For example, in FM and PSK signal systems, these intelligible interferences in r.f. become unintelligible through nonlinear demodulation schemes of FM and PSK signals. But, in this system, the intelligible interferences in r.f. stay intelligible even after the demodulation into the baseband, since the demodulation scheme is linear.

Therefore, the companders (explained in Section 4.1 of Volume I) have been introduced to this system to compensate these disadvantages. However, even after the introduction of companders, the existence of intelligible interferences must be very carefully avoided, since the effects of the intelligible crosstalks on SSB signals are very severe (see Chapter 5).

2.3 PSK SIGNAL TRANSMISSION

In Section 4.3 of Volume I, the sketches of the PSK (phase shift keying) modulation are explained simply. In this section, more detailed theoretical analyses are shown from the transmission point of view.

In Section 2.3.1, the effects of thermal noise on PSK signal transmission are analyzed. Section 2.3.2 discussed the effects of intersymbol interferences (due to filters) and, Section 2.3.3, the combined effects of thermal noise, intersymbol interferences and non-linear devices.

In Section 2.3.4, the transmission analysis of staggered PSK and MSK signals is shown. In Section 2.3.5, the DPSK signal transmission is analyzed and, in Section 2.3.6, the TDMA signal transmission is shown.

2.3.1 Effects of Thermal Noise

As shown in Section 4.3 of Volume I, the ideal PSK signals are represented by

$$A \cos(\omega_0 t + \phi(t) + \theta) \qquad (2.3.1.1)$$

where

$$\phi(t) = \frac{\pi}{4} + \frac{2\pi}{L} l \begin{array}{l} (l = 1, 2, \ldots, L) \\ (L = 2^M) \end{array} \quad |t - kT| < \frac{T}{2}$$

$$(k = 0, \pm1, \pm2, \ldots) \qquad (2.3.1.2)$$

and θ is an arbitrary phase.

If $M = 1, 2, 3$, each becomes respectively the binary, quarterly and octal phase cases. It is assumed here that the value of $\phi(t)$ in each time interval defined

by Equation 2.3.1.2 is statistically independent for different values of k.
If thermal noise is added to Equation 2.3.1.1, it becomes

$$A \cos(\omega_0 t + \phi(t) + \theta) + N_c(t) \cos(\omega_0 t) + N_s(t) \sin(\omega_0 t) \qquad (2.3.1.3)$$

where N_c and N_s are respectively the inphase and quadrature components of the r.f. noise.

2.3.1.1 Binary Case

Instead of analyzing a purely ideal case, let us assume that the amplitude and the phase are distorted. In a purely ideal case, the error occurs when

$$A + N_c < 0. \qquad (2.3.1.1.1)$$

In a distorted case, the error occurs when

$$(A + \Delta A) \cos \Delta\theta + N_c < 0. \qquad (2.3.1.1.2)$$

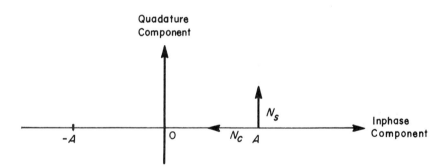

Figure 2.3.1.1.1(a)   Signal Space of BPSK (Purely Ideal Case)

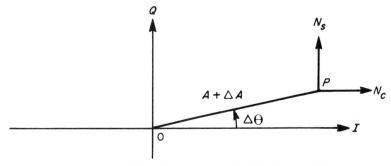

Figure 2.3.1.1.1(b)   Signal Space of BPSK (Distorted Case)

Since the probability density function of N_c is given by

$$P(x) = \frac{1}{\sqrt{2\pi}\,\sigma}\, e^{-\frac{x^2}{2\sigma^2}}, \tag{2.3.1.1.3}$$

the error probability of Equation 2.3.1.1.2 is given by

$$P_e = \int_{-\infty}^{-(A+\Delta A)\cos(\Delta\theta)} P(x)\,dx = \frac{1}{\sqrt{2\pi}\,\sigma} \int_{-\infty}^{-(A+\Delta A)\cos(\Delta\theta)} e^{-\frac{x^2}{2\sigma^2}}\,dx$$

$$= \frac{1}{\sqrt{2\pi}} \int_{-\infty}^{-\frac{(A+\Delta A)}{\sigma}\cos(\Delta\theta)} e^{-\frac{x^2}{2}}\,dx = \frac{1}{2}\,\mathrm{erfc}\left(\frac{A+\Delta A}{\sigma}\cos(\Delta\theta)\right)$$

$$= \frac{1}{2}\,\mathrm{erfc}\left(\sqrt{2\left(\frac{C}{N}\right)}\left\{1 + \sqrt{\frac{D}{C}}\right\}\cos(\Delta\theta)\right) \tag{2.3.1.1.4}$$

where, since the carrier power is $C = A^2/2$ and noise power is σ^2,

$$\frac{C}{N} = \frac{A^2}{2\sigma^2} \tag{2.3.1.1.5}$$

$$\frac{C}{D} = \frac{\left(\frac{A^2}{2}\right)}{\frac{(\Delta A)^2}{2}}. \tag{2.3.1.1.6}$$

and

$$\mathrm{erfc}(z) = \frac{2}{\sqrt{2\pi}} \int_z^{\infty} e^{-\frac{x^2}{2}}\,dx \tag{2.3.1.1.7}$$

2.3.1.2 Quarterly Case

In the ideal case, when

$$A\cos\left(\frac{\pi}{4}\right) + N_c < 0$$

or/and

$$A\cos\left(\frac{\pi}{4}\right) + N_s < 0 \tag{2.3.1.2.1}$$

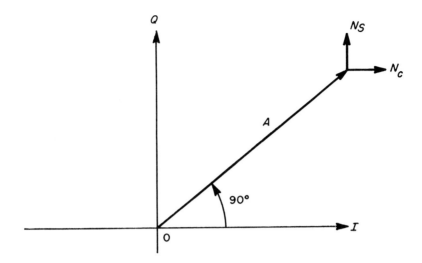

Figure 2.3.1.2.1(a)   Signal Space of QPSK (Ideal Case)

the error occurs. In the distorted case, when

$$(A + \Delta A) \cos\left(\frac{\pi}{4} + \Delta\theta\right) + N_c < 0$$

or/and $$(A + \Delta A) \sin\left(\frac{\pi}{4} + \Delta\theta\right) + N_s < 0 \qquad (2.3.1.2.2)$$

the error occurs.

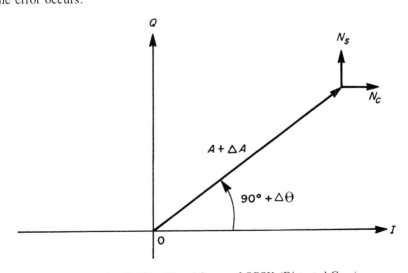

Figure 2.3.1.2.1(b)   Signal Space of QPSK (Distorted Case)

Then, the probability of the correct decision is

$$(A + \Delta A) \cos\left(\frac{\pi}{4} + \Delta\theta\right) + N_c > 0$$

and
$$(A + \Delta A) \sin\left(\frac{\pi}{4} + \Delta\theta\right) + N_s > 0. \qquad (2.3.1.2.3)$$

Since the joint probability density function of N_c and N_s is given by

$$P(x, y) = \frac{1}{(\sqrt{2\pi}\,\sigma)^2}\, e^{-\frac{x^2 + y^2}{2\sigma^2}}, \qquad (2.3.1.2.4)$$

then, the probability of errors is given by

$$P_e = 1 - \int_{-a}^{\infty} \int_{-b}^{\infty} P(x, y)\, dx\, dy \qquad (2.3.1.2.5)$$

where

$$a = (A + \Delta A) \cos\left(\frac{\pi}{4} + \Delta\theta\right) = A\left(1 + \sqrt{\frac{D}{C}}\right)\frac{1}{\sqrt{2}}$$

$$\cdot\, [\cos\Delta\theta - \sin\Delta\theta]$$

$$b = A\left(1 + \sqrt{\frac{D}{C}}\right)\frac{1}{\sqrt{2}}\, [\cos\Delta\theta + \sin\Delta\theta]. \qquad (2.3.1.2.6)$$

Thus,

$$P_e = 1 - \int_{-\frac{a}{\sigma}}^{\infty} \int_{-\frac{b}{\sigma}}^{\infty} \frac{1}{(2\pi)}\, e^{-\frac{(x^2 + y^2)}{2}}\, dx\, dy$$

$$= 1 - \left[1 - \frac{1}{2}\,\text{erfc}\left(\frac{a}{\sigma}\right)\right]\left[1 - \frac{1}{2}\,\text{erfc}\left(\frac{b}{\sigma}\right)\right]$$

$$= \frac{1}{2}\,\text{erfc}\left(\frac{a}{\sigma}\right) + \frac{1}{2}\,\text{erfc}\left(\frac{b}{\sigma}\right) - \frac{1}{4}\,\text{erfc}\left(\frac{a}{\sigma}\right)\text{erfc}\left(\frac{b}{\sigma}\right) \qquad (2.3.1.2.7)$$

where

$$\frac{a}{\sigma} = \sqrt{\frac{C}{N}}\left(1 + \sqrt{\frac{D}{C}}\right)[\cos\Delta\theta - \sin\Delta\theta]$$

$$\frac{b}{\sigma} = \sqrt{\frac{C}{N}}\left(1 + \sqrt{\frac{D}{C}}\right)[\cos\Delta\theta + \sin\Delta\theta]. \qquad (2.3.1.2.8)$$

In the ideal case where $\Delta A = \Delta \theta = 0$,

$$P_e = \text{erfc}\left(\sqrt{\frac{C}{N}}\right) - \frac{1}{4}\left[\text{erfc}\left(\sqrt{\frac{C}{N}}\right)\right]^2$$

$$\simeq \text{erfc}\left(\sqrt{\frac{C}{N}}\right). \qquad (2.3.1.2.9)$$

Since the error probability for an ideal BPSK case is given, from Equation 2.3.1.1.4 with $\Delta A = 0$ and $\Delta \theta = 0$, by

$$P_e = \frac{1}{2}\text{erfc}\left(\sqrt{2\left(\frac{C}{N}\right)}\right), \qquad (2.3.1.2.10)$$

the difference between the BPSK and QPSK errors (ideal cases) is factor 1/2 before the error function and factor 2 attached to (C/N) for the BPSK case.

Since the error function erfc (Z) very quickly decreases when Z increases, the factor difference 1/2 before the erfc (Z) is very easily compensated by increasing the value of (C/N) by a very small amount. In order to obtain the same P_e in the BPSK and QPSK, the (C/N) value of the QPSK must be approximately 3 dB larger than that of the BPSK for the same symbol rate T^{-1}.

Note that, from Section 5.6.1 of Volume I, the power spectra of the BPSK and QPSK are equal as far as T is equal in both cases. Therefore, the QPSK can transmit double information with the same frequency bandwidth and with approximately 3 dB more power (compared with BPSK).

However, in practice, because of modem impairments, intersymbol interference degradation, nonlinear effects, etc., the QPSK needs better (C/N) than the ideal 3 dB explained above. This is explained in later sections.

2.3.1.3 Octal and Higher Order PSK Case

The cases of the BPSK and QPSK are especially simple for the evaluation of error probabilities, since these cases are essentially single integrals of Gaussian functions as seen from Equations 2.3.1.1.4 and 2.3.1.2.6.

But, in the octal or higher order PSK cases, double integrals must be evaluated as explained in the following. For example, in an ideal octal PSK signal, the error probability is given by

$$P_e = 1 - \int_0^\infty \int_{-x\sin\left(\frac{\pi}{8}\right)}^{x\sin\left(\frac{\pi}{8}\right)} \frac{1}{2\pi\sigma^2} e^{-\frac{(x-A)^2 + y^2}{2\sigma^2}} \, dy \, dx. \qquad (2.3.1.3.1)$$

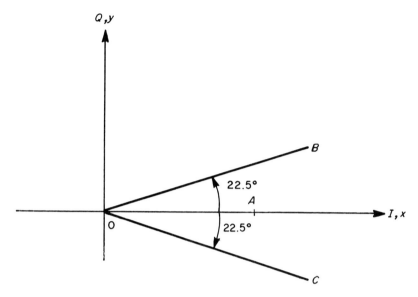

Figure 2.3.1.3.1   Signal Space of OPSK

Let us modify this further as

$$P_e = 1 - \int_0^\infty \frac{1}{\sqrt{2\pi}} e^{-\frac{1}{2}\left(x - \frac{A}{\sigma}\right)^2} dx \int_{-x\sin\left(\frac{\pi}{8}\right)}^{x\sin\left(\frac{\pi}{8}\right)} \frac{1}{\sqrt{2\pi}} e^{-\frac{y^2}{2}} dy$$

$$= 1 - \int_0^\infty \frac{1}{\sqrt{2\pi}} e^{-\frac{\left(x - \frac{A}{\sigma}\right)^2}{2}} \left[1 - \text{erfc}\left(x \sin\left(\frac{\pi}{8}\right)\right)\right] dx$$

$$= 1 - \int_{-\frac{A}{\sigma}}^\infty \frac{1}{\sqrt{2\pi}} e^{-\frac{x^2}{2}} \left[1 - \text{erfc}\left\{\left(x + \frac{A}{\sigma}\right) \sin\left(\frac{\pi}{8}\right)\right\}\right] dx$$

$$= \frac{1}{2}\text{erfc}\left(\frac{A}{\sigma}\right) + \int_{-\frac{A}{\sigma}}^\infty \frac{1}{\sqrt{2\pi}} e^{-\frac{x^2}{2}} \text{erfc}\left\{\left(x + \frac{A}{\sigma}\right) \sin\left(\frac{\pi}{8}\right)\right\} dx.$$

$$(2.3.1.3.2)$$

The explicit solution of this integral is not simple but the following approximation can be done in most practical cases.

Let us start from Equation 2.3.1.3.1, which can be rewritten as

$$P_e = 1 - \int_0^\infty \int_{-x \sin\left(\frac{\pi}{8}\right)}^{x \sin\left(\frac{\pi}{8}\right)} \frac{1}{2\pi} e^{-\frac{\left(x - \frac{A}{\sigma}\right)^2 + y^2}{2}} \, dx \, dy. \qquad (2.3.1.3.3)$$

Using the polar coordinate transformation

$$x = r \cos \theta$$

$$y = r \sin \theta \qquad (2.3.1.3.4)$$

then,

$$P_e = 1 - \int_{-\frac{\pi}{8}}^{\frac{\pi}{8}} \frac{1}{2\pi} e^{-\frac{1}{2}\left(\frac{A}{\sigma}\right)^2 \sin^2\theta} \, d\theta$$

$$\cdot \int_0^\infty e^{-\frac{\left(r - \frac{A}{\sigma}\cos\theta\right)^2}{2}} r \, dr = 1 - \int_{-\frac{\pi}{8}}^{\frac{\pi}{8}} \frac{1}{2\pi}$$

$$\cdot e^{-\frac{1}{2}\left(\frac{A}{\sigma}\right)^2 \sin^2\theta} \, d\theta \int_{-\frac{A}{\sigma}\cos\theta}^\infty \left[r + \frac{A}{\sigma}\cos\theta\right] e^{-\frac{r^2}{2}} \, dr$$

$$= 1 - \int_{-\frac{\pi}{8}}^{\frac{\pi}{8}} \frac{1}{2\pi} e^{-\frac{1}{2}\left(\frac{A}{\sigma}\right)^2 \sin^2\theta} \, d\theta \int_{-\frac{A}{\sigma}\cos\theta}^\infty r e^{-\frac{r^2}{2}} \, dr$$

$$- \int_{-\frac{\pi}{8}}^{\frac{\pi}{8}} \frac{1}{\sqrt{2\pi}} e^{-\frac{1}{2}\left(\frac{A}{\sigma}\right)^2 \sin^2\theta} \left(\frac{A}{\sigma}\right) \cos\theta \int_{-\frac{A}{\sigma}\cos\theta}^\infty \frac{1}{\sqrt{2\pi}}$$

$$\cdot e^{-\frac{r^2}{2}} \, dr = 1 - \frac{1}{8} e^{-\frac{1}{2}\left(\frac{A}{\sigma}\right)^2}$$

$$- \int_{-\frac{\pi}{8}}^{\frac{\pi}{8}} \frac{1}{\sqrt{2\pi}} e^{-\frac{1}{2}\left(\frac{A}{\sigma}\right)^2 \sin^2\theta} \left(\frac{A}{\sigma}\right) \cos\theta \left[1 - \frac{1}{2}\operatorname{erfc}\left(\frac{A}{\sigma}\cos\theta\right)\right] d\theta.$$

$$(2.3.1.3.5)$$

In the last integral of this result, when θ changes from $-\pi/8$ to $\pi/8$,

$$1 - \frac{1}{2} \mathrm{erfc}\left(\frac{A}{\sigma}\cos\left(\frac{\pi}{8}\right)\right) \leq 1 - \frac{1}{2}\mathrm{erfc}\left(\frac{A}{\sigma}\cos\theta\right) \leq 1 - \frac{1}{2}\mathrm{erfc}\left(\frac{A}{\sigma}\right).$$

$$(2.3.1.3.6)$$

Therefore, P_e is smaller than

$$1 - \frac{1}{8}e^{-\frac{1}{2}\left(\frac{A}{\sigma}\right)^2} - \left[1 - \mathrm{erfc}\left(\frac{A}{\sigma}\sin\left(\frac{\pi}{8}\right)\right)\right]\left[1 - \frac{1}{2}\mathrm{erfc}\left(\frac{A}{\sigma}\right)\right]$$

$$\simeq \mathrm{erfc}\left(\frac{A}{\sigma}\sin\left(\frac{\pi}{8}\right)\right) \qquad (2.3.1.3.7)$$

since, in most practical cases,[†]

$$\mathrm{erfc}\left(\frac{A}{\sigma}\sin\left(\frac{\pi}{8}\right)\right) \gg \frac{1}{8}e^{-\frac{1}{2}\left(\frac{A}{\sigma}\right)^2}, \mathrm{erfc}\left(\frac{A}{\sigma}\right) \qquad (2.3.1.3.8)$$

and larger than

$$1 - \frac{1}{8}e^{-\frac{1}{2}\left(\frac{A}{\sigma}\right)^2} - \left[1 - \mathrm{erfc}\left(\frac{A}{\sigma}\sin\left(\frac{\pi}{8}\right)\right)\right]\left[1 - \frac{1}{2}\mathrm{erfc}\left(\frac{A}{\sigma}\cos\left(\frac{\pi}{8}\right)\right)\right]$$

$$\simeq \mathrm{erfc}\left(\frac{A}{\sigma}\sin\left(\frac{\pi}{8}\right)\right) \qquad (2.3.1.3.9)$$

because, in most practical cases,

$$\mathrm{erfc}\left(\frac{A}{\sigma}\sin\left(\frac{\pi}{8}\right)\right) \gg \frac{1}{8}e^{-\frac{1}{2}\left(\frac{A}{\sigma}\right)^2}, \mathrm{erfc}\left(\frac{A}{\sigma}\cos\left(\frac{\pi}{8}\right)\right). \qquad (2.3.1.3.10)$$

Thus, in most practical cases,

$$P_e \simeq \mathrm{erfc}\left(\frac{A}{\sigma}\sin\left(\frac{\pi}{8}\right)\right)$$

$$\simeq \mathrm{erfc}\left(\sqrt{2\left(\frac{C}{N}\right)}\sin\left(\frac{\pi}{8}\right)\right). \qquad (2.3.1.3.11)$$

[†]This means that the error probabilities are small enough, so that the communication may be possible in practice.

2.3.1.4 L-ary PSK Case

Using a similar approach, the error probabilities of L-ary PSK is given by (approximately),[†]

$$
\begin{aligned}
P_e &\simeq \frac{1}{2}\operatorname{erfc}\left\{\frac{(A+\Delta A)}{\sigma}\sin\left(\frac{\pi}{L}-\Delta\theta\right)\right\} \\
&\quad + \frac{1}{2}\operatorname{erfc}\left\{\frac{(A+\Delta A)}{\sigma}\sin\left(\frac{\pi}{L}+\Delta\theta\right)\right\} \\
&= \frac{1}{2}\operatorname{erfc}\left\{\sqrt{2\left(\frac{C}{N}\right)}\left(1+\sqrt{\frac{D}{C}}\right)\sin\left(\frac{\pi}{L}-\Delta\theta\right)\right\} \\
&\quad + \frac{1}{2}\operatorname{erfc}\left\{\sqrt{2\left(\frac{C}{N}\right)}\left(1+\sqrt{\frac{D}{C}}\right)\sin\left(\frac{\pi}{L}+\Delta\theta\right)\right\} \cdot \quad (2.3.1.4.1)
\end{aligned}
$$

[†]Also, this approximation is only valid when the error probabilities are small (i.e., practically usable).

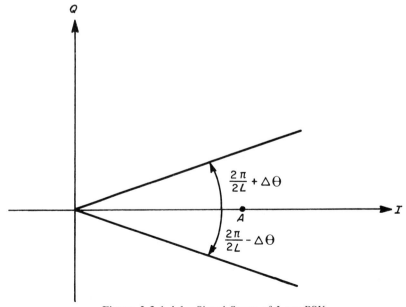

Figure 2.3.1.4.1 Signal Space of L-ary PSK

2.3.2   Effects of Filters (Intersymbol Interferences)

The following analyses the effects of intersymbol interferences in linear channel and then the next section shows how the intersymbol interference effects are modified by nonlinear devices.

The last section explains how thermal noise can cause symbol errors.

Represent the ideal PSK signal (not filtered) by

$$e_i(t) = A\, e^{j\omega_0 t + j\phi(t) + j\theta}$$

$$= A\, e^{j\omega_0 t + j\theta} \sum_{k=-\infty}^{\infty} V(t - kT)\, e^{j\phi_k} \tag{2.3.2.1}$$

where

$$V(t) = 1, \qquad |t| \le \frac{T}{2}$$

$$= 0 \qquad \text{elsewhere.} \tag{2.3.2.2}$$

T is the symbol time period ($1/T$ is the symbol rate). Because of the square wave form of $V(t)$ defined by Equation 2.3.2.2, the envelope of $e_i(t)$ is a constant A, i.e.,

$$|e_i| = A. \tag{2.3.2.3}$$

ϕ_k is the random phase variable in the k-th symbol period, $(kT - T/2, kT + T/2)$ and takes four values for QPSK cases as

$$\phi_k = \frac{\pi}{4}, \frac{3\pi}{4}, \frac{5\pi}{4}, \frac{7\pi}{4}. \tag{2.3.2.4}$$

It is also assumed that all ϕ_k's are statistically independent. This assumption is valid from a practical point of view if a good bit sequence scrambler is used.

It is also very important to maintain this randomness to make sure (as described in later Sections) that the carrier and bit recoveries work and that the power spectrum of the PSK signal is smoothly distributed. This is important from an interference point of view. Since the PSK signal spectrum is very much spread as described in later Sections, some filters require cutting the sidelobes off. The output of the modem *IF* filters (F_1) is

$$e_0(t) = A\, e^{j\omega_0 t + j\theta} \sum_{k=-\infty}^{\infty} S(t - kT)\, e^{j\phi_k} \tag{2.3.2.5}$$

where $S(t)$ is given by

$$S(t) = \int_{-\infty}^{\infty} V(t)\, h_1(t - x)\, dx \tag{2.3.2.6}$$

and is a complex function of t in general (if the filter is not symmetric around the carrier frequency f_0). $h_1(t)$ is the low pass analog impulse response of filter F_1. Note here that the analysis in this Section can be applied to any filter other than F_1.

In the ideal PSK of Equation 2.3.2.1, the window function is confined to each symbol period and it never interacts with the other symbols or square waves. Therefore, it is called "intersymbol interference free."

However, after the filter F_1, the pulse $S(t)$ is no longer confined to the symbol period $(-T/2, T/2)$ and spreads into adjacent symbol intervals, which creates effects of intersymbol interferences. Because of this invasion of the skirt of adjacent pulses, the degradation of the error probabilities occurs. Note that the intersymbol interference itself does not cause any error in the phase detection of the PSK signal at the demodulator in normal cases, if there is no thermal noise (or other types of interference).

$e^{j\phi_k}$ in Equation 2.3.2.1 can be shown in complex coordinate as in Figure 2.3.2.1. In a symbol period, the phase of $V(t - kT) e^{j\phi_k}$ stays at one of P_1, P_2, P_3 and P_4 and the amplitude stays at a constant amplitude for the ideal QPSK case. However, for the complex signal after the filter,

$$\sum_{k=-\infty}^{\infty} S(t - kT)e^{j\phi_k} \qquad (2.3.2.7)$$

in a symbol period, e.g., $(kT - T/2, kT + T/2)$, the invasion of the other pulses into this interval makes the phase and amplitude of this signal variable dependent on the random values of the adjacent $\phi_l (l \neq k)$ as shown in Figure 2.3.2.2. In case the amplitude of the vector becomes smaller or the phase drifts from $45°$ (with the amplitude staying the same or decreasing for the case of P_1), the thermal noise (or the interferences) gives worse error probabilities than an ideal case. Therefore, the effect of the intersymbol interferences on the sampled values of the received signals at the demodulator must be minimized. Thus, the theory of Nyquist has been established [11].

In Section 3.2.1 of Volume I, the Nyquist condition is analyzed, and the way by which to obtain the effects of intersymbol interference on the error probabilities of a QPSK signal is shown here, since the Nyquist condition is never satisfied in practical cases and, even if it is after F_1, the HPA and F_2 will damage this condition. Now, take the real part of Equation 2.3.2.5 so as to make the analysis realistic

$$\text{Re}\{e_0(t)\} = \left(A \sum_{k=-\infty}^{\infty} [S_r(t - kT) \cos \phi_k - S_i(t - kT) \sin \phi_k] \right)$$

$$\cdot \cos(\omega_0 t + \theta)$$

$$- \left(A \sum_{k=-\infty}^{\infty} [S_r(t - kT) \sin \phi_k + S_i(t - kT) \cos \phi_k] \right)$$

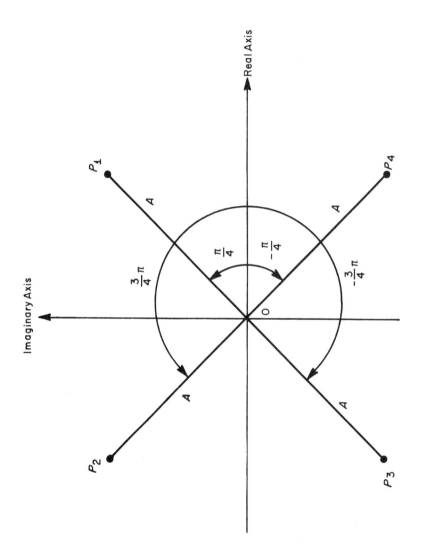

Figure 2.3.2.1   Complex Representation of $Ae^{j\phi k}$

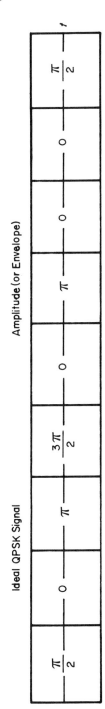

Ideal QPSK Signal

Amplitude (or Envelope)

Distortion of Square
Wave Pulses Due to Filters
Inphase or Quadrature Component

Figure 2.3.2.2 PSK Signal Distortions Due to Filters

$$\cdot \sin(\omega_0 t + \theta)$$

$$= x(t)\cos(\omega_0 t + \theta) + A[S_r(t)\cos\phi_0 - S_i(t)\sin\phi_0]\cos(\omega_0 t + \theta)$$

$$- y(t)\sin(\omega_0 t + \theta) - A[S_r(t)\sin\phi_0 + S_i(t)\cos\phi_0]\sin(\omega_0 t + \theta)$$

$$(2.3.2.8)$$

where

$$S(t) = S_r(t) + j\,S_i(t) \qquad\qquad (2.3.2.9)$$

where

$$x(t) = A \sum_{\substack{k=-\infty \\ (k\neq 0)}}^{\infty} [S_r(t - kT)\cos\phi_k - S_i(t - kT)\sin\phi_k]$$

$$y(t) = A \sum_{\substack{k=-\infty \\ (k\neq 0)}}^{\infty} [S_r(t - kT)\sin\phi_k + S_i(t - kT)\cos\phi_k]. \quad (2.3.2.10)^\dagger$$

For abbreviation, use the following notations for $S_r(t - kT)$ and $S_i(t - kT)$,

$$S_r(t - kT) = S_r^{(k)}(t),\ S_i(t - kT) = S_i^{(k)}(t) \qquad (2.3.2.11)$$

$x(t)$ and $y(t)$ are called respectively the inphase and quadrature components. The k-th terms of $x(t)$ and $y(t)$ take the following values, according to the values of ϕ_k, i.e.,

(i)

$$\phi_k = \pi/4,\ 1/\sqrt{2}\ (S_r^{(k)} - S_i^{(k)}) = h_k^{(1)} \qquad \text{for } x$$

$$1/\sqrt{2}\ (S_r^{(k)} + S_i^{(k)}) = h_k^{(2)} \qquad \text{for } y.$$

(ii)

$$\phi_k = 3/4\pi,\ -1/\sqrt{2}\ (S_r^{(k)} + S_i^{(k)}) = -h_k^{(2)} \qquad \text{for } x.$$

$$1/\sqrt{2}\ (-S_r^{(k)} + S_i^{(k)}) = -h_k^{(1)} \qquad \text{for } y.$$

(iii)

$$\phi_k = 5/4\pi,\ 1/\sqrt{2}\ (-S_r^{(k)} + S_i^{(k)}) = -h_k^{(1)}$$

$$1/\sqrt{2}\ (-S_r^{(k)} - S_i^{(k)}) = -h_k^{(2)}$$

$^\dagger x(t)$ and $y(t)$ give the intersymbol interferences to the sampled value of 0-th time interval $(-T/2, T/2)$.

(iv)

$$\phi_k = 7/4\pi, \quad 1/\sqrt{2}\ (S_r^{(k)} + S_i^{(k)}) = h_k^{(2)}$$

$$1/\sqrt{2}\ (S_r^{(k)} - S_i^{(k)}) = h_k^{(1)} \qquad (2.3.2.12)$$

In other terms, it is assumed here that (x, y) can take the following pairs

$$(h_k^{(1)}, h_k^{(2)}), (-h_k^{(2)}, -h_k^{(1)}), (-h_k^{(1)}, -h_k^{(2)})\ \text{and}\ (h_k^{(2)}, h_k^{(1)})\ (2.3.2.13)$$

and they occur independently with equal probability.

At the demodulation of ground terminal, $x(t)$ and $y(t)$ are detected and sampled in each symbol interval. The sampling point of each symbol interval is decided so that the error probability may become the smallest possible, but it usually happens around the center point $(t = kT)$.[†] In order to obtain the joint probability density function of x and y, the characteristic function of x and y excluding the value for $k = 0$ will be first analyzed at a sampling time of t in

$$C_I(u, v) = E\{e^{jux + jvy}\} = E_\phi\left\{\prod_{\substack{k=-\infty \\ (k\neq0)}}^{\infty} \exp[ju(S_r^{(k)}\cos\phi_k\right.$$

$$\left. - S_i^{(k)}\sin\phi_k)A + jv(S_r^{(k)}\sin\phi_k + S_i^{(k)}\cos\phi_k)A]\right\}$$

$$= \prod_{\substack{k=-\infty \\ (k\neq0)}}^{\infty} \cos\left(\frac{A}{\sqrt{2}}u\,S_r^{(k)} + \frac{v}{\sqrt{2}}S_i^{(k)}\right)$$

$$\cdot \cos\left(-\frac{A}{\sqrt{2}}u\,S_i^{(k)} + \frac{A}{\sqrt{2}}v\,S_r^{(k)}\right) \qquad (2.3.2.14)$$

At the demodulator, in addition to the distorted signal of Equation 2.3.2.5, thermal noise exists. The input to the receiver is

$$A e^{j\omega_0 t + j\theta}\ S(t)\ e^{j\phi_0}$$

$$+ A e^{j\omega_0 t + j\theta} \sum_{\substack{k=-\infty \\ (k\neq0)}}^{\infty} S(t - kT)e^{j\phi_k}$$

$$+ N(t)e^{j\omega_0 t + j\theta} \qquad (2.3.2.15)$$

[†]It is assumed here that the group delay of the filter is normalized to be zero at the center frequency of the passband of the filter.

and Equation 2.3.2.8 becomes

$$[A(S_r^{(0)} \cos \phi_0 - S_i^{(0)} \sin \phi_0)] \cos(\omega_0 t + \theta)$$
$$- [A(S_r^{(0)} \sin \phi_0 + S_i^{(0)} \cos \phi_0)] \sin(\omega_0 t + \theta)$$
$$+ (x + N_c) \cos(\omega_0 t + \theta)$$
$$- (y + N_s) \sin(\omega_0 t + \theta). \tag{2.3.2.16}$$

At the demodulator output, $x + N_c + A(S_r^{(0)} \cos \phi_0 - S_i^{(0)} \sin \phi)$ and $y + N_S + A(S_r^{(0)} \sin \phi_0 + S_i^{(0)} \cos \phi_0)$ are respectively detected and, from them, the value of ϕ_k is determined in each symbol period after the sampling. The characteristic function of N_c and N_s is given by

$$C_N(u, v) = E\{e^{juN_c + jvN_s}\}_N = e^{-\frac{\sigma_N^2}{2}(u^2 + v^2)} \tag{2.3.2.17}$$

where σ_N^2 is the average power of N_c or N_s or that of

$$N_c \cos \omega_0 t - N_s \sin \omega_0 t. \tag{2.3.2.18}$$

Thus, the characteristic function of $x + N_c$ and $y + N_s$ is given by

$$C(u, v) = C_I(u, v) C_N(u, v)$$

$$= e^{-\frac{\sigma_N^2}{2}(u^2 + v^2)} \prod_{\substack{k = -\infty \\ (k \neq 0)}}^{\infty} \cos\left[\frac{A}{\sqrt{2}} u S_r^{(k)} + \frac{A}{\sqrt{2}} v S_i^{(k)}\right]$$

$$\cdot \cos\left(\frac{-A}{\sqrt{2}} u S_i^{(k)} + \frac{A}{\sqrt{2}} v S_r^{(k)}\right). \tag{2.3.2.19}$$

The error probabilities when the signal point is located at P_4, P_1, P_2 and P_3 are all the same since the effects of the thermal noise and intersymbol interferences have all the same distribution at any point. Therefore, let us assume that the signal point is located at P_1, i.e.,

$$(Ah_0^{(1)}, Ah_0^{(2)}) = \left(A \frac{S_r^{(0)} - S_i^{(0)}}{\sqrt{2}}, A \frac{S_r^{(0)} + S_i^{(0)}}{\sqrt{2}}\right). \tag{2.3.2.20}$$

Represent the probability density function of $X(= x + N_C)$ and $Y(= y + N_S)$ by $P(X, Y)$. Then, the error probability in which the wrong symbols are obtained, when the signal of the first quadrant $(Ah_0^{(1)}, Ah_0^{(2)})$ is sent from the transmitter, is given by

$$P_e = 1 - \int_0^\infty \int_0^\infty P(X - Ah_0^{(1)}, Y - Ah_0^{(2)}) dX \, dY. \tag{2.3.2.21}$$

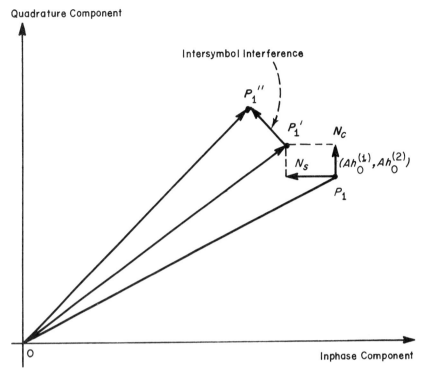

Figure 2.3.2.3   Signal Space Modification Due to Thermal Noise and Intersymbol Interference

Using the characteristic function of X and Y given by Equation 2.3.2.19, the above equation can be rewritten as

$$
P_e = 1 - \frac{1}{(2\pi)^2} \int_0^\infty \int_0^\infty \int_{-\infty}^\infty \int_{-\infty}^\infty
$$

$$
\cdot e^{-\frac{\sigma_N^2}{2}(u^2 + v^2)} \prod_{\substack{k=-\infty \\ (k \neq 0)}}^{\infty} \cos\left(\frac{A}{\sqrt{2}} S_r^{(k)} u + \frac{A}{\sqrt{2}} S_i^{(k)} v \right)
$$

$$
\cdot \cos\left(-\frac{A}{\sqrt{2}} S_i^{(k)} u + \frac{A}{\sqrt{2}} S_r^{(k)} v \right)
$$

$$
\cdot e^{-ju(X - Ah_0^{(1)}) - jv(Y - Ah_0^{(2)})} \, du \, dv \, dX \, dY .
$$

(2.3.2.22)

The straightforward integral of Equation 2.3.2.22 is very difficult to evaluate and there are several ways to evaluate it up to now. One way is to do it by expanding the characteristic functions $C(u, v)$ by a power series of u and v, and other ones are to obtain the bound of P_e by simple representations [12, 13, 14].

Approach by Power Series Expansion of Characteristic Function

Expand $C_I(u, v)$ of Equation 2.3.2.19 by power series of u and v as

$$C_I(u, v) = \sum_{k_1=0}^{\infty} \sum_{k_2=0}^{\infty} a_{k_1, k_2} u^{k_1} v^{k_2} \qquad (2.3.2.23)$$

where an approach to obtain a_{k_1, k_2} will be mentioned later in this Section.

Then,

$$P_e = 1 - \frac{1}{(2\pi)} \int_0^{\infty} \int_{-\infty}^{\infty} e^{-\frac{\sigma_N^2}{2} u^2} e^{-ju(x - Ah_0^{(1)})} \, dx \, du$$

$$\cdot \frac{1}{2\pi} \int_0^{\infty} \int_{-\infty}^{\infty} e^{-\frac{\sigma_N^2}{2} v^2} e^{-jv(y - Ah_0^{(2)})} \, dy \, dv$$

$$- \sum_{k_1=0}^{\infty}{}' \sum_{k_2=0}^{\infty}{}' a_{k_1, k_2} \frac{1}{(2\pi)} \int_0^{\infty} \int_{-\infty}^{\infty} e^{-\frac{\sigma_N^2}{2} u^2} u^{k_1} e^{-ju(x - Ah_0^{(1)})}$$

$$\cdot dx \, du \frac{1}{(2\pi)} \int_0^{\infty} \int_{-\infty}^{\infty} e^{-\frac{\sigma_N^2}{2} v^2} e^{-jv(y - Ah_0^{(2)})} \, dy \, dv. \qquad (2.3.2.24)^\dagger$$

Use the formula

$$\frac{1}{\sqrt{2\pi}} \frac{1}{\sigma_N} e^{-\frac{1}{2} \frac{x^2}{\sigma_N^2}} = \frac{1}{2\pi} \int_{-\infty}^{\infty} e^{-\frac{\sigma_N^2}{2} u^2} e^{jux} \, du \qquad (2.3.2.25)$$

and define the error function

$$\frac{1}{\sqrt{2\pi}} \int_z^{\infty} e^{-\frac{x^2}{2}} \, dx = \frac{1}{2} \operatorname{erfc}(z) \qquad (2.3.2.26)$$

where

$$\operatorname{erfc}(0) = 1. \qquad (2.3.2.27)$$

---

†The double summation $\Sigma'\Sigma'$ means that the cases $k_1 = 0$ and $k_2 = 0$ are excluded in the summation.

$$P_e = 1 - \left\{ 1 - \frac{1}{2} \operatorname{erfc}\left(\frac{Ah_0^{(1)}}{\sigma_N}\right) \right\} \left\{ 1 - \frac{1}{2} \operatorname{erfc}\left(\frac{Ah_0^{(2)}}{\sigma_N}\right) \right\}$$

$$- \sideset{}{'}\sum_{k_1=0}^{\infty} \sideset{}{'}\sum_{k_2=0}^{\infty} a_{k_1,k_2} \frac{1}{\sigma_N^{k_1+k_2}} \frac{1}{(-j)^{k_1+k_2}}$$

$$\cdot \int_0^{\infty} \int_0^{\infty} \left[\frac{\partial^{k_1}}{\partial x^{k_1}} \left\{ \frac{1}{\sqrt{2\pi}} e^{-\frac{1}{2}\left(x - \frac{Ah_0^{(1)}}{\sigma_N}\right)^2} \right\} \right]$$

$$\cdot \left[\frac{\partial^{k_2}}{\partial y^{k_2}} \left\{ \frac{1}{\sqrt{2\pi}} e^{-\frac{1}{2}\left(y - \frac{Ah_0^{(2)}}{\sigma_N}\right)^2} \right\} \right] dx\, dy. \qquad (2.3.2.28)^{\dagger}$$

Define the Hermite functions as

$$\phi_{k_1}(z) = (-1)^k \frac{\partial^{k_1}}{\partial z^{k_1}} \left\{ \frac{1}{\sqrt{2\pi}} e^{-\frac{z^2}{z}} \right\} \qquad (2.3.2.29)$$

$$P_e = \frac{1}{2} \operatorname{erfc}\left(\frac{Ah_0^{(1)}}{\sigma_N}\right) + \frac{1}{2} \operatorname{erfc}\left(\frac{Ah_0^{(2)}}{\sigma_N}\right)$$

$$- \frac{1}{4} \operatorname{erfc}\left(\frac{Ah_0^{(1)}}{\sigma_N}\right) \operatorname{erfc}\left(\frac{Ah_0^{(2)}}{\sigma_N}\right)$$

$$- \sideset{}{'}\sum_{k_1=0}^{\infty} \sideset{}{'}\sum_{k_2=0}^{\infty} a_{k_1,k_2} \frac{1}{(\sigma_N)^{k_1+k_2}} \frac{1}{(j)^{k_1+k_2}}$$

$$\cdot \int_0^{\infty} \phi_{k_1}\left(x - \frac{Ah_0^{(1)}}{\sigma_N}\right) dx \int_0^{\infty} \phi_{k_2}\left(y - \frac{Ah_0^{(2)}}{\sigma_N}\right) dy. \qquad (2.3.2.30)$$

Using the relation (from Equation 2.3.2.30 and Equation 2.3.2.26)

$$\int \phi_{k_1}(z)\, dz = -\phi_{k_1-1}(z) \quad (k_1 > 0)$$

$$\phi_{-1}(z) = \operatorname{erfc}(z) \qquad (2.3.2.31)$$

---

†If one of k_1 or k_2 is zero, use the definition of Equation 2.2.9 of Volume I for the integrals.

$$P_e = \frac{1}{2} \phi_{-1}\left(\frac{Ah_0^{(1)}}{\sigma_N}\right) + \frac{1}{2} \phi_{-1}\left(\frac{Ah_0^{(2)}}{\sigma_N}\right)$$

$$- \frac{1}{4} \phi_{-1}\left(\frac{Ah_0^{(1)}}{\sigma_N}\right) \phi_{-1}\left(\frac{Ah_0^{(2)}}{\sigma_N}\right)$$

$$- \sum_{k_1=0}^{\infty}{}' \sum_{k_2=0}^{\infty}{}' a_{k_1,k_2} \frac{(-j)^{k_1+k_2}}{(\sigma_N)^{k_1+k_2}} \phi_{k_1-1}\left(-\frac{Ah_0^{(1)}}{\sigma_N}\right)$$

(Exclude $k_1 = k_2 = 0$)

$$\cdot \phi_{k_2-1}\left(-\frac{Ah_0^{(2)}}{\sigma_N}\right). \tag{2.3.2.32}$$

There is a convenient recurrence relationship to obtain all the values of $\phi_k(z)$

$$\phi_{n+1}(z) = n\phi_n(z) - z\,\phi_{n-1}(z) \tag{2.3.2.33}$$

where

$$\phi_0(z) = \frac{1}{\sqrt{2\pi}} e^{-\frac{z^2}{2}}$$

$$\phi_1(z) = \frac{1}{\sqrt{2\pi}} z\, e^{-\frac{z^2}{2}}. \tag{2.3.2.34}$$

All the other higher order functions ϕ_k can be obtained from the above two functions using Equation 2.3.2.33.

There is also a convenient recurrence relation to obtain a_{k_1,k_2}. See References [41] and [43] for the detailed approach for a_{k_1,k_2}, but the author will explain here a simpler case whose approach is fundamentally the same as that of a_{k_1,k_2}. Instead of the second dimensional case, the single dimensional case (that corresponds to the binary case) will be shown here. In the binary case where ϕ_k can take only two values, 0 and π in Equation 2.3.2.7, the probability of symbol errors is given by:

$$P_e = \mathrm{erfc}\left(\frac{Ah_0}{\sigma_N}\right) - \sum_{k=1}^{\infty} a_k \frac{(-j)^k}{(\sigma_N)^k} \phi_{k-1}\left(-\frac{h_0}{\sigma_N}\right) \tag{2.3.2.35}$$

where the coefficients a_k's are given by

$$C_I(u) = \prod_{k=1}^{\infty} \cos(h_k\, u) = \sum_{k=0}^{\infty} a_k\, u^k \tag{2.3.2.36}$$

where

$$a_{2k+1} = 0 \qquad (2.3.2.37)$$

$$h_k = S(t_0 + kT) \qquad (2.3.2.38)$$

where t_0 is the sampling point in the symbol period $(-T/2, T/2)$ (which makes P_e smaller).

The way to obtain the a_k's is as follows (Section 3.2.1 of Volume I):

$$\frac{d}{du} C_I(u) = -\sum_{k=1}^{\infty} h_k \sin(h_k u) \prod_{\substack{p=1 \\ (p \neq k)}}^{\infty} \cos(h_p u)$$

$$= -\prod_{p=1}^{\infty} \cos(h_p u) \sum_{k=1}^{\infty} h_k \tan(h_k u)$$

$$= -C_I(u) \sum_{k=1}^{\infty} h_k \tan(h_k u). \qquad (2.3.2.39)$$

Substituting the expansion of Equation 2.3.2.36 into this result, we have

$$\sum_{k=0}^{\infty} a_{2k+2}(2k+2)u^{2k+1} = \left(\sum_{k_1=0}^{\infty} a_{2k_1} u^{2k_1} \right)$$

$$\cdot \left(\sum_{k_2=0}^{\infty} b_{2k_2+1} u^{2k_2+1} \right) \qquad (2.3.2.40)$$

where the b_{2k+1} are given by

$$b_{2k_2+1} = -\eta_{k_2} \sum_{p=1}^{\infty} h_p^{(2k_2+2)} \qquad (2.3.2.41)$$

$$\tan z = \sum_{k=0}^{\infty} \eta_k z^{2k+1}. \qquad (2.3.2.42)$$

The η_k's are Bernouli's numbers. From the above equations,

$$a_{2k+2} = \sum_{k_1=0}^{k} a_{2k_1} b_{2(k-k_1)+1}, \text{ i.e.,}$$

$$a_2 = a_0 b_1 = b_1 \ (a_0 = 1)$$

$$a_4 = a_0 b_3 + a_2 b_1.$$

.

.

.

$$(2.3.2.43)$$

Thus, the higher order a_{2k} can be obtained by the lower order a_{2k}, since the values of the b_{2k+1}'s are known.

The QPSK case is more complicated than the BPSK and it is recommended to look at References [41] [43] for the recurrence relation for a_{k_1,k_2}. A numerical example of P_e versus (C/N) ($= A^2/2\sigma_N^2$) for a particular filter is shown in Figure 2.3.2.4.

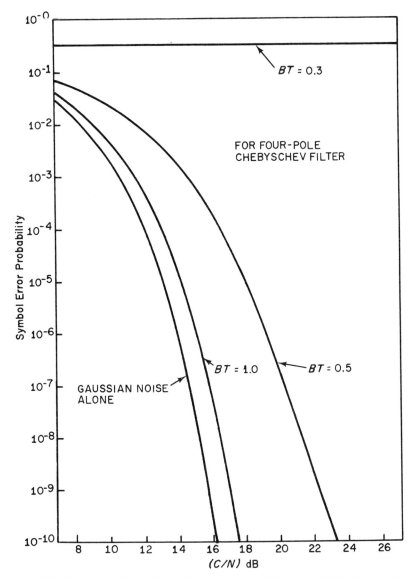

Figure 2.3.2.4(a)   Error Probability of Quaternary PSK System with Fourth-order Chebyshev Filter

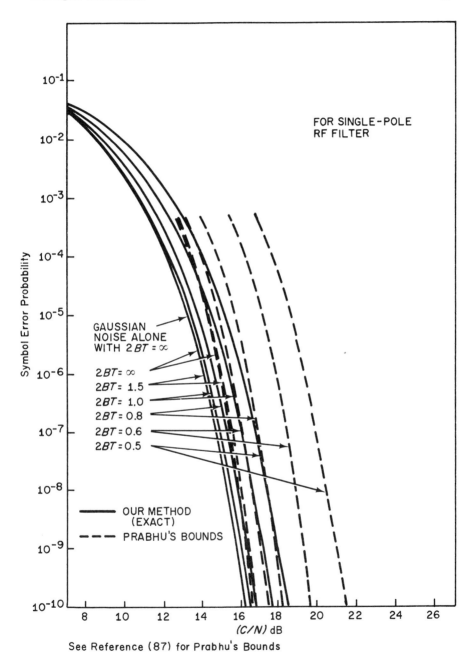

Figure 2.3.2.4(b) Error Probability of Quaternary PSK System with Single-Pole RF Filter

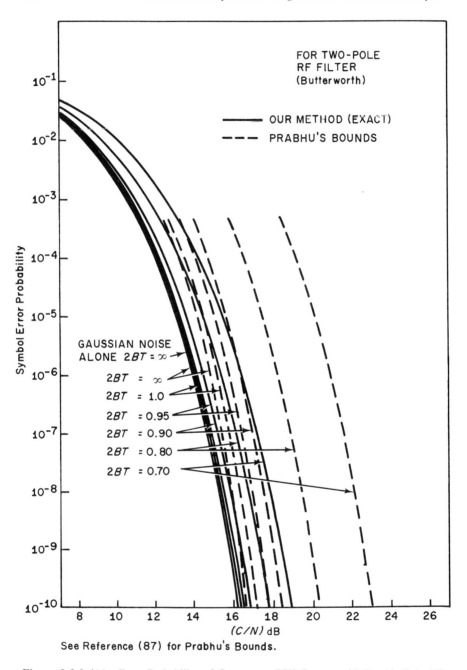

Figure 2.3.2.4(c)   Error Probability of Quaternary PSK System with Double-Pole RF
Filter

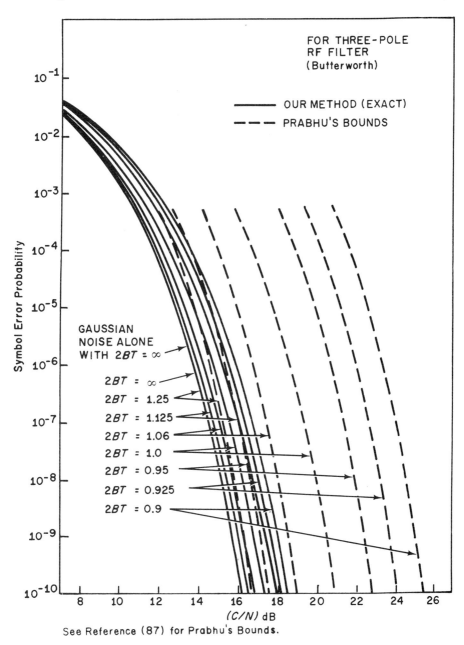

Figure 2.3.2.4(d)   Error Probability of Quaternary PSK System with Triple-Pole RF Filter

2.3.3   Combined Effects of Thermal Noise, Intersymbol Interferences and Nonlinear Effects

For an ideal QPSK signal represented by Equation 2.3.2.1, the amplitude A is always constant and the phase of $\phi(t)$ is also always constant (ϕ_k) in every symbol period. At this time instant of $kT \pm T/2$, the phase ϕ suddenly changes into another phase value whose transitional time length is zero, i.e., the phase jump from P_1 to P_2, P_3 or P_4 is instantaneous. Therefore, the envelope of $e_i(t)$ (Equation 2.3.2.1) stays as a constant A. Then, when this ideal PSK signal is filtered (e.g., F_1), the window function $V(t)$ is modified into $s(t)$ and this instantaneous phase jump becomes impossible because of the higher frequency components cut-off. Thus, the jump from P_1 to P_2, P_3 or P_4 takes some finite time length as shown in Figure 2.3.3.1.

In case the phase change from P_1 into P_3 is π ($180°$), the signal vector point P moves crossing the neighbor of 0 point, i.e., the envelope $|e_0(t)|$ becomes very small at the phase transitional time $t = kT \pm T/2$. When the phase change from P_1 into P_4 (or P_2) is $\pm \pi/2$, the vector P moves crossing the I coordinate almost perpendicularly. Thus, the envelope of the signal $|e_0(t)|$ after the filter becomes

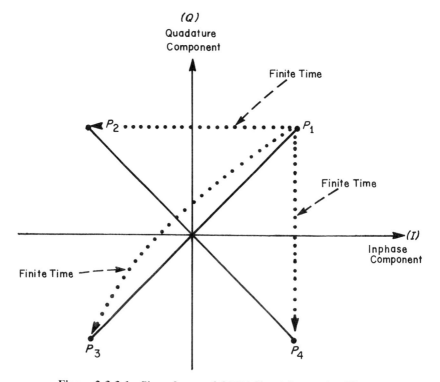

Figure 2.3.3.1   Phase Jumps of QPSK Signal Space after Filters

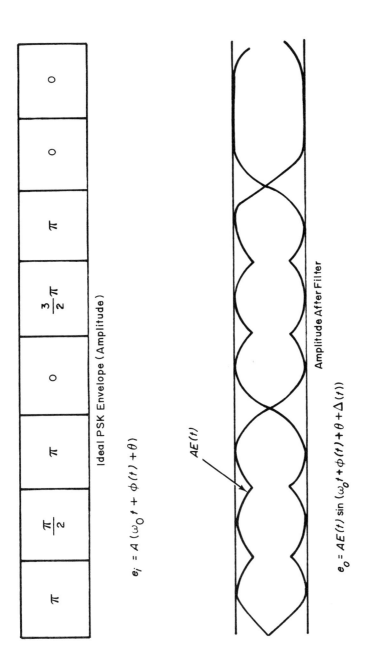

Ideal PSK Envelope (Amplitude)

$$e_i = A \left(\omega_0 t + \phi(t) + \theta \right)$$

$AE(t)$

Amplitude After Filter

$$e_0 = AE(t) \sin \left(\omega_0 t + \phi(t) + \theta + \Delta(t) \right)$$

Figure 2.3.3.2 Amplitude Fluctuation of QPSK Signals Due to Filters

respectively almost zero at the $\pi(180°)$ phase change point and $1/\sqrt{2}$ times smaller (3 dB decrease) at the $\pm \pi/2$ ($\pm 90°$) phase change point.

The exact shape of the envelope $|e_0(t)|$ also depends on the random phase values of the adjacent symbol intervals, i.e., on intersymbol interferences. Because of this random fluctuation of the envelope of the PSK signal at the input of a nonlinear device (with AM/AM and AM/PM), the output of the nonlinear device receives the following distortion. The output of the nonlinear device for the input $e_0(t)$ is given by

$$\frac{g(AE(t))}{AE(t)} e^{jf(AE(t))} e_0(t)$$

$$= \frac{g(AE(t))}{AE(t)} e^{jf(AE(t))} A e^{j\omega_0 t + j\theta} \sum_{k=-\infty}^{\infty} s(t - kT) e^{j\phi_k} \quad (2.3.3.1)$$

where

$$E(t) = \left| \sum_{k=-\infty}^{\infty} s(t - kT) e^{j\phi_k} \right|. \quad (2.3.3.2)$$

Because of the nature of the memoryless nonlinearity, the phase and amplitude values of Equation 2.3.3.1 are not much affected by the nonlinear device at the sampling points, since the sampling points are usually always almost at the peak points of the envelope, which are not much changed from symbol interval to interval except for the small change due to the intersymbol interferences. First the envelope of Equation 2.3.3.1 is changed by a factor $g(AE(t))/AE(t)$ after the nonlinear device and the phase is changed by the factor $f(AE(t))$. As described above, $AE(t)$ does not vary much at each sampling point except for the effects of the intersymbol interferences. However, if this signal is passed by another filter, the factor

$$\frac{g(AE(t))}{AE(t)} e^{jf(AE(t))} \quad (2.3.3.3)$$

becomes very much distorted and this distorted randomly modulated factor of Equation 2.3.3.3 causes much greater degradation to the signal. The output of the post-nonlinear filter is given by

$$\text{Re}\left\{ A e^{j\omega_0 t + j\theta} \int_{-\infty}^{\infty} \left[\frac{g(AE(x))}{AE(x)} e^{jf(AE(x))} \right] \right.$$

$$\left. \left[\sum_{k=-\infty}^{\infty} s(x - kT) e^{j\phi_k} \right] h_2(t - x) \, dx \right\}. \quad (2.3.3.4)^{\dagger}$$

$^{\dagger}h_2(t)$ is the lowpass analog impulse response of the post nonlinear filter.

If the factor of Equation 2.3.3.3 is constant (a linear case), Equation 2.3.3.4 becomes the cascaded case of the h_1 and h_2 filters. The amplitude and phase random modulation due to the factor of Equation 2.3.3.3 causes much more degradation than the linear case after an h_2 filter. This is called "emphasized intersymbol interferences by nonlinear devices and filters." For SCPC/PSK signals (64 Kbits/s) and continuous QPSK (1.44 Mbits/s ~ 10 Mbits/s) signals, the operating points of the HPA and TWTA are at low levels where the nonlinear characteristics are almost linear and the effects of the nonlinear devices can usually be ignored. However, for the TDMA signals which usually occupy the whole transponder and whose TWTA backoff is usually small (operating at or over-driving mode of TWTA in some cases), this type of degradation cannot be ignored.

In C-Band TDMA cases, the out-of-band signal power spectrum spill over due to the power spectrum sideband regrowth, because of HPA nonlinearity, is important and the input backoff of the HPA must usually be around 10 dB (in order to satisfy the CCIR criterion on outband emission). Therefore, in this case, only the degradation due to the satellite TWTA is important. However, for some K-Band TDMA systems (as in SBS), in order to reduce the ground terminal cost, the HPA and TWTA are both operating close to saturating power (the TWTA is overdriven in the SBS case) and the degradation caused by the filters and the cascaded nonlinear devices (HPA and TWTA) is even larger. Normally, this degradation is around 0.5 or 1.5 dB for the former single nonlinear case (TWTA only) and 1.5 dB ~ 2.5 dB for the two nonlinear cases (HPA and TWTA).

For the FDM/FM single carrier transmission which operates close to the saturating point of the HPA or/and TWTA, Section 2.1.1 showed that the filter equalization is still possible by adjusting the characteristics of $Y_{c+}^{(1)}$ and of $Y_{c+}^{(4)}$ (F_1 and F_4) as explained in Equation 2.1.3.19, since the instantaneous operating point of the FM signal is not changed very much because the envelope of the FM signal is not caused to fluctuate much by filter distortion. However, in the TDMA case, as explained in Figure 2.3.3.2, the TDMA signal envelope fluctuates a lot because of filter distortion. An analysis similar to that used when Equation 2.1.3.19 is derived is no longer applicable.

This is the reason why transmission analysis for a TDMA signal through cascaded filters and nonlinear devices (see Figure 2.1) is extremely difficult. For this purpose, a computer simulation is used, in which the random symbol pulse sequence is generated by the computer and the nonlinear characteristics and filter effects (convolution of $h(t)$ or Fourier-transform in frequency domain) are calculated. Figure 2.3.3.4 shows how the scattering diagram of the signal vector is obtained after the whole chain (F_1, HPA, F_2, TWTA, F_3, F_4).

For each scattered point of Figure 2.3.3.4 due to the filters and nonlinear devices, the error probability is analytically calculated for each point considering the up- and downlink noises and these error probabilities are averaged. This is

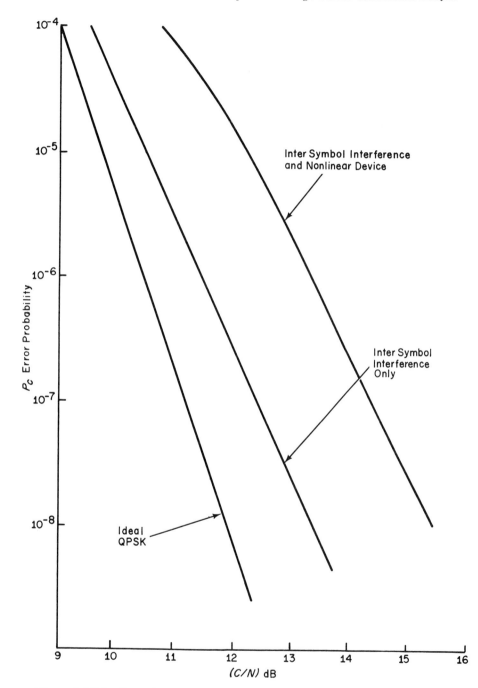

Figure 2.3.3.3   Example of Nonlinear Effects on Modem Performance (Measured Results)

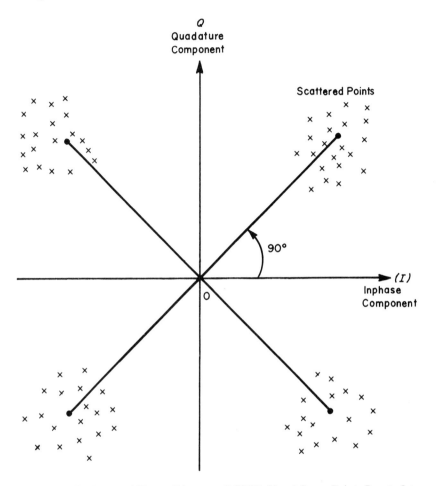

Figure 2.3.3.4 Scattered Vector Diagram of QPSK Signal Space Points Due to Inter-Symbol Interference and Nonlinear Effects (at the Sampling Points)

the final averaged error probability. In this way, the nonlinear effects on the uplink noise are ignored (all the noise effects are linearly considered).[†] In order to obtain accurate error probabilities, especially in the areas of small value of P_e, the symbol sequence must be long enough, since in the error probability calculation, the worst case prevails, and may not happen in a short sequence length. Bennedetto established an analytical approach [44] which handles this problem analytically but the result is not elegant.

[†]If the uplink noise is created by computer, the nonlinear effects on the uplink noise can be considered but the computer uses more time.

The effects of intersymbol interferences and nonlinear devices on octal and M-ary PSK signals can be analyzed as in Sections 2.3.2 and 2.3.3.

From the analysis of Section 2.3.1, the error probabilities of the octal or higher order PSK signals are larger than for the QPSK (or BPSK) with the same thermal noise. Similarly, the octal PSK or higher order PSK signals are weaker than QPSK (or OPSK) against the intersymbol interferences and against nonlinearities. Although M-ary PSK signals ($M \geqq 8$) are more complicated with thermal noise, intersymbol interferences and nonlinearities, since they are very similar to QPSK signal cases, they are not analyzed in this book.

2.3.4   Transmission of Staggered QPSK and MSK Signals

As explained in Section 4.3 of Volume I, the ideal staggered QPSK and MSK can be represented as:

$$
\begin{aligned}
e(t) &= \frac{A}{\sqrt{2}} \sin(\omega_0 t) \sum_{n=-\infty}^{\infty} a_n s(t - nT) \\
&\quad + \frac{A}{\sqrt{2}} \cos(\omega_0 t) \sum_{n=-\infty}^{\infty} b_n s\left(t - nT - \frac{T}{2}\right) \\
&= \frac{A}{\sqrt{2}} \left[\sin(\omega_0 t) x(t) + \cos(\omega_0 t) y\left(t - \frac{T}{2}\right) \right]
\end{aligned} \qquad (2.3.4.1)
$$

where

$$
s(t) = V(t) = \begin{cases} 1, & |t| \leq \dfrac{T}{2} \\[2mm] 0, & |t| > \dfrac{T}{2} \end{cases} \qquad (2.3.4.2)
$$

for the staggered QPSK and

$$
s(t) = \begin{cases} \cos(\dfrac{\pi}{T} t), & |t| \leq \dfrac{T}{2} \\[2mm] 0, & |t| \geqq \dfrac{T}{2} \end{cases} \qquad (2.3.4.3)
$$

for MSK.

a_n and b_n take ± 1 independently with equal probability of 1/2. From Equation 2.3.4.1,

$$x(t) = \sum_{n=-\infty}^{\infty} a_n s(t - nT)$$

$$y(t) = \sum_{n=-\infty}^{\infty} b_n s(t - nT). \qquad (2.3.4.4)$$

Rewrite Equation 2.3.4.1 as

$$e(t) = B \sin\{\omega_0 t + \phi(t)\} \qquad (2.3.4.5)$$

where

$$B = A \quad \text{for QPSK}$$

$$B = \frac{A}{\sqrt{2}} \quad \text{for MSK.} \qquad (2.3.4.6)$$

At the transmitter modulator, two bit streams $x(t)$ and $y(t - T/2)$ are created and $B \sin(\omega_0 t)$ and $B \cos(\omega_0 t)$ are multiplied, respectively, to $x(t)$ and $y(t - T/2)$. Then, $e(t)$ goes through a filter for the band limitation.

At the receiving side demodulator, $\cos(\omega_0 t)$ and $\sin(\omega_0 t)$ are first recovered and multiplied to $e(t)$. Thus, $x(t)$ and $y(t)$ are recovered (see Section 4.3.4 of Volume I).

As explained in Section 4.3 of Volume I, in this case, $\phi(t)$ of Equation 2.3.4.5 of Volume II can change only $\pm 90°$ at a time. In the conventional QPSK, $\phi(t)$ can change $\pm 90°$ or $180°$ at $t = nT + T/2$ $(n = 0, \pm 1, \ldots)$. But, in these systems, when ϕ changes $180°$ from $t = nT + T/2$ to $t = (n+1)T + T/2$, ϕ changes first $\pm 90°$ from $t = nT + T/2$ to $t = nT + T$ and then changes again $\pm 90°$ from $t = nT + T$ to $t = (n+1)T + T/2$ so that it finally changes to $180°$ after T is passed.

Therefore, $180°$ phase changes never occur in these systems and thus the amplitude fluctuation of these signals due to filtering becomes at most 3 dB (see Section 4.3 of Volume I). This helps the transmission of these signals through nonlinear devices with AM/PM conversion as explained in Section 4.3 of Volume I.

In linear transmission channels, the performances of these signal transmissions are similar to those of the conventional systems, as long as the carrier and bit synchronizations are properly done, i.e., $x(t)$ and $y(t)$ are correctly recovered. Since there are some difficulties in carrier recovery of these systems, the following will cover the subject.

2.3.4.1 MSK Signal

As explained in Section 4.3.5 of Volume I, when the phase of a conventional QPSK signal changes as 0, $\pm 90°$ or $180°$, the phase of this system always

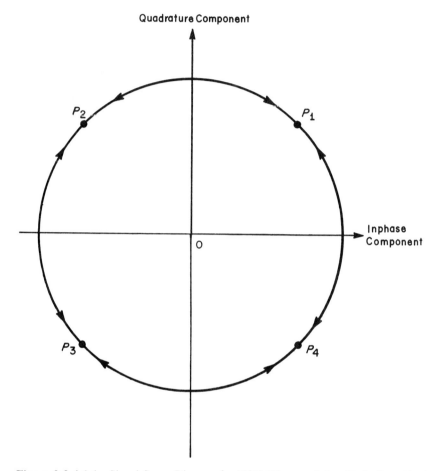

Figure 2.3.4.1.1   Signal Space Diagram for MSK (Phase and Amplitude Transition)

moves only $\pm$ 90° at the same speed, as shown in Figure 2.3.4.1.1. Therefore, the instantaneous frequency of this signal is always $f_0 \pm 1/2T$.

Thus the carrier frequency always becomes $f_0 \pm 1/2T$.

In such a case, making $e^4(t)$ by a nonlinear device and taking $4f_0$ components does not create the carrier frequency f_0 but creates 4 ($f_0 \pm 1/2T$).

Therefore, the carrier recovery becomes more difficult. One way of solving this problem is as follows. First, obtain 4 ($f_0 \pm 1/2T$) components through a nonlinear device plus filters and pass these two components through a mixer to obtain $8f_0$ ($=4f_0 + 4/2T + 4f_0 - 4/2T$). The bit recovery cannot be achieved through the conventional approach which is the amplitude fluctuation detection produced by the band width limitation,[†] since the MSK signal amplitude fluctuation is not large because there is only $\pm\, 90°$ phase at a time and the power spectrum spread is much less than that of the conventional QPSK (it decreases with f^{-4} in this case instead of f^{-2} in the conventional QPSK), which produces less amplitude fluctuations due to filters.

2.3.4.2 *Staggered QPSK*

In the ideal staggered QPSK, the phase change occurs instantaneously and therefore the conventional carrier recovery approach can be applied without any problem. However, after it is passed through the bandwidth limitation filters (transmission bandlimitation filter at the transmission side and noise cut filter at the receiving side), the wave form $V(t)$ is distorted and is no longer a square wave shape. As explained in Section 4.3.4 of Volume I, when the signal point moves from P_1 to P_2 (or P_4), or from P_2 to P_3, it takes a finite time (approximately $T/2$). Thus, a phenomenon similar to the MSK case discussed in the preceding section occurs,[‡] although the carrier frequency does not become exactly ($f_0\, \pm\, 1/2T$).

Using the mixer for the two components $4\,f_0\, \pm\, 4/2T$ to obtain $8\,f_0$ becomes less efficient since the carrier frequency does not take exactly ($f_0\, \pm\, 1/2T$).

2.3.5 Transmission of Differential PSK Signals

The recovered carriers at the PSK demodulator sometimes suffer from the so-called cycle skipping, especially when the carrier-to-noise power ratio is low. This is essentially the same phenomenon as that of the click noise explained in Section 2.1.5 where the carrier phase jumps suddenly $\pm\, 2\pi$ ($\pm\, 360°$).

Since the recovered carrier has a frequency $4\,f_0$ after the phase modulation elimination and before the frequency division into f_0, this phase change of $\pm\, 2\pi$ gives $\pm\, \pi/2$ ($\pm\, 90°$) after the frequency division into f_0, which is needed for the demodulation of the QPSK signal into the inphase and quadrature components. This sudden change of the recovered carrier phase ($\pm\, 90°$) generates a type of errors in which one of the I and Q streams becomes erroneous after the phase jump, as can easily be seen. This phenomenon is called "phase ambiguity."

One of the ways to avoid this problem is to use the so-called differential encoding in which the difference between the adjacent bits in the bit streams carries the information, i.e., whether a_n and a_{n+1} ($n = 0, \pm1, \pm2, \ldots$) (or

---

[†]Rigorously speaking, it should be said that it becomes harder to obtain the bit synchronization practically in this case.

[‡]In this case, some carrier frequency component always exists (if the randomness of the symbol sequence is good enough), although it is not so in a MSK case.

b_n and b_{n+1}) have the same sign or not is important (the signs of a_n and a_{n+1} themselves are not important). For example, if a_n and a_{n+1} have the same signs, $+1$ is sent and if not, -1 is sent. In this differential encoding system, the errors caused by the produced phase ambiguity (by the click noise of the recovered carrier) do not propagate after this error. However, in this system, once an error happens, two bit contiguous errors always occur. This reduces coding efficiency very much in many cases. But this system is robust against the phase ambiguity problem and has been used in some applications. This differentially encoded PSK signal can obviously be demodulated by coherent PSK demodulators (with carrier recovery). However, there is another convenient demodulation scheme for this system, i.e. differential PSK demodulation (DPSK), which will be analyzed in the following.

When the received PSK carrier suffers from low frequency phase noise, the conventional PSK demodulation system is not good in low bit rate signal transmission. A typical case is satellite communication where the local oscillator for the uplink and downlink frequency conversion has a large amount of low frequency phase noise.

Suppose that a PSK signal has a phase noise whose power spectrum is given by Figure 2.3.5.1 which is a typical satellite communication case. Ignoring temporarily thermal noise, represent the PSK signal by

$$A \sin(\omega_0 t + \phi(t) + \theta(t)) \qquad (2.3.5.1)$$

where ϕ is the phase modulation and $\theta(t)$ is the phase noise of Figure 2.3.5.1. Then the recovered carrier can be represented as

$$B \sin(\omega_0 t + \theta_1(t)) \quad \text{or} \quad B \cos(\omega_0 t + \theta_1(t)) \qquad (2.3.5.2)$$

where $\theta_1(t)$ is the phase noise whose power spectrum is that of $\theta(t)$ except for the fact that the components between $f_0 - f_1$ and $f_0 + f_1$ are eliminated. $(f_0 - f_1, f_0 + f_1)$ is the narrow band of the carrier recovery circuit (to cut the noise components and decrease the click noise or phase noise). Thus, the demodulated inphase and quadrature components of the signal are

$$A \cos(\phi(t) + \theta(t) - \theta_1(t)),$$

$$A \sin(\phi(t) + \theta(t) - \theta_1(t)). \qquad (2.3.5.3)$$

The power spectrum of $\theta(t) - \theta_1(t)$ is given by Figure 2.3.5.2 where the components of $\theta(t)$ in Figure 2.3.5.1 inside $(f_0 - f_1, f_0 - f_1)$ are eliminated as shown in Figure 2.3.5.2. When the bit rate is higher, the power of the phase noise $\theta(t) - \theta_1(t)$ becomes smaller and, when it is lower, the power becomes larger (the smaller the bit rate, the smaller f_1 becomes). When the power spectrum of $\theta(t)$ is given by Figure 2.3.5.1, if the bit rate is 500 bits/sec and $f_1 = 10$ Hz, for example, the power of $[\theta(t) - \theta_1(t)]$ becomes a large number, which causes serious degradation to the signal. In order to avoid this problem, the DPSK

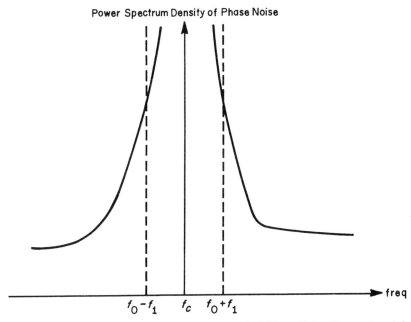

Figure 2.3.5.1   Power Spectrum Density of a Typical Phase Noise (Due to Local Oscillators)

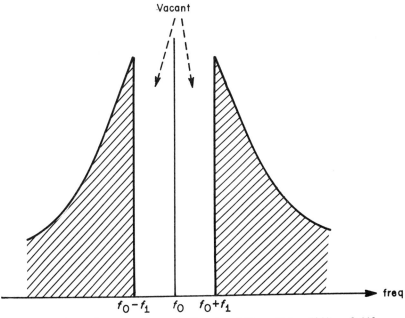

Figure 2.3.5.2   Power Spectrum Density of Phase Noise, $[\theta(t) - \theta_1(t)]$

demodulation for the differential encoded PSK signals or FSK systems are recommended for low bit rate transmission. Although the incoherent FSK signals (see Section 2.1.6) are very strong against the phase noise, as easily seen, and the demodulation scheme is simpler than the DPSK demodulation, the (C/N) value required for the FSK is 3 dB higher than the DPSK demodulation case as explained in the following. Therefore, from the power saving point of view, which is important in satellite communications, the DPSK demodulation is better, although the demodulation scheme becomes more complicated for the DPSK case.

The following analyses the DPSK demodulation case with a phase noise. As is well known [3], the FSK and DPSK demodulations are analytically related and therefore offer an interesting analysis.

Representing the differentially encoded BPSK signal (only the BPSK case is analyzed here for simplicity's sake) by

$$e(t) = A \cos\{\omega_0 t + \phi(t) + \theta(t)\}$$
$$+ N_c(t) \cos(\omega_0 t) - N_s(t) \sin(\omega_0 t) \qquad (2.3.5.4)$$

where $\phi(t)$ is the phase modulation (takes o or π) and $\theta(t)$ is the phase noise.

In the DPSK demodulation systems, the signal $e(t)$ time-delayed by T is multiplied by $e(t)$. Then, the low pass filter eliminates the $2 f_0$ component without distorting the low frequency component. For simplicity's sake, look at the case with no thermal and no phase noise. Then,

$$e(t)e(t - T) = \frac{A^2}{2} \cos\{\omega_0 T + \phi(t) - \phi(t - T)\}$$
$$- \frac{A^2}{2} \cos\{2\omega_0 t - \omega_0 T + \phi(t) + \phi(t - T)\} \qquad (2.3.5.5)$$

after the low pass filter, this becomes

$$e_0(t) = \left(\frac{A^2}{2}\right) \cos\{\omega_0 T + \phi(t) - \phi(t - T)\}. \qquad (2.3.5.6)$$

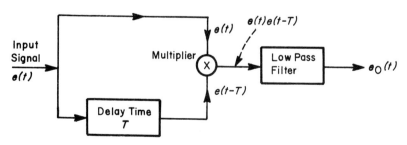

Figure 2.3.5.3 DPSK Receiver Block Diagram

If $\phi(t)$ and $\phi(t - T)$ are in equal phase,

$$e_0(t) = \left(\frac{A^2}{2}\right) \cos(\omega_0 t) \qquad (2.3.5.7)$$

and if $\phi(t)$ and $\phi(t - T)$ are in different phase,

$$e_0(t) = -\left(\frac{A^2}{2}\right) \cos(\omega_0 t). \qquad (2.3.5.8)$$

Since the noise, interferences and phase noise exist in practice, it is obvious that

$$\omega_0 T = n\pi \left(f_0 = \frac{n}{2T}\right) \qquad (2.3.5.9)$$

should be chosen. In such a case,

$$e_0(t) = \left(\frac{A^2}{2}\right)(-1)^n \quad \text{for same } \phi(t) \text{ and } \phi(t - T)$$

$$= -\left(\frac{A^2}{2}\right)(-1)^n \quad \text{for different } \phi(t) \text{ and } \phi(t - T). \quad (2.3.5.10)$$

Thus, the differential phase demodulation becomes possible.

The choice of $f_0 = n(2T)^{-1}$ at the ground terminal is useless in satellite communications, since the local oscillator frequency of satellite for the uplink and downlink frequency conversion drifts very much ($\pm$ 15 KHz), so that it is almost impossible to maintain the relation of $f_0 = n(2T)^{-1}$. Therefore, some method to make $f_0 = n(2T)^{-1}$ at the receiving ground terminal must be created. Since one can choose $f_0 = (2n)(2T)^{-1}$ (i.e., n is even in Equation 2.3.5.9) without deviating from any theoretical general rule, factor $(-1)^n$ of Equation 2.3.5.10 is taken away in the following analysis.

Rewrite $e(t)$ as

$$e(t) = \text{Re } \{(x_1 + jy_1)e^{j\omega_0 t}\} \qquad (2.3.5.11)$$

where

$$x_1(t) = A \cos\{\phi(t) + \theta(t)\} + N_c(t)$$

$$y_1(t) = A \sin\{\phi(t) + \theta(t)\} + N_s(t) \qquad (2.3.5.12)$$

$$e(t - T) = \text{Re } \{(x_2 + jy_2)e^{j\omega_0(t - T)}\} \qquad (2.3.5.13)$$

where

$$x_2 = x_1(t - T)$$

$$y_2 = y_1(t - T). \qquad (2.3.5.14)$$

Let us obtain

$$e(t)\,e(t\,-\,T).\tag{2.3.5.15}$$

Using the formula

$$\mathrm{Re}\,(a)\,\mathrm{Re}\,(b)\,=\,\frac{1}{2}\,\mathrm{Re}\{ab^*\,+\,ab\}.\tag{2.3.5.16}$$

If

$$a\,=\,(x_1\,+\,jy_1)\,e^{\,j\omega_0 t}$$

$$b\,=\,(x_2\,+\,jy_2)\,e^{\,j\omega_0(t-T)}\tag{2.3.5.17}$$

$$e(t)\,e(t\,-\,T)\,=\,\frac{1}{2}\,\mathrm{Re}\{ab^*\,+\,ab\}.\tag{2.3.5.18}$$

Since ab is the component of $2\omega_0 t$, $e_0(t)$ does not include it, i.e.,

$$e_0(t)\,=\,\frac{1}{2}\,\mathrm{Re}\{e^{\,j\omega_0 T}(x_1\,+\,jy_1)(x_2\,-\,jy_2)\}$$

$$=\,\frac{1}{2}(x_1 x_2\,+\,y_1 y_2).\tag{2.3.5.19}$$

Thus, the probability of errors, when $\phi(t)$ and $\phi(t\,-\,T)$ take the same phases, is given by

$$P_e^{(+)}\,=\,\mathrm{Prob}\{(x_1 x_2\,+\,y_1 y_2)\,<\,0\,|\,\phi(t)\,-\,\phi(t\,-\,T)\,=\,0\}.\tag{2.3.5.20}$$

Similarly, the probability of errors of the different $\phi(t)$ and $\phi(t\,-\,T)$ values is given by

$$P_e^{(-)}\,=\,\mathrm{Prob}\{(x_1 x_2\,+\,y_1 y_2)\,>\,0\,|\,\phi(t)\,-\,\phi(t\,-\,T)\,=\,\pm\pi\}.\tag{2.3.5.21}$$

To make the analysis simpler, the following coordinate transformation is used here.

$$X_1\,=\,\frac{x_1\,+\,x_2}{\sqrt{2}},\quad X_2\,=\,\frac{x_1\,-\,x_2}{\sqrt{2}},$$

$$Y_1\,=\,\frac{y_1\,+\,y_2}{\sqrt{2}},\quad Y_2\,=\,\frac{y_1\,-\,y_2}{\sqrt{2}},$$

$$y_1\,=\,\frac{Y_1\,+\,Y_2}{\sqrt{2}},\quad y_2\,=\,\frac{Y_1\,-\,Y_2}{\sqrt{2}},$$

$$x_1\,=\,\frac{X_1\,+\,X_2}{\sqrt{2}},\quad x_2\,=\,\frac{X_1\,-\,X_2}{\sqrt{2}}.\tag{2.3.5.22}$$

Then,

$$P_e^{(+)} = \text{Prob}\{(X_1^2 + Y_1^2) < (X_2^2 + Y_2^2) \mid \phi(t) - \phi(t - T) = 0\}$$

$$P_e^{(-)} = \text{Prob}\{(X_1^2 + Y_1^2) > (X_2^2 + Y_2^2) \mid \phi(t) - \phi(t - T) = \pm\pi\}.$$

$$(2.3.5.23)$$

Assuming that $\phi(t) - \phi(t - T) = 0$ and $\phi(t) - \phi(t - T) = \pm\pi$ occur with equal probabilities 1/2, the average error probability is given by

$$P_e = \frac{1}{2}P_e^{(+)} + \frac{1}{2}P_e^{(-)}. \qquad (2.3.5.24)$$

The following shows that $(X_1 - \overline{X}_1)$, $(X_2 - \overline{X}_2)$, $(Y_1 - \overline{Y}_1)$ and $(Y_2 - \overline{Y}_2)$ are all mutually independent zero-mean Gaussian processes and

$$\overline{(X_1 - \overline{X}_1)^2} = \overline{(Y_1 - \overline{Y}_1)^2} = \sigma_1^2$$

$$\overline{(X_2 - \overline{X}_2)^2} = \overline{(Y_2 - \overline{Y}_2)^2} = \sigma_2^2$$

$$(\sigma_1 \neq \sigma_2). \qquad (2.3.5.25)$$

Also, $\overline{X}_1$, $\overline{Y}_1$, $\overline{X}_2$ and $\overline{Y}_2$ change with $\phi(t) - \phi(t - T) = 0$ or $\pm\pi$ where the notation $^-$ means the average.

Define A_1 and A_2 as

$$A_1 = \sqrt{(\overline{X}_1)^2 + (\overline{Y}_1)^2}$$

$$A_2 = \sqrt{(\overline{X}_2)^2 + (\overline{Y}_2)^2}. \qquad (2.3.5.26)$$

Note that A_1 and A_2 change with $\phi(t) - \phi(t - T) = 0$ or $\pm\pi$.

Therefore, from Equation 2.3.5.23 and from the above facts, this system is equivalent to an incoherent FSK system as shown by Figure 2.1.5 of Volume I where the signal amplitudes of A_1 and A_2 are given by the above equation and the noise power after the filters I and II are respectively σ_1^2 and σ_2^2 given above.

Therefore, $P_e^{(+)}$ and $P_e^{(-)}$ are given by Equation 2.1.82 of Volume I. From Equations 2.3.5.12, 2.3.5.14, and 2.3.5.22 of Volume II,

$$\overline{X}_1 = \frac{\pm A}{\sqrt{2}} [\cos \theta(t) + \cos \theta(t - T)],$$

$$\overline{Y}_1 = \frac{\pm A}{\sqrt{2}} [\sin \theta(t) + \sin \theta(t - T)],$$

$$\overline{X}_2 = \frac{\pm A}{\sqrt{2}} [\cos \theta(t) - \cos \theta(t - T)],$$

$$\overline{Y}_2 = \frac{\pm A}{\sqrt{2}} [\sin \theta(t) - \sin \theta(t - T)] \qquad (2.3.5.27)$$

for $\phi(t) - \phi(t - T) = 0$ (same phase)

$$\overline{X}_1 = \frac{\pm A}{\sqrt{2}} [\cos \theta(t) - \cos \theta(t - T)],$$

$$\overline{Y}_1 = \frac{\pm A}{\sqrt{2}} [\sin \theta(t) - \sin \theta(t - T)],$$

$$\overline{X}_2 = \frac{\pm A}{\sqrt{2}} [\cos \theta(t) + \cos \theta(t - T)],$$

$$\overline{Y}_2 = \frac{\pm A}{\sqrt{2}} [\sin \theta(t) + \sin \theta(t - T)] \tag{2.3.5.28}$$

for $\phi(t) - \phi(t - T) = \pm \pi$ (different phase)

$$X_1 - \overline{X}_1 = \frac{N_c(t) + N_c(t - T)}{\sqrt{2}}, \quad Y_1 - \overline{Y}_1 = \frac{N_s(t) + N_s(t - T)}{\sqrt{2}}$$

$$X_2 - \overline{X}_2 = \frac{N_c(t) - N_c(t - T)}{\sqrt{2}}, \quad Y_2 - \overline{Y}_2 = \frac{N_s(t) - N_s(t - T)}{\sqrt{2}}.$$

$$\tag{2.3.5.29}$$

Therefore,

$$\sigma_1^2 = (R_N(0) + R_N(T))$$

$$\sigma_2^2 = (R_N(0) - R_N(T)) \tag{2.3.5.30}$$

where

$$R_N(\tau) = \overline{N_c(t) N_c(t + T)} = \overline{N_s(t) N_s(t + T)}. \tag{2.3.5.31}$$

Using

$$\overline{N_c(t) N_s(t)} = \overline{N_c(t - T) N_s(t - T)} = 0 \tag{2.3.5.32}$$

and

$$\overline{N_c(t) N_s(t - T)} = \overline{N_c(t + T) N_s(t)} = 0 \tag{2.3.5.33}$$

where it is assumed that the power spectrum of the DPSK thermal noise given by Equation 2.3.5.4 is symmetric around f_0 (to satisfy Equation 2.3.5.33).

Since $P_e^{(+)}$ and $P_e^{(-)}$ are symmetric to each other in the analysis, $P_e^{(+)}$ is first obtained. Note here that σ_1^2 and σ_2^2 do not change with $\phi(t) - \phi(t - T) = 0$

or $\pm\pi$ and that A_1 and A_2 become different as seen from Equations 2.3.5.27 and 2.3.5.28, i.e.,

$$A_1 = A[1 + \cos\Delta\theta]^{\frac{1}{2}} = \sqrt{2}A\left|\cos\left(\frac{\Delta\theta}{2}\right)\right|$$

$$A_2 = A[1 - \cos\Delta\theta]^{\frac{1}{2}} = \sqrt{2}A\left|\sin\left(\frac{\Delta\theta}{2}\right)\right| \qquad (2.3.5.34)$$

for $\phi(t) - \phi(t - T) = 0$ (same phase)

where

$$\Delta\theta = \theta(t) - \theta(t - T) \qquad (2.3.5.35)$$

$$A_1 = \sqrt{2}A\left|\sin\left(\frac{\Delta\theta}{2}\right)\right|$$

$$A_2 = \sqrt{2}A\left|\cos\left(\frac{\Delta\theta}{2}\right)\right| \qquad (2.3.5.36)$$

for $\phi(t) - \phi(t - T) = \pm\pi$ (different phase).

Thus, using the formula of Equation 2.1.82 of Volume I,

$$P_e^{(+)} = -\frac{1}{2}\left[1 + \frac{R_N(T)}{R_N(0)}\right]e^{-\left(\frac{C}{N}\right)}I_0\left(\left(\frac{C}{N}\right)\sin(\Delta\theta)\right)$$

$$+ Q\left(\sqrt{2}\sqrt{\frac{C}{N}}\sin\left(\frac{\Delta\theta}{2}\right), \sqrt{2}\sqrt{\frac{C}{N}}\cos\left(\frac{\Delta\theta}{2}\right)\right) \qquad (2.3.5.37)$$

where (C/N) is the carrier-to-noise-power ratio of the DPSK demodulator input, i.e.,

$$(C/N) = \frac{(A^2/2)}{R_N(0)} . \qquad (2.3.5.38)$$

Since, in case of $\phi(t) - \phi(t - T) = \pm\pi$ (different phase), A_1 and A_2 are exchanged and also σ_1^2, σ_2^2 are exchanged, the error probability is given by

$$P_e^{(-)} = \text{Prob}\{(X_1^2 + Y_1^2) > (X_2^2 + Y_2^2) \mid \phi(t) - \phi(t - T) = \pm\pi\}$$

$$= -\frac{1}{2}\left[1 - \frac{R_N(T)}{R_N(0)}\right]e^{-\left(\frac{C}{N}\right)}I_0\left(\left(\frac{C}{N}\right)\sin(\Delta\theta)\right)$$

$$+ Q\left(\sqrt{2}\sqrt{\frac{C}{N}}\sin\left(\frac{\Delta\theta}{2}\right), \sqrt{2}\sqrt{\frac{C}{N}}\cos\left(\frac{\Delta\theta}{2}\right)\right). \qquad (2.3.5.39)$$

Therefore,

$$P_e = \frac{1}{2}P_e^{(+)} + \frac{1}{2}P_e^{(-)}$$

$$= -\frac{1}{2}e^{-\left(\frac{C}{N}\right)}I_0\left(\left(\frac{C}{N}\right)\sin(\Delta\theta)\right)$$

$$+ Q\left(\sqrt{2}\sqrt{\frac{C}{N}}\sin\left(\frac{\Delta\theta}{2}\right), \sqrt{2}\sqrt{\frac{C}{N}}\cos\left(\frac{\Delta\theta}{2}\right)\right). \quad (2.3.5.40)$$

When there is no phase noise ($\Delta\theta = 0$),

$$P_e = \frac{1}{2}e^{-\left(\frac{C}{N}\right)} \quad (2.3.5.41)$$

where the formulas

$$I_0(0) = 1$$

$$Q(0, b) = e^{-\frac{b^2}{2}} \quad (2.3.5.42)$$

were used to obtain Equation 2.3.5.41.

Compare the result of Equation 2.3.5.41 with that of Equation 2.1.6.11, the DPSK demodulation scheme is 3 dB better than that of the FSK case. For the small phase noise case,

$$P_e = \frac{1}{2}e^{-\left(\frac{C}{N}\right)}\left[\sum_{k=0}^{\infty}d_k\tan^{2k}\left(\frac{\Delta\theta}{2}\right)\right.$$

$$\left. \cdot I_k\left(\left(\frac{C}{N}\right)\sin(\Delta\theta)\right)\right] \quad (2.3.5.43)$$

where

$$d_0 = 1$$

$$d_k = 2 \quad (k = 1, 2, 3, \ldots) \quad (2.3.5.44)$$

giving a good convergence for the computation.

The formula

$$Q(a, b) = e^{-\frac{a^2 + b^2}{2}}\sum_{k=0}^{\infty}\left(\frac{a}{b}\right)^k I_k(ab) \quad (2.3.5.45)$$

was used to obtain Equation 2.3.5.43 [3].

The average degradation of $P_e(\Delta\theta)$ is given by

$$\overline{P}_e = \int_{-\infty}^{\infty} P_e(\Delta\theta)\,\mathrm{Prob}(\Delta\theta)\,d\theta \qquad (2.3.5.46)$$

where $\mathrm{Prob}(\Delta\theta)$ is the probability density function of $\Delta\theta$.

Figure 2.3.5.4 shows the characteristics of P_e (C/N) with and without the phase noise. (It is assumed in this case that the phase noise is Gaussian.)

2.3.6 Transmission of TDMA/PSK Signals

In TDMA signal transmission, it is important to consider the carrier and bit recoveries, the frame identification and phase ambiguity resolution by unique words (see Section 4.5 of Volume I), filter distortions and nonlinear distortions (or combination of both), etc. As shown in Fig. 2.3.6.1, the TDMA signal consists of a repetition of frames. Within a frame, a number of bursts are arranged in time division. In Figure 2.3.6.1, the burst '1' comes from the transmitter A, the burst '2' comes from the transmitter B, etc. Each burst in most cases is a modulated PSK carrier. This TDMA (time division multiple access)/PSK signal has some merits in satellite communication transmission. In FDMA (frequency division multiple access) cases of satellite communications, a transponder amplifies many modulated carriers together (PSK or FDM/FM carriers). In order to utilize the transponder power efficiently, the input power of these PSK and FDM/FM signals, etc. should be as close as possible to the transponder saturating power in which the signal transmission becomes very nonlinear. Then, as analyzed in Chapter 3, the intermodulation products or modulation transfer deteriorate the signal qualities. Therefore, it becomes necessary to reduce the input power of the transponder to reduce these effects (increase the transponder back-off). If the TDMA systems are used, the saturating power (maximum power) of the transponder becomes available without causing any deterioration of these signals, since only one burst is amplified at a time. The only disadvantages of using such a transponder are

(i) the transponder antenna or power (HPA) must be larger than the FDMA, since the transponder is operated at maximum power and
(ii) the receiver antenna must be larger, since the transmitted bit rates are much higher than those required to send special data or messages.

For example, in order to transmit only 32 kbits/sec signal from an earth station, the bit rate to be transmitted from this station must still be 120 Mbits/sec, for example. Accordingly, the disadvantages of the above (i) and (ii) occur. Also, the modems become more expensive, since the 32 kbits/sec must be picked from the 120 Mbits/sec signal.

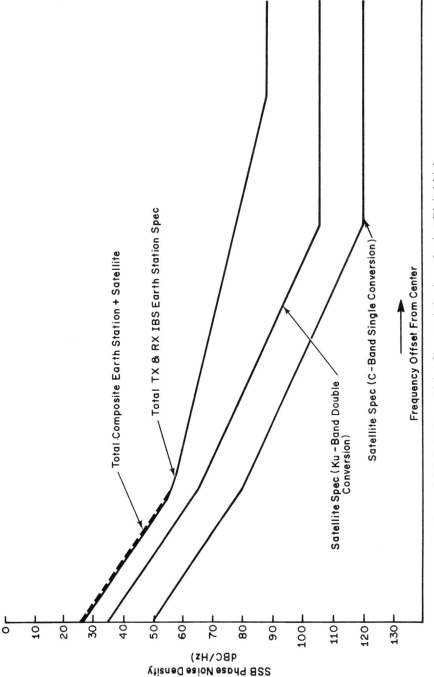

Figure 2.3.5.4(a)   Phase Noise Characteristics in an Intelsat Digital Link

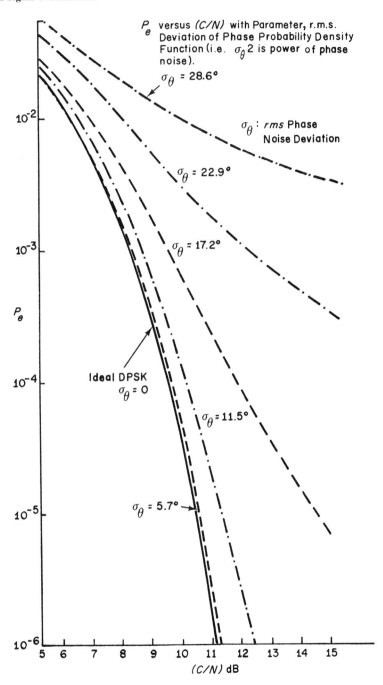

Figure 2.3.5.4(b)   Averaged BER for DPSK as a Function of RMS Phase Noise σ_θ and (C/N)

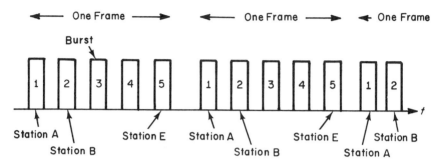

Figure 2.3.6.1 Repetition of Frames of TDMA Signal

Figure 2.3.6.2 shows the structure of each burst. In TDMA systems, at each burst, the carrier and bit timing must be recovered. Therefore, the carrier recovery and bit timing recovery filters have much wider bandwidths than those of the continuous mode PSK cases (see Sections 4.5.1 and 4.5.2 of Volume I), in which the PSK signal is continuously sent from the transmitter and where there is no need for quick carrier and bit timing recoveries at each burst. Because of these wider carrier and bit timing recovery filters, the phase ambiguity resolution (if the absolute encoding is used) becomes very important (see Section 4.5 of Volume I), since the signal-to-noise-power ratios after these filters are much lower than those of the continuous mode PSK signal cases. For example, in the Intelsat TDMA/PSK system, the carrier recovery filter bandwidth is almost 700 kHz (the symbol rate of QPSK signal is 60 M bauds/sec). Since the signal bandwidth of this case is approximately 1.1×60 MHz, the improvement of the carrier-to-noise-power ratio of the carrier recovery case is $10 \log_{10} (1.1 \times 60 \times 10/700) = 19.7$ dB.

Normally, the signal-carrier-to-noise ratio is about 17 dB and there is a 12 dB degradation of the (C/N) ratio due to the elimination of the phase modulation (for QPSK cases) (see Section 4.5.1 of Volume I). Therefore, (C/N) of the output of this carrier recovery filter becomes (C/N) $= 17 \, dB + 19.7 \, dB - 12 \, dB = 24.7 \, dB$.

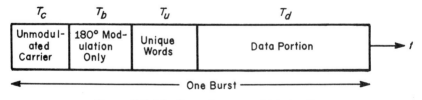

Figure 2.3.6.2 Burst Structure of TDMA Signal

This result is large enough to keep the occurrences of cycle skipping effects small enough, even under fading. Thus, the first portion of each burst (T_c period) (e.g., 48 symbol period) is unmodulated, which helps the carrier recovery, since the carrier component takes the maximum level in comparison with that of the modulated case. T_c must be long enough so that the carrier is recovered almost completely at the end of T_c. Next, in the period of T_b (e.g., 128 symbols), the carrier is modulated by 180° so that the bit recovery is most efficiently done and a fairly good amount of carrier components still exists. As explained in Section 4.5 of Volume I, the bit recovery is usually done by detecting the amplitude of the modulated carrier which receives the largest modulation when the 180° phase changes occur. If the receiver is modulated by 180°, the carrier component still exists, although the level is smaller than that of the modulated carrier, since the power decreases because of the amplitude modulation due to filters. In the third period of T_u, the unique words are arranged, which tell when the data frame portion started in the demodulation and resolve the phase ambiguity caused by the recovered carrier. The phase ambiguity resolution is only important for the absolutely encoded cases as explained in Section 4.5 of Volume I. After all these are done, in the T_d period, the data bits are filled. In this period, it is very important for the transmitter to use a good scrambler so that no modulation bit patterns or 90° phase change patterns continue for a long time (the former is harmful for the bit recovery and the latter is harmful for the carrier recovery) (see Section 4.5 of Volume I).

2.4 ANALOG HYBRID MODULATION

In Figure 2.4.1, $\phi^{(1)}(t)$ is the source signal which must be transmitted to the other station. F_1 is a low pass filter to cut excess higher frequency components to avoid the interference into other signals. L is a linear circuit to give a modulation gain of this system. g_0 is the gain amplification (or less) that gives modulation sensitivity to the modulator. Since the effect of F_1 is trivial for analytical purposes, the author starts from $\phi^{(2)}$, the output of F_1. The conversion from $\phi^{(2)}$ to $\phi^{(3)}$ is a linear operation (this operation is L) and it is easy to achieve this conversion. In FM signals, the transfer function of L is $(jf)^{-1}$ ($2\pi \int dt$ in time domain), i.e., the conversion from the frequency to the phase. g_0 is the gain to adjust the modulation sensitivity. In FM cases, it is the modulation index or the frequency deviation. In the modulator, using this input $\phi^{(3)}$ (or $g_0\phi^{(3)}$), the inphase and quadrature components respectively are produced as

$$I(\phi^{(3)}) \cos(\omega_0 t + \theta)$$

and

$$+ Q(\phi^{(3)}) \sin(\omega_0 t + \theta). \qquad (2.4.1)$$

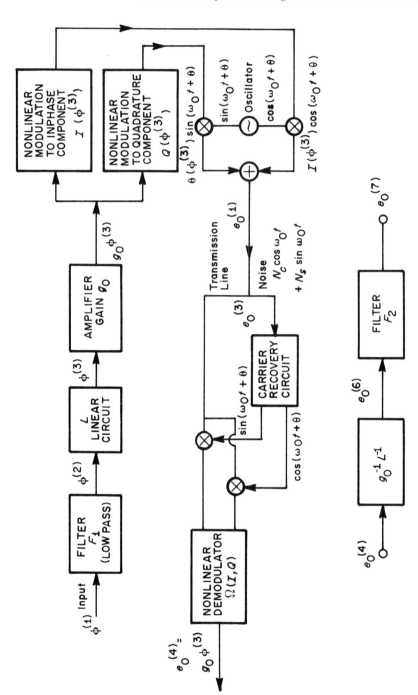

Figure 2.4.1 Idealized Analog APM Transmission Chain

Thus, the output of the modulator is given by

$$e_0^{(1)} = I(\phi^{(3)}) \cos(\omega_0 t + \theta)$$

$$+ Q(\phi^{(3)}) \sin(\omega_0 t + \theta) \qquad (2.4.2)$$

where ω_0 is the angular frequency of the r.f. carrier and θ is an arbitrary phase.

If there is no thermal noise and HPA + satellite is a linear channel, the output of the demodulator is

$$e_0^{(4)} = \Omega(I(\phi^{(3)}), Q(\phi^{(3)})) = g_0 \phi^{(3)}. \qquad (2.4.3)$$

In other terms, in the demodulator, I and Q are obtained by recovering $\cos(\omega_0 t)$ and $\sin(\omega_0 t)$ (carrier recovery) as it is done in QPSK cases. The function Ω is the inverse function of $(I(\phi^{(3)}), Q(\phi^{(3)}))$, as seen from Equations 2.4.1 and 2.4.3. However, in reality, there are thermal noise interferences, nonlinear effects of HPA, and filter distortions in transmission.

First, for simplicity's sake, assume that there is only thermal noise in transmission channel. Then, the input to the demodulator is

$$e_0^{(3)} = [I(\phi^{(3)}) + N_c] \cos(\omega_0 t + \theta)$$

$$+ [Q^{(3)}(\phi^{(3)}) + N_s] \cos(\omega_0 t + \theta). \qquad (2.4.4)$$

Then, the output of the demodulator is given by

$$e_0^{(4)} = \Omega(I(\phi_0^{(3)}) + N_c, Q(\phi_0^{(3)}) + N_s)$$

$$\simeq \Omega(I(\phi^{(3)}), Q(\phi^{(3)}))$$

$$+ \Omega^{(I)}(I(\phi^{(3)}))N_c + \Omega^{(Q)}(Q(\phi^{(3)}))N$$

$$= g_0 \phi^{(3)} + \Omega^{(I)}N_c + \Omega^{(Q)}N_s \qquad (2.4.5)^\dagger$$

where

$$\Omega^{(I)}(x, y) = \frac{\partial \Omega(x, y)}{\partial x}$$

$$\Omega^{(Q)}(x, y) = \frac{\partial \Omega(x, y)}{\partial y}. \qquad (2.4.6)$$

In an FM case,

$$\Omega(x, y) = \tan^{-1}\left(\frac{y}{x}\right). \qquad (2.4.7)$$

---

†It is assumed here that the signal is operating above threshold.

Thus, the final demodulated output is given by

$$e_0^{(6)} = g_0^{-1} L^{-1} [g_0 \phi^{(3)} + \Omega^{(I)} N_c + \Omega^{(Q)} N_s]$$

$$= \phi^{(2)} + g_0^{-1} L^{-1} [\Omega^{(I)} N_c + \Omega^{(Q)} N_s] \qquad (2.4.8)$$

where L^{-1} is $1/2\pi \; d/dt$ in time domain (jf in frequency domain) in an FM modulation case.

In an FM case, from Equations 2.4.6 and 2.4.7 using

$$I(\phi^{(3)}) = A \cos g_0 \phi^{(3)}, \quad Q(\phi^{(3)}) = A \sin g_0 \phi^{(3)} \qquad (2.4.9)$$

$$\Omega^{(I)} = \frac{-A \sin(g_0 \phi^{(3)})}{(A \cos g_0 \phi^{(3)})^2 + (A \sin g_0 \phi^{(3)})^2} = \frac{-\sin(g_0 \phi^{(3)})}{A}$$

$$\Omega^{(Q)} = \frac{A \cos(g_0 \phi^{(3)})}{(A \cos g_0 \phi^{(3)})^2 + (A \sin g_0 \phi^{(3)})^2} = \frac{\cos(g_0 \phi^{(3)})}{A}. \qquad (2.4.10)$$

In this case, the demodulated output of the Equation is given by

$$e_0^{(6)} = \frac{1}{2\pi} \phi^{(2)}(t)' + g_0^{-1} \frac{1}{2\pi} \frac{d}{dt}$$

$$\cdot \left[\frac{N_s \cos(g_0 \phi^{(3)}) - N_c \sin(g_0 \phi^{(3)})}{A} \right]$$

$$= g_0^{-1} \left[\frac{1}{2\pi} g_0 \phi^{(2)}(t)' + \frac{1}{2\pi} \frac{d}{dt} \; Im\left\{ \frac{N e^{-j g_0 \phi^{(3)}}}{A} \right\} \right]. \qquad (2.4.11)$$

This result is the same as that of Equation 2.1.5.9 if ϕ of Equation 2.1.5.9 is replaced by $g_0 \phi(t)$. From the above analysis, it can be concluded that:

(a) The linear circuit L should be chosen in such a way that, after the inverse operation L^{-1} in the demodulation process, the noise output $g_0^{-1} L^{-1} (\Omega^{(I)} N_c + \Omega^{(Q)} N_s)$ in Equation 2.4.8 should be suppressed in some frequency components for which the signal is sensitive, and emphasized in other frequency components for which the signal is less sensitive. Note here that the signal component after the demodulator goes back to the original one (before the L operator at the transmitter) because of L^{-1} at the receiver as seen from Equation 2.4.3, while the noise component only receives the inverse operation L^{-1} (and does not receive L). For example, in an FM case, L is the combination of $1/j2\pi f$ and of the pre-emphasis circuit (frequency domain), where the above analysis should be applied to the pre-emphasis portion.

(b) g_0 should be of such a size that the transmission bandwidth required is not excessive and the carrier power/noise ratio does not fall below threshold because of an excess of bandwidth required due to too large a value of g_0. Note here that the larger g_0, the more bandwidth is required but the noise power in $e_0^{(7)}$ stays the same, since it is cut by the filter F_2 (above threshold). In FM cases, a larger g_0 corresponds to a larger frequency deviation (linear proportional).

(c) Since the power of $\Omega^{(I)}N_c + \Omega^{(Q)}N_s$ (Equation 2.4.5) is $[(\Omega^{(I)})^2 + (\Omega^{(Q)})^2]$ $2\sigma_N^2$ (σ_N^2 is the power of $N_c(t)$ or $N_s(t)$ or r.f. noise power), if the modulation is chosen so that $[(\Omega^{(I)})^2 + (\Omega^{(Q)})^2]$ may be small, a noise reduction can be obtained. In an FM case, from Equation 2.4.11 $(\Omega^{(I)})^2 + (\Omega^{(Q)})^2 = 1/A^2$ which is independent of g_0.

The hybrid modulated signals receive some distortions by the filters. Suppose the output of the modulator ($e_0^{(1)}$) is filtered by a filter whose low pass analog impulse response is given by $h(t)$. Then, this filtered output is given (in the complex form) by:

$$e^{j\omega_0 t + j\theta} \int_{-\infty}^{\infty} M(\phi^{(3)}(x))\, h(t - x)\, dx \tag{2.4.12}$$

where

$$M(\phi^{(3)}(x)) = I(\phi^{(3)}(x)) + jQ(\phi^{(3)}(x)). \tag{2.4.13}$$

In normal operating conditions, the distortion due to filters is small and therefore, Equation 2.4.12 can be represented by

$$[(I(\phi^{(3)}) + \Delta I) + j(Q(\phi^{(3)}) + \Delta Q)]. \tag{2.4.14}$$

Note here that the transfer function of the filter is normalized as done in Section 2.1.1 to make ΔI and ΔQ small.

If the result of Equation 2.4.14 goes through the demodulator, the output $e_0^{(4)}$ is given in a way similar to Equation 2.4.5 by

$$e_0^{(4)} \simeq \phi^{(3)} + \Omega^{(I)} \cdot \Delta I + \Omega^{(Q)} \cdot \Delta Q. \tag{2.4.15}$$

Then, the final output before the low pass filter F_2 is given by

$$e_0^{(6)} = \phi^{(1)} + g_0^{-1} L^{-1}(\Omega^{(I)}\Delta I + \Omega^{(Q)}\Delta Q). \tag{2.4.16}$$

The similar optimization on g_0, L and $(\Omega^{(I)}, \Omega^{(Q)})$ explained in the thermal noise case can be done in this case. However, note that ΔI and ΔQ are dependent on g_0 and L, while N_c and N_s are not dependent on g_0 and L in the thermal noise case.

For the nonlinear effects on the hybrid modulated signals, let us see first what happens if there is no noise and no filter distortion. In Figure 2.4.1, the output of HPA, when the input is given by $e_0^{(1)}$ (in the complex form), is

$$
\begin{aligned}
e_0^{(2)} &= \frac{g_H(|M(\phi^{(3)})|)}{|M(\phi^{(3)})|} e^{jf_H(|M(\phi^{(3)})|)} \cdot e_0^{(1)} \\
&= \frac{g_H(|M|)}{|M|} M e^{j\omega_0 t + j\theta + jf_H(|M|)}.
\end{aligned}
\tag{2.4.17}
$$

Then, the output of the TWTA is

$$
\begin{aligned}
e^{(2)} &= \frac{g_T(g_H(|M|))}{|M|} e^{jf_T(g_H(|M|)) + jf_H(|M|)} \\
&\quad \cdot M e^{j\omega_0 t + j\theta} \\
&= (I_{ND} + jQ_{ND}) \cdot e^{j\omega_0 t + j\theta}
\end{aligned}
\tag{2.4.18}
$$

where

$$
M_{ND} = g_T(g_H(|M|)) \cdot e^{jf_T(g_H(|M|)) + jf_H(|M|)} \cdot \frac{M}{|M|}
\tag{2.4.19}
$$

$$
I_{ND} = \mathrm{Re}\{M_{ND}\}
$$

$$
Q_{ND} = \mathrm{Im}\{M_{ND}\}.
\tag{2.4.20}
$$

In order to obtain the undistorted signal after the demodulator, the following relation must be satisfied instead of Equation 2.4.3,

$$
\begin{aligned}
\phi^{(3)} &= \Omega_{ND}(I_{ND}, Q_{ND}) \\
&= \Omega_N(I(\phi^{(3)}), Q(\phi^{(3)}))
\end{aligned}
\tag{2.4.21}
$$

where, from Equations 2.4.13 and 2.4.19, the function Ω_N can be obtained. The author relies on readers for this task. Because of the nonlinear devices, the demodulator mapping function Ω must now be replaced by the new function Ω_N. The effects of the thermal noise and filter distortion can be analyzed using this function Ω_N in a way similar to the approaches shown in the linear cases above.

2.5 DIGITAL HYBRID MODULATION

In the digital hybrid modulation case, the transmission chain is much simpler than that of the analog case as shown in Figure 2.5.1. The original signal to be sent to other ground terminals is

$$
e_i^{(0)} = \sum_{k=-\infty}^{\infty} a_k V(t - kT)
\tag{2.5.1}
$$

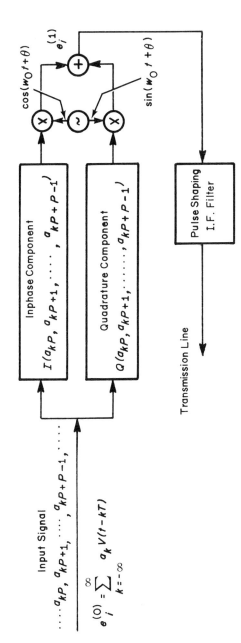

Figure 2.5.1 Modulation Scheme of Digital APM Signal

where a_k can take ± 1, i.e., this is a binary sequence. The function of the modulation is shown in Figure 2.5.1 Receiving $e_1^{(0)}$ given above, it sends out

$$e_i^{(1)} = \text{Re} \left\{ \sum_{k=-\infty}^{\infty} [I(a_{kP}, a_{kP+1}, \ldots, a_{kP+P-1}) \right.$$

$$+ jQ(a_{kP}, a_{kP+1}, \ldots, a_{kP+P-1})] \left. \right\}$$

$$\cdot V_P(t - kPT) e^{j(\omega_0 t + \theta)} \tag{2.5.2}$$

where $V_P(t)$ is the window-function of Equation 2.3.2.2 whose symbol period is now PT. (I, Q) is a mapping function of the random sequence $(\ldots a_{-2}, a_{-1}, a_0, a_1, a_2, a_3 \ldots)$, i.e., the multiple (non-overlapping) $(a_{kP}, a_{kP+1}, \ldots, a_{kP+P-1}) = b_k$ $(k = 0, \pm 1, \pm 2, \ldots)$ of Equation 2.5.2 is mapped into a single point of the complex plain, (I_k, Q_k). Therefore, the total number of the points of (I_k, Q_k) must be 2^P. Thus, the symbol rate of this modulation becomes $1/P$ times that of the BPSK using the same binary sequence of Equation 4.3.1.2 of Volume I, which leads us to a bandwidth reduction.

Rewrite Equation 2.5.2 by

$$e_i^{(1)} = \left(\sum_{k=-\infty}^{\infty} [I(b_k) + jQ(b_k)] \right)$$

$$\cdot V_P(t - kPT) e^{j(\omega_0 t + \theta)} \tag{2.5.3}†$$

Because of the multi-level amplitude and phase modulation, the signal is more vulnerable to filter distortion, nonlinear distortion and thermal noise than the FM and QPSK signals. The output of the pulse-shaping filter F_1 is now given by

$$e_i^{(2)} = e^{j\omega_0 t + j\theta} \sum_{k=-\infty}^{\infty} [I(b_k) + jQ(b_k)]$$

$$\cdot S_P(t - kpT) \tag{2.5.4}$$

where

$$S_P(t) = \int_{-\infty}^{\infty} V_P(t) h_1(t - x) \, dx \tag{2.5.5}$$

$h_1(t)$ is the low pass analog impulse response of F_1. As explained in Section 2.3.2, $S_P(t)$ is not restricted in the time interval $(-P \, T/2, P \, T/2)$ (one symbol period corresponding to $k = 0$) and the intersymbol interferences degrade the

---

†The complex form is used in this case for mathematical convenience.

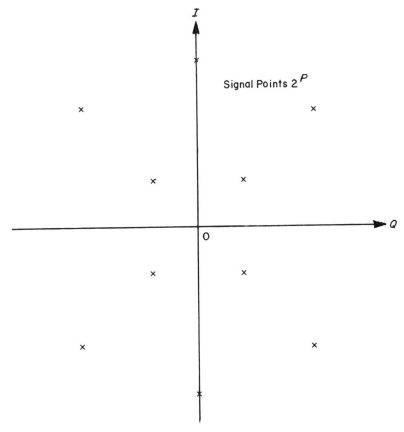

I

Signal Points 2^P

Q

O

Figure 2.5.2   Signal Space of Digital APM Signal (Example)

transmission performance (error probabilities) even in linear channel cases. The analysis of the effects of the intersymbol interferences and the thermal noise is similar to that in Section 2.3.2, except for the fact that the characteristic function of the intersymbol interference is now different and that the integral domain of x and y in Equation 2.3.2.22 is also complicated.

Now, $C_I(u, v)$ is given as

$$C_I(u, v) = \prod_{k=-\infty}^{\infty} \underset{a \text{ or } b}{E} \{\exp[(jI_k S_{pr}^{(k)} - Q_k S_{pi}^{(k)})u$$

$$+ (I_k S_{pi}^{(k)} + Q_k S_{pr}^{(k)})v\} \qquad (2.5.6)$$

where $S_{pr}^{(k)}$ and $S_{pi}^{(k)}$ are respectively the real part and imaginary part of $S_P(t - kPT)$ at the sampling point t_0 and

$$I(b_k) = I_k$$

$$Q(b_k) = Q_k \qquad (2.5.7)$$

In this case, $C_I(u, v)$ is more complicated than the QPSK case given by Equation 2.3.2.19, since I_k and Q_k are variable not only in inphase but in amplitude as seen in Figure 2.5.2. The domain of x and y integrals in Equation 2.3.2.22 is no more $(x \geqslant 0, y \geqslant 0)$ as in a QPSK case, and it is much more complicated because of the changes of amplitudes. While, in the QPSK case, the error probabilities obtained by assuming that $\phi_0 = \pi/4$, $3/4\pi$, $5/4\pi$ or $7/4\pi$ are all the same, there is no such analytical convenience in this case. However, the evaluation of the effects of thermal noise and intersymbol interference is still possible, although it is beyond the scope of this book. The combined effects of the nonlinear characteristics and intersymbol interference for this signal can be analyzed in a way similar to that of Section 2.3.3. For the same reason as that described in Section 2.3.3, the degradation of the error probability due to the combined effects is much greater than that of the intersymbol interference alone.

2.2 EXERCISES

1. In Equations 2.1.1.3.14 and 2.1.1.3.15, the terms of $(k_1 = 0, k_2 = 0)$, $(k_1 = 1, k_2 = 0)$, $(k_1 = 0, k_2 = 1)$, and $(k_1 = 1, k_2 = 1)$, should be evaluated as exercises.

2. Applying the approach of Equation 2.1.1.2.1 to the case of Equation 2.1.2.5, obtain the FM signal distortion due to the echo distortion of this case.

3. Based on Equation 2.1.3.3, derive Equation 2.1.3.5.

4. For an FDM/FM signal, obtain the worst value of a NPR channel frequency produced by interferences whose power spectrum has a Gaussian shape, for various frequency distances. Find the cases where the worst NPR is not at the highest frequency channel.

5. For the nonlinear characteristics of TWTA given by Figure 2.1.3.1, obtain the value of $1 + (\beta F(x_A)')^2$ in Equation 2.1.5.45 and show $(\beta F(x_A)')^2 \ll 1$ for various backoffs between 0 dB and 15 dB. Find when the largest value occurs.

6. Study the analytical approach shown in [37]. Understand the analysis to obtain the zero crossing probability for the Gaussian noise using reference shown in [37].

7. Prove Equation 2.1.5.61 using the representation of Equation 2.1.1 for the Gaussian noises.

8. Derive Equation 2.1.5.77 yourself.

9. Derive Equation 2.1.5.78 from Equation 2.1.5.77.

10. Prove Equation 2.1.5.80.

11. Prove Equation 2.1.5.90 using Equations 2.3.32 and 2.3.10 of Volume I.

12. Prove Equation 2.1.5.101.

13. Prove the results of Figures 2.1.6.3(a) and (b) using the formula established in Section 5.6.4 of Volume I.

14. Prove the result of equation 2.1.7.12.

15. Prove Equation 2.3.1.4.1.

16. Read References [41] and [43] and understand how to obtain a_{k_1, k_2}.

Chapter 3

TRANSMISSION IMPAIRMENTS: MULTI-CARRIER ANALYSIS

3.0 INTRODUCTION

Chapter 3 discusses the case where a number of carriers go through nonlinear devices with AM/AM and AM/PM, i.e., intermodulation products and modulation transfers. Chapter 3 covers cases of various signal input to various nonlinear device for the intermodulation analysis. Special cases, two or three carrier input cases, small carriers cases and a large carrier case, cases of coherent intermodulation products and FM demodulation, etc., are discussed in detail.

For modulation transfers, three combination cases between FM and digital (PSK) signals, i.e., modulation transfers from FM to FM, digital to digital, and digital to FM, are discussed. The case of modulation transfer from FM to digital is ignored here, since its effect is almost negligible.

All the analyses in Chapter 3 are entirely based on the general formula shown in Sections 2.13 of Volume I and in Chapter 3 of Volume II.

In Chapter 2, it is assumed that only a single carrier is transmitted through a transponder, and the effects of thermal noise and of distortions due to filters and nonlinear effects are only considered. There is accordingly no consideration of the effects of intermodulation products, modulation transfers and interferences from other signals which come from other transponders or other satellites. This chapter consists of two Sections, one discussing intermodulation products and one, modulation transfer produced by multi-carrier transmission per transponder. Thus, the analysis is limited, in this case, to mutual effects between carriers transmitted through a common transponder (or HPA). The other important effect from the adjacent transponders and other satellites is described in later sections.

3.1 DEVELOPMENT OF GENERAL THEORY

This sub-section shows a general theoretical model of nonlinear devices for multi-carrier transmission. The results obtained in this sub-section will be applied later in Sections 3.2 and 3.3 to analyze the intermodulation products and modulation transfers. The nonlinear devices are, in this section, HPA, TWTA, SSPA, etc. As assumed in Section 2.13 of Volume I, these devices are taken as memoryless in this section. This assumption is valid except for some cases of HPA whose bandwidth is usually 500 MHz and in which the frequency separations between carriers are more than 100 MHz. For such cases with memory, there are few successful (experimentally proved) theories up to now [52] and the published results are hard to apply to practical cases.

The simplest data obtainable from experimental laboratory tests which characterize these nonlinear devices, are the amplitude and phase versus input power explained in Section 2.1.3. Based on this single carrier amplitude and phase characteristics (AM/AM and AM/PM), all the multi-carrier transmission analyses must be derived (excluding the cases with memory). Represent the input to the nonlinear device by,

$$e_i^{(0)}(t) = A \sin(\omega_0 t + \theta) \qquad (3.1.1)$$

where the amplitude A and phase θ are assumed to be constants.

Then, the output of the nonlinear device is given by[†]

$$e_0^{(1)}(t) = \sum_{k=1}^{\infty} a_k \sin(2\pi k f_0 t + k\theta)$$

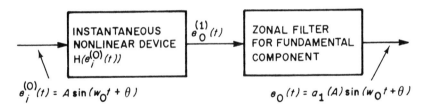

Figure 3.1.1(a)   Instantaneous Model of Nonlinear Device

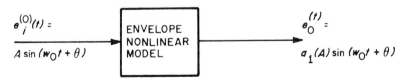

Figure 3.1.1(b)   Envelope Model of Nonlinear Device

[†]It is obvious that $e_0^{(1)}$ is a periodic function whose period is $2\pi/\omega_0 = f_0^{-1}$.

$$+ \sum_{k=1}^{\infty} b_k \cos(2\pi k f_0 t + k\theta) + b_0 \qquad (3.1.2)$$

where

$$a_k = \frac{1}{\pi} \int_0^{2\pi} H(A \sin x) \sin(kx) dx$$

$$b_k = \frac{1}{\pi} \int_0^{2\pi} H(A \sin x) \cos(kx) dx$$

$$(k \neq 0). \qquad (3.1.3)^{\ddagger}$$

It is easy to prove here that

$$a_{2k} = 0 \text{ and } b_{2k+1} = 0 \ (k = 0, 1, 2, \ldots) \qquad (3.1.4)$$

and that a_{2k+1} is an odd function of A and b_{2k} is an even function of A, i.e.,

$$a_{2k+1} = \frac{2}{\pi} \int_0^{\pi} \frac{H(A \sin x) - H(-A \sin x)}{2} \sin((2k+1)x) dx$$

$$b_{2k} = \frac{2}{\pi} \int_0^{\pi} \frac{H(A \sin x) + H(-A \sin x)}{2} \cos(2kx) dx. \qquad (3.1.5)$$

This is a simple Fourier series expansion. The function $H(e_i^{(0)})$ is called a "Nonlinear function of instantaneous model." In laboratories, the fundamental components are usually only measured and the d.c. and higher harmonics are attenuated by the devices around nonlinear device H. Thus, the output of the zonal filter is

$$e_0(t) = a_1(A) \sin(\omega_0 t + \theta) \qquad (3.1.6)$$

where a_1 is an odd function of A. As seen from this result, the instantaneous nonlinear characteristic cannot give the AM/PM nonlinearity explained in Section 2.1.3 (i.e., $f(A)$), which exists in reality.

In order to explain the AM/AM and AM/PM characteristics $g(A)e^{jf(A)}$, two instantaneous nonlinear devices must be considered, i.e.,

$$a_{1I}(A) = \frac{1}{\pi} \int_0^{2\pi} H_I(A \sin x) \sin x \, dx$$

$$a_{1Q}(A) = \frac{1}{\pi} \int_0^{2\pi} H_Q(A \sin x) \sin x \, dx. \qquad (3.1.7)$$

---

‡The value of b_0 is half that of Equation 3.1.3 for $k = 0$.

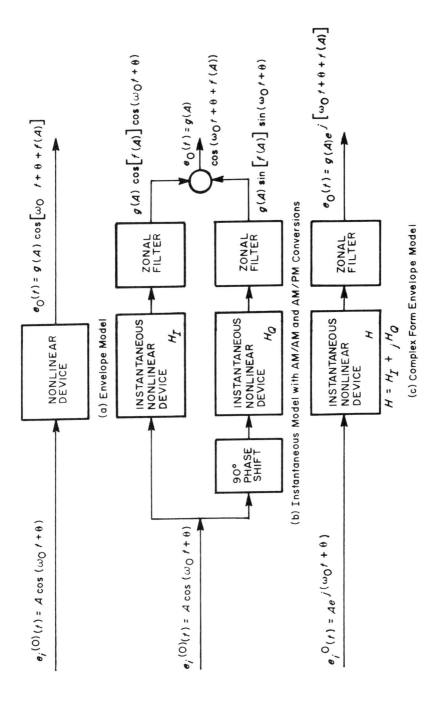

Figure 3.1.2   Nonlinear Model for Fundamental Component with AM/AM and AM/PM

Thus, the outputs of the zonal filters, F_1 and F_2 are respectively

$$a_{1I}(A) \sin(\omega_0 t + \theta)$$

$$a_{1Q}(A) \cos(\omega_0 t + \theta). \tag{3.1.8}$$

Thus, the final sum e_0 is given by

$$e_0 = a_{1I}(A) \sin(\omega_0 t + \theta)$$

$$+ a_{1Q}(A) \cos(\omega_0 t + \theta)$$

$$= \sqrt{(a_{1I})^2 + (a_{1Q})^2} \, \sin\left\{\omega_0 t + \theta + \tan^{-1} \frac{a_{1Q}}{a_{1I}}\right\}. \tag{3.1.9}$$

It is assumed that the zonal filters cut d.c. components and higher harmonics and do not cause any distortion to the fundamental components. Define new functions

$$g(A) = \sqrt{(a_{1I})^2 + (a_{1Q})^2}$$

$$f(A) = \tan^{-1}\left(\frac{a_{1Q}}{a_{1I}}\right). \tag{3.1.10}$$

Thus, the output of the zonal filter is now represented by

$$e_0 = g(A) \sin(\omega_0 t + \theta + f(A)) \tag{3.1.11}$$

This is the same result as that of Equation 2.1.3.2. Laboratories measurements give this $g(A)$ and $f(A)$ but not in this form, i.e.,

$$y_A = 10 \log_{10}\left[\frac{1}{2}\left\{g\left(\sqrt{2} \, 10^{\frac{x_A}{20}}\right)\right\}^2\right]$$

$$= G(x_A) \tag{3.1.12}$$

where (x_A and A) and (y_A and A) are related by Equation 2.1.3.4, i.e., x_A and $G(x_A)$ are given in dB. Also, for $f(A)$,

$$f(\sqrt{2} \, 10^{\frac{x_A}{20}}) = F(x_A) \tag{3.1.13}$$

where $F(x_A)$ is degree/dB. Again, the laboratory measurements give $G(x_A)$ and $F(x_A)$ as in Figure 2.1.3.1.

Before going to the general analysis, a simple example will be analyzed. Instead of handling a single carrier as above, consider now a two carrier input into the nonlinear device.

$$e_i^{(0)} = A_1 \sin((\omega_0 + \omega_1)t + \theta_1)$$

$$+ A_2 \sin((\omega_0 + \omega_2)t + \theta_2) \tag{3.1.14}$$

where ω_0 is a midband angular frequency and ω_1 and ω_2 are respectively the differences from it. For example, f_0 is 6 GHz, f_1 ($= \omega_1/2\pi$) $= 15$ MHz and f_2 ($= \omega_2/2\pi$) $= -15$ MHz. The representation of $f_0 + f_1$ and $f_0 + f_2$ is just made for analytical convenience. Combining two tones of Equation 3.1.14 into one,

$$e_i^{(0)} = [A_1 \cos(\omega_1 t + \theta_1) + A_2 \cos(\omega_2 t + \theta_2)] \sin(\omega_0 t)$$

$$+ [A_1 \sin(\omega_1 t + \theta_1) + A_2 \sin(\omega_2 t + \theta_2)]$$

$$\cdot \cos(\omega_0 t). \tag{3.1.15}$$

Rewrite this as

$$e_i^{(0)} = A(t) e^{j\omega_0 t + j\theta(t)} \tag{3.1.16}$$

where

$$A(t) = [\{A_1 \cos(\omega_1 t + \theta_1) + A_2 \cos(\omega_2 t + \theta_2)\}^2$$

$$+ \{A_1 \sin(\omega_1 t + \theta_1) + A_2 \sin(\omega_2 t + \theta_2)\}^2]^{1/2}$$

$$= [A_1^2 + A_2^2 + 2A_1 A_2 \cos\{(\omega_1 - \omega_2)t + \theta_1 - \theta_2\}]^{1/2}$$

$$\theta(t) = \tan^{-1}\left\{\frac{A_1 \sin(\omega_1 t + \theta_1) + A_2 \sin(\omega_2 t + \theta_2)}{A_1 \cos(\omega_1 t + \theta_1) + A_2 \cos(\omega_2 t + \theta_2)}\right\}. \tag{3.1.17}$$

From the assumption of memorylessness,

$$e_0(t) = g(A(t)) \sin\{\omega_0 t + \theta(t) + f(A(t))\}. \tag{3.1.18}$$

If the complex forms are used,

$$e_i^{(0)} = [A_1 e^{j\omega_1 t + j\theta_1} + A_2 e^{j\omega_2 t + \theta_2}] e^{j\omega_0 t}$$

$$e_0 = \frac{g(A)}{A} e^{jf(A)} A e^{j\omega_0 t + j\theta}$$

$$= \frac{g(A)}{A} e^{jf(A)} e_i^{(0)}. \tag{3.1.19}$$

Assume for simplicity's sake the following nonlinear characteristics

$$g(A) e^{jf(A)} = \alpha_0 A + \alpha_1 A^3 \tag{3.1.20}$$

where α_0 and α_1 are complex coefficients in general. The function $g(A)e^{jf(A)}$ must be an odd function of A which will be proved later.

Thus, from Equation 3.1.19,

$$e_0 = (\alpha_0 + \alpha_1 A^2) e_i^{(0)} \tag{3.1.21}$$

$$A^2 = A_1^2 + A_2^2 + A_1 A_2 \, e^{j(\omega_1 - \omega_2)t + j(\theta_1 - \theta_2)}$$

$$+ A_1 A_2 \, e^{-j(\omega_1 - \omega_2)t - j(\theta_1 - \theta_2)} \tag{3.1.22}$$

from Equation 3.1.17.

Therefore, from Equation 3.1.21,

$$e_0 = [\alpha_0 + \alpha_1 A_1^2 + \alpha_1 A_2^2 + \alpha_1 A_1 A_2 \, e^{j(\omega_1 - \omega_2)t + j(\theta_1 - \theta_2)}$$

$$+ \alpha_1 A_1 A_2 e^{-j(\omega_1 - \omega_2)t - j(\theta_1 - \theta_2)}]$$

$$\cdot [A_1 e^{j(\omega_0 + \omega_1)t + \theta_1} + A_2 e^{j(\omega_0 + \omega_2)t + j\theta_2}]$$

$$= [\alpha_0 A_1 + \alpha_1 (A_1^3 + 2A_1 A_2^2)] \, e^{j(\omega_0 + \omega_1)t + j\theta_1}$$

$$+ [\alpha_0 A_2 + \alpha_1 (A_2^3 + 2A_1^2 A_2)] \, e^{j(\omega_0 + \omega_2)t + j\theta_2}$$

$$+ \alpha_1 A_1^2 A_2 e^{j(\omega_0 + 2\omega_1 - \omega_2)t + j(2\theta_1 - \theta_2)}$$

$$+ \alpha_1 A_1 A_2^2 e^{j(\omega_0 - \omega_1 + 2\omega_2)t + j(-\theta_1 + 2\theta_2)} \tag{3.1.23}$$

where the first two terms are the signal components at the output and the last two terms are intermodulations, which are called third order intermodulation products. Note here that, for the constant envelope modulations as in FM signals, the output signals do not receive any distortions and only the levels are changed (except for the fact that the intermodulations appear). But, for the amplitude modulations or hybrid modulations where A_1 and A_2 are time functions (or even the filtered PSK signals), the signal components (the first two terms of Equation 3.1.23) receive the amplitude and phase distortions, since α_0, α_1 are complex numbers. In practical cases, the power series expansion needs much more terms than that of Equation 3.1.20 and in many cases the power series expansion is not a good approach (e.g. small backoff areas). There are also much more than two carriers in most cases. Furthermore, the higher order intermodulation products (5th, 7th, etc., orders) are required in some cases. Thus, it is important to obtain a general solution, which can easily be applied to many kinds of practical cases. Thus, the input signal $e_i^{(0)}$ is assumed to be

$$e_i^{(0)} = \sum_{k=1}^{n} A_k(t) e^{j(\omega_0 + \omega_k)t + j\phi_k(t)}$$

$$= A(t) e^{j\omega_0 t + j\phi(t)} \tag{3.1.24}$$

where

$$A(t) e^{j\phi(t)} = \sum_{k=1}^{n} A_k(t) e^{j\omega_k t + j\phi_k(t)} \tag{3.1.25}$$

where A and ϕ are real functions. Then, the output of the zonal filter F_1 (in Figure 3.1.1) is

$$e_0(t) = \frac{g(A(t))}{A(t)} e^{jf(A(t))} e_i^{(0)}(t)$$

$$= \frac{g(A(t))}{A(t)} e^{jf(A(t))} \sum_{k=1}^{n} A_k(t) e^{j(\omega_0 + \omega_k)t + j\phi_k(t)}. \qquad (3.1.26)$$

As seen from this result, the difference between the output and input is the factor $g(A)e^{jf(A)}/A$ and, noting A is the envelope of the composite signal of $e_i^{(0)}$, the model using Equation 3.1.26 is called "envelope model", while the model using the function $H(e_i^{(0)})$ (the output of the nonlinear device before the zonal filter) is called "instantaneous model", since $e_i^{(0)}$ changes much faster than $A(t)$ (the change of $e_i^{(0)}$ is $\sin(\omega_0 t)$ and that of $A(t)$ is only $\sin(\omega_k t)$ as seen from Equation 3.1.25).

The relationship between the instantaneous nonlinear model and the envelope model is the Tschebycheff transformations (see Equation 3.1.7),

$$g(A) \cos f(A) = \frac{1}{\pi} \int_0^{2\pi} H_I(A \sin x) \sin x \, dx$$

$$g(A) \sin f(A) = \frac{1}{\pi} \int_0^{2\pi} H_Q(A \sin x) \sin x \, dx \quad \text{or}$$

$$g(A)e^{jf(A)} = \frac{1}{\pi} \int_0^{2\pi} [H_I + jH_Q] \sin x \, dx. \qquad (3.1.27)$$

Although, in previous analyses, H_I and H_Q have been used to solve problems, a general solution based on $g(A)$ and $f(A)$ (or measured $G(X_A)$ and $F(X_A)$) must be found, since $g(A)$ and $f(A)$ are only available in reality. As seen in the following, the introduction of H_I and H_Q is not required for the analysis. The problem is now to obtain a general formula for the evaluation of all the intermodulation products based on $g(A)$ and $f(A)$ (or $G(X_A)$ and $F(X_A)$) measured by single tone tests. Rewrite Equation 3.1.24 for the input to the nonlinear device of Equation 3.1.27 as

$$e_i^{(0)} = [x(t) + jy(t)] e^{j\omega_0 t}$$

$$= \sqrt{x^2 + y^2} \, e^{j\omega_0 t + j \tan^{-1}\left(\frac{y}{x}\right)} \qquad (3.1.28)$$

where

$$x(t) = \sum_{k=1}^{n} A_k(t) \cos(\omega_k t + \phi_k)$$

$$y(t) = \sum_{k=1}^{n} A_k(t) \sin(\omega_k t + \phi_k). \tag{3.1.29}$$

Using this x and y, the output of the zonal filter is given by

$$e_0(t) = g(\sqrt{x^2 + y^2}) \, e^{jf(\sqrt{x^2 + y^2})} \, \frac{(x + jy)}{\sqrt{x^2 + y^2}} \, e^{j\omega_0 t}. \tag{3.1.30}$$

Define the double Fourier transform

$$L(u, v) = \int_{-\infty}^{\infty} \frac{g(\sqrt{x^2 + y^2})}{\sqrt{x^2 + y^2}} \, e^{jf(\sqrt{x^2 + y^2})}$$

$$(x + jy) e^{-jux - jvy} \, dx \, dy \tag{3.1.31}$$

i.e.,

$$g(\sqrt{x^2 + y^2}) \, e^{jf(\sqrt{x^2 + y^2})} \, \frac{(x + jy)}{\sqrt{x^2 + y^2}}$$

$$= \frac{1}{(2\pi)^2} \int_{-\infty}^{\infty} \int_{-\infty}^{\infty} L(u, v) e^{jux + jvy} \, du \, dv. \tag{3.1.32}$$

Substituting x and y of Equation 3.1.29 into Equation 3.1.32, e_0 becomes

$$e_0(t) = (2\pi)^{-2} \, e^{j\omega_0 t} \int_{-\infty}^{\infty} \int_{-\infty}^{\infty} L(u, v) \prod_{k=1}^{n}$$

$$\cdot \exp\left[jA_k \sqrt{u^2 + v^2} \sin\left\{ \omega_k t + \phi_k + \tan^{-1}\left(\frac{u}{v}\right) \right\} \right] du \, dv =$$

$$(2\pi)^{-2} \, e^{j\omega_0 t} \sum_{k_1 = -\infty}^{\infty} \sum_{k_2 = -\infty}^{\infty} \cdots \sum_{k_n = -\infty}^{\infty}$$

$$\cdot \int_{-\infty}^{\infty} \int_{-\infty}^{\infty} L(u, v) \prod_{p=1}^{n} J_{k_p}(A_p \sqrt{u^2 + v^2})$$

$$\cdot \exp\left[jk_p \left\{ \omega_p t + \phi_p + \tan^{-1}\left(\frac{v}{u}\right) \right\} \right] du \, dv \tag{3.1.33}$$

where the formula

$$e^{jz \sin \theta} = \sum_{k=-\infty}^{\infty} J_k(z) \, e^{jk\theta} \tag{3.1.34}$$

was used. The result of Equation 3.1.33 can be rewritten as

$$e_0(t) = \exp[j\omega_0 t] \sum_{k_1 = -\infty}^{\infty} \sum_{k_2 = -\infty}^{\infty} \cdots \sum_{k_n = -\infty}^{\infty}$$

$$\cdot \exp[jk_1(\omega_1 t + \phi_1) + jk_2(\omega_2 t + \phi_2) + \cdots + jk_n(\omega_n t + \phi_n)]$$

$$\cdot M(k_1, k_2, \ldots, k_n; A_1, A_2, \ldots, A_n) \tag{3.1.35}$$

where

$$M = (2\pi)^{-2} \int_{-\infty}^{\infty}\int_{-\infty}^{\infty}\int_{-\infty}^{\infty}\int_{-\infty}^{\infty} \frac{g(\sqrt{x^2 + y^2})}{\sqrt{x^2 + y^2}}$$

$$\cdot \exp[jf(\sqrt{x^2 + y^2})]\,(x+jy) \prod_{p=1}^{n} J_{k_p}(A_p\sqrt{u^2 + v^2})$$

$$\cdot \exp\left[j \sum_{p=1}^{n} k_p \tan^{-1}\left(\frac{u}{v}\right)\right] e^{-jux-jvy}\, dx\, dy\, du\, dv. \tag{3.1.36}$$

Using the polar coordinate transformations,

$$x = \rho \cos \xi, \qquad u = \gamma \sin \eta$$
$$y = \rho \sin \xi, \qquad v = \gamma \sin \eta \tag{3.1.37}$$

$$M(k_1, k_2, \ldots, k_n; A_1, A_2, \ldots, A_n)$$

$$= \int_0^{\infty}\int_0^{\infty} \left[\gamma \prod_{p=1}^{n} J_{k_p}(A_p\gamma)\right] \rho g(\rho)\, e^{jf(\rho)}$$

$$\cdot J(\gamma\rho)\, d\gamma\, d\rho \qquad \text{for } k_1 + k_2 + \cdots + k_n = 1$$

and

$$M = 0 \qquad \text{for } k_1 + k_2 + \cdots + k_n \neq 1 \tag{3.1.38}$$

i.e., the output of the zonal filter is finally given by

$$e_0(t) = \sum_{k_1 = -\infty}^{\infty} \sum_{k_2 = -\infty}^{\infty} \cdots \sum_{k_n = -\infty}^{\infty} e^{j\omega_0 t}$$

$$\cdot M(k_1, k_2, \ldots, k_n; A_1, A_2, \ldots, A_n) \prod_{p=1}^{n} e^{j(k_p\omega_p + k_p\phi_p)} \tag{3.1.39}$$

where

$$M = \int_0^{\infty}\int_0^{\infty} \gamma \left[\prod_{p=1}^{n} J_{k_p}(A_p\gamma)\right] J_1(\gamma\rho)\rho g(\rho)\, e^{jf(\rho)}\, d\gamma\, d\rho \tag{3.1.40}$$

where only the components (in the sums of k_p) satisfying

$$k_1 + k_2 + \cdots + k_n = 1 \tag{3.1.41}$$

are taken. This condition physically comes from the fact that only the fundamental components after the nonlinear device are considered, i.e.,

$$k_1(\omega_0 + \omega_1) + k_2(\omega_0 + \omega_2) + \cdots + k_n(\omega_0 + \omega_n)$$

$$= \omega_0 + k_1\omega_1 + k_2\omega_2 + \cdots + k_n\omega_n$$

$$\text{for } k_1 + k_2 + \cdots + k_n = 1. \quad (3.1.42)$$

The result of Equation 3.1.39 is very useful, although it looks difficult to evaluate the double integral of Equation 3.1.40. However, as shown later, it can be integrated for many important cases.

According to the commonly used terminology, the components satisfying

$$|k_1| + |k_2| + \cdots + |k_n| = k \quad (3.1.43)$$

are called "k-th order intermodulation products." It is very easily proved from the condition of Equation 3.1.42 that k must be an odd integer and therefore, there is no even order intermodulation product. This also comes from the fact that the zonal filter takes only the fundamental components of ω_0. As simple examples, take the first order ($k = 1$) intermodulation products (the signals) and third order intermodulation products ($k = 3$).

In the case of $k = 1$, the only solution is the case where only one of $k_p(p = 1, 2, \ldots, n)$ is 1 and others are zero. In the case of $k = 3$, there are two types of intermodulation products

(i) Two of them take 1, another takes -1 and all the others take zero, e.g., $k_1 = k_2 = 1, k_3 = -1$ and $k_4 = k_5 \cdots k_n = 0$.
(ii) One of them takes $+2$, another takes -1 and the others take zero, e.g., $k_1 = 2, k_2 = -1, k_3 = k_4 = \cdots = k_n = 0$.

The number of intermodulation products of type (i) is

$$_{n-1}C_2 = \frac{n(n-1)(n-2)}{2} \quad (3.1.44)$$

and that of type (ii) is

$$_{n-1}C_1 = n(n-1). \quad (3.1.45)$$

Therefore, the total number of the third order intermodulation products is

$$_{n-1}C_2 + {}_{n-1}C_1 = \frac{n^2(n-1)}{2}. \quad (3.1.46)$$

For the reader's interest, the case of the linear device where there should not be any intermodulation product is analyzed.

In this case,

$$g(\rho) = g_0\rho(g_0; \text{constant}), f(\rho) = 0 \quad (3.1.47)$$

$$M(k_1, k_2, \ldots, k_n; A_1, \ldots, A_n)$$

$$= g_0 \int_0^\infty \int_0^\infty \gamma J_{k_1}(A_1 r) J_{k_2}(A_2 r) \cdots J_{k_n}(A_n \gamma)$$

$$\cdot J_1(\rho\gamma)\rho^2 \, d\gamma \, d\rho. \tag{3.1.48}$$

In order to obtain this double integral, Equation 3.1.48 is modified as

$$M = g_0 \lim_{\sigma \to 0} \int_0^\infty \int_0^\infty \gamma \prod_{p=1}^n J_{k_p}(A_p \gamma) J_1(\gamma\rho) e^{-\frac{\sigma^2}{2}\rho^2} \rho^2 \, d\gamma \, d\rho \tag{3.1.49}$$

where

$$\int_0^\infty \rho^2 J_1(\rho\gamma) e^{-\frac{\sigma^2}{2}\rho^2} = \frac{\gamma}{\sigma^4} e^{-\frac{\gamma^2}{2\sigma^2}}. \tag{3.1.50}$$

Thus,

$$M = g_0 \lim_{\sigma \to 0} \int_0^\infty \frac{\gamma^2}{\sigma^4} \prod_{p=1}^n J_{k_p}(A_p \gamma) e^{-\frac{\gamma^2}{2\sigma^2}} \, d\gamma$$

$$= g_0 \lim_{\sigma \to 0} \int_0^\infty \frac{x^2}{\sigma} \prod_{p=1}^n J_{k_p}(\sigma A_p x) e^{-\frac{x^2}{2}} \, dx \tag{3.1.51}$$

Since

$$\lim_{\sigma \to 0} \frac{1}{\sigma} \prod_{p=1}^n J_{k_p}(\sigma A_p x) = 0 \tag{3.1.52}$$

if $|k_1| + |k_2| + \cdots + |k_n| \geq 3$ and

$$\lim_{\sigma \to 0} \frac{1}{\sigma} \prod_{p=1}^n J_{k_p}(\sigma A_p x) = \frac{A_\ell}{2} x$$

if $|k_1| + |k_2| + \cdots + |k_n| = 1$ and

$$k_1 = 0, k_2 = 0, \ldots, k_\ell = 1, k_{\ell+1} = 0, \ldots, k_n = 0.$$

Thus,

$$M(0, 0, \ldots, 0, \overset{\ell\text{-th}}{1}, 0, \ldots, 0) = \frac{A_\ell}{2} g_0 \int_0^\infty x^3 e^{-\frac{x^2}{2}} \, dx = g_0 A_\ell. \tag{3.1.53}$$

This is the expected result for a linear case. The general formula established above can be usefully applied to the intermodulation and modulation transfer problems in the following Sections.

3.2   INTERMODULATION ANALYSIS

The general formula obtained in the preceding Section 3.1 is too difficult to apply to practical cases. In this Section, it will be approximated into practically usable forms by means of convenient expansions, and many important cases will be discussed.

3.2.1   Power Series Expansion of Nonlinear Characteristics

The power series expansion of the nonlinear characteristics has been most commonly used [53] [54] but it is not really a good approximation for the smaller backoff areas (close to saturating power), since a great many terms are needed to approximate the nonlinear characteristics. Assume that

$$g(\rho)e^{jf(\rho)} = \sum_{m=0}^{L} \alpha_m \rho^{2m+1}. \qquad (3.2.1.1)$$

Then, the complex amplitude M of Equation 3.1.40 can be exactly obtained as follows:

$$M(k_1, k_2, \ldots, k_n; A_1, A_2, \ldots, A_n)$$

$$= \sum_{m=0}^{\infty} \alpha_m \int_0^{\infty} \int_0^{\infty} \left[\gamma \prod_{p=1}^{n} J_{k_p}(A_p\gamma) \right] J_1(\gamma\rho)\rho^{2(m+1)} \, d\gamma \, d\rho. \qquad (3.2.1.2)$$

These integrals do not exist for some cases. Therefore, Equation 3.2.1.1 is modified as

$$g(\rho)e^{jf(\rho)} = \lim_{\beta \to 0} \sum_{m=0}^{L} \alpha_m \, \rho^{2m+1} \, e^{-\beta\rho^2}. \qquad (3.2.1.3)$$

Thus,

$$M = \lim_{\beta \to 0} \sum_{m=0}^{L} \alpha_m \left[(-1)^m \frac{\partial^m}{\partial \beta^m} \int_0^{\infty} \int_0^{\infty} \left[\prod_{p=1}^{n} J_{k_p}(A_p \gamma) \right] \right.$$

$$\left. \cdot \gamma J_1(\gamma\rho)e^{-\beta\rho^2}\rho^2 \, d\gamma \, d\rho. \right. \qquad (3.2.1.4)$$

Using Equation 3.1.50, this becomes

$$M = \lim_{\beta \to 0} \sum_{m=0}^{L} \alpha_m(-1)^m \frac{\partial^m}{\partial \beta^m} \int_0^{\infty} \frac{\gamma^2}{(2\beta)^2} \, e^{-\frac{\gamma^2}{4\beta}} \prod_{p=1}^{n} J_{k_p}(A_p\gamma) \, d\gamma. \qquad (3.2.1.5)$$

Replacing $\gamma = \sqrt{2\beta} \, x$, M becomes again

$$M = \sum_{m=0}^{L} \alpha_m \int_0^{\infty} x^2 e^{-\frac{x^2}{2}} \left[\frac{(-1)^{m'} \partial^m}{\partial \beta^m} \right.$$

$$\cdot \left\{ \frac{1}{\sqrt{2\beta}} \prod_{p=1}^{n} J_{k_p}(\sqrt{2\beta}\, A_p x) \right\} \Bigg|_{\beta \to 0}. \tag{3.2.1.6}$$

To evaluate these integrals, expand

$$\prod_{p=1}^{n} J_{k_p}(A_p \gamma) = \sum_{q=1}^{\infty} e_q \gamma^{2q-1} \tag{3.2.1.7}$$

where it is easy to prove that this is an odd function of γ from the condition of Equation 3.1.42. Now,

$$\left[\frac{\partial^m}{\partial \beta^m} \left\{ \frac{1}{\sqrt{2\beta}} \prod_{p=1}^{n} J_{k_p}(\sqrt{2\beta}\, A_p x) \right\} \right]_{\beta \to 0} = e_{m+1}\, 2^m\, m!\, x^{2m+1}. \tag{3.2.1.8}$$

Substituting this result into Equation 3.2.1.6, M is given by

$$M = \sum_{m=0}^{L} \alpha_m (-1)^m e_{m+1}\, 2^m m! \int_0^{\infty} x^{2m+3} e^{-\frac{x^2}{2}}\, dx$$

$$= \sum_{m=0}^{L} \alpha_m (-1)^m e_{m+1}\, 2^{2m+1}\, m!\, (m+1)! \tag{3.2.1.9}$$

where e_{m+1} is a fuinction of $A_1, A_2, \ldots, A_n$, and determined by $k_1, k_2, \ldots, k_n$.

To show how to use this formula, two examples are given here:

(i) $n = 1$ for single carrier input cases. In this case, from Equation 3.1.43, only the $k_1 = 1$ case exists (only one output). Thus, $M(1; A_1)$ is given by

$$M(1; A_1) = \int_0^{\infty} \int_0^{\infty} \rho g(\rho) e^{jf(\rho)} J_1(A_1 \gamma) J_1(\rho\gamma)\gamma\, d\gamma\, d\rho. \tag{3.2.1.10}$$

Using the formula from Equation 2.4.31 of Volume I,

$$\int_0^{\infty} \int_0^{\infty} Q(\rho) J_p(\gamma\rho) J_p(B\gamma)\gamma d\,\gamma d\rho = \frac{Q(B)}{B} \tag{3.2.1.11}$$

$$M(1; A_1) = \frac{A_1 g(A_1) e^{jf(A_1)}}{A_1} = g(A_1) e^{jf(A_1)}. \tag{3.2.1.12}$$

Now, for the case of Equation 3.2.1.1, from Equation 3.2.1.7,

$$J_1(A_1\gamma) = \sum_{m=1}^{\infty} \frac{(-1)^{m-1}\left(\frac{1}{2}\right)^{2m-1}}{(m-1)!\, m!} A_1^{2m-1}\, \gamma^{2m-1}$$

$$= \sum_{q=1}^{\infty} e_q \, \gamma^{2q-1} \tag{3.2.1.13}$$

$$e_{m+1} = \frac{(-1)^m \left(\dfrac{1}{2}\right)^{2m+1}}{(m+1)! \, m!} \, A_1^{2m+1}. \tag{3.2.1.14}$$

Therefore, from Equation 3.2.1.9,

$$M(1; A_1) = \sum_{m=0}^{L} \alpha_m \, 2^{2m+1} \, m! \, (m+1)! \, (-1)^m$$

$$\cdot \frac{(-1)^m \, 2^{-2m-1}}{m! \, (m+1)!} \, A_1^{2m+1}$$

$$= \sum_{m=0}^{L} \alpha_m A_1^{2m+1}. \tag{3.2.1.15}$$

From Equation 3.2.1.1, this must be equal to the result of Equation 3.2.1.12.

(ii) Two carrier case. Under the expansion of Equation 3.1.20, a two carrier case is analyzed using the above result.

The coefficients e_q's of Equation 3.2.1.7 for the signal component ($k_1 = 1$, $k_2 = 0$) are given by

$$J_1(A_1 \gamma) J_0(A_2 \gamma) = \sum_{q=1}^{n} e_q \, \gamma^{2q-1} \tag{3.2.1.16}$$

In this case, only e_1 and e_2 are required to calculate M from Equation 3.2.1.9.

$$J_1(A_1 \gamma) J_0(A_2 \gamma) = \left[\frac{A_1}{2} \gamma - \frac{A_1^3}{16} \gamma^3 + \cdots \right]$$

$$\cdot \left[1 - \frac{A_2^2}{4} \gamma^2 + \cdots \right]$$

$$= \frac{A_1}{2} \gamma - \left(\frac{A_1 A_2^2}{8} + \frac{A_1^3}{16} \right) \gamma^3 + \cdots . \tag{3.2.1.17}$$

Therefore,

$$e_1 = \frac{A_1}{2}, \, e_2 = - \left(\frac{A_1 A_2^2}{8} + \frac{A_1^3}{16} \right). \tag{3.2.1.18}$$

From Equation 3.1.20,

$$M(1, 0; A_1, A_2) = \alpha_0 \frac{A_1}{2} 2$$

$$+ \alpha_1(-1)(-1) \left(\frac{A_1 A_2^2}{8} + \frac{A_1^3}{16} \right) 2^3 \, 2!$$

$$= \alpha_0 A_1 + \alpha_1 (A_1^3 + 2A_1 A_2^2) \qquad (3.2.1.19)$$

This is the same as Equation 3.1.23. The result for ($k_2 = 1$, $k_1 = 0$) case can be obtained by exchanging A_1 and A_2 because of the symmetricity of A_1 and A_2. The third order distortions are given as follows: The component for ($k_1 = 2$, $k_2 = -1$)

$$J_2(A_2\gamma)J_{-1}(A_2\gamma) = \left[\frac{A_1^2}{8} \gamma^2 - \cdots \right] (-1) \left[\frac{A_2}{2} \gamma \cdots \right]$$

$$= - \frac{A_1^2 A_2}{16} \gamma^3 + \cdots . \qquad (3.2.1.20)$$

Therefore, in this case,

$$e_1 = 0, \ e_2 = - \frac{A_1^2 A_2}{16} . \qquad (3.2.1.21)$$

From Equation 3.2.1.9,

$$M(2, -1; A_1, A_2) = \alpha_1(-1)2^3 2! \, (-1) \frac{A_1^2 A_2}{16} = \alpha_1 A_1^2 A_2. \quad (3.2.1.22)$$

This result is the same as that of Equation 3.1.23. The component $M(-1, 2; A_1, A_2)$ is given by exchanging A_1 and A_2 as seen from Equation 3.1.23. By measurements, we have $G(x_A)$ and $F(x_A)$ (single carrier characteristic). From Equations 2.1.3.3 and 2.1.3.4, calculate $g(A)$ and $f(A)$ and fit the characteristic $g(A)e^{jf(A)}$ by a polynomial as in Equation 3.2.1.1 ($\alpha_1, \alpha_2, \ldots, \alpha_L$ are obtained). Using the Bessel expansion,

$$J_k(z) = \left(\frac{k}{|k|} \right)^{|k|} \sum_{m=0}^{\infty} \frac{(-1)^m \left(\frac{1}{2} \right)^{2m+|k|}}{m! \, (m+|k|)!} z^{2m+|k|} \quad (k \neq 0) \quad (3.2.1.23)^{\dagger}$$

the coefficients of Equation 3.2.1.7 are obtained. Thus, the complex amplitude $M(k_1, \ldots, k_n; A_1, \ldots, A_n)$ can be calculated by Equation 3.2.1.9.

---

†In case of $k = 0$, the factor before the summation is unity and $k = 0$.

3.2.2 Bessel Expansion

If the nonlinear characteristic $g(\rho)e^{jf(\rho)}$ is expanded by a Bessel series, many complicated problems can be easily solved, e.g.,

$$g(\rho)e^{jf(\rho)} = \sum_{k=1}^{L} b_k J_1(\alpha k \rho) \qquad (0 < L \le \infty). \qquad (3.2.2.1)$$

This expansion corresponds to a Fourier series expansion in the instantaneous model. Expand the instantaneous model nonlinear function as

$$H(X) = H_I(X) + j H_Q(X)$$

$$= \sum_{k=-\infty}^{\infty} C_k \exp\left[-j\frac{2\pi}{D}kx\right] \qquad (3.2.2.2)$$

where, in order to obtain a good result, D must be larger than the dynamic range of the input signal $e_i^{(0)}$ (or the probability of $\left|e_i^{(0)}\right|$ exceeding D must be very small so that the error caused by this approximation is small enough).

$$C_k = \frac{1}{D}\int_{-\frac{D}{2}}^{\frac{D}{2}} H(x)\, e^{j2\pi \frac{k}{D}x}\, dx. \qquad (3.2.2.3)$$

From Equation 3.1.7,

$$g(\rho)e^{jf(\rho)} = \frac{2}{\pi}\int_{-\frac{\pi}{2}}^{\frac{\pi}{2}} \sin\theta\, H(\rho\sin\theta)\, d\theta$$

$$= \frac{2}{\pi}\sum_{k=-\infty}^{\infty} C_k \int_{-\frac{\pi}{2}}^{\frac{\pi}{2}} e^{j\frac{2\pi}{D}k\rho\sin\theta}\sin\theta\, d\theta$$

$$= (-2j)\sum_{k=1}^{\infty} (C_k - C_{-k})J_1\left(\frac{2\pi}{D}k\rho\right) \qquad (3.2.2.4)$$

where Equations 2.3.11 and 2.3.13 of Volume I were used to obtain this result. This sum must be terminated in practical cases at some number (say L).

If b_k is defined as

$$b_k = (-2j)(C_k - C_{-k})$$

$$\alpha = \frac{2\pi}{D}. \qquad (3.2.2.5)$$

the result of Equation 3.2.2.1 is obtained. This simply means that the Bessel and Fourier series expansions are related by the Tschebycheff transformations as explained in Section 3.1.

Under the expansion of Equation 3.2.2.1, the integrals of Equation 3.1.40 is given by

$$M(k_1, \ldots, k_n; A_1, \ldots, A_n)$$

$$= \sum_{s=1}^{L} b_s \int_0^\infty \int_0^\infty \gamma \prod_{p=1}^{n} J_{k_p}(A_p \rho) J_1(\gamma \rho) J_1(\alpha s \rho) \rho \, d\rho \, d\gamma$$

$$= \sum_{s=1}^{L} b_s \prod_{p=1}^{n} J_{k_p}(\alpha s \, A_p) \qquad (3.2.2.6)$$

where the formula of Equation 3.2.1.11 is used to obtain the result. The coefficients b_s can be evaluated by Fletcher Powell or Bessel (or by a general) approach [56]. It has been shown that the Bessel expansion is a very suitable approach for the HPA or TWTA applications [61], [55], [66]. The following shows that this approach can be applicable even to the ideal hardlimiter case.

The instantaneous model function $H(X)$ is assumed here

$$H(X) = H_0 \qquad X \geq 0$$

$$= -H_0 \quad X < 0. \qquad (3.2.2.7)$$

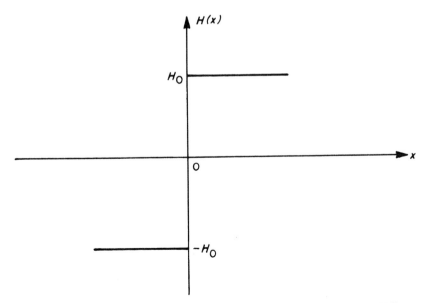

Figure 3.2.2.1   Instantaneous Model for Ideal Hardlimiter (WithoutAM/PM)

Then, from

$$g(A)e^{jf(A)} = \frac{1}{\pi} \int_0^{2\pi} H(A \sin x) \sin x \, dx$$

$$= \frac{4}{\pi} H_0, \qquad A > 0$$

$$= -\frac{4}{\pi} H_0, \quad A < 0 \qquad (3.2.2.8)$$

where A must be ≥ 0 in normal conditions, i.e., the hardlimiter characteristic is unchanged in both models but only the constant $4/\pi$ factor is different. In this case, the C_k's of Equation 3.2.2.3 are given by

$$C_k = \frac{1}{D} \int_{-\frac{D}{2}}^{\frac{D}{2}} H(x) e^{-j\frac{2\pi}{D}kx} \, dx$$

$$= \frac{2}{\pi k j} H_0 \qquad\qquad \text{for odd } k$$

$$= 0 \qquad\qquad \text{for even } k. \qquad (3.2.2.9)$$

Thus, the Bessel coefficients, b_k's are given by Equation 3.2.2.5

$$b_k = (-2j) \frac{4}{j\pi k} = \frac{(-8)}{\pi k} H_0 \qquad \text{for odd } k$$

$$= 0 \qquad\qquad \text{for even } k \qquad (3.2.2.10)$$

From Equation 3.2.2.8, so that

$$g(\rho)e^{jf(\rho)} = g_0 \text{ (a real number)}, \qquad\qquad \rho > 0, \qquad (3.2.2.11)$$

$$H_0 = \frac{\pi}{4} g_0 \qquad\qquad\qquad\qquad (3.2.2.12)$$

$$b_k = \frac{(-8)}{\pi k} H_0 = \frac{(-8)}{\pi k} \frac{\pi}{4} g_0 = \frac{(-2g_0)}{k} \qquad \text{for odd } k$$

$$= 0 \qquad\qquad\qquad\qquad \text{for even } k. \qquad (3.2.2.13)$$

Therefore, Equation 3.2.2.6 becomes

$$M(k_1, k_2, \ldots, k_n; A_1, A_2, \ldots, A_n)$$

$$= g_0 \sum_{s=1}^{\infty} \frac{(-2)}{(2s-1)} \prod_{p=1}^{n} J_{k_p}(\alpha(2s-1)A_p). \qquad (3.2.2.14)$$

This series is very quickly convergent for the sum of s. Another reason why the Bessel expansion is convenient for the analysis is that all the A_p's are separable as a product of the Bessel functions in Equation 3.2.2.6, which is very convenient for the derivative, integral and other operations of A_p. The author will finish this sub-section by providing an example to show this convenience. Suppose that n carriers are the input to a nonlinear device as in Equation 3.1.26. Then, the signal components at the output have the amplitudes $B_1, B_2, \ldots, B_n$.

Now, the problem is how to obtain the input power of each carrier when the output power of each carrier is given, assuming the intermodulation products can be ignored. From the theory established in this section,

$$B_k = M(0, 0, \ldots, \overset{k\text{-th}}{1}, 0, \ldots, 0; A_1, A_2, \ldots, A_n)$$

$$(k = 1, 2, \ldots, n). \tag{3.2.2.15}$$

Thus, the input and output powers of each carrier are respectively given by

$$P_{ik} = \frac{1}{2} A_k^2$$

$$P_{0k} = \frac{1}{2} |B_k(A_1, A_2, \ldots, A_n)|^2. \tag{3.2.2.16}$$

The problem is again mathematically that, when $P_{01}, P_{02}, \ldots, P_{0n}$ are given, we obtain $P_{i1}, P_{i2}, \ldots, P_{in}$. It is very difficult to solve this problem analytically. Therefore, define function

$$\lambda(A_1, A_2, \ldots, A_n) = \sum_{k=1}^{n} \left[P_{0k} - \frac{1}{2} |B_k(A_1, A_2, \ldots, A_n)|^2 \right]^2. \tag{3.2.2.17}$$

The problem is to obtain $A_1, A_2, \ldots, A_n$ so that

$$\text{Mini}\{\lambda(A_1, A_2, \ldots, A_n)\}. \tag{3.2.2.18}$$

To minimize $\lambda(A_1, A_2, \ldots, A_n)$, many approaches are available but the problem becomes much easier if the partial derivations of λ with respect to A_k ($k = 1, \ldots, n$) are available. As shown by Equation 3.2.2.6,

$$B_k(A_1, A_2, \ldots, A_n) = \sum_{s=1}^{L} b_s J_0(A_1 \alpha s) J_0(A_2 \alpha s) \cdots$$

$$J_0(A_{k-1} \alpha s) J_1(A_k \alpha s) J_0(A_{k+1} \alpha s) \cdots J_0(A_n \alpha s). \tag{3.2.2.19}$$

Therefore,

$$\frac{\partial B_k}{\partial A_\ell} = -\sum_{s=1}^{L} b_s(\alpha s) J_0(A_1 \alpha s) \cdots J_1(A_\ell \alpha s) \cdots$$

$$J_1(A_k \alpha s) \cdots J_0(A_n \alpha s) \ (\ell \neq k) \tag{3.2.2.20}$$

$$\frac{\partial B_k}{\partial x_k} = \sum_{s=1}^{L} b_s(\alpha s)\, J_0(A_1 \alpha s) \cdots$$

$$\frac{1}{2}\,[J_0(A_k \alpha s) - J_2(A_k \alpha s)] \cdots J_0(A_n \alpha s) \quad (3.2.2.21)$$

where $J_0(A_\ell \alpha S)$ is replaced by $-J_1(A_\ell \alpha S)\,(\alpha S)$ in the product of Equation 3.2.2.19 for the first case and $J_1(A_k \alpha S)$ is replaced by $1/2\,[J_0(A_k \alpha S) - J_2(A_k \alpha S)]$ (αS) for the second case. This availability of the partial derivative of λ makes the minimization of λ much simpler. See Reference [60] for the detailed description. It is very difficult to obtain $\partial\lambda/\partial A_\ell$ by other means of expansion of $g(\rho)e^{jf(\rho)}$. Using $\partial B_k/\partial A_\ell$ of Equations 3.2.2.20 and 3.2.2.21, $\partial B_k/\partial A_\ell$ is given by

$$\frac{\partial\lambda}{\partial A_\ell} = 2 \sum_{k=1}^{n} \left[P_{0k} - \frac{1}{2}|B_k|^2 \right] (-1)\, \mathrm{Re}\left\{ B_k^* \frac{\partial B_k}{\partial A_\ell} \right\}$$

$$= -2\,\mathrm{Re}\left\{ \sum_{k=1}^{n} B_k^* \frac{\partial B_k}{\partial A_\ell} \left[P_{0k} - \frac{1}{2}|B_k|^2 \right] \right\}. \quad (3.2.2.22)$$

Thus, the availability of the analytical derivatives shown in Equation 3.2.2.22 makes the minimization of Equation 3.2.2.18 by softwares much simpler and much more accurate. See Reference [60] for detailed practical applications.

3.2.3 Fourier Series Expansion

In this case, the envelope model nonlinear characteristic is expanded by a Fourier series instead of the instantaneous model expanded by a Fourier series as in Equation 3.2.2.2, i.e.,

$$g(\rho)e^{jf(\rho)} = \sum_{m=1}^{L} a_m \sin(2\pi m D\rho). \quad (3.2.3.1)$$

D must be chosen considering the dynamic range of $e_i^{(0)}$, as before. Then, from Equation 3.1.38,

$$M(k_1, k_1, \ldots, k_n; A_1, A_2, \ldots, A_n)$$

$$= \sum_{m=1}^{L} a_m \int_0^\infty \gamma \prod_{p=1}^{n} J_{k_p}(A_p \gamma) \left[\int_0^\infty \rho \sin(2\pi m D\rho)\, J_1(\gamma\rho)\, d\rho \right] d\gamma. \quad (3.2.3.2)$$

Since we have

$$\int_0^\infty \left[\int_0^\infty \rho \sin(2\pi m D\rho) J_1(\gamma\rho)\, d\rho \right] \gamma \prod_{p=1}^{n} J_{k_p}(A_p \gamma)\, d\gamma$$

$$= \int_0^\infty \left[\int_0^\infty \sin(2\pi mD\rho) J_0(\gamma\rho) d\rho \right] \frac{d}{d\gamma} \left[\gamma \prod_{p=1}^n J_{k_p}(A_p\gamma) d\gamma \right] d\gamma$$

$$= \int_0^{2\pi mD} \frac{1}{\sqrt{(2\pi mD)^2 - \gamma^2}} \left[\frac{d}{d\gamma} \left\{ \gamma \prod_{p=1}^n J_{k_p}(A_p\gamma) \right\} \right] d\gamma.$$

$$(3.2.3.3)$$

Therefore, applying the partial integral to Equation 3.2.3.2,

$$M = \sum_{m=1}^L a_m \int_0^{2\pi mD} \frac{1}{\sqrt{(2\pi mD)^2 - \gamma^2}} \left[\frac{d}{d\gamma} \left\{ \gamma \prod_{p=1}^n J_{k_p}(A_p\gamma) \right\} \right] d\gamma.$$

$$(3.2.3.4)$$

Achieving the differentiation with respect to γ in this result and replacing

$$\gamma = 2\pi mD \sin\theta, \qquad\qquad (3.2.3.5)$$

$$M = \sum_{m=1}^L a_m \int_0^{\frac{\pi}{2}} \left[\prod_{p=1}^n J_{k_p}(A_p 2\pi mD \sin\theta) + \frac{2\pi mD \sin\theta}{2} \right.$$

$$\cdot \sum_{\ell=1}^n \left\{ \prod_{\substack{p=1 \\ (p\neq\ell)}}^n J_{k_p}(A_p 2\pi mD \sin\theta) \right\}$$

$$\left. \cdot \left\{ J_{k_\ell-1}(A_p 2\pi mD \sin\theta) - J_{k_\ell+1}(A_p 2\pi mD \sin\theta) \right\} A_\ell \right] d\theta.$$

$$(3.2.3.6)$$

The evaluation of this result is easy to do by computer.

3.2.4 Special Expansion

As shown in some cases, another simple type of approximation has been done, which is enough to calculate the intermodulation products of some simple cases. In this case,

$$g(\rho) e^{jf(\rho)} = (a_0\rho + a_1\rho^3 + a_2\rho^5) e^{-\beta\rho^2} \qquad (3.2.4.1)$$

where a_1, a_2, a_3 and β are complex and $\mathrm{Re}\{\beta\}$ = a positive number.

This is a special case of Equation 3.2.1.3 ($L = 2$) with the exclusion of $\beta \to 0$, i.e.,

$$M = \sum_{m=0}^2 a_m \int_0^\infty x^2 e^{-\frac{x^2}{2}}$$

$$\cdot \left[\frac{(-1)^m \partial^m}{\partial \beta^m} \left\{ \frac{1}{\sqrt{2\beta}} \prod_{p=1}^{n} J_{k_p}(\sqrt{2\beta} A_p x) \right\} \right] dx. \qquad (3.2.4.2)$$

Using the coefficients of e_q's of Equation 3.2.1.16,

$$M = 2a_0 e_1 + 16(a_0 \beta - a_1) e_2 + \sum_{q=3}^{\infty} 2^{2q-1} q! \beta^{q-3} e_q$$

$$\cdot [a_0 \beta^2 - (q-1) a_1 \beta + (q-1)(q-2) a_2]. \qquad (3.2.4.3)$$

This approach is useful for the cases where the signal input at the back is more than -5 dB.

3.2.5   Hardlimiter Case

In many military applications, the transponder nonlinear characteristics are the hardlimiters. Therefore, the envelope model nonlinear characteristic is assumed as in Equation 3.2.2.11, although the AM/PM effects exist in the real hardlimiters. For the case of the hardlimiter with a AM/PM effect, the Bessel or Fourier series expansions are applicable. In this case, we have, from Equation 3.1.38,

$$M = g_0 \int_0^{\infty} \int_0^{\infty} \left[\gamma \prod_{p=1}^{n} J_{k_p}(A_p \gamma) \right] J_1(\gamma \rho) \rho \, d\gamma \, d\rho. \qquad (3.2.5.1)$$

The integral with respect to ρ does not exist in this case, and this integral can be obtained as a limit, i.e., replace $g(\rho) e^{jf(\rho)}$ of Equation 3.1.38 by $g_0 e^{-\alpha\rho}$ instead of g_0. Then,

$$\int_0^{\infty} \rho \, J_1(\gamma \rho) e^{-\alpha\rho} \, d\rho = \frac{\gamma}{(\gamma^2 + \alpha^2)^{3/2}} \cdot \qquad (3.2.5.2)$$

Therefore,

$$M = \lim_{\alpha \to 0} g_0 \int_0^{\infty} \gamma^2 \prod_{p=1}^{n} J_{k_p}(A_p \gamma)(\gamma^2 + \alpha^2)^{-\frac{3}{2}} \, d\gamma$$

$$= g_0 \int_0^{\infty} \prod_{p=1}^{n} J_{k_p}(A_p \gamma) \frac{1}{\gamma} \, d\gamma. \qquad (3.2.5.3)$$

The close form of this integral solution is difficult to obtain in general but it is possible to obtain the numerical integral by computer. If n is a large number and none of the carriers dominates the others (the input $e_i^{(0)}$ becomes a Gaussian process in this case through the central limiting theorem), the signal components and the third order intermodulations can be obtained as follows (note here that the third order intermodulation products and signal components occupy respectively 9.8% and 78.5% of the total output power and the rest of the higher order intermodulation power is 11.7%).

The l-th signal component has the amplitude, from Equation 3.2.5.3,

$$M_l^{(1)} \simeq \frac{g_0}{2} A_l \int_0^\infty e^{-\frac{\sigma^2}{2}\gamma^2} \, d\gamma$$

$$= \frac{g_0}{2} A_l \frac{\sqrt{2\pi}}{2} \frac{1}{\sigma}$$

$$= \left(\frac{1}{2} \sqrt{\frac{\pi}{2}} g_0 \right) \frac{A_l}{\sigma} \qquad (3.2.5.4)$$

where

$$\sigma^2 = \sum_{k=1}^n \left(\frac{A_k^2}{2} \right) \quad \text{(total input power)}$$

and

$$\int_0^\infty e^{-\frac{\sigma^2}{2}\gamma^2} \, d\gamma = \sqrt{\frac{\pi}{2}} \frac{1}{\sigma}. \qquad (3.2.5.5)$$

When there are many carriers, the percentage of the l-th carrier power is very small in the total power σ^2. Therefore,

$$\frac{J_1(A_l\gamma)}{J_0(A_l\gamma)} \prod_{k=1}^n J_0(A_k\gamma) \simeq \left(\frac{A_l}{2}\gamma \right) e^{-\frac{\sigma^2}{2}\gamma^2} \qquad (3.2.5.6)$$

where

$$\frac{J_1(A_l\gamma)}{J_0(A_l\gamma)} \simeq \frac{1}{2}A_l\gamma,$$

$$\prod_{k=1}^n J_0(A_k\gamma) \simeq e^{-\frac{\sigma^2}{2}\gamma^2}. \qquad (3.2.5.7)$$

Namely, the output signal is

$$M_1^{(l)} e^{j(\omega_0 + \omega_l)t + j\phi(t)} = \left(\frac{1}{2}\sqrt{\frac{\pi}{2}} \right) g_0 \frac{A_l}{\sigma} e^{j\omega_0 t + j\phi_l(t)}. \qquad (3.2.5.8)$$

In this case, the pure signal components do not receive any distortion (if there is no amplitude modulation, i.e., if A_k is a constant) and the relative levels are unchanged, i.e., all the components receive

$$\frac{1}{2}\sqrt{\frac{\pi}{2}} g_0 \frac{1}{\sigma} \quad \text{factor change.}$$

The total power of the pure signal components is

$$\sum_{k=1}^{n} \frac{1}{2} \left(\frac{1}{2} \sqrt{\frac{\pi}{2}} \right)^2 g_0^2 \frac{A_l^2}{\sigma^2} = \frac{\pi}{8} g_0^2 \frac{\sum_{k=1}^{n} \left(\frac{A_l^2}{2} \right)}{\sigma^2}$$

$$= \frac{\pi}{8} g_0^2 . \tag{3.2.5.9}$$

Now, the total power of all the components is, from Equation 3.1.24

$$\frac{1}{2} |g_0 e^{j\omega_0 t + j\phi(t)}|^2 = \frac{1}{2} g_0^2 \tag{3.2.5.10}$$

where the output of the hardlimiter is

$$g_0 e^{j\omega_0 t + j\phi(t)}. \tag{3.2.5.11}$$

Therefore, the percentage of pure signal component power in the total power is

$$\frac{\frac{\pi}{8} g_0^2}{\frac{1}{2} g_0^2} \times 100 = \frac{\pi}{4} \times 100 = 78.5\%. \tag{3.2.5.12}$$

The case of the third order intermodulation products is analyzed as follows:

(i) Type $A + B - C$ or $f_1 + f_2 - f_3$ (see Equation 3.1.40). In this case,

$$M_3^{(p,q,r)} = -g_0 \frac{A_p A_q A_r}{8} \int_0^\infty e^{-\frac{\sigma^2}{2}\gamma^2} \gamma^2 \, d\gamma$$

$$= -g_0 \frac{A_p A_q A_r}{8\sigma^3} \sqrt{\frac{\pi}{2}} . \tag{3.2.5.13}$$

If the amplitudes of all the input components are equal, i.e., if $A_1 = A_2 \ldots = A_n = A$, the total power of this type of intermodulation products is, from Equation 3.1.44

$$\frac{1}{2} \left(\frac{g_0}{8} \right)^2 \left(\frac{\pi}{2} \right) \frac{A^6 n(n-1)(n-2)}{\sigma^6 2} = \frac{\pi}{64} g_0^2 \left(1 - \frac{1}{n} \right) \left(1 - \frac{2}{n} \right) \tag{3.2.5.14}$$

where

$$\sigma^2 = \frac{A^2 n}{2}$$

(see Equation 3.2.5.5). Therefore, the percentage of this type of intermodulation power is, from Equation 3.2.5.9,

$$\frac{\dfrac{\pi}{64}g_0^2}{\dfrac{1}{2}g_0^2} \times 100 = \frac{\pi}{32} \times 100 = 9.8\%.$$

(ii) Type $2A - B$ or $2f_1 - f_2$

$$M_3^{(2p,q)} = -g_0\frac{A_p^2 A_q}{16}\int_0^\infty e^{-\frac{\sigma^2}{2}\gamma^2}\gamma^2\,d\gamma$$

$$= -g_0\frac{A_p^2 A_q}{16\sigma^3}\sqrt{\frac{\pi}{2}}. \tag{3.2.5.15}$$

Assuming all carrier powers are equal as in (i), the total power of this, from Equation 3.1.45, is:

$$\frac{1}{2}\left(\frac{g_0}{16}\right)^2\frac{A^6}{\sigma^6}\left(\frac{\pi}{2}\right)n(n-1) = \frac{1}{2}\left(\frac{g_0}{16}\right)^2\left(\frac{\pi}{2}\right)2^3\frac{n(n-1)}{n^3}$$

$$= 2\left(\frac{g_0}{16}\right)^2\pi\left(1 - \frac{1}{n}\right)\frac{1}{n} \simeq 0 \tag{3.2.5.16}$$

since n is assumed to be very large. This type of third order intermodulations can be ignored for many carrier cases (none of them is dominant, i.e., a Gaussian process case). In Section 3.2.6, the Gaussian input case (including the hardlimiter case) will be analyzed, and more general results including the above results will be obtained.

3.2.6 Gaussian Input

Although, in Section 3.2.5, the Gaussian input to the hardlimiter case was analyzed using an inductive approach, a more direct deductive approach will be used by means of Gaussian process properties in this Section. Using the same approach as explained in Section 3.2.5, assuming that there are many carriers and that none of them dominates the others in Equation 3.1.38, the l-th signal component is given by

$$M_1^{(l)} \simeq \frac{A_l}{2}\int_0^\infty\int_0^\infty \gamma^2 e^{-\frac{\sigma^2}{2}\gamma^2}J_1(\gamma\rho)\rho\,g(\rho)\,e^{jf(\rho)}\,d\gamma\,d\rho. \tag{3.2.6.1}$$

Using the formula from Equation 2.3.41 of Volume I for the integral with respect to γ, $M_1^{(l)}$ becomes

$$M_1^{(l)} \simeq A_l \left[\frac{1}{2\sigma} \int_0^\infty \rho^2 e^{-\frac{\rho^2}{2}} g(\sigma\rho) e^{jf(\sigma\rho)} \, d\rho \right]$$

where σ^2 is given by

$$\sigma^2 = \frac{1}{2} \sum_{k=1}^n A_k^2. \tag{3.2.6.2}$$

Therefore, all the signal components combined at the output of the envelope model are

$$e_0^{(s)} \simeq \left[\frac{1}{2\sigma} \int_0^\infty \rho^2 e^{-\frac{\rho^2}{2}} g(\sigma\rho) e^{jf(\sigma\rho)} \, d\rho \right] e_i^{(0)} \tag{3.2.6.3}$$

where $e_i^{(0)}$ is the input signal (Equation 3.1.24). Now, the third order intermodulation products (one component) is given by, in a way similar to Equation 3.2.5.13,

$$M_3^{(p,q,r)} = -\frac{A_p A_q A_r}{8} \int_0^\infty \int_0^\infty \gamma^4 e^{-\frac{\sigma^2}{2}\gamma^2} J_1(\gamma\rho) \rho g(\rho) e^{jf(\rho)} \, d\gamma \, d\rho$$

$$= \frac{A_p A_q A_r}{4} \int_0^\infty \left[\frac{\partial}{\partial R_0} \int_0^\infty \gamma^2 e^{-\frac{R_0}{2}\gamma^2} J_1(\gamma\rho) \, d\gamma \right]_{R_0=\sigma^2}$$

$$\cdot \rho g(\rho) e^{jf(\rho)} \, d\rho \tag{3.2.6.4}$$

where, from Equation 2.3.41 of Volume I,

$$\left[\frac{\partial}{\partial R_0} \int_0^\infty \gamma^2 e^{-\frac{R_0}{2}\gamma^2} J_1(\gamma\rho) \, d\gamma \right]_{R_0=\sigma^2}$$

$$= \frac{1}{2\sigma^5} \left(\frac{\rho}{\sigma} \right) e^{-\frac{1}{2}\left(\frac{\rho}{\sigma}\right)^2} \left[\left(\frac{\rho}{\sigma} \right)^2 - 4 \right]. \tag{3.2.6.5}$$

Thus,

$$M_3^{(p,q,r)} \simeq \frac{A_p A_q A_r}{8\sigma^3} \int_0^\infty \rho^2 g(\sigma\rho) e^{jf(\sigma\rho)} (\rho^2 - 4) \, d\rho \tag{3.2.6.6}$$

where the frequency of this component is

$$f_o + f_p + f_q - f_r. \tag{3.2.6.7}$$

Therefore, all the third order intermodulation products falling on the above frequency must be collected to obtain the intermodulation at the frequency $f_o + f_p + f_q - f_r$. In the following, more general results will be obtained, including the above results.

Let us assume that the input to the nonlinear device is a narrowband Gaussian process (the bandwidth of the Gaussian signal or noise is much smaller than the center frequency). Then, it is represented by

$$e_i^{(0)} = N(t) e^{j\omega_0 t} \tag{3.2.6.8}$$

where

$$N(t) = N_c(t) + jN_s(t). \tag{3.2.6.9}$$

N_c and N_s are respectively inphase and quadrature components of $e_i^{(0)}$. The output of the envelope nonlinear device is given by

$$e_0(t) = g(\sqrt{N_c^2 + N_s^2}) e^{jf(\sqrt{N_c^2 + N_s^2})} e^{j\tan^{-1}\left(\frac{N_s}{N_c}\right) + j\omega_0 t}$$

$$= e^{j\omega_0 t} \int_0^\infty \int_0^\infty \gamma J_1(\sqrt{N_c^2 + N_s^2}\,\gamma) e^{j\tan^{-1}\left(\frac{N_s}{N_c}\right)}$$

$$\cdot J_1(\rho\gamma)\rho g(\rho) e^{jf(\rho)} \, dr \, d\rho \tag{3.2.6.10}$$

where Equation 3.2.1.11 is used to obtain this result. The autocorrelation function of Equation 3.2.6.10 is given as follows

$$Re_0(\tau) = \frac{1}{2} E\{e_0(t) e_0(t + \tau)^*\}$$

$$= \frac{e^{j\omega_0\tau}}{2} \int_0^\infty \int_0^\infty \int_0^\infty \int_0^\infty \gamma_1 \gamma_2 \rho_1 \rho_2$$

$$\cdot J_1(\gamma_1 \rho_1) J_1(\gamma_2 \rho_2) g(\rho_1) e^{jf(\rho_1)} g(\rho_2)$$

$$\cdot e^{jf(\rho_2)} E\left\{ J_1(\sqrt{N_c^2(t) + N_s(t)^2}\,\gamma_1) \right.$$

$$\cdot J_1(\sqrt{N_c(t+\tau)^2 + N_s(t+\tau)^2}\,\gamma_2) \exp\left[j \tan^{-1} \frac{N_s(t)}{N_c(t)} \right.$$

$$\left. \left. - j \tan^{-1} \frac{N_s(t+\tau)}{N_c(t+\tau)} \right] \right\} \, d\gamma_1 \, d\gamma_2 \, d\rho_1 \, d\rho_2.$$

$$\tag{3.2.6.11}$$

The statistical average $E\{\ \}$ in Equation 3.2.6.11 can be obtained as follows:
Define

$$R_r(\tau) = \int_{-\infty}^{\infty} W_N(f) \cos(2\pi f\tau)\, df \qquad (3.2.6.12)$$

$$R_i(\tau) = \int_{-\infty}^{\infty} W_N(f) \sin(2\pi f\tau)\, df \qquad (3.2.6.13)$$

$$R(\tau) = |R_r(\tau) + jR_i(\tau)|. \qquad (3.2.6.14)$$

$W_N(f)$ is the power spectrum of the input signal e_i (i.e., $N(t)\,e^{j\omega_0 t}$) whose center frequency is shifted to zero. Therefore, $W_N(f)$ is not necessarily symmetric around zero frequency, since e_i is not necessarily so around f_0. Then, $E\{\ \}$ is obtained as follows:

$$E\left\{ J_k(\sqrt{N_c^2(t) + N_s^2(t)}\,\gamma_1)\, J_k(\sqrt{N_c(t+\tau)^2 + N_s(t+\tau)^2}\,\gamma_2) \right.$$
$$\left. \cdot \exp\left[jk\tan^{-1}\left(\frac{N_s(t)}{N_c(t)}\right) - jk\tan^{-1}\left(\frac{N_s(t+\tau)}{N_c(t+\tau)}\right)\right]\right\}$$

$$= \int_{-\infty}^{\infty}\int_{-\infty}^{\infty}\int_{-\infty}^{\infty}\int_{-\infty}^{\infty} (\sqrt{2\pi})^{-4}\{R(0)^2 - R(\tau)^2\}^{-1}$$

$$\cdot J_k(\sqrt{x_1^2 + y_1^2}\,\gamma_1)\, J_k(\sqrt{x_2^2 + y_2^2}\,\gamma_2)$$

$$\cdot \exp\left[j\tan^{-1}\frac{y_1}{x_1} - j\tan^{-1}\frac{y_2}{x_2}\right]$$

$$\cdot \exp\left[-\frac{R(0)(x_1^2 + y_1^2 + x_2^2 + y_2^2)}{R(0)^2 - R(\tau)^2}\right]$$

$$\cdot \exp\left[\frac{R_r(\tau)(x_1 x_2 + y_1 y_2)}{R(0)^2 - R(\tau)^2} + \frac{R_i(\tau)(x_1 y_2 - x_2 y_1)}{R(0)^2 - R(\tau)^2}\right]. \qquad (3.2.6.15)$$

Applying the polar coordinates

$$x_1 = \xi_1 \cos\eta_1 \qquad x_2 = \xi_2 \cos\eta_2$$
$$y_1 = \xi_1 \sin\eta_1 \qquad y_2 = \xi_2 \sin\eta_2, \qquad (3.2.6.16)$$

Equation 3.2.6.15 becomes

$$(2\pi)^{-2}(R(0)^2 - R(\tau)^2)^{-1} \int_0^{\infty}\int_0^{\infty}\int_0^{2\pi}\int_0^{2\pi} J_k(\xi_1\gamma_1)$$

$$\cdot\, J_k(\xi_2\gamma_2)\xi_1\xi_2 \exp[j(\eta_1 - \eta_2)] \exp\left[-\frac{R(0)(\xi_1^2 + \xi_2^2)}{2(R(0)^2 - R(\tau)^2)}\right]$$

$$\exp\left[\frac{\xi_1\xi_2 R(\tau) \cos\left\{\eta_2 - \eta_1 + \tan^{-1}\left(\dfrac{R_i(\tau)}{R_r(\tau)}\right)\right\}}{\{R(0)^2 - R(\tau)^2\}}\right]$$

$$\cdot\, d\xi_1\, d\xi_2\, d\eta_1\, d\eta_2. \tag{3.2.6.17}$$

Using the formula from Equation 3.1.34 for the last exponential factor of Equation 3.2.6.17, the integrals with respect to η_1 and η_2 can be done simply and the result is given by

$$(R(0)^2 - R(\tau)^2)^{-1} \exp\left[jk \tan^{-1}\left(\frac{R_i(\tau)}{R_r(\tau)}\right)\right]$$

$$\cdot \int_0^\infty \int_0^\infty J_k(\xi_1\gamma_1) J_k(\xi_2\gamma_2) \exp\left[-\frac{R(0)(\xi_1^2 + \xi_2^2)}{2(R(0)^2 - R(\tau)^2)}\right]$$

$$\cdot\, I_k\left(\frac{\xi_1\xi_2 R(\tau)}{R(0)^2 - R(\tau)^2}\right) \xi_1\xi_2\, d\xi_1\, d\xi_2. \tag{3.2.6.18}$$

This double integral can be integrated out and the result is (the formula of Equation 2.3.47 of Volume I was used twice to obtain this result):

$$e^{-\frac{R(0)}{2}(\gamma_1^2 + \gamma_2^2)} I_k(R(\tau)\gamma_1\gamma_2)\, e^{jk \tan^{-1}\left(\frac{R_i(\tau)}{R_r(\tau)}\right)}. \tag{3.2.6.19}$$

Thus,

$$Re_0(\tau) = \frac{1}{2}E\{e_0(t)e_0(t+\tau)\}$$

$$= \frac{1}{2}e^{-j\omega_0\tau} \int_0^\infty \int_0^\infty \int_0^\infty \int_0^\infty \rho_1\rho_2\, g(\rho_1)$$

$$\cdot\, e^{jf(\rho_1)} g(\rho_2)\, e^{jf(\rho_2)}\, e^{-\frac{R(0)}{2}(\gamma_1^2 + \gamma_2^2)} I_1(R(\tau)\gamma_1\gamma_2)$$

$$\cdot\, J_1(\gamma_1\rho_1) J_1(\gamma_2\rho_2) \exp\left[j\frac{R_i(\tau)}{R_r(\tau)}\right]\gamma_1\gamma_2$$

$$\cdot\, d\gamma_1\, d\gamma_2\, d\rho_1\, d\rho_2$$

$$= \frac{1}{2}e^{-j\omega_0\tau}\left[\frac{R_r(\tau) + jR_i(\tau)}{R(\tau)}\right] \int_0^\infty \int_0^\infty \int_0^\infty \int_0^\infty$$

$$\cdot J_1(\gamma_1\rho_1)\, J_1(\gamma_2\rho_2)\rho_1 g(\rho_1)\,\gamma_1\, e^{\,jf(\rho_1)}\, e^{-\frac{R(0)}{2}\gamma_1^2}\rho_2 g(\rho_2)$$

$$\cdot\, e^{\,jf(\rho_2)}\, e^{-\frac{R(0)}{2}\gamma_2^2}\gamma_2\, I_1(R(\tau)\gamma_1\gamma_2)\, d\gamma_1\, d\gamma_2\, d\rho_1\, d\rho_2 \qquad (3.2.6.20)$$

where, from Equation 3.2.6.14,

$$R(0) = R_r(0) = \int_{-\infty}^{\infty} W_N(f)\, df = \sigma^2, \qquad (3.2.6.21)$$

σ^2 = the power of the Gaussian input. The fourth integral of Equation 3.2.6.20 is difficult and, therefore, let us expand $I_1(R(\tau)\gamma_1\gamma_2)$ by a power series, i.e.,

$$I_1(R(\tau)\gamma_1\gamma_2) = \sum_{m=0}^{\infty} \frac{\left(\frac{1}{2}\right)^{2m+1}}{m!(m+1)!}[R(\tau)]^{2m+1}\,\gamma_1^{2m+1}\,\gamma_2^{2m+1}. \qquad (3.2.6.22)$$

Using this expansion,

$$\mathrm{Re}_0(\tau) = \frac{1}{2}e^{-j\omega_0\tau}[R_r(\tau) + jR_i(\tau)]$$

$$\cdot \sum_{m=0}^{\infty} \frac{1}{m!(m+1)!}\left(\frac{1}{2}\right)^{2m+1}[R(\tau)]^{2m}$$

$$\cdot \left| \int_0^{\infty}\int_0^{\infty} J_1(\gamma\rho)\rho\, g(\rho)\, e^{\,jf(\rho)}\, e^{-\frac{R(0)}{2}\gamma^2}\gamma^{2m+2}\, d\rho\, d\gamma \right|^2$$

$$= \frac{1}{2}e^{-j\omega_0\tau}[R_r(\tau) + jR_i(\tau)] \sum_{m=0}^{\infty} \frac{1}{m!(m+1)!}$$

$$\cdot \frac{1}{2}[R(\tau)]^{2m}\left| \frac{(-1)^m\partial^m}{\partial R(0)^m}\int_0^{\infty}\int_0^{\infty} \right.$$

$$\cdot\, J_1(\gamma\rho)\rho\, g(\rho)\, e^{\,jf(\rho)}\, e^{-\frac{R(0)}{2}\gamma^2}\gamma^2\, d\rho\, d\gamma \bigg|^2. \qquad (3.2.6.23)$$

Using the formula from Equation 3.1.50,

$$\mathrm{Re}_0(\tau) = \frac{1}{4}e^{-j\omega_0\tau}[R_r(\tau) + jR_i(\tau)] \sum_{m=0}^{\infty}$$

$$\cdot \frac{1}{m!(m+1)!}[R(\tau)]^{2m}\left| (-1)^m \int_0^{\infty} \rho^2 g(\rho)\, e^{\,jf(\rho)} \right.$$

$$\cdot \left[\frac{\partial^m}{\partial R(0)^m}\left\{ \frac{1}{(R(0))^2}e^{-\frac{\rho^2}{2R(0)}} \right\} \right] d\rho \bigg|^2. \qquad (3.2.6.24)$$

The component of $m = 0$ corresponds to the signal component, i.e.,

$$\mathrm{Re}_0^{(s)}(\tau) = e^{-j\omega_0\tau}[R_r(\tau) + jR_i(\tau)]$$

$$\cdot \left| \frac{1}{2} \int_0^\infty \rho^2 g(\rho) e^{jf(\rho)} \frac{1}{\sigma^4} e^{-\frac{\rho^2}{2\sigma^2}} d\rho \right|^2$$

$$= e^{-j\omega_0\tau}[R_r(\tau) + jR_i(\tau)]$$

$$\cdot \left| \frac{1}{2\sigma} \int_0^\infty \rho^2 \{g(\sigma\rho) e^{jf(\sigma\rho)}\} e^{-\frac{\rho^2}{2}} d\rho \right|^2 \qquad (3.2.6.25)$$

where $R(0)$ is replaced by σ^2 (Equation 3.2.6.21). The Fourier-transform of Equation 3.2.6.25 is given by

$$W_N(f - f_0) \left| \frac{1}{2\sigma} \int_0^\infty \rho^2 e^{-\frac{\rho^2}{2}} \{g(\sigma\rho) e^{jf(\sigma\rho)}\} d\rho \right|^2$$

$$(0 < f < \infty). \qquad (3.2.6.26)$$

Since the power spectrum of $e_i^{(0)}(t)$ is $W_N(f - f_0)$, this result is equal to Equation 3.2.6.3, i.e., the approximation used to obtain Equation 3.2.6.3 was correct.

The term of $m = 1$ in Equation 3.2.6.24 corresponds to the third order intermodulation products, i.e.,

$$\mathrm{Re}_0(\tau) = \frac{1}{8} e^{-j\omega_0\tau}[R_r(\tau) + jR_i(\tau)][R(\tau)]^2$$

$$\cdot \left| \frac{1}{\sigma^3} \int_0^\infty \rho^2 \left(\frac{\rho^2}{2} - 2\right) e^{-\frac{\rho^2}{2}} \{g(\sigma\rho) e^{jf(\sigma\rho)}\} d\rho \right|^2 \qquad (3.2.6.27)$$

where the Fourier-transform of $[R_r(\tau) + jR_i(\tau)][R(\tau)]^2$ is given by

$$W_N(f) \circledast W_N(f) \circledast W_N(-f) \qquad (3.2.6.28)$$

(where $\circledast$ denotes the convolution).

Therefore, the power spectrum of the third order intermodulation is

$$\frac{1}{8} \left| \frac{1}{\sigma^3} \int_0^\infty \rho^2 \left(\frac{\rho^2}{2} - 2\right) e^{-\frac{\rho^2}{2}} \{g(\sigma\rho) e^{jf(\sigma\rho)}\} d\rho \right|^2$$

$$\cdot [W_N(x) \circledast W_N(x) \circledast W_N(-x)] \quad (x = f - f_0) \qquad (3.2.6.29)$$

where after two convolutions, x is replaced by $(f - f_0)$. This result is equal to Equation 3.2.6.6, although it is not a complete solution.

If the nonlinear characteristic is given by the Bessel expansion as in Equation 3.2.2.1, Equation 3.2.6.20 is given by

$$
\mathrm{Re}_0(\tau) = \frac{1}{2} e^{-j\omega_0\tau} \left[\frac{R_r(\tau) + jR_i(\tau)}{R(\tau)} \right] \sum_{s_1=1}^{L} \sum_{s_2=1}^{L} b_{s_1} b_{s_2}^*
$$

$$
\cdot \int_0^\infty \int_0^\infty \int_0^\infty \int_0^\infty J_1(\gamma_1 \rho_1) J_1(\gamma_2 \rho_2) \rho_1 \rho_2
$$

$$
\cdot \exp\left[-\frac{R(0)}{2}(\gamma_1^2 + \gamma_2^2) \right] J_1(\alpha s_1 \rho_1)
$$

$$
\cdot J_1(\alpha s_2 \rho_2) \gamma_1 \gamma_2 I_1(R(\tau)\gamma_1 \gamma_2) \, d\gamma_1 \, d\gamma_2 \, d\rho_1 \, d\rho_2. \quad (3.2.6.30)
$$

Applying the formula of Equation 3.2.1.11 for the integral ρ_1 first and doing the same thing again for ρ_2,

$$
\mathrm{Re}_0(\tau) = \frac{1}{2} e^{-j\omega_0\tau} \left[\frac{R_r(\tau) + jR_i(\tau)}{R(\tau)} \right]
$$

$$
\cdot \left[\sum_{s_1=1}^{L} \sum_{s_2=1}^{L} b_{s_1} b_{s_2}^* e^{-\frac{\alpha^2}{2}(s_1^2 + s_2^2)R(0)} I_1(\alpha^2 s_1 s_2 R(\tau)) \right]
$$

$$
= \frac{1}{2} e^{-j\omega_0\tau} \left[\frac{R_r(\tau) + jR_i(\tau)}{R(\tau)} \right] \sum_{m=0}^{\infty} \frac{1}{m!(m+1)!}
$$

$$
\cdot \left(\frac{1}{2} \right)^{2m+1} \left| \sum_{s=1}^{L} b_s(\alpha s)^{2m+1} e^{-\frac{R(0)}{2}\alpha^2 s^2} \right|^2 [R(\tau)]^{2m+1}. \quad (3.2.6.31)
$$

In the hardlimiter case, $g(\rho) e^{jf(\rho)}$ is replaced by Equation 3.2.2.11 in Equation 3.2.6.20

$$
\mathrm{Re}_0(\tau) = \frac{g_0^2}{2} e^{-j\omega_0\tau} \left[\frac{R_r(\tau) + jR_i(\tau)}{R(\tau)} \right] \int_0^\infty \int_0^\infty \int_0^\infty \int_0^\infty \rho_1 \rho_2
$$

$$
\cdot J_1(\gamma_1 \rho_1) J_1(\gamma_2 \rho_2) \gamma_1 \gamma_2 I_1(R(\tau)\gamma_1 \gamma_2) \, d\rho_1 \, d\rho_2 \, d\gamma_1 \, d\gamma_2. \quad (3.2.6.32)
$$

Using the same approach as in Equation 3.2.5.3 for ρ_1 and ρ_2, this becomes

$$
\mathrm{Re}_0(\tau) = \frac{g_0^2}{2} e^{-j\omega_0\tau} \left[\frac{R_r(\tau) + jR_i(\tau)}{R(\tau)} \right]
$$

$$
\cdot \int_0^\infty \int_0^\infty e^{-\frac{R(0)}{2}(\gamma_1^2 + \gamma_2^2)} \frac{I_1(R(\tau)\gamma_1 \gamma_2)}{\gamma_1 \gamma_2} \, d\gamma_1 \, d\gamma_2. \quad (3.2.6.33)
$$

The first term of the power series expansion of $I_1(R\gamma_1 \gamma_2)$ (Equation 3.2.6.22) gives the signal component, i.e.,

$$\text{Re}_0^{(s)}(\tau) = \frac{g_0^2}{2} e^{-j\omega_0\tau} \left[\frac{R_r(\tau) + jR_i(\tau)}{R(\tau)} \right] R(\tau)$$

$$\cdot \frac{1}{2} \left[\int_0^\infty e^{-\frac{R(0)}{2}\gamma^2} d\gamma \right]^2$$

$$= \frac{g_0^2}{4} e^{-j\omega_0\tau} [R_r(\tau) + jR_i(\tau)] \frac{\pi}{2} \frac{1}{\sigma^2}$$

$$= \frac{\pi}{8} g_0^2 \left[\frac{R_r(\tau) + jR_i(\tau)}{R(0)} \right]. \qquad (3.2.6.34)$$

This is the same result as that of Equation 3.2.5.8 and if $\tau = 0$ (which gives the total output power of the signal components), it becomes equal to the result of Equation 3.2.5.9. If $g(\sigma\rho)e^{jf(\sigma\rho)}$ is replaced by g_0 in Equation 3.2.6.26, the same result also can be obtained.

The second term of the expansion of $I_1(R\gamma_1\gamma_2)$ gives the autocorrelation function of the third order intermodulation at the output, i.e.,

$$\text{Re}_0^{(3)}(\tau) = \frac{g_0^2}{32} e^{-j\omega_0\tau} [R_r(\tau) + jR_i(\tau)][R(\tau)]^2$$

$$\cdot \left[\int_0^\infty e^{-\frac{R(0)}{2}\gamma^2} \gamma^2 d\gamma \right]^2$$

$$= \frac{g_0^2 \pi}{64[R(0)]^3} e^{-j\omega_0\tau} [R_r(\tau) + jR_i(\tau)][R(\tau)]^2. \qquad (3.2.6.35)$$

This is the same as in Equation 3.2.5.14. In most commercial satellite communications, it is enough to evaluate the signal component outputs and third order intermodulation products except for the SSPA case, where the AM/PM characteristic has an irregular shape. However, in the hardlimiter case, as explained in Section 3.2.5, it is necessary to include the higher order intermodulation products. The explicit solution of the integral of Equation 3.2.6.33 has been obtained. Expanding $I_1(R_{\gamma_1\gamma_2})$ by the power series and integrating each term with respect to γ_1 and γ_2, $\text{Re}_0(\tau)$ is given by

$$\text{Re}_0(\tau) = \frac{\pi}{2} g_0^2 e^{-j\omega_0\tau} \left[\frac{R_r(\tau) + jR_i(\tau)}{R(0)} \right]$$

$$\cdot \frac{1}{4} \sum_{m=0}^\infty \frac{1}{(m+1)} \frac{[(2m)!]^2}{[m!\,2^m]^4} \left[\frac{R(\tau)}{R(0)} \right]^{2m}. \qquad (3.2.6.36)$$

It is now easy to prove that the above is equal to

$$\frac{1}{2} g_0^2 e^{-j\omega_0 \tau} \left[\frac{R_r(\tau) + jR_i(\tau)}{R(0)} \right] \left[\frac{R(\tau)}{R(0)} \right]^{-2}$$

$$\cdot \left[E\left(\frac{R(\tau)}{R(0)} \right) - \left\{ 1 - \left(\frac{R(\tau)}{R(0)} \right)^2 \right\} K\left(\frac{R(\tau)}{R(0)} \right) \right] \qquad (3.2.6.37)$$

where

$$K(x) = \int_0^{\frac{\pi}{2}} \frac{d\theta}{\sqrt{1 - x^2 \sin^2 \theta}}$$

$$E(x) = \int_0^{\frac{\pi}{2}} \sqrt{1 - x^2 \sin^2 \theta} \, d\theta \qquad (3.2.6.38)$$

where $K(x)$ and $E(x)$ are the Jacobi elliptic integrals. The elliptic integrals are well known and there are many approximate functions.

3.2.7 Signal Components of Two Carrier Inputs

In many occasions, measurements of two carrier intermodulation are important to specify the nonlinear performance of devices used in satellite communications. The reason is mainly due to the simplicity of the experimental analysis. Therefore, this case of practical importance is explained here.

In this case, $n = 2$ in Equation 3.1.25. Then, the output of the nonlinear device is given from Equations 3.1.39 and 3.1.40 by,

$$e_0(t) = \sum_{k_1 = -\infty}^{\infty} \sum_{k_2 = -\infty}^{\infty} M(k_1, k_2; A_1, A_2) e^{j(\omega_0 + k_1\omega_1 + k_2\omega_2)t + jk_1\phi_1 + jk_2\phi_2}$$
$$\scriptstyle (k_1 + k_2 = 1) \qquad\qquad\qquad\qquad\qquad\qquad\qquad\qquad (3.2.7.1)$$

where

$$M(k_1, k_2; A_1, A_2) = \int_0^{\infty} \int_0^{\infty} \gamma J_{k_1}(A_1 \gamma) J_{k_2}(A_2 \gamma)$$

$$\cdot J_1(\rho\gamma)\rho g(\rho) e^{jf(\rho)} \, d\gamma \, d\rho. \qquad (3.2.7.2)$$

Because of the condition, $k_1 + k_2 = 1$, Equation 3.2.7.1 becomes a single summation, i.e.,

$$e_0(t) = \sum_{k_1 = -\infty}^{\infty} M(k_1, 1 - k_1; A_1, A_2)$$

$$\cdot e^{j[\omega_0 + \omega_2 + k_1(\omega_1 - \omega_2)]t} e^{jk_1\phi_1 + j(1 - k_1)\phi_2} \qquad (3.2.7.3)$$

where,

$$M(k_1, 1 - k_1; A_1, A_2) = \int_0^{\infty} \int_0^{\infty} \gamma J_{k_1}(A_1 \gamma) J_{1 - k_1}(A_2 \gamma)$$

$$\cdot J_1(\gamma\rho)\rho g(\rho)e^{jf(\rho)} \, d\gamma \, d\rho. \qquad (3.2.7.4)$$

The signal components at the output can be obtained as follows (only the $k_1 = 1$ case is shown, since the $k_2 = 1$ case is obtained by replacing A_1 and A_2).

$$M(1,0;A_1,A_2) = \int_0^\infty \int_0^\infty \gamma J_1(A_1\gamma)J_0(A_2\gamma)$$

$$\cdot J_1(\gamma\rho)\rho g(\rho)e^{jf(\rho)} \, d\gamma \, d\rho \qquad (3.2.7.5)$$

where the integral with respect to γ is given as

$$\int_0^\infty \gamma J_1(A_1\gamma)J_0(A_2\gamma)J_1(\gamma\rho) \, d\gamma$$

$$= \frac{(\rho^2 + A_1^2 - A_2^2)}{\pi A_1 \rho \sqrt{(2A_1A_2)^2 - (\rho^2 - A_1^2 - A_2^2)^2}}$$

$$|A_1 - A_2| \le \rho \le A_1 + A_2$$

$$= 0 \qquad \text{Elsewhere} \qquad (3.2.7.6)$$

Thus,

$$M(1,0)$$

$$= \int_{|A_1-A_2|}^{A_1+A_2} \frac{(\rho^2 + A_1^2 - A_2^2)g(\rho)e^{jf(\rho)}}{\pi A_1 \sqrt{(2A_1A_2)^2 - (\rho^2 - A_1^2 - A_2^2)^2}} \, d\rho$$

$$= \frac{1}{\pi} \int_0^\pi (A_1 - A_2 \cos\theta) \left[\frac{g(\sqrt{A_1^2 + A_2^2 - 2A_1A_2\cos\theta})}{\sqrt{A_1^2 + A_2^2 - 2A_1A_2\cos\theta}} \right]$$

$$\cdot \exp[jf(\sqrt{A_1^2 + A_2^2 - 2A_1A_2\cos\theta})] \, d\theta$$

$$= \frac{1}{\pi A_1} \int_{|A_1-A_2|}^{A_1+A_2} \cos^{-1}\left[\frac{A_2^2 - A_1^2 + \rho^2}{2A_2\rho} \right]$$

$$\cdot \left[\frac{d}{d\rho}\{\rho g(\rho)e^{jf(\rho)}\} \right] d\rho. \qquad (3.2.7.7)$$

Since this is only a single integral, it can be easily evaluated by a computer when $g(\rho)$ and $f(\rho)$ are given. However, there is no such simple form for the intermodulation product. Since the intermodulation product carrier frequencies are located at $\omega_0 + \omega_1 - l\Delta\omega$ and $\omega_0 + \omega_2 + l\Delta\omega$ ($l = 1, 2, 3, \ldots$), assuming $\omega_1 < \omega_2$, $(\omega_2 - \omega_1 = \Delta\omega)$, they do not usually fall on the signal carrier frequencies and therefore, the intermodulation products are not important in many cases, especially in cases where the output filter of the nonlinear device exists. However, as an exercise for power series expansion, the complex amplitude M for the intermodulation products will be analyzed. Assume $g(\rho)e^{jf(\rho)}$ is expanded by a power series as in Equation 3.2.1.1. In this case, the $M(k_1, 1-k; A_1 A_2)$'s are given by Equation 3.2.1.9 using the coefficients e_q of Equation 3.2.1.7. Therefore, the problem is how to obtain e_q in this case. In Section 3.2, Example (ii), the case of the simplest possible nonlinear characteristic of Equation 3.1.20 has been shown to explain how to apply the general formula derived in Section 3.1. The reason why the power series expansion case is only shown here is that the physical insight can be acquired more easily than with the other cases. For the other expansions, the results can be obtained by making $n = 2$, $k_2 = 1 - k_1$ in Equations 3.2.2.6, 3.2.3.6 and 3.2.4.3. Now, using the formula from Equation 3.2.1.23,

$$J_{k_1}(A_1 \gamma) J_{1-k_1}(A_2 \gamma)$$

$$= \sum_{q=1}^{\infty} e_q \gamma^{2q-1}$$

$$= \left(\frac{k_1}{|k_1|} \right)^{k_1} \left(\frac{1-k_1}{|1-k_1|} \right)^{1-k_1} \sum_{m_1=0}^{\infty} \sum_{m_2=0}^{\infty}$$

$$\cdot \frac{\left(\dfrac{1}{2} \right)^{2(m_1+m_2)+(|k_1|+|1-k_1|)}}{m_1!(m_1+|k_1|)! \, m_2!(m_2+|1-k_1|)!}$$

$$\cdot A_1^{2m_1+|k_1|} A_2^{2m_2+|1-k_1|} \gamma^{2(m_1+m_2)+(|k_1|+|1-k_1|)}. \qquad (3.2.7.8)$$

Therefore, the e_q's are given by

$$e_q = \left(\frac{k_1}{|k_1|} \right)^{|k_1|} \left(\frac{1-k_1}{|1-k_1|} \right)^{|1-k_1|} \left(\frac{1}{2} \right)^{|k_1|+|1-k_1|}$$

$$\cdot A_1^{|k_1|} A_2^{|1-k_1|} \sum_{m_1=0}^{q-\frac{1}{2}\{|k_1|+|1-k_1|+1\}} \left(\frac{1}{2} \right)^{2m_1} \frac{A_1^{2m_1}}{m_1!(m_1+|k_1|)!}$$

$$\cdot \left(\frac{1}{2} \right)^{2m_2} \frac{A_2^{2m_2}}{m_2!(m_2+|1-k_1|)!} \qquad (3.2.7.9)$$

where

$$m_2 = q - \left\{ \frac{|k_1|+|1-k_1|+1}{2} \right\} - m_1. \qquad (3.2.7.10)$$

Since Equation 3.2.7.9 is represented by a finite single sum, the analysis is very simple.

3.2.8 One or Two Signals Plus a Gaussian Input

The case where one or two carriers occupy a substantial portion of the total input power and the rest of the signals only occupy small portions of the total power, when there are many carriers, will be analzyed. Therefore, the total input is not a Gaussian process but the rest, excluding the above mentioned one or two carriers can be assumed as a Gaussian process. Thus, the input to the nonlinear device is given by

$$e_i^{(0)} = A_1 e^{j(\omega_0 + \omega_1)t + j\phi_1(t) + j\theta_1} + A_2 e^{j(\omega_0 + \omega_2)t + j\phi_2(t) + j\theta_2}$$

$$+ N(t) e^{j\omega_0 t}$$

$$= A_1 \exp[j(\omega_0 + \omega_1)t + j\phi_1(t) + j\theta_1]$$

$$+ A_2 \exp[j(\omega_0 + \omega_2)t + j\phi_2(t) + j\theta_2]$$

$$+ \sqrt{N_c^2 + N_s^2}\, e^{j\omega_0 t + \tan^{-1}\frac{N_s}{N_c}}. \tag{3.2.8.1}$$

Then, the output component whose angular frequency is $\omega_0 + k_1\omega_1 + k_2\omega_2$, is

$$e^{j(\omega_0 + k_1\omega_1 + k_2\omega_2)t + j(k_1\phi_1 + k_2\phi_2)} e^{jk_3 \tan^{-1}\left(\frac{N_s}{N_c}\right)} \int_0^\infty \int_0^\infty \gamma J_{k_1}(A_1\gamma)$$

$$\cdot J_{k_2}(A_2\gamma) J_{k_3}(\sqrt{N_c^2 + N_s^2}\,\gamma) J_1(\gamma\rho)\rho\, g(\rho)\, e^{jf(\rho)}\, d\gamma\, d\rho \tag{3.2.8.2}$$

where

$$k_3 = 1 - k_1 - k_2. \tag{3.2.8.3}$$

Let us obtain the signal components from Equation 3.2.8.2, which are the components $k_1 = 1, k_2 = 0, k_3 = 0$ (the case of $k_1 = 0, k_2 = 1, k_3 = 0$ can be obtained by replacing A_1 and A_2) and $k_1 = 0, k_2 = 0, k_3 = 1$.

(i) $k_1 = 1, \ k_2 = k_3 = 0$:

$$e^{j(\omega_0 + \omega_1)t + j\phi_1} \int_0^\infty \int_0^\infty \gamma J_1(A_1\gamma) J_0(A_2\gamma)$$

$$\cdot J_0(\sqrt{N_c^2 + N_s^2}\,\gamma) J_1(\rho\gamma)\rho\, g(\rho)\, e^{jf(\rho)}\, d\gamma\, d\rho. \tag{3.2.8.4}$$

This is not the signal component still because of the time variation factor $J_0(\sqrt{N_c^2 + N_s^2}\,\gamma)$. To obtain the real signal component, the average on this must be taken

$$\underset{N}{E}\{J_0(\sqrt{N_c^2 + N_s^2}\,\gamma)\} = e^{-\frac{R(0)}{2}\gamma^2} \tag{3.2.8.5}$$

Thus, the signal component in this case is

$$
e^{j(\omega_0 + \omega_1)t + j\phi_1} \int_0^\infty \int_0^\infty \gamma J_1(A_1 \gamma) J_0(A_2 \gamma) e^{-\frac{R(0)}{2}\gamma^2}
$$

$$
\cdot J_1(\gamma\rho)\rho g(\rho) e^{jf(\rho)} \, d\gamma \, d\rho. \tag{3.2.8.6}
$$

If $A_2 = 0$, this can be simplified, i.e., by using the formula

$$
\int_0^\infty \gamma J_k(A_1 \gamma) J_k(\gamma\rho) e^{-\frac{R(0)}{2}\gamma^2} \, d\gamma
$$

$$
= \frac{1}{R(0)} e^{-\frac{(A_1^2 + \rho^2)}{2R(0)}} I_k\!\left(\frac{A_1 \rho}{R(0)}\right). \tag{3.2.8.7}
$$

Therefore, in this case, Equation 3.2.8.6 becomes

$$
e^{j(\omega_0 + \omega_1)t + j\phi_1} \, e^{-\frac{A_1^2}{2\sigma^2}} \int_0^\infty e^{-\frac{\rho^2}{2}} I_1\!\left(\frac{A_1}{\sigma}\rho\right)
$$

$$
\cdot \rho g(\sigma\rho) e^{jf(\sigma\rho)} \, d\rho. \tag{3.2.8.8}
$$

If the Gaussian signal is small, i.e.,

$$
\left(\frac{A_1}{\sigma}\right) \gg 1 \tag{3.2.8.9}
$$

$$
I_1\!\left(\frac{A_1}{\sigma}\rho\right) \simeq \frac{e^{\frac{A_1}{\sigma}\rho}}{\sqrt{2\pi\left(\frac{A_1}{\sigma}\right)\rho}}, \tag{3.2.8.10}
$$

the integral of Equation 3.2.8.8 can be approximated by

$$
e^{-\frac{A_1^2}{2\sigma^2}} \int_0^\infty e^{-\frac{\rho^2}{2} + \frac{A_1}{\sigma}\rho} \sqrt{\rho}\, g(\sigma\rho) e^{jf(\sigma\rho)} \frac{1}{\sqrt{2\pi}} \sqrt{\frac{\sigma}{A_1}}
$$

$$
= \sqrt{\frac{\sigma}{2\pi A_1}} \int_0^\infty e^{-\frac{1}{2}\left(\rho - \frac{A_1}{\sigma}\right)^2} \sqrt{\rho}\, g(\sigma\rho) e^{jf(\sigma\rho)} \, d\rho. \tag{3.2.8.11}
$$

Because of Equation 3.2.8.9 and $g(\sigma\rho) e^{jf(\sigma\rho)}$ does not change much when ρ changes as $A_1/\sigma \pm a$ (a should be the smallest possible number since $e^{-a^2/2}$ is very small), the above result can be further approximated as

$$\sqrt{\frac{\sigma}{2\pi A_1}} \sqrt{\frac{A_1}{\sigma}} \, g(A_1) \, e^{jf(A_1)} \int_{-\infty}^{\infty} e^{-\frac{\rho^2}{2}} \, d\rho$$

$$= \frac{1}{\sqrt{2\pi}} \times \sqrt{2\pi} \, g(A_1) \, e^{jf(A_1)}$$

$$= g(A_1) \, e^{jf(A_1)}. \tag{3.2.8.12}$$

Then, Equation 3.2.8.8 becomes

$$g(A_1) \, e^{jf(A_1)} \, e^{j(\omega_0 + \omega_1)t + j\phi_1} \tag{3.2.8.13}$$

This result is expected, since the Gaussian signal is small and can be ignored.

(ii) $k_1 = k_2 = 0$, $k_3 = 1$; Equation 3.2.8.2 becomes

$$e^{j\omega_0 t} \, e^{j\tan^{-1}\left(\frac{N_s}{N_c}\right)} \int_0^\infty \int_0^\infty \gamma J_0(A_1\gamma) J_0(A_2\gamma)$$

$$\cdot J_1(\sqrt{N_c^2 + N_s^2}\,\gamma) J_1(\gamma\rho) \rho \, g(\rho) \, e^{jf(\rho)} \, d\gamma \, d\rho. \tag{3.2.8.14}$$

The autocorrelation function of

$$e^{j\tan^{-1}\left(\frac{N_s}{N_c}\right)} J_1(\sqrt{N_c^2 + N_s^2}\,\gamma)$$

is given by Equation 3.2.6.19 and by expanding $I_1(R(\tau)\gamma_1\gamma_2)$ by a power series, it is easily determined by deriving that the signal component of the Gaussian signal is given by

$$[N_c(t) + jN_s(t)] \, e^{j\omega_0 t} \frac{1}{2} \int_0^\infty \int_0^\infty \gamma^2 J_0(A_1\gamma)$$

$$\cdot J_0(A_2\gamma) J_1(\gamma\rho) \, e^{-\frac{R(0)}{2}\gamma^2} \rho \, g(\rho) \, e^{jf(\rho)} \, d\gamma \, d\rho. \tag{3.2.8.15}$$

As mentioned before, if there are many signals and none of them dominates the other, then the input signal is a Gaussian process and the signal components for this are given by Equation 3.2.6.3. The rest of the components of Equation 3.2.8.14 consists of the intermodulation products among the Gaussian input whose level is changed by the existence of A_1 and A_2. If $A_2 = 0$, then Equation 3.2.8.15 becomes

$$N(t) \, e^{j\omega_0 t} \frac{1}{2\sigma} \, e^{-\frac{A_1^2}{2\sigma^2}} \int_0^\infty e^{-\frac{\rho^2}{2}}$$

$$\cdot \rho \left[\rho I_0\left(\frac{A_1}{\sigma}\rho\right) - \left(\frac{A_1}{\sigma}\right) I_1\left(\frac{A_1}{\sigma}\rho\right) \right] g(\sigma\rho)\, e^{\,jf(\sigma\rho)}\, d\rho \quad (3.2.8.16)$$

where the formula was used,

$$\int_0^\infty \gamma^2 J_0(A_1\gamma)\, J_1(\gamma\rho)\, e^{-\frac{R(0)}{2}\gamma^2}\, d\gamma$$

$$= \frac{1}{\sigma^3} e^{-\frac{(A_1^2 + \rho^2)}{2\sigma^2}} \left[\left(\frac{\rho}{\sigma}\right) I_0\left(\frac{A_1\rho}{\sigma^2}\right) - \left(\frac{A_1}{\sigma}\right) I_1\left(\frac{A_1\rho}{\sigma^2}\right) \right]. \quad (3.2.8.17)$$

Now, the autocorrelation function of Equation 3.2.8.2 is given, using derivations similar as those in Equations 3.2.6.11 and 3.2.6.12 by,

$$\frac{1}{2} e^{-j(\omega_0 + k_1\omega_1 + k_2\omega_2)\tau} \; \underset{\phi}{E} \left\{ e^{jk_1(\phi_1(t) - \phi_1(t+\tau))} \; e^{jk_2(\phi_2(t) - \phi_2(t+\tau))} \right\}$$

$$\cdot [R_r(\tau) + jR_i(\tau)]^{k_3} [R(\tau)]^{-k_3} \int_0^\infty \int_0^\infty \int_0^\infty \int_0^\infty \gamma_1 \gamma_2$$

$$\cdot J_{k_1}(A_1\gamma_1) J_{k_2}(A_2\gamma_1) J_{k_1}(A_1\gamma_2) J_{k_2}(A_2\gamma_2)$$

$$\cdot J_1(\rho_1\gamma_1) J_1(\rho_2\gamma_2) \rho_1 \rho_2 g(\rho_1) g(\rho_2)$$

$$\cdot \exp[\,jf(\rho_1) - jf(\rho_2)] I_{k_3}(R(\tau)\gamma_1\gamma_2)\, e^{-\frac{R(0)}{2}(\gamma_1^2 + \gamma_2^2)}$$

$$\cdot d\gamma_1\, d\gamma_2\, d\rho_1\, d\rho_2. \quad (3.2.8.18)$$

Using the following expansion,

$$I_{k_3}(R(\tau)\gamma_1\gamma_2) = \sum_{m=0}^\infty \frac{\left(\frac{1}{2}\right)^{2m + |k_3|}}{m!(m + |k_3|)!} [R(\tau)]^{2m + |k_3|}$$

$$\cdot \gamma_1^{2m + |k_3|} \gamma_2^{2m + |k_3|}, \quad (3.2.8.19)$$

Equation 3.2.8.18 becomes

$$\frac{1}{2} e^{-j(\omega_0 + k_1\omega_1 + k_2\omega_2)\tau} \; \underset{\phi_1}{E} \left\{ e^{jk_1(\phi_1(t) - \phi_1(t+\tau))} \right\}$$

$$\cdot \underset{\phi_2}{E} \left\{ e^{jk_2(\phi_2(t) - \phi_2(t+\tau))} \right\} [R_r(\tau) + jR_i(\tau)]^{k_3}$$

$$\cdot [R(\tau)]^{-k_3 + |k_3|} \sum_{m=0}^\infty \frac{\left(\frac{1}{2}\right)^{2m + |k_3|}}{m!(m + |k_3|)!} [R(\tau)]^{2m} \left| \int_0^\infty \int_0^\infty \gamma^{2m + |k_3| + 1} \right.$$

$$\cdot J_{k_1}(A_1\gamma)J_{k_2}(A_2\gamma)J_1(\gamma\rho)\rho g(\rho)\,e^{jf(\rho)}\,e^{-\frac{R(0)}{2}\gamma^2}\,d\gamma\,d\rho\bigg|^2. \qquad (3.2.8.20)$$

These integrals are very difficult to evaluate unless the function $g(\rho)e^{jf(\rho)}$ is given in an especially convenient form as in a Bessel expansion (Equation 3.2.2.1), which will be analyzed later in this Section. However, if $A_2 = 0$, all the terms of $k_2 \neq 0$ disappear and now $k_1 + k_3 = 1$ instead of $k_1 + k_2 + k_3 = 1$. In this case, the terms corresponding to $|k_1| + |k_3| > 1$ (the intermodulation products) are out of the band in most cases as shown in Figure 3.2.8.1, i.e., $k_1 = 1$, $k_3 = 0$, $A_2 = 0$ ($k_2 = 0$). From Equation 3.2.8.20, the autocorrelation function of this component is given by

$$\frac{1}{2}e^{-j(\omega_0+\omega_1)\tau}\,\underset{\phi}{E}\left\{e^{j\phi_1(t)-j\phi_1(t+\tau)}\right\}\sum_{m=0}^{\infty}[m!]^{-2}[R(\tau)]^{2m}$$

$$\cdot\left|\int_0^\infty\frac{\partial^m}{\partial R(0)^m}\int_0^\infty\int_0^\infty\gamma J_1(A_1\gamma)J_1(\gamma\rho)\,e^{-\frac{R(0)}{2}\gamma^2}\,d\gamma\right.$$

$$\left.\cdot\,\rho g(\rho)\,e^{jf(\rho)}\,d\rho\right|^2$$

$$= \frac{1}{2}e^{-j(\omega_0+\omega_1)\tau}\,\underset{\phi_1}{E}\left\{e^{j\phi_1(t)-j\phi_1(t+\tau)}\right\}\sum_{m=0}^{\infty}[m!]^{-2}$$

$$\cdot\left|\int_0^\infty\rho g(\rho)\,e^{jf(\rho)}\frac{\partial^m}{\partial R(0)^m}\left[\frac{1}{R(0)}e^{-\frac{A_1^2+\rho^2}{2R(0)}}\right.\right.$$

$$\left.\left.\cdot I_1\!\left(\frac{A_1\rho}{R(0)}\right)\right]d\rho\right|^2[R(\tau)]^{2m} \qquad (3.2.8.21)$$

where the formula of Equation 3.2.8.7 was used to derive this result. The term $m = 0$ is the pure signal component which is independent from the autocorrelation function of the Gaussian process, and the term $m = 1$ gives the noise components falling around $\omega_0 + \omega_1$. The term of $m = 0$ is

$$\frac{1}{2}e^{-j(\omega_0+\omega_1)\tau}\,\underset{\phi_1}{E}\left\{e^{j\phi_1(t)-j\phi_1(t+\tau)}\right\}$$

$$\cdot\left|\exp\!\left(-\frac{A_1^2}{2\sigma^2}\right)\int_0^\infty\rho e^{-\frac{\rho^2}{2}}I_1\!\left(\frac{A_1}{\sigma}\rho\right)\{g(\sigma\rho)\,e^{jf(\sigma\rho)}\}\,d\rho\right|^2. \qquad (3.2.8.22)$$

This is the same result as in Equation 3.2.8.8 but Equation 3.2.8.8 is the time function. That of $m = 1$ in Equation 3.2.8.21 is

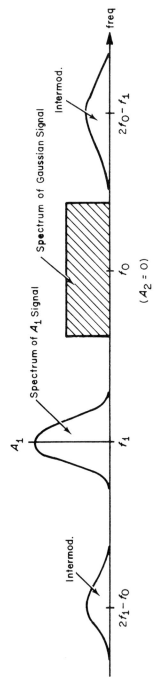

Figure 3.2.8.1 Power Spectra of Signals and Intermodulation Products

$$\frac{1}{8} e^{-j(\omega_0 + \omega_1)\tau} \underset{\phi_1}{E} \left\{ e^{j\phi_1(t) - j\phi_1(t+\tau)} \right\} \left[\frac{R(\tau)}{R(0)} \right]^2$$

$$\cdot \left| \int_0^\infty \rho \left[\left(\frac{A_1}{\sigma} \rho \right) I_0 \left(\frac{A_1}{\sigma} \rho \right) + \left\{ 2 - \rho^2 - \left(\frac{A_1}{\sigma} \right)^2 \right\} I_1 \left(\frac{A_1}{\sigma} \rho \right) \right. \right.$$

$$\left. \left. + \left(\frac{A_1}{\sigma} \rho \right) I_2 \left(\frac{A_1}{\sigma} \rho \right) \right] e^{-\frac{A_1^2}{2\sigma^2}} e^{-\frac{\rho^2}{2}} g(\sigma\rho) \, e^{jf(\sigma\rho)} \, d\rho \right|^2. \qquad (3.2.8.23)$$

This is the third order intermodulation product and it is only important from a practical point of view in most commercial satellite communications. Since the result of Equation 3.2.8.23 is given by a single integral of ρ, the evaluation is easy to realize by computer. The autocorrelation function of the ($k_3 = 1$, $k_1 = 0$) component is given (assuming $A_2 = 0$) (See Figure 3.2.8.1), from Equation 3.2.8.20, by

$$\frac{1}{2} [R_r(\tau) + jR_i(\tau)] e^{-j\omega_0\tau} \sum_{m=0}^\infty \frac{[R(\tau)]^{2m}}{2^{2m+1} m!(m+1)!}$$

$$\cdot \left| \int_0^\infty \int_0^\infty \gamma^{2m+2} J_0(A_1\gamma) J_1(\rho\gamma) e^{-\frac{R(0)}{2}\gamma^2} \rho g(\rho) \right.$$

$$\left. \cdot e^{jf(\rho)} \, d\gamma \, d\rho \right|^2$$

$$= \frac{1}{4} [R_r(\tau) + jR_i(\tau)] e^{-j\omega_0\tau} \sum_{m=0}^\infty \frac{[R(\tau)]^{2m}}{m!(m+1)!}$$

$$\cdot \left| \int_0^\infty \left\{ \frac{\partial^m}{\partial R(0)^m} \frac{\partial}{\partial \rho} \int_0^\infty \gamma J_0(A_1\gamma) J_0(\rho\gamma) \right. \right.$$

$$\left. \left. \cdot e^{-\frac{R(0)}{2}\gamma^2} \, d\gamma \right\} \rho g(\rho) e^{jf(\rho)} \, d\rho \right|^2$$

$$= \frac{1}{4} [R_r(\tau) + jR_i(\tau)] e^{-j\omega_0\tau} \sum_{m=0}^\infty \frac{[R(\tau)]^{2m}}{m!(m+1)!}$$

$$\cdot \left| \int_0^\infty \frac{\partial^m}{\partial R(0)^m} \left\{ \left[\frac{\rho}{R(0)^2} I_0 \left(\frac{A_1\rho}{R(0)} \right) - \frac{A_1}{R(0)^2} I_1 \left(\frac{A_1\rho}{R(0)} \right) \right] \right. \right.$$

$$\left. \left. \cdot e^{-\frac{A_1^2 + \rho^2}{2R(0)}} \right\} \rho g(\rho) e^{jf(\rho)} \, d\rho \right|^2 \qquad (3.2.8.24)$$

where, using the formula of Equation 3.2.8.7,

$$\frac{\partial}{\partial \rho} \int_0^\infty \gamma J_0(A_1 \gamma) J_0(\rho \gamma) e^{-\frac{R(0)}{2}\gamma^2} d\gamma$$

$$= \left[-\frac{\rho}{R(0)^2} I_0\left(\frac{A_1 \rho}{R(0)}\right) + \frac{A_1}{R(0)^2} I_1\left(\frac{A_1 \rho}{R(0)}\right) \right]. \qquad (3.2.8.25)$$

In Equation 3.2.8.24, the term $m = 0$ gives the pure signal component for the Gaussian signal, i.e.,

$$\frac{1}{4}\left[\frac{R_r(\tau) + j R_i(\tau)}{R(0)} \right] e^{-j\omega_0 \tau} \left| \int_0^\infty \rho \left[\rho I_0\left(\frac{A_1}{\sigma}\rho\right) \right. \right.$$

$$\left. \left. - \left(\frac{A_1}{\sigma}\right) I_1\left(\frac{A_1}{\sigma}\rho\right) \right] e^{-\frac{\rho^2}{2}} e^{-\frac{A_1^2}{2\sigma^2}} g(\sigma \rho) e^{jf(\sigma \rho)} d\rho \right|^2. \qquad (3.2.8.26)$$

Thus, the power spectrum of this component is proportional to that of the input and only the level changes with A_1. The third order intermodulation products for the inband Gaussian process (see Figure 3.2.8.1) is given by the term of $m = 1$ in Equation 3.2.8.24, i.e.,

$$\frac{1}{8} e^{-j\omega_0 \tau} \left[\frac{R_r(\tau) + j R_i(\tau)}{R(0)} \right] \left[\frac{R(\tau)}{R(0)} \right]^2 \left| e^{-\frac{A_1^2}{2\sigma^2}} \right.$$

$$\cdot \int_0^\infty \rho \left[\left\{ -2\rho + \frac{A_1^2}{\sigma^2}\rho + \frac{\rho^3}{2} \right\} I_0\left(\frac{A_1}{\sigma}\rho\right) \right.$$

$$+ \left\{ -\frac{3}{2}\frac{A_1}{\sigma}\rho^2 + 2\frac{A_1}{\sigma} - \frac{1}{2}\frac{A_1^3}{\sigma^3} \right\} I_1\left(\frac{A_1}{\sigma}\rho\right)$$

$$\left. \left. + \frac{1}{2}\frac{A_1^2}{\sigma^2}\rho I_2\left(\frac{A_1}{\sigma}\rho\right) \right] e^{-\frac{\rho^2}{2}} g(\sigma \rho) e^{jf(\sigma \rho)} d\rho \right|^2. \qquad (3.2.8.27)$$

As repeatedly explained, in most commercial satellite communications, the terms for $m \geq 2$ can be ignored. The Bessel expansion of Equation 3.2.2.1 makes the calculation of the general solution for the output autocorrelation function in Equation 3.2.8.18 much easier, i.e., by substituting Equation 3.2.2.1 into Equation 3.2.8.18, the integral of Equation 3.2.8.18 is given by

$$\sum_{S_1 = 1}^L \sum_{S_2 = 1}^L b_{S_1} b_{S_2}^* \int_0^\infty \int_0^\infty \int_0^\infty \int_0^\infty \gamma_1 \gamma_2$$

$$\cdot J_{k_1}(A_1 \gamma_1) J_{k_2}(A_2 \gamma_1) J_{k_1}(A_1 \gamma_2) J_{k_2}(A_2 \gamma_2) J_1(\rho_1 \gamma_1)$$

$$\cdot J_1(\rho_2 \gamma_2) \rho_1 \rho_2 J_1(\alpha S_1 \rho_1) J_1(\alpha_2 S_2 \rho_2) I_{k_3}(R(\tau) \gamma_1 \gamma_2)$$

$$\cdot \, e^{-\frac{R(0)}{2}(\gamma_1^2 + \gamma_2^2)} \, d\gamma_1 \, d\gamma_2 \, d\rho_1 \, d\rho_2$$

$$= \sum_{S_1=1}^{L} \sum_{S_2=1}^{L} b_{S_1} b_{S_2}^* J_{k_1}(A_1 \alpha S_1) J_{k_1}(A_1 \alpha S_2)$$

$$\cdot \, J_{k_2}(A_2 \alpha S_1) J_{k_2}(A_2 \alpha S_2) \, e^{-\frac{R(0)}{2}(S_1^2 + S_2^2)\alpha^2}$$

$$\cdot \, I_{k_3}(R(\tau)\alpha^2 S_1 S_2). \tag{3.2.8.28}$$

Thus, in this case, Equation 3.2.8.18 becomes

$$\frac{1}{2} e^{-j(\omega_0 + k_1\omega_1 + k_2\omega_2)t} \, \mathop{E}_{\phi} \left\{ e^{jk_1(\phi_1(t) - \phi_1(t+\tau))} \, e^{jk_2(\phi_2(t) - \phi_2(t+\tau))} \right\}$$

$$\cdot \, [R_r(\tau) + jR_i(\tau)]^{k_3}[R(\tau)]^{-k_3} \sum_{S_1=1}^{L} \sum_{S_2=1}^{L} b_{S_1} b_{S_2}^*$$

$$\cdot \, J_{k_1}(A_1 \alpha S_1) J_{k_1}(A_1 \alpha S_2) J_{k_2}(A_2 \alpha S_1) J_{k_2}(A_2 \alpha S_2)$$

$$\cdot \, e^{-\frac{R(0)}{2}(S_1^2 + S_2^2)\alpha^2} I_{k_3}(R(\tau)\alpha^2 S_1 S_2). \tag{3.2.8.29}$$

The result of Equation 3.2.8.28 can be obtained by using twice the formula of Equation 3.2.1.11 for ρ_1 and ρ_2. Once the coefficients b_S's are obtained, which can be done easily [55], it is not difficult to evaluate this sum. This result can be simply expanded to an arbitrary number of carriers (instead of two) plus a Gaussian case (see the details in [55]).

Expanding $I_{k_3}(R(\tau)\alpha^2 S_1 S_2)$ by a power series as in Equation 3.2.8.19, the double sum can be reduced into the single summation as

$$\frac{1}{2} e^{-j(\omega_0 + k_1\omega_1 + k_2\omega_2)\tau} \, \mathop{E}_{\phi} \left\{ e^{jk_1(\phi_1(t) - \phi_1(t+\tau))} \, e^{jk_2(\phi_2(t) - \phi_2(t+\tau))} \right\}$$

$$\cdot \, [R_r(\tau) + jR_i(\tau)]^{k_3}[R(\tau)]^{-k_3 + |k_3|} 2^{-|k_3|} \sum_{m=0}^{\infty} \frac{[R(\tau)]^{2m}}{m!(m + |k_3|)! \, 2^{2m}}$$

$$\cdot \left| \sum_{S=1}^{L} b_S J_{k_1}(A_1 \alpha S) J_{k_2}(A_2 \alpha S) \, e^{-\frac{R(0)}{2}\alpha^2 S^2} (\alpha S)^{2m + |k_3|} \right|^2. \tag{3.2.8.30}$$

In a hardlimiter case, the integrals of ρ_1 and ρ_2 in Equation 3.2.8.18 can be done, using the formula of Equation 3.2.5.2 or 3.2.5.3, i.e.,

$$\int_0^{\infty} \int_0^{\infty} J_1(\rho_1 \gamma_1) J_1(\rho_2 \gamma_2) \rho_1 \rho_2 g(\rho_1) g(\rho_2) \, e^{jf(\rho_1) - jf(\rho_2)} \, d\rho_1 \, d\rho_2$$

$$= \frac{1}{(\gamma_1 \gamma_2)^2} . \qquad (3.2.8.31)$$

Then, Equation 3.2.8.18 becomes

$$\frac{g_0^2}{2} e^{-j(\omega_0 + k_1\omega_1 + k_2\omega_2)\tau} \; \underset{\phi}{E} \; \{ e^{j(\phi_1(t) - \phi_1(t+\tau))} \; e^{j(\phi_2(t) - j\phi_2(t+\tau))} \}$$

$$\cdot [R_r(\tau) + jR_i(\tau)]^{k_3} [R(\tau)]^{-k_3} \int_0^\infty \int_0^\infty (\gamma_1 \gamma_2)^{-1}$$

$$\cdot J_{k_1}(A_1\gamma_1) J_{k_2}(A_2\gamma_1) J_{k_1}(A_1\gamma_2) J_{k_2}(A_2\gamma_2) e^{-\frac{R(0)}{2}(\gamma_1^2 + \gamma_2^2)}$$

$$\cdot I_{k_3}(R(\tau)\gamma_1\gamma_2) \; d\gamma_1 \; d\gamma_2$$

$$= \frac{g_0^2}{2} e^{-j(\omega_0 + k_1\omega_1 + k_2\omega_2)\tau}$$

$$\cdot \underset{\phi}{E} \; \{ e^{jk_1(\phi_1(t) - \phi_1(t+\tau))} \; e^{jk_2(\phi_2(t) - \phi_2(t+\tau))} \}$$

$$\cdot [R_r(\tau) + jR_i(\tau)]^{k_3} [R(\tau)]^{-k_3 + |k_3|} 2^{-|k_3|}$$

$$\cdot \sum_{m=0}^{\infty} \frac{[R(\tau)]^{2m}}{m!(m + |k_3|)! 2^{2m}}$$

$$\cdot \left| \int_0^\infty \gamma^{2m + |k_3| - 1} J_{k_1}(A_1\gamma) J_{k_2}(A_2\gamma) e^{-\frac{R(0)}{2}\gamma^2} d\gamma \right|^2 . \qquad (3.2.8.32)$$

The integrals with respect to γ can be evaluated by a computer (only a single integral).

As explained in Figure 3.2.8.1, only the intermodulation products that are falling in bands will be shown in more detail as shown above.

(i) $k_1 = 1$, $k_2 = k_3 = 0$ $(A_2 = 0)$ and $m = 0$;

$$\frac{g_0^2}{2} e^{-j(\omega_0 + \omega_1)\tau} \; \underset{\phi_1}{E} \; [e^{j(\phi_1(t) - \phi_1(t+\tau))}] \left| \int_0^\infty \frac{J_1\left(\frac{A_1}{\sigma}\gamma\right)}{\gamma} e^{-\frac{\gamma^2}{2}} d\gamma \right|^2$$

$$= \frac{g_0^2}{2} e^{-j(\omega_0 + \omega_1)\tau} \; \underset{\phi_1}{E} \; \{ e^{j(\phi_1(t) - \phi_1(t+\tau))} \}$$

$$\cdot \left| \sqrt{\frac{\pi}{2}} \sum_{m=0}^{\infty} \frac{(-1)^m (2m)!}{2(m+1)(2^m m!)^3} \left(\frac{A_1}{\sigma}\right)^{2m+1} \right|^2 . \qquad (3.2.8.33)$$

In this case, if $m = 1$ (third order intermodulation),

$$\frac{g_0^2}{2} e^{-j(\omega_0 + \omega_1)\tau} \underset{\phi_1}{E} \{e^{j\phi_1(t) - j\phi_1(t+\tau)}\}$$

$$\cdot \frac{1}{4}[R(\tau)]^2 \left| \int_0^\infty \gamma J_1(A_1 \gamma) e^{-\frac{R(0)}{2}\gamma^2} d\gamma \right|^2 \qquad (3.2.8.34)$$

where

$$\int_0^\infty \gamma J_1(A_1 \gamma) e^{-\frac{R(0)}{2}\gamma^2} d\gamma = \sqrt{\frac{\pi}{2}} \frac{1}{(2\sigma^2)} \left(\frac{A_1}{\sigma}\right)$$

$$\cdot e^{-\frac{A_1^2}{4\sigma^2}} \left[I_0\left(\frac{A_1^2}{4\sigma^2}\right) - I_1\left(\frac{A_1^2}{4\sigma^2}\right) \right]. \qquad (3.2.8.35)$$

Therefore, Equation 3.2.8.34 becomes

$$\frac{g_0^2}{8} e^{-j(\omega_0 + \omega_1)\tau} \underset{\phi_1}{E} \{e^{j\phi_1(t) - j\phi_1(t+\tau)}\} \left[\frac{R(\tau)}{R(0)}\right]^2$$

$$\cdot \left\{ \frac{1}{2} \sqrt{\frac{\pi}{2}} \left(\frac{A_1}{\sigma}\right) e^{-\frac{A_1^2}{4\sigma^2}} \left[I_0\left(\frac{A_1^2}{4\sigma^2}\right) - I_1\left(\frac{A_1^2}{4\sigma^2}\right) \right] \right\}^2. \qquad (3.2.8.36)$$

(ii) $k_1 = k_2 = 0$ ($A_2 = 0$), $k_3 = 1$ ($m = 0$) (pure signal of the Gaussian signal);

$$\frac{g_0^2}{4} e^{-j\omega_0\tau}[R_r(\tau) + jR_i(\tau)] \left| \int_0^\infty J_0(A_1 \gamma) e^{-\frac{R(0)}{2}\gamma^2} d\gamma \right|^2$$

$$= \frac{g_0^2}{4} e^{-j\omega_0\tau} \left[\frac{R_r(\tau) + jR_i(\tau)}{R(0)}\right] \left[\sqrt{\frac{\pi}{2}} e^{-\frac{A_1^2}{4R(0)}} I_0\left(\frac{A_1^2}{4R(0)}\right) \right]^2 \qquad (3.2.8.37)$$

where the formula

$$\int_0^\infty J_0(A_1 \gamma) e^{-\frac{R(0)}{2}\gamma^2} d\gamma = \sqrt{\frac{\pi}{2}} \frac{1}{\sqrt{R(0)}} e^{-\frac{A_1^2}{4R(0)}} I_0\left(\frac{A_1^2}{4R(0)}\right) \qquad (3.2.8.38)$$

was used to obtain Equation 3.2.8.37. The component for $m = 1$ (third order intermodulation for the Gaussian signal) is given by

$$\frac{g_0^2}{32} e^{-j(\omega_0 + \omega_1)\tau}[R_r(\tau) + jR_i(\tau)][R(\tau)]^2$$

$$\left| \int_0^\infty \gamma^2 J_0(A_1 \gamma) e^{-\frac{R(0)}{2}} \, d\gamma \right|^2$$

$$= \frac{g_0^2}{32} e^{-j(\omega_0 + \omega_1)\tau} \left[\frac{R_r(\tau) + jR_i(\tau)}{R(0)} \right] \left[\frac{R(\tau)}{R(0)} \right]^2 \left(\frac{\pi}{2} \right)$$

$$\cdot \left[\left\{ 1 - \frac{1}{2} \left(\frac{A_1^2}{R(0)} \right) \right\} I_0 \left(\frac{A_1^2}{4R(0)} \right) + \frac{1}{2} \left(\frac{A_1^2}{R(0)} \right) I_1 \left(\frac{A_1^2}{4R(0)} \right) \right]^2$$

$$\cdot e^{-\frac{A_1^2}{2R(0)}} \tag{3.2.8.39}$$

where the formula

$$\int_0^\infty \gamma^2 J_0(A_1 \gamma) e^{-\frac{R(0)}{2} \gamma^2} \, d\gamma$$

$$= -\frac{2\partial}{\partial R(0)} \int_0^\infty J_0(A_1 \gamma) e^{-\frac{R(0)}{2} \gamma^2} \, d\gamma$$

$$= (-2) \frac{\partial}{\partial R(0)} \left[\sqrt{\frac{\pi}{2}} \frac{1}{\sqrt{R(0)}} e^{-\frac{A_1^2}{4R(0)}} I_0 \left(\frac{A_1^2}{4R(0)} \right) \right]$$

$$= \frac{\left(\sqrt{\frac{\pi}{2}} \right)}{[R(0)]^{3/2}} \left[\left\{ 1 - \frac{A_1^2}{2R(0)} \right\} I_0 \left(\frac{A_1^2}{4R(0)} \right) \right.$$

$$\left. + \left(\frac{A_1^2}{2R(0)} \right) I_1 \left(\frac{A_1^2}{4R(0)} \right) \right]. \tag{3.2.8.40}$$

3.2.9 Large Backoff Areas

It is very useful to know about intermodulation products in a large backoff area where a simple formula can be applied and where the results for a smaller backoff area can be extended from those in the large backoff and are not very different from the real values. Therefore, the intermodulation analysis for the large backoff areas will be done in this Section. In large backoff areas (the input backoff below -10 dB), the phase change of the nonlinear devices is proportional to the input power (except in some SSPA or linearized TWTA or HPA cases probably) and the amplitude characteristics are linear, i.e., $g(A)$ and $f(A)$ of Equation 3.1.26 are given by

$$g(A) = g_0 A \quad (g_0 \text{ is a constant})$$

$$f(A) = \beta A^2 \quad (\text{radian}). \tag{3.2.9.1}$$

Thus,

$$g(A) e^{jf(A)} = g_0 A e^{j\beta A^2}. \tag{3.2.9.2}$$

Usually, in large backoff areas, the value of βA^2 (radian) is small and therefore,

$$g(A) e^{jf(A)} \simeq g_0 A(1 + j\beta A^2)$$

$$= g_0 A + j g_0 \beta A^3. \tag{3.2.9.3}$$

In this case, considering the third order intermodulation product is enough, since the higher order intermodulation products are much smaller. The result of Equation 3.2.1.9 can be used now directly with the coefficients α_m, i.e.,

$$\alpha_0 = g_0$$

$$\alpha_1 = j g_0 \beta$$

$$\alpha_m = 0 \quad (m \geqslant 2). \tag{3.2.9.4}$$

For simplicity's sake, it is assumed here that all the signal amplitudes are the same ($A_1 = A_2 = A_3, \ldots, = A_n$). Thus, the coefficients e_q's of Equation 3.2.1.7 are given, from Equation 3.2.1.7, by

(i) $k_1 = 1$, $k_2 = 1$, $k_3 = -1$, all the others zero:

$$-[J_1(A\gamma)]^3 [J_0(A\gamma)]^{n-3} = \sum_{q=1}^{\infty} e_q \gamma^{2q-1}. \tag{3.2.9.5}$$

(ii) $k_1 = 2$, $k_2 = -1$, all the others zero:

$$-[J_2(A\gamma) J_1(A\gamma)][J_0(A\gamma)]^{n-2} = \sum_{q=1}^{\infty} e_q \gamma^{2q-1}. \tag{3.2.9.6}$$

From Equations 3.2.9.4 and 3.2.1.9, it is clear that only e_1 and e_2 have to be evaluated.

(i) $e_1 = 0$:

$$e_2 = -\frac{1}{8} A^3. \tag{3.2.9.7}$$

(ii) $e_1 = 0$:

$$e_2 = -\frac{1}{16} A^3. \tag{3.2.9.8}$$

Thus,

(i) $$M(1, 1, -1, 0, \ldots, 0) = j2 g_0 \beta A^3. \tag{3.2.9.9}$$

All the other cases give the same results for this type.

(ii) $$M(2, 1, -0, 0, \ldots, 0) = jg_0\beta A^3.$$ (3.2.9.10)

All the other cases give the same results for this type. (*Note:* Type (i) is 6 dB larger than Type (ii).)

Based on the above results, for two equal amplitude carrier cases ($n = 2$), C/I (single signal power versus single intermodulation power) (no type (i) in this case) at the output, is given by

$$(\text{C/I}) = \left| \frac{M(1,0;A,A)}{M(2,-1;A,A)} \right|^2 \simeq \left| \frac{g_0 A}{j g_0 \beta A^3} \right|^2 = \frac{1}{(\beta A^2)^2}$$

$$= \frac{1}{[f(A)]^2} = \frac{1}{[F(X_A)]^2} \times \left(\frac{180}{\pi} \right)^2$$ (3.2.9.11)

where $F(X_A)$ is the single carrier phase given in degree and X_A is the input backoff of a carrier in dB. Thus,

$$(\text{C/I}) \ (\text{dB}) = 35.168 \ \text{dB} - 20 \log_{10}(F(X_A)).$$ (3.2.9.12)

For three equal amplitude cases ($A_1 = A_2 = A_3$) ($n = 3$) and spaced at equal frequency (e.g., $\omega_2 - \omega_1 = \omega_3 - \omega_2$), the signal power at the center frequency ($\omega_0 + \omega_2$) versus the intermodulation power falling on the frequency ($\omega_0 + \omega_2$), (C/I) is given by

$$(\text{C/I}) = \left| \frac{g_0 A}{2 j g_0 \beta A^3} \right|^2 = \frac{1}{(2\beta A^2)^2} = \left| \frac{M(1,0,0;A,A,A)}{M(1,1,-1;A,A,A)} \right|^2$$

$$= \frac{1}{4} \left[\frac{1}{F(X_A)} \right]^2 \times \left(\frac{180}{\pi} \right)^2,$$ (3.2.9.13)

i.e.,

$$(\text{C/I}) \ (\text{dB}) = 29.16 \ \text{dB} - 20 \log_{10}[F(X_A)]$$ (3.2.9.14)

where $F(X_A)$ is the single carrier phase given in degrees and X_A is the input backoff of a carrier in dB. Since the total input power for two carrier and three carrier cases is $2A^2/2$ and $3A^2/2$ respectively, Equation 3.2.9.11 becomes

$$(\text{C/I}) = \frac{1}{(\beta P_i)^2}.$$ (3.2.9.15)

Equation 3.2.9.13 becomes

$$(\text{C/I}) = \frac{9}{16} \frac{1}{(\beta P_i)^2}.$$ (3.2.9.16)

This result shows that the value of (C/I) for a three carrier case is 2.5 dB worse than for a two carrier case if the total input power (backoff) is equal in both cases. Note here that there is only one intermodulation product falling on $\omega_0 + \omega_2$ (center frequency) in this case. Since obtaining the number of the intermodulation products falling on the center frequency in general is tedious (even if one assumes that the levels and the frequency spacings are equal), the case with a great number of carriers is analyzed as follows. Substituting Equation 3.2.9.3 for Equation 3.2.6.26, the signal output power spectrum of this case is given by

$$W_N(f - f_0) \left| \frac{1}{2\sigma} \int_0^\infty \rho^2 e^{-\frac{\rho^2}{2}} \{g_0 \sigma \rho + jg_0 \beta \sigma^3 \rho^3\} d\rho \right|^2$$

$$\simeq W_N(f - f_0) \left| \frac{g_0}{2\sigma} \int_0^\infty \sigma \rho^3 e^{-\frac{\rho^2}{2}} d\rho \right|^2$$

$$= g_0^2 W_N(f - f_0). \tag{3.2.9.17}$$

The third order intermodulation product power spectrum of this case is, from Equation 6.2.6.29,

$$\frac{1}{8} W_N(f) \circledast W_N(f) \circledast W_N(-f) \times 64 g_0^2 \beta^2$$

$$= 8 g_0^2 \beta^2 W_N(f) \circledast W_N(f) \circledast W_N(-f). \tag{3.2.9.18}$$

Since it is assumed that all the carriers have equal power levels, the output carrier power at the center frequency is

$$g_0^2 \frac{P_i}{n} \tag{3.2.9.19}$$

and the intermodulation power of all the components falling at the center frequency is given by

$$8 g_0^2 \beta^2 \times \frac{3}{4} P_i^3 \frac{1}{n}. \tag{3.2.9.20}$$

Therefore,

$$\left(\frac{C}{I}\right) = \frac{g_0^2 \dfrac{P_i}{n}}{6 g_0^2 (\beta P_i)^2 \dfrac{P_i}{n}} = \frac{1}{6(\beta P_i)^2}. \tag{3.2.9.21}$$

Comparing the result with Equation 3.2.9.15, it can be said that (C/I) of many equal power and equal frequency spacing carrier case levels is 6 times worse (7.78 dB) than a carrier case with 2 equal power levels. As seen from Figure 3.2.9.1, the (C/I) values at the band center frequency become worse and worse

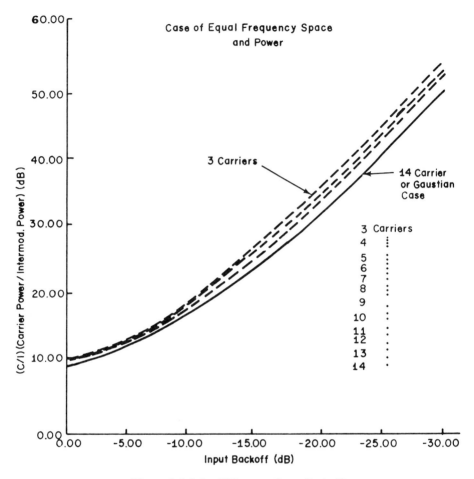

Figure 3.2.9.1   (C/I) versus Input Backoff

when the number of carriers increases in large backoff areas and converges into the limiting values in cases where there is a great number of carriers (Gaussian input case). In small backoff areas, the (C/I) values become almost independent from the number of carriers.

3.2.10   Coherent Intermodulation Products and FM Demodulation

In the previous sections, the time domain representations and autocorrelation functions (the Fourier-transforms give the power spectra) of the intermodulation products and signal components for various nonlinear devices, are shown. Since some intermodulation products and signals are coherent with one another, the evaluation of the effects of the intermodulation on FM signals demodulation leads to errors if the power spectrum of the intermodulation products only is used where the coherency is lost. Therefore, as an illustration of typical cases, a three carrier case and a carrier with a Gaussian signal case are analyzed for simplicity's sake. Precautions in dealing with general cases will be discussed.

3.2.10.1 Three Carrier Case

Consider the case of $n = 3$ in Equation 3.1.24.
  The input to the nonlinear device is

$$e_i(t) = \sum_{k=1}^{3} A_k \, e^{j(\omega_0 + \omega_k)t + j\phi_k(t)}. \qquad (3.2.10.1.1)$$

Let us take the intermodulation products ($k_1 = 1$, $k_2 = 1$, $k_3 = -1$) and ($k_1 = 1$, $k_2 = -1$, $k_3 = 1$), i.e.,

$$M(1, 1, -1; A_1, A_2, A_3) \, e^{j(\omega_0 + \omega_1 + \omega_2 - \omega_3)t + j\phi_1 + j\phi_2 - j\phi_3}$$

and

$$M(1, -1, 1; A_1, A_2, A_3) \, e^{j(\omega_0 + \omega_1 - \omega_2 + \omega_3)t + j\phi_1 - j\phi_2 + j\phi_3} \qquad (3.2.10.1.2)$$

where

$$M(1, 1, -1; A_1, A_2, A_3)$$

$$= M(1, -1, 1; A_1, A_2, A_3)$$

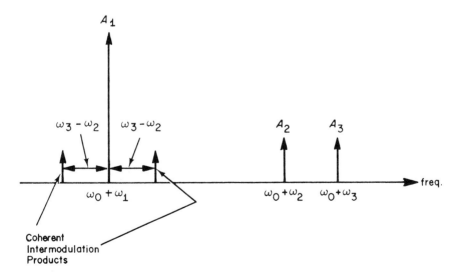

Figure 3.2.10.1.1   Three Carrier Coherent Intermodulation Model

$$= -\int_0^\infty \int_0^\infty \gamma J_1(A_1\gamma)J_1(A_2\gamma)J_1(A_3\gamma)J_1(\gamma\rho)\rho g(\rho)\, e^{jf(\rho)}\, d\rho\, d\gamma$$

$$(3.2.10.1.3)$$

where

$$J_{-1}(\tau) = -J_1(\tau) \tag{3.2.10.1.4}$$

is used.

The two intermodulation products considered above are located at the frequencies $\omega_0 + \omega_1 \pm \Delta\omega$ ($\Delta\omega = \omega_3 - \omega_2$) and it is assumed that these intermodulation products fall in the signal band of the A_1 carrier as seen from Figure 3.2.10.1.1. From Equation 3.2.10.1.3, the complex amplitudes of these intermodulations are in the same level and same phase. Therefore, represent them by M_3 as

$$M_3 = M(1, 1, -1; A_1, A_2, A_3)$$

$$= M(1, -1, 1; A_1, A_2, A_3). \tag{3.2.10.1.5}$$

Then, the total of the signal A_1 plus these intermodulations becomes

$$M_1 e^{j(\omega_0 + \omega_1)t + j\phi_1}$$

$$+ M_3 e^{j(\omega_0 + \omega_1 + \omega_2 - \omega_3)t + j(\phi_1 + \phi_2 - \phi_3)}$$

$$+ M_3 e^{j(\omega_0 + \omega_1 - \omega_2 + \omega_3)t + j(\phi_1 - \phi_2 + \phi_3)} \tag{3.2.10.1.6}$$

where

$$M(1, 0, 0; A_1, A_2, A_3)$$

$$= \int_0^\infty \int_0^\infty \gamma J_1(A_1\gamma)J_0(A_2\gamma)J_0(A_3\gamma)J_1(\gamma\rho)\rho g(\rho)e^{jf(\rho)}\, d\gamma\, d\rho = M_1.$$

$$(3.2.10.1.7)$$

To consider the demodulation of the A_1 carrier with these intermodulations, rewrite Equation 3.2.10.1.6 as

$$M_1 e^{j(\omega_0 + \omega_1)t + j\phi_1} \left[1 + \frac{M_3}{M_1} e^{-j\Delta\omega t - j(\phi_3 - \phi_2)} + \frac{M_3}{M_1} e^{j\Delta\omega t + j(\phi_3 - \phi_2)} \right]$$

$$= M_1 B(t)\, \exp[j(\omega_0 + \omega_1)t + j\phi_1 + j\theta(t)] \tag{3.2.10.1.8}$$

where

$$B(t) = \left| 1 + 2\frac{M_3}{M_1}\cos(\Delta\omega t + \phi_3 - \phi_2) \right|,$$

$$\theta(t) = \text{Im}\left\{\log\left[1 + \frac{2M_3}{M_1}\cos(\Delta\omega t + \phi_3 - \phi_2)\right]\right\}. \qquad (3.2.10.1.9)$$

After the hardlimiter of the FM receiver, $B(t)$ becomes a constant and since $|M_3/M_1| \ll 1$ in normal operating conditions,

$$\theta(t) \simeq \left\{\text{Im}\left[2\left(\frac{M_3}{M_1}\right)\right]\right\}\cos(\Delta\omega_3 t + \phi_3 - \phi_2). \qquad (3.2.10.1.10)$$

Therefore, the demodulated intermodulation products are given by

$$\frac{1}{2\pi}\frac{d}{dt}\theta(t) \simeq \frac{1}{2\pi}\frac{d}{dt}\left[\left\{\text{Im}\left[2\frac{M_3}{M_1}\right]\right\}\cos(\Delta\omega t + \phi_3 - \phi_2)\right]. \qquad (3.2.10.1.11)$$

The power spectrum of this component is given by

$$\left[\text{Im}\left(\frac{M_3}{M_1}\right)^2\right]f^2\{[W_2(x) \circledast W_3(x)]_{x=f-\Delta f} + [W_2(x) \circledast W_3(x)]_{x=f+\Delta f}\}.$$

$$(3.2.10.1.12)$$

where $-\infty < f < \infty$, $W_2(f)$ and $W_3(f)$ are respectively the power spectra of the A_2 and A_3 carriers whose center frequencies are shifted to zero and whose total powers are normalized to unity. If the above coherences are not considered in the FM demodulation, the power spectrum of the demodulated intermodulation products is quite different from Equation 3.2.10.1.12. The power spectrum of the intermodulation products given by Equation 3.2.10.1.2 (both added), is

$$\frac{1}{2}|M_3|^2[W_1(x) \circledast W_2(x) \circledast W_3(x)]_{x=f-f_0-f_1-\Delta f}$$

$$+ \frac{1}{2}|M_3|^2 [W_1(x) \circledast W_2(x) \circledast W_3(x)]_{x=f-f_0-f_1+\Delta f} \qquad (0 < f)$$

$$(3.2.10.1.13)$$

where $W_3(f)$ is the power spectrum of the A_3 carrier whose center is shifted to zero and whose power is normalized to unity. Considering Equation 3.2.10.1.12 as the power spectrum of the interferences to the signal (A_1 carrier), the demodulated interference power spectrum is given by

$$\frac{1}{2}\left|\frac{M_3}{M_1}\right|^2 \{[W_1(x) \circledast W_2(x) \circledast W_3(x) \circledast W_3(f)]_{x=f+\Delta f}$$

$$+ [W_1(x) \circledast W_2(x) \circledast W_3(x) \circledast W_3(f)]_{x=f-\Delta f}\} \qquad (-\infty < f < \infty).$$

$$(3.2.10.1.14)$$

The difference between the correct result in Equation 3.2.10.1.12 and the incorrect one in Equation 3.2.10.1.14 is very clear.

3.2.10.2   Large FM Carrier and Many Small Carriers

This case corresponds from a practical point of view to a large FM carrier (FDM/FM or FM/TV) plus many SCPC carrier cases. As explained in Figure 3.2.8.1, only the inband intermodulation products will be analyzed (i.e., $k_1 = 1$, $k_2 = 0$, $k_3 = 0$ and $k_1 = 0$, $k_2 = 0$, $k_3 = 1$ with $A_2 = 0$ in Section 3.2.8). In this case, the input to the transponder is

$$e_i(t) = A_1 e^{j(\omega_0 + \omega_1)t + j\phi_1(t)} + N(t) e^{j\omega_0 t}. \qquad (3.2.10.2.1)$$

Then, the output is

$$e_0(t) = \sum_{k_1 = -\infty}^{\infty} M(k_1, 1 - k_1; A_1, |N|) e^{j(\omega_0 + k_1\omega_1)t + jk_1\phi_1 + j(1 - k_1)\tan^{-1}\frac{N_s}{N_c}}$$

$$(3.2.10.2.2)$$

where

$$M(k_1, 1 - k_1; A_1, |N|)$$

$$= \int_0^\infty \int_0^\infty \gamma J_{k_1}(A_1\gamma)\, J_{1-k_1}(\sqrt{N_C^2 + N_S^2}\,\gamma)J_1(\gamma\rho)\rho g(\rho)e^{jf(\rho)}\, d\rho.$$

$$(3.2.10.2.3)$$

From Equation 3.2.8.8, the pure signal component of the large FM carrier is

$$M_S e^{j(\omega_0 + \omega_1)t + j\phi_1(t)} \qquad (3.2.10.2.4)$$

where M_S is

$$M_S = e^{-\frac{A_1^2}{2\sigma^2}} \int_0^\infty e^{-\frac{\rho^2}{2}} I_1\left(\frac{A_1}{\sigma\rho}\right) \rho g(\sigma\rho)e^{jf(\sigma\rho)}\, d\rho. \qquad (3.2.10.2.5)$$

Thus, $e_0(t)$ for e_i of Equation 3.2.10.2.1 (only the components of $k_1 = 1$ and $k_2 = 0$) can be represented as

$$M_S e^{j(\omega_0 + \omega_1)t + j\phi_1(t)} + [M(1, 0; A_1, |N|) - M_S]\, e^{j(\omega_0 + \omega_1)t + j\phi_1(t)}$$

$$= B(t)M_S e^{j(\omega_0 + \omega_1)t + j\phi_1(t) + j\theta(t)} \qquad (3.2.10.2.6)$$

where, in a way similar to Section 3.2.10.1,

$$\theta(t) \simeq \mathrm{Im}\left\{\frac{M(1, 0; A_1, |N|) - M_S}{M_S}\right\}$$

$$= \mathrm{Im}\left\{\frac{M(1, 0; A_1, |N|)}{M_S}\right\}. \qquad (3.2.10.2.7)$$

The autocorrelation function of this $\theta(t)$ is given by

$$E\{\theta(t)\theta(t+\tau)\} = \mathop{E}_{N}\left[\mathrm{Im}\left\{\frac{M(1,0;A_1,|N(t)|)}{M_S}\right\}\mathrm{Im}\left\{\frac{M(1,0;A_1,|N(t+\tau)|)}{M_S}\right\}\right]$$

$$= \frac{1}{2}\mathop{E}_{N}\left[\mathrm{Re}\left\{\frac{M(1,0;A_1,|N(t)|)\,M(1,0;A_1,|N(t+\tau)|)^*}{|M_S|^2}\right\}\right.$$

$$\left. - \frac{1}{2}\mathrm{Re}\left\{\frac{M(1,0;A_1,|N(t)|)\,M(1,0;A_1,|N(t+\tau)|)}{M_S^2}\right\}\right].$$

$$(3.2.10.2.8)$$

Using the formula from Equation 3.2.6.17,

$$\mathop{E}_{N}\{M(1,0;A_1,|N(t)|)\,M(1,0;A_1,|N(t+\tau)|)^*\}$$

$$= \int_0^\infty \int_0^\infty \int_0^\infty \int_0^\infty \gamma_1\gamma_2 J_1(A_1\gamma)\,J_1(A_1\gamma_2)\,J_1(\rho_1\gamma_1)\,J_1(\rho_2\gamma_2)\,\rho_1\rho_2$$

$$\cdot g(\rho_1)g(\rho_2)e^{jf(\rho_1)}e^{-jf(\rho_2)}e^{-\frac{R(0)}{2}(\gamma_1^2+\gamma_2^2)}$$

$$\cdot I_0(R(\tau)\gamma_1\gamma_2)\,d\gamma_1\,d\gamma_2\,d\rho_1\,d\rho_2.$$

$$(3.2.10.2.9)$$

The second term of Equation 3.2.10.2.8 is given by replacing $e^{-jf(\rho_2)}$ by $e^{jf(\rho_2)}$ in this result. Thus, an average $\{\theta(t)\theta(t+\tau)\}$ becomes

$$\mathop{E}_{N}\{\theta(t)\theta(t+\tau)\} = \int_0^\infty \int_0^\infty \int_0^\infty \int_0^\infty \gamma_1\gamma_2$$

$$\cdot J_1(A_1\gamma_1)J_1(A_1\gamma_2)J_1(\rho_1\gamma_1)J_1(\rho_2\gamma_2)\rho_1\rho_2 g(\rho_1)g(\rho_2)$$

$$\cdot e^{-\frac{R(0)}{2}(\gamma_1^2+\gamma_2^2)}I_0(R(\tau)\gamma_1\gamma_2)\left[\mathrm{Im}\left\{\frac{e^{jf(\rho_1)}}{M_S}\right\}\right]$$

$$\cdot \left[\mathrm{Im}\left\{\frac{e^{jf(\rho_2)}}{M_S}\right\}\right]d\gamma_1\,d\gamma_2\,d\rho_1\,d\rho_2.$$

$$(3.2.10.2.10)$$

Expanding $I_0(R(\tau)\gamma_1\gamma_2)$ by a power series,

$$E\{\theta(t)\theta(t+\tau)\} = \sum_{m=0}^{\infty}(2^m m!)^{-2}[R(\tau)]^{2m}$$

$$\cdot \left[\int_0^\infty \int_0^\infty \gamma^{2m+1}J_1(A_1\gamma)J_1(\gamma\rho)e^{-\frac{R(0)}{2}\gamma^2}\rho g(\rho)\right.$$

$$\cdot \, \mathrm{Im} \left\{ \frac{e^{jf(\rho)}}{M_S} \right\} d\gamma \, d\rho \right]^2 \tag{3.2.10.2.11}$$

where the term of $m = 0$, i.e.,

$$\left[e^{-\frac{A_1^2}{2\sigma^2}} \int_0^\infty \rho e^{-\frac{\rho^2}{2}} I_1 \left(\frac{A_1}{\sigma} \rho \right) g(\sigma \rho) \, \mathrm{Im} \left\{ \frac{e^{jf(\sigma \rho)}}{M_S} \right\} d\rho \right]^2 \tag{3.2.10.2.12}$$

is the direct current component.

The formula of Equation 3.2.8.7 was used to obtain the integral of γ for $m = 0$ in Equation 3.2.10.2.11. The term from Equation 3.2.10.2.11 of $m = 1$ gives the third order intermodulation product of the inband for the A_1 carrier. Using the same formula as that of Equation 3.2.8.21 (for $m = 1$), this inband third order intermodulation product is

$$\frac{1}{4} \left[e^{-\frac{A_1^2}{2\sigma^2}} \int_0^\infty \rho \left[\left(\frac{A_1}{\sigma} \rho \right) I_0 \left(\frac{A_1}{\sigma} \rho \right) + \left\{ 2 - \rho^2 - \left(\frac{A_1}{\sigma} \right)^2 \right\} \right. \right.$$

$$\left. \cdot I_1 \left(\frac{A_1}{\sigma} \rho \right) + \left(\frac{A_1}{\sigma} \rho \right) I_2 \left(\frac{A_1}{\sigma} \rho \right) \right] e^{-\frac{\rho^2}{2}}$$

$$\left. \cdot g(\sigma \rho) \, \mathrm{Im} \left\{ \frac{e^{jf(\sigma \rho)}}{M} \right\} d\rho \right]^2 \left[\frac{R(\tau)}{R(0)} \right]^2 . \tag{3.2.10.2.13}$$

The Fourier transform of this result gives the power spectrum of this intermodulation, where the Fourier transform of $\{R(\tau)\}^2$ is $W_N(t) \circledast W_N(-f)$ and the other factors are constants (see the definition of $W_N(f)$ just below Equation 3.2.6.12). If $g(\rho)e^{jf(\rho)}$ is expanded by a Bessel expansion (Equation 3.2.2.1), the fourth-fold integral of Equation 3.2.10.2.10 can be simply done as in Equation 3.2.8.28, i.e.,

$$E\{\theta(t)\theta(t+\tau)\} = \sum_{s_1=1}^{L} \sum_{s_2=1}^{L} \mathrm{Im} \left\{ \frac{b_{s_1}}{M} \right\} \mathrm{Im} \left\{ \frac{b_{s_2}}{M} \right\} e^{-\frac{R(0)}{2}(s_1^2 + s_2^2)\alpha^2}$$

$$\cdot J_1(A_1 \alpha s_1) J_1(A_1 \alpha s_2) I_0(R(\tau)\alpha^2 s_1 s_2). \tag{3.2.10.2.14}$$

As seen from the analysis done in this section (or as in Section 3.2.10.1)), the coherences of the signals and intermodulation products must be considered in the analysis of the demodulation. Otherwise, the analysis becomes misleading. In the next section, the precautions for treating this problem will be discussed in general cases.

3.2.10.3   General Coherent Intermodulation and FM Demodulation

In Sections 3.2.10.1 and 3.2.10.2, two special cases were analyzed to show the importance of the coherent intermodulation products. In order to analyze general cases, let us go back to Equations 3.1.24 and 3.1.39. In Equation 3.1.39,

$$M(1, 0, 0, \ldots, 0)e^{j(\omega_0 + \omega_1)t} e^{j\phi_1(t)} = M_s e^{j(\omega_0 + \omega_1)t + j\phi_1(t)} \quad (3.2.10.3.1)$$

is assumed to be an FM signal at the output of the nonlinear device. Now, Equation 3.1.39 can be rewritten as

$$M_s e^{j(\omega_0 + \omega_1)t + j\phi_1(t)}$$

$$+ \sum_{k_1 = -\infty}^{\infty} \sum_{k_2 = -\infty}^{\infty} \cdots \sum_{k_n = -\infty}^{\infty}{}'$$

$$(k_1 + k_2 + \cdots + k_n = 1)$$

$$\cdot M(k_1, k_2, \ldots, k_n; A_1, A_2, \ldots, A_n)$$

$$\cdot e^{j(\omega_0 + k_1\omega_1 + \cdots + k_n\omega_n)t + j(k_1\phi_1 + k_2\phi_2 + \cdots + k_n\phi_n)}$$

$$= M_s e^{j(\omega_0 + \omega_1)t + j\phi_1(t)} \left[1 + \frac{1}{M_s} \sum_{k_1 = -\infty}^{\infty} \cdots \sum_{k_n = -\infty}^{\infty}{}' \right.$$

$$(k_1 + k_2 + \cdots + k_n = 1)$$

$$\cdot M(k_1, k_2, \ldots, k_n; A_1, A_2, \ldots, A_n)e^{j(k_1 - 1)(\omega_1 t + j\phi_1)}$$

$$\left. \cdot \prod_{p=2}^{n} e^{jk_p\omega_p t + jk_p\phi_p} \right] = M_s B(t) e^{j(\omega_0 + \omega_1)t + j\phi_1} \quad (3.2.10.3.2)$$

where " $'$ " in the summations means "to exclude the component of M_s." In a way similar to Sections 3.2.10.1 and 3.2.10.2, $\theta(t)$ can be approximated as

$$\theta(t) \simeq \text{Im}\left\{ \frac{1}{M_s} \sum_{k_1 = -\infty}^{\infty} \cdots \sum_{k_n = -\infty}^{\infty}{}' M(k_1, k_2, \ldots, k_n; A_1, \ldots, A_n) \right.$$

$$(k_1 + k_2 + \cdots + k_n = 1)$$

$$\left. \cdot e^{j(k_1 - 1)\omega_1 t + j(k_1 - 1)\phi_1} \prod_{p=2}^{\infty} e^{jk_p\omega_p t + jk_p\phi_p} \right\} \cdot \quad (3.2.10.3.3)$$

Since the demodulated intermodulation products are $1/2\pi \, d/dt \, \theta(t)$, the power spectrum of the demodulated intermodulation products is the power spectrum of

$\theta(t)$ multiplied by f^2. In order to obtain the power spectrum of $\theta(t)$, the autocorrelation function of $\theta(t)$ must be obtained, i.e.,

$$\frac{1}{2} \operatorname{Re} E \left\{ \frac{1}{|M_s|^2} \sum_{k_1 = -\infty}^{\infty} \cdots \sum_{k_n = -\infty}^{\infty}{}' \sum_{\ell_1 = -\infty}^{\infty} \cdots \sum_{\ell_n = -\infty}^{\infty}{}' \right.$$

$$(k_1 + \cdots + k_n = 1) \quad (\ell_1 + \cdots + \ell_2 = 1)$$

$$\cdot \, M(k_1, \ldots, k_n; A_1, \ldots, A_n) \, M(\ell_1, \ldots, \ell_n; A_1, \ldots, A_n)^*$$

$$\cdot \, e^{j(k_1 - 1)\omega_1 t - j(\ell_1 - 1)\omega_1 (t + \tau)} \, e^{j(k_1 - 1)\phi_1(t) - j(\ell_1 - 1)\phi_1(t + \tau)}$$

$$\cdot \, \prod_{p_1 = 2}^{n} e^{jk_{p_1} t + \phi_{p_1}(t))} \, \prod_{p_2 = 2}^{n} e^{-j\ell_{p_2} (\omega_{p_2}(t + \tau) + \phi_{p_2}(t + \tau))} \left. \right\}$$

$$- \frac{1}{2} \operatorname{Re} E \left\{ \frac{1}{M_s^2} \sum_{k_1 = -\infty}^{\infty} \cdots \sum_{k_n = -\infty}^{\infty}{}' \sum_{\ell_1 = -\infty}^{\infty} \cdots \sum_{\ell_n = -\infty}^{\infty}{}' \, e^{j(k_1 - 1)\omega_1 t + j(\ell_1 - 1)\omega_1(t + \tau)} \right.$$

$$(k_1 + \cdots + k_n = 1) \quad (\ell_1 + \cdots + \ell_n = 1)$$

$$\cdot \, e^{j(k_1 - 1)\phi_1(t) + j(\ell_1 - 1)\phi_1(t + \tau)} \, M(k_1, k_2, \ldots, k_n; A_1, A_2, \ldots, A_n)$$

$$\cdot \, M(\ell_1, \ldots, \ell_n; A_1, \ldots, A_n) \, \prod_{p_1 = 2}^{n} e^{jk_{p_1}(\omega_{p_1} t + \phi_{p_1}(t))}$$

$$\cdot \, \prod_{p_2 = 2}^{\infty} e^{j\ell_{p_2}(\omega_{p_2}(t + \tau) + \phi_{p_2}(t + \tau))}. \tag{3.2.10.3.4}$$

In order for each component of the first term not to be zero,

$$k_{p_1} = \ell_{p_2}$$

$$p_1 = p_2. \tag{3.2.10.3.5}$$

Also, for the second term,

$$k_{p_1} = -\ell_{p_2} \quad (\text{but } \ell_1 + k_1 = 2)$$

$$p_1 = p_2. \tag{3.2.3.10.3.6}$$

Equation 3.2.10.3.4 becomes

$$\operatorname{Re} \frac{1}{2} E \left\{ \frac{1}{|M_s|^2} \sum_{k_1 = -\infty}^{\infty} \cdots \sum_{k_n = -\infty}^{\infty}{}' \, |M(k_1, \ldots, k_n; A_1, \ldots, A_n)|^2 \right.$$

$$\cdot \, e^{-j(k_1 - 1)\omega_1 \tau} \, e^{j(k_1 - 1)\{\phi_1(t) - \phi_1(t + \tau)\}} \, \prod_{p = 2}^{n} e^{-jk_p \omega_p \tau} \, e^{jk_p\{\phi_p(t) - j\phi_p(t + \tau)\}} \left. \right\}$$

$$-\frac{1}{2}\operatorname{Re} E\left\{\frac{1}{M_s^2}\sum_{k_1=-\infty}^{\infty}\cdots\sum_{k_n=-\infty}^{\infty}{}' e^{-j(k_1-1)\omega_1\tau}\,e^{j(k_1-1)(\phi_1(t)-\phi_1(t+\tau))}\right.$$

$$\prod_{p=2}^{n} e^{-jk_p\omega_p\tau}\,e^{jk_p\{\Phi_{p(t)}-j\Phi_{p(t+\tau)}\}}$$

$$\cdot M(k_1,k_2,\ldots,k_n;A_1,A_2,\ldots,A_n)$$

$$M(2-k_1,-k_1,\ldots,-k_n;A_1,A_2,\ldots,A_n). \tag{3.2.10.3.7}$$

Since all the ϕ_k's are interdependent in most practical cases,

$$E\{\theta(t)\theta(t+\tau)\} \simeq \frac{1}{2}\operatorname{Re}\left\{\sum_{k_1=-\infty}^{\infty}\cdots\sum_{k_n=-\infty}^{\infty} e^{-j(k_1-1)\omega_1\tau}\right.$$

$$\cdot \prod_{p=2}^{n} e^{-jk_p\omega_p\tau} E\{e^{j(k_1-1)(\phi_1(t)-\phi_1(t+\tau))}\}\right\}$$

$$\cdot E\left\{\prod_{p=2}^{n} e^{jk_p[\phi_p(t)-\phi_p(t+\tau)]}\left[\left|\frac{M(k_1,\ldots,k_n;A_1,\ldots,A_n)}{M_s}\right|^2-\right.\right.$$

$$M(k_1,k_2,\ldots,k_n;A_1,\ldots,A_n)$$

$$\cdot\left.\left.\left.\frac{M(2-k_1,-k_2,\ldots,-k_n;A_1,\ldots,A_n)}{M_s^2}\right]\right\}\right\}. \tag{3.2.10.3.8}$$

The case of Section 3.2.10.2 is a special case of this result, where $n=3$ and the components ($k_1=1$, $k_2=1$ and $k_3=-1$) and ($k_1=1$, $k_2=-1$ and $k_3=1$) are only considered in the summation Σ'. In the computation of the demodulation intermodulation product power spectrum, the averages in Equation 3.2.10.3.8 must be done first, where if $\phi_p(t)$ is a Gaussian process as in FDM/FM cases,

$$E_\phi\{e^{jk[\phi(t)-\phi(t+\tau)]}\} = e^{-k^2[R_\phi(0)-R_\phi(0)]} \tag{3.2.10.3.9}$$

$R_\phi(\tau)$ is the autocorrelation function of $\phi(t)$. Then, the Fourier-transform of Equation 3.2.10.3.8 with respect to τ gives the power spectrum to be obtained, where the Fourier-transform of Equation 3.2.10.3.9 is the power spectrum of the FM signal

$$\sqrt{2}\,\sin(\omega_0 t + k\phi(t)) \tag{3.2.10.3.10}$$

whose total power is unity.

3.2.11 Effects of a Large Carrier on Small Carriers

When a large carrier and a number of small carriers pass together through a nonlinear device, the small carriers are very much affected in their phases and amplitudes by the large carrier, while the large ones receive only very small effects. This type of cases happens very commonly in practice and it is important to evaluate this effect precisely. The case of a large carrier and a small carrier will be discussed first.

3.2.11.1 Two Carrier Case

The case of $n = 2$ in Equation 3.1.24 is analyzed here under the condition that

$$A_1 \gg A_2. \tag{3.2.11.1.1}$$

Then, the smaller component is given by

$$M(0, 1; A_1, A_2) e^{j(\omega_0 + \omega_2)t + j\phi_2(t)} = M_{A_2} e^{j(\omega_0 + \omega_2)t + j\phi_2(t)} \tag{3.2.11.1.2}$$

where

$$M_{A_2} = M(0, 1; A_1, A_2). \tag{3.2.11.1.3}$$

Let us use the result of Equation 3.2.7.7

$$M_{A_2} = \frac{1}{\pi A_2} \int_{A_1 - A_2}^{A_1 + A_2} \cos^{-1}\left[\frac{A_1^2 - A_2^2 + \rho^2}{2A_1\rho}\right] \left[\frac{d}{d\rho}\{\rho g(\rho)\, e^{jf(\rho)}\}\right] d\rho.$$

$$\tag{3.2.11.1.4}$$

Because of the condition of Equation 3.2.11.1.1, $d/d\rho\{\rho g(\rho)e^{jf(\rho)}\}$ does not change much within $\rho = A_1 \pm A_2$, and therefore,

$$M_{A_2} \simeq \left[\frac{d}{d\rho}\{\rho g(\rho)e^{jf(\rho)}\}\right]_{\rho = A_1}$$

$$\cdot \frac{1}{\pi A_2} \int_{A_1 - A_2}^{A_1 + A_2} \cos^{-1}\left[\frac{A_1^2 - A_2^2 + \rho^2}{2A_1\rho}\right] d\rho \tag{3.2.11.1.5}$$

where

$$\frac{1}{\pi A_2} \int_{A_1 - A_2}^{A_1 + A_2} \cos^{-1}\left[\frac{A_1^2 - A_2^2 + \rho^2}{2A_1\rho}\right] d\rho$$

$$= \left[\frac{\rho}{\pi A_2} \cos^{-1}\left\{\frac{A_1^2 - A_2^2 + \rho^2}{2A_1\rho}\right\}\right]_{\rho = A_1 - A_2}^{\rho = A_1 + A_2}$$

$$- \frac{1}{\pi A_2} \int_{A_1 - A_2}^{A_1 + A_2} \rho \frac{d}{d\rho} \cos^{-1}\left\{\frac{A_1^2 - A_2^2 + \rho^2}{2A_1\rho}\right\} d\rho$$

$$= \frac{1}{\pi A_2} \int_{A_1 - A_2}^{A_1 + A_2} \frac{(\rho^2 - A_1^2 + A_2^2)}{\sqrt{(2A_1A_2)^2 - (\rho^2 - A_1^2 - A_2^2)^2}} d\rho. \tag{3.2.11.1.6}$$

Doing the variable conversion, $x = (\rho^2 - A_1^2 - A_2^2)/2A_1A_2$ and using the polar coordinate transformation for x, Equation 3.2.11.1.6 becomes

$$\frac{A_2}{\pi} \int_{-\frac{\pi}{2}}^{\frac{\pi}{2}} \frac{d\theta}{\sqrt{A_1^2 + A_2^2 + 2A_1A_2 \sin \theta}} d\theta$$

$$+ \frac{A_1}{\pi} \int_{-\frac{\pi}{2}}^{\frac{\pi}{2}} \frac{\sin \theta}{\sqrt{A_1^2 + A_2^2 + 2A_1A_2 \sin \theta}} d\theta \qquad (3.2.11.1.7)$$

where

$$\frac{1}{\sqrt{A_1^2 + A_2^2 + 2A_1A_2 \sin \theta}} = \frac{1}{A_1} \frac{1}{\sqrt{1 + \left(\frac{A_2}{A_1}\right)^2 + 2\left(\frac{A_2}{A_1}\right) \sin \theta}}$$

$$\simeq \frac{1}{A_1} \left[1 - \left(\frac{A_2}{A_1}\right) \sin \theta\right] \cdot$$

$$(3.2.11.1.8)$$

Substituting this approximation into Equation 3.2.11.1.7, Equation 3.2.11.1.6 becomes

$$\frac{A_2}{A_1} \frac{1}{\pi} \int_{-\frac{\pi}{2}}^{\frac{\pi}{2}} \left[1 - \left(\frac{A_2}{A_1}\right) \sin \theta\right] d\theta$$

$$+ \frac{1}{\pi} \int_{-\frac{\pi}{2}}^{\frac{\pi}{2}} \left[1 - \left(\frac{A_2}{A_1}\right) \sin \theta\right] \sin \theta d\theta = \frac{1}{2}\left(\frac{A_2}{A_1}\right) \cdot \qquad (3.2.11.1.9)$$

Thus, from Equation 3.2.11.1.5,

$$M_{A_2} \simeq \left[\frac{d}{d\rho} \{\rho g(\rho)e^{jf(\rho)}\}\right]\left(\frac{A_2}{2A_1}\right) \qquad (\rho = A_1). \quad (3.2.11.1.10)$$

Using $F'(x_{A_1})$, $G(x_{A_1})'$ and β defined by Equation 2.1.3.5,

$$M_{A_2} \simeq g(A_1)e^{jf(A_1)} [\{1 + G(x_{A_1})'\} + j\beta F(x_{A_1})]\left(\frac{A_2}{2A_1}\right)$$

$$= A_2 \left[\frac{g(A_1)}{2A_1}\right] \sqrt{\{1 + G(x_{A_1})'\}^2 + \{\beta F(x_{A_1})'\}^2} \; e^{jf(A_1)}$$

$$\cdot e^{j \tan^{-1}\left\{\frac{\beta F(x_{A_1})'}{1 + G(x_{A_1})'}\right\}} \cdot \qquad (3.2.11.1.11)$$

An interesting thing to see here is that, if A_1 appears and disappears, the amplitude of the smaller carrier changes as follow:

$$g(A_2) \quad \Leftrightarrow \quad A_2 \left[\frac{g(A_1)}{2A_1} \right] \sqrt{\{1 + G(x_{A_1})'\}^2 + \{\beta F(x_{A_1})'\}^2}$$

(no A_1)   (with A_1)

(3.2.11.1.12)

and the phase changes as

$$f(A_2) \quad \Leftrightarrow \quad f(A_1) + \tan^{-1}\left\{ \frac{\beta F(x_{A_1})'}{1 + G(x_{A_1})'} \right\}$$

(no A_1)   (with A_1).

(3.2.11.1.13)

Two examples are:

(i) Ideal Hardlimiter Case:
    In this case $g(\rho) = g_0$, $f(\rho) = 0$, $G(x_A)' = 0$, and $F(x_{A_1})' = 0$, then,

$$g_0 \quad \Leftrightarrow \quad \frac{A_2}{2A_1} g_0$$

(no A_1)   (with A_1).

(3.2.11.1.14)

Thus, the amplitude decreases by 6 dB when the large carrier appears. In this case, the phase of the smaller carrier suffers no change (because of $f = 0$). In a practical hardlimiter case, there is some phase shift. In this case, $g(A_1) = g_0$, $f(A_1) \neq 0$, $G(x_{A_1})' = 0$, $F(x_{A_1})' \neq 0$. In this case,

$$g_0 \quad \Leftrightarrow \quad \frac{A_2}{2A_1} g_0 \sqrt{1 + \{\beta F(x_{A_1})'\}^2}$$

(no A_1)   (with A_1)

(3.2.11.1.15)

where the amplitude suppression is less than 6 dB because of the factor $\{\beta F(x_{A_1})\}^2$. The phase changes as

$$f(A_2) \quad \Leftrightarrow \quad f(A_1) + \tan^{-1}\{\beta F(x_{A_1})'\}$$

(no A_1)   (with A_1).

(3.2.11.1.16)

(ii) Large Backoff Case
    In this case

$$g(\rho) = g_0\rho, \quad f(A_1) = \theta_0 A_1^2 \text{ (radian)}.$$

(3.2.11.1.17)

The amplitude changes as

$$(g_0 A_2) \Leftrightarrow (g_0 A_2) \sqrt{1 + (\theta_0 A_1^2)^2}$$

$$\text{(no } A_1) \qquad\qquad \text{(with } A_1). \qquad (3.2.11.1.18)$$

In this, the amplitude increases when there is a larger carrier. The phase changes as

$$f(A_2) \Leftrightarrow f(A_1) + \tan^{-1}(\theta_0 A_1^2) \simeq 2\theta_0 A_1^2 = 2f(A_1) \quad (3.2.11.1.19)$$

where the value of $\theta_0 A_1^2$(radian) is small for large backoff areas and, therefore,

$$\tan^{-1}(\theta_0 A_1^2) \simeq \theta_0 A_1^2. \qquad (3.2.11.1.20)$$

For the readers' interest, M_{A_2} in this case, can be solved exactly as follows:

$$M_{A_2} = g_0 \int_0^\infty \int_0^\infty \gamma J_1(A_2\gamma) J_0(A_1\gamma) J_1(\rho\gamma) \rho^2 \, e^{j\theta_0 \rho^2} \, d\gamma \, d\rho$$

$$= -g_0 \int_0^\infty \gamma^2 \frac{1}{(2\theta_0)^2} J_1(A_2\gamma) J_0(A_1\gamma) \, e^{-j\frac{\gamma^2}{4\theta_0}} \, d\gamma$$

$$= (2\theta_0)^{-2} g_0 \frac{\partial}{\partial A_2} \int_0^\infty \gamma \, J_0(A_2\gamma) J_0(A_1\gamma) \, e^{-j\frac{\gamma^2}{4\theta_0}} \, d\gamma \qquad (3.2.11.1.21)$$

where the formula

$$\int_0^\infty J_1(\rho\gamma) \rho^2 \, e^{j\theta_0 \rho^2} \, d\rho = \frac{-\gamma}{(2\theta_0)^2} e^{-j\frac{\gamma^2}{4\theta_0}} \qquad (3.2.11.1.22)$$

was used to obtain Equation 3.2.11.1.21. Equation 3.2.11.1.21 can be further integrated out

$$M_{A_2} = (2\theta_0)^{-2} g_0 \frac{\partial}{\partial A_2} [(2\theta_0)(-j) J_0(2\theta_0 A_1 A_2) \, e^{j\theta_0(A_1^2 + A_2^2)}]$$

$$= g_0 \left[A_2 J_0(2\theta_0 A_1 A_2) + j A_1 J_1(2\theta_0 A_1 A_2) \right] e^{j\theta_0(A_1^2 + A_2^2)}. \qquad (3.2.11.1.23)$$

With the same reason as how Equation 3.2.11.1.20 is obtained, this can be approximated as

$$M_{A_2} \simeq g_0 [A_2 + j\theta_0 A_1^2 A_2] \, e^{j\theta_0(A_1^2 + A_2^2)} \qquad (3.2.11.1.24)$$

where

$$J_0(2\theta_0 A_1 A_2) \simeq 1, \; J_1(2\theta_0 A_1 A_2) \simeq \theta_0 A_1 A_2. \qquad (3.2.11.1.25)$$

Thus,

$$M_{A_2} \simeq (g_0 A_2) \sqrt{1 + (\theta_0 A_1^2)^2} \; e^{j\theta_0(A_1^2 + A_2^2)} \; e^{j\theta_0 A_1^2}$$

$$\simeq (g_0 A_2) \sqrt{1 + (\theta_0 A_1^2)^2} \; e^{j2\theta_0 A_1^2} \qquad (3.2.11.1.26)$$

where, from Equation 3.2.11.1.1, $2A_1^2 \gg A_2^2$, this result is the same as in Equation 3.2.11.1.19.

3.2.11.2 A Large Carrier and Many Small Carriers

In Equation 3.1.24, the power of the first carrier ($k = 1$) is assumed to be much larger than that of the total of the rest of the carrier power, i.e.,

$$\frac{A_1^2}{2} \gg \sigma^2 \left(= \sum_{k=2}^{n} \left(\frac{A_k^2}{2} \right) \right). \qquad (3.2.11.2.1)$$

Consider now one of the smaller carriers, say the A_ℓ carrier whose output signal component is given by

$$M(0, 0, \ldots, \overset{\ell\text{-th}}{1}, 0, \ldots, 0) \quad e^{j(\omega_0 + \omega_\ell)t + j\phi_\ell} \qquad (3.2.11.2.2)$$

where

$$M(0, 0, \ldots, 0, \overset{\ell\text{-th}}{1}, 0, \ldots, 0) = M_\ell$$

$$= \int_0^\infty \int_0^\infty \gamma J_1(A_\ell \gamma) \prod_{\substack{p=2 \\ (p \neq \ell)}}^{n} J_0(A_p \gamma) \rho g(\rho) e^{jf(\rho)}$$

$$\cdot J_1(\gamma\rho) J_0(A_1 \gamma) d\gamma \, d\rho \simeq \int_0^\infty \int_0^\infty \frac{A_\ell}{2} \gamma^2 e^{-\frac{\sigma^2}{2}\gamma^2} \rho g(\rho)$$

$$\cdot e^{jf(\rho)} J_1(\gamma\rho) J_0(A_1 \gamma) d\gamma \, d\rho \qquad (3.2.11.2.3)$$

where the approximation of Equation 3.2.5.7 was used to obtain the above result, whose validity is proved later in the same Section. Equation 3.2.11.2.3 can be written as

$$M_\ell = \frac{A_\ell}{2} \int_0^\infty \left\{ -\frac{d}{d\rho} \int_0^\infty \gamma J_0(A_1 \gamma) J_0(\gamma\rho) \gamma^2 \, e^{-\frac{\sigma^2}{2}\gamma^2} d\gamma \right\} \rho g(\rho)$$

$$e^{jf(\rho)} d\rho = -\frac{A_\ell}{2} \int_0^\infty \left[\frac{d}{d\rho} \left\{ \frac{1}{\sigma^2} e^{-\frac{(A_1^2 + \rho^2)}{2\sigma^2}} I_0 \left(\frac{A_1 \rho}{\sigma^2} \right) \right\} \right]$$

$$\int [\rho g(\rho) e^{jf(\rho)}] \, d\rho = \left[-\frac{A_\ell}{2\sigma^2} e^{-\frac{(A_1^2 + \rho^2)}{2\sigma^2}} I_0\left(\frac{A_1 \rho}{\sigma^2}\right) g(\rho) e^{jf(\rho)} \right]_{\rho=0}^{\infty}$$

$$+ \frac{A_\ell}{2\sigma^2} e^{-\frac{A_1^2}{2\sigma^2}} \int_0^\infty e^{-\frac{\rho^2}{2\sigma^2}} I_0\left(\frac{A_1 \rho}{\sigma^2}\right) \left[\frac{d}{d\rho}\{\rho g(\rho) e^{jf(\rho)}\}\right] d\rho$$

$$= \left(\frac{A_\ell}{2\sigma}\right) \int_0^\infty \left[\sqrt{2\pi}\left(\frac{A_1}{\sigma}\rho\right)^{1/2} e^{-\frac{A_1}{\sigma}\rho} I_0\left(\frac{A_1}{\sigma}\rho\right)\right]$$

$$\cdot (2\pi)^{-\frac{1}{2}} \left(\frac{A_1}{\sigma}\rho\right)^{-1/2} e^{-\frac{\left(\rho - \frac{A_1}{\sigma}\right)^2}{2}} \left[\frac{d}{dx}\{xg(x) e^{jf(x)}\}\right]_{x=\sigma\rho} d\rho.$$

$$(3.2.11.2.4)$$

Suppose

$$\frac{A_1}{\sigma} >> 3. \qquad (3.2.11.2.5)$$

Then, the integral of Equation 3.2.11.2.4 can be approximated as

(i) In the outside of the interval of ρ, $(A_1/\sigma - 3, A_1/\sigma + 3)$, the function $1/\sqrt{2\pi} \, e^{-(\rho - A_1/\sigma)^2/2}$ becomes very small.

(ii) In the same interval, $(A_1/\sigma - 3, A_1/\sigma + 3)$,

$$\sqrt{2\pi}\left(\frac{A_1}{\sigma}\rho\right)^{1/2} I_0\left(\frac{A_1}{\sigma}\rho\right) e^{-\frac{A_1}{\sigma}\rho} \cong 1. \qquad (3.2.11.2.6)$$

(iii) In $(A_1/\sigma - 3, A_1/\sigma + 3)$, $x = \sigma\rho$ changes $(x = A_1 - 3\sigma, x = A_1 + 3\sigma)$ and, in this range of x,

$$\left[\frac{d}{dx}\{xg(x) e^{jf(x)}\}\right]_{x=\sigma\rho} \cong \left[\frac{d}{d\rho}\{\rho g(\rho) e^{jf(\rho)}\}\right]_{\rho=A_1} \qquad (3.2.11.2.7)$$

Therefore,

$$
M_\ell \simeq \frac{A_\ell}{2A_1} \left[\frac{d}{d\rho} \{ \rho g(\rho) e^{jf(\rho)} \} \right]_{\rho = A_1} \int_0^\infty \frac{1}{\sqrt{2\pi}} e^{-\frac{\left(\rho - \frac{A_1}{\sigma}\right)^2}{2}} \left(\frac{A_1}{\sigma} \rho \right)^{-1/2} d\rho
$$

$$
\simeq \frac{A_\ell}{2A_1} \left[\frac{d}{d\rho} \{ \rho g(\rho) e^{jf(\rho)} \} \right]_{\rho = A_1} . \qquad (3.2.11.2.8)
$$

This is the same result as in Equation 3.2.11.1.10.

3.3   MODULATION TRANSFERS

When a number of carriers pass together through nonlinear devices, in addition to the intermodulation products produced, there will be modulation transfers between the signals (which are not intermodulation products) mainly because of the AM/PM nonlinearities, although there exist some effects due to the AM/AM nonlinearities. However, note here that, if there is no AM/PM characteristics, no modulation transfer exists. In cases of FM and PSK signals, the envelope fluctuation caused by filters (the ideal FM and continuous PSK signals have flat envelopes) creates this problem. In TDMA cases, because of the burst mode of the TDMA signals, the modulation transfer also occurs. In hybrid modulation, the ideal signal already has envelope fluctuations and the modulation transfer is essentially unavoidable. In this section, the intelligible crosstalk from FDM/FM signals to FDM/FM signals is analyzed first in Section 3.3.1. Then, the modulation transfer from digital carriers to FDM/FM signals is analyzed in Section 3.3.2. The effect of the TDMA signal burst mode on FDM/FM signals will also be explained in Section 3.3.2. In the last Section 3.3.3, the effects of the envelope fluctuation of the PSK signal (due to filters) into other digital carriers (PSK) will be explained.

3.3.1   Intelligible Crosstalk Between Two FDM/FM Signals

Section 3.3.1.1 analyzes the single nonlinear transmission channel and, in Section 3.3.1.2, the double cascaded nonlinear device case will be discussed.

3.3.1.1   Single Nonlinear Devices

The transmission chain of this case is explained in Figure 3.3.1.1.1. Filter F_{11} is the combination of the ground terminal filter and the satellite input filter for the first signal $e_{i1}^{(0)}$, which will be considered here as the interfering FM signal. The filter F_{12} is the combination of the ground terminal filter and satellite input filter for the second signal $e_{i2}^{(0)}$, which will be considered as the main signal to be demodulated at the ground terminal. Since the satellite input filter is usually common to the first and second signals although both use different portions of the passband, the characteristics of these portions can be respectively included in F_{11} and F_{12}.

The inputs to F_{11} and F_{12} are, respectively,

$$e_{i1}^{(0)} = A_1 e^{j(\omega_0 + \omega_1)t + j\phi_1(t)} \qquad \text{and}$$

$$e_{i2}^{(0)} = A_2 e^{j(\omega_0 + \omega_2)t + j\phi_2(t)}. \qquad (3.3.1.1.1)$$

Then, the outputs of these filters are, respectively,

$$e_{i1}^{(1)} = A_1\{1 + \epsilon_1(t)\} e^{j(\omega_0 + \omega_1)t + j\phi_1(t) + j\Delta_1(t)} \qquad \text{and}$$

$$e_{i2}^{(1)} = A_2\{1 + \epsilon_2(t)\} e^{j(\omega_0 + \omega_2)t + j\phi_2(t) + j\Delta_2(t)} \qquad (3.3.1.1.2)$$

where ϵ_1, ϵ_2 and Δ_1, Δ_2 are the amplitude and phase distortions of the first and second carrier. It is assumed here that ϵ_1, ϵ_2 and Δ_1, Δ_2 are much smaller than 1, normalizing the amplitudes and group delays of F_{11} and F_{12} as in Section 2.1.1. The output signal component of the nonlinear device corresponding to $e_{i2}^{(1)}$ is given by

$$M(0, 1; A_1(1 + \epsilon_1), A_2(1 + \epsilon_2)) e^{j(\omega_0 + \omega_2)t + j\phi_2 + j\Delta_2} \qquad (3.3.1.1.3)$$

where, from Equation 3.1.38,

$$M(0, 1; A_1(1 + \epsilon_1), A_2(1 + \epsilon_2))$$

$$= \int_0^\infty \int_0^\infty \gamma J_1(A_2(1 + \epsilon_2)\gamma) \, J_0(A_1(1 + \epsilon_1)\gamma) J_1(\gamma\rho) \rho g(\rho) e^{jf(\rho)} \, d\gamma \, d\rho$$

$$(3.3.1.1.4)$$

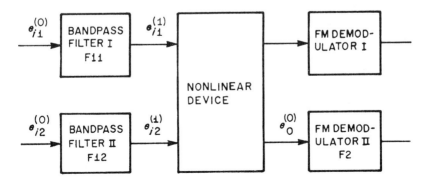

Figure 3.3.1.1.1 Intelligible Crosstalk of FM Signals Due to Single Nonlinear Device

where considering the second signal is enough, since it is assumed to be the main signal to be demodulated. The function M of Equation 3.3.1.1.4 can be approximated, since ϵ_1 and e_2 are much smaller than 1, as

$$M(0, 1; A_1(1 + \epsilon_1), A_2(1 + \epsilon_2))$$

$$\simeq M(0, 1; A_1, A_2) + A_1\epsilon_1 \frac{\partial}{\partial A_1} M(0, 1; A_1, A_2)$$

$$+ A_2\epsilon_2 \frac{\partial}{\partial A_2} M(0, 1; A_1, A_2) \qquad (3.3.1.1.5)$$

where ϵ_1 and ϵ_2 respectively contain their own signal components, (i.e., ϕ_1 and ϕ_2). However, the portion ϵ_2 proportional to ϕ_2 is not considered to be an "intelligible crosstalk," since it is the same as ϕ_2. The contribution of ϵ_2 after the nonlinear device can be handled as a distortion as in Section 2.1.1. Thus, only the portion of ϵ_1 which is proportional to ϕ_1 is considered here, since this component is the "intelligible crosstalk" to the second carrier (A_2). Because the cross terms of ϵ_1 and ϵ_2 are much smaller than ϵ_1 and ϵ_2, these terms in Equation 3.3.1.1.5 will be ignored, i.e.,

$$M(0, 1; A_1(1 + \epsilon_1), A_2(1 + \epsilon_2))$$

$$\simeq M(0, 1; A_1, A_2) + \epsilon_1 A_1 \frac{\partial}{\partial A_1} M(0, 1; A_1, A_2)$$

$$= M_s + \epsilon_1 M_1 A_1 \qquad (3.3.1.1.6)$$

where

$$M_s = M(0, 1; A_1, A_2)$$

$$= \int_0^\infty \int_0^\infty \gamma J_1(A_2\gamma) J_0(A_1\gamma) J_1(\gamma\rho)\rho g(\rho)e^{jf(\rho)} \, d\gamma \, d\rho \qquad (3.3.1.1.7)$$

$$M_1 = \frac{\partial}{\partial A_1} M(0, 1; A_1, A_2)$$

$$= -\int_0^\infty \int_0^\infty \gamma^2 J_1(A_1\gamma) J_1(A_2\gamma) J_1(\gamma\rho)\rho g(\rho)e^{jf(\rho)} \, d\rho \, d\gamma. \qquad (3.3.1.1.8)$$

M_s has been obtained in several forms, in Section 3.2. However, it is not easy to evaluate the integral of Equation 3.3.1.18 in general, particularly in the areas closer to the saturating power of the nonlinear device. In a large backoff area where $g(\rho)e^{jf(\rho)}$ is expanded by Equation 3.1.20 (or 3.2.9.2),

$$M_s = \alpha_0 A_2 + \alpha_1 (A_2^3 + 2 A_1^2 A_2)$$

$$\simeq \alpha_0 A_2 = g_0 A_2 \qquad (3.3.1.1.9)$$

$$M_1 = \frac{\partial}{\partial A_1} [\alpha_0 A_2 + \alpha_1 (A_2^3 + 2A_1^2 A_2)]$$

$$= 4 \alpha_1 A_1 A_2 = j4g_0 \beta A_1 A_2 . \qquad (3.3.1.1.10)$$

In other areas, the best approach is the Bessel expansion of Equation 3.2.2.1. In this case,

$$M_s = \sum_{s=1}^{L} b_s J_1(A_2 \alpha s) J_0(A_1 \alpha s). \qquad (3.3.1.1.11)$$

Therefore,

$$M_1 = \frac{\partial M_s}{\partial A_1} = - \sum_{s=1}^{L} (\alpha s) b_s J_1(A_2 \alpha s) J_1(A_1 \alpha s). \qquad (3.3.1.1.12)$$

The approach to obtain the coefficients b_s is explained in [55]. In other approaches, it is difficult to obtain $\partial/\partial A_1 \, M_s$ in general. Now, the output signal of the nonlinear device (for A_2) is

$$e_0^{(0)} = (M_s + A_1 \epsilon_1 M_1) e^{j(\omega_0 + \omega_2)t + j\phi_2 + j\Delta_2}$$

$$= |M_s + A_1 \epsilon_1 M_1| e^{j(\omega_0 + \omega_2)t + j\phi_2 + j\Delta_2 + j\theta_2} \qquad (3.3.1.1.13)$$

where

$$\theta_2(t) = \text{Im} \log(M_s + A_1 \epsilon_1 M_1) = \text{Im} \log(M_s) + \text{Im} \log\left(1 + \frac{A_1 M_1}{M_s} \epsilon_1\right)$$

$$\simeq \text{Im} \log(M_s) + \text{Im}\left\{\frac{A_1 M_1}{M_s} \epsilon_1\right\} .$$

$$(3.3.1.1.14)$$

Since $|M_1/M_s| \, \epsilon_1$ is much smaller than 1,

$$\text{Im} \log\left[1 + \frac{M_1}{M_s} A_1 \epsilon_1\right] \simeq \text{Im}\left\{\frac{M_1}{M_s}\right\} \epsilon_1 A_1. \qquad (3.3.1.1.15)$$

After the FM demodulator of the signal of Equation 3.3.1.1.13, the modulation transfer which contains the intelligible crosstalk from the A_1 carrier is

$$(2\pi)^{-1} \text{Im}\left\{\frac{A_1 M_1}{M_s}\right\} \frac{d}{dt} \epsilon_1(t) \qquad (3.3.1.1.16)$$

where $\epsilon_1(t)$ is given by

$$\epsilon_1(t) \simeq \text{Re} \left\{ e^{-j\phi_1(t)} \int_{-\infty}^{\infty} e^{j\phi_1(x)} h_{11}(t-x)dx - 1 \right\} \qquad (3.3.1.1.17)$$

(see Equation 2.1.3.7). $h_{11}(t)$ is the low pass analog impulse response of the filter F_{11} (Y_{11} is also the lowpass analog, i.e. the Fourier transform of $h_{11}(t)$). Note here that the filter F_2, which is the combination of the satellite output filter and of the ground terminal receiver filter, gives the distortions to the signal of Equation 3.3.1.1.13 and this distorted signal goes to the FM receiver of the ground terminal for the demodulation. The distortion produced by F_2 does not affect the analysis of the intelligible crosstalk component. θ_2 is the one which contains the intelligible crosstalk from ϕ_1.

In large backoff areas,

$$\text{Im} \left\{ \frac{M_1}{M_s} \right\} = 4\beta A_1. \qquad (3.3.1.1.18)$$

In a Bessel expansion case,

$$\text{Im} \left\{ \frac{M_1}{M_s} \right\} = -\text{Im} \left[\frac{\sum_{s=1}^{L} b_s(\alpha s) J_1(A_1 \alpha s) J_1(A_2 \alpha s)}{\sum_{s=1}^{L} b_s J_1(A_2 \alpha s) J_0(A_1 \alpha s)} \right] . \qquad (3.3.1.1.19)$$

In FDM/FM signals, the power spectrum of Equation 3.3.1.1.17 must be evaluated to obtain the crosstalk ratio of each channel as shown in the following. The power spectrum of $1/2\pi \, d/dt \, \epsilon_1$ is that of ϵ_1 multiplied by f^2. Therefore, the autocorrelation function of Equation 3.3.1.1.15 whose Fourier transform gives the power spectrum, will be obtained.

From this autocorrelation function, the signal component of the A_1 carrier which is the intelligible crosstalk will be separated. Note that the separation of the A_1 signal component from Equation 3.3.1.1.17 in time domain representation is very difficult.

$$A_1^2 E \left[\text{Im} \left(\frac{M_1}{M_s} \right) \epsilon_1(t) \, \text{Im} \left(\frac{M_1}{M_s} \right) \epsilon_1(t+\tau) \right]$$

$$= \left[\text{Im} \left(\frac{M_1}{M_s} \right) \right]^2 A_1^2 E[\epsilon_1(t)\epsilon_1(t+\tau)]. \qquad (3.3.1.1.20)$$

From Equation 3.3.1.1.17,

$$\{\epsilon_1(t)\epsilon_1(t+\tau)\} = \frac{1}{2} \text{Re} \left\{ \int_{-\infty}^{\infty} \int_{-\infty}^{\infty} E_{\phi_1} \left[e^{-j\phi_1(t) + j\phi_1(x) + j\phi_1(t+\tau) - j\phi_1(y)} \right] \right.$$

$$\cdot\, h_{11}(t-x)\, h_{11}(t+\tau-y)^*\, dx\, dy$$

$$+ \int_{-\infty}^{\infty}\int_{-\infty}^{\infty} E_{\phi_1}\, [e^{-j\phi_1(t)+j\phi_1(x)-j\phi_1(t+\tau)+j\phi_1(y)}]$$

$$\left.\cdot\, h_{11}(t-x)h_{11}(t+\tau-y)\, dx\, dy\right\} \qquad (3.3.1.1.21)$$

where the formula for any complex numbers a and b

$$\mathrm{Re}(a)\,\mathrm{Re}(b) = \frac{1}{2}\,\mathrm{Re}\{ab^* + ab\} \qquad (3.3.1.1.22)$$

was used. a corresponds to $\epsilon_1(t)$ and b, to $\epsilon_1(t+\tau)$. All the terms which are not functions of τ and t are neglected in the result of Equation 3.3.1.1.21, since these contribute only to the D.C. components. It is also assumed here that $\phi_1(t)$ is a stationary Gaussian process as in FDM/FM cases. The averages in Equation 3.3.1.1.21 are obtained in Section 2.1.1.3. Thus,

$$E\{\epsilon_1(t)\epsilon_1(t+\tau)\} \Rightarrow \mathrm{Re}\left\{\int_{-\infty}^{\infty}\int_{-\infty}^{\infty} \frac{1}{2}\, e^{-2R_{\phi_1}(0)+R_{\phi_1}(x)+k_{\phi_1}(y)}\right.$$

$$\left.\cdot\, [h_{11}(x)\, h_{11}(y)^*\, e^{R_v(\tau,x,y)} + h_{11}(x)\, h_{11}(y)\, e^{-R_v(\tau,x,y)}]\, dx\, dy\right\} \cdot$$

$$(3.3.1.1.23)$$

In the expansion

$$e^{\pm R_v(\tau,x,y)} = \sum_{k=0}^{\infty} \frac{1}{k!}\, [\pm R_v(\tau,\, x,\, y)]^k. \qquad (3.3.1.1.24)$$

The term of $k = 1$ only gives the intelligible crosstalk and the terms of $k \geq 2$ gives the non-intelligible crosstalks. Therefore, only the term of $k = 1$ is considered here.

$$E[\epsilon_1(t)\epsilon_1(t+\tau)] \Rightarrow \int_{-\infty}^{\infty}\int_{-\infty}^{\infty} e^{-2R_{\phi_1}(0)+R_{\phi_1}(x)+R_{\phi_1}(y)}$$

$$\cdot\, [\mathrm{Im}\{h_{11}(x)\}]\, [\mathrm{Im}\{h_{11}(y)\}]\, R_v(\tau,\, x,\, y)\, dx\, dy \qquad (3.3.1.1.25)$$

where, from Equation 2.1.1.3.3

$$R_v(\tau,\, x,\, y) = R_{\phi_1}(\tau) - R_{\phi_1}(\tau+x) - R_{\phi_1}(\tau-y) + R_{\phi_1}(\tau + x - y). \qquad (3.3.1.1.26)$$

Let us use the Fourier transform of Equation 3.3.1.1.25 to obtain the power spectrum of the intelligible crosstalk, where

$$\int_{-\infty}^{\infty} R_v(\tau,x,y) e^{-j2\pi f\tau} \, d\tau = (1 - e^{j2\pi fx})(1 - e^{-j2\pi fy}) W_{\phi_1}(f) \quad (3.3.1.1.27)$$

where $W_{\phi_1}(f)$ is the power spectrum of $\phi_1(f)$. Thus, the power spectrum of the intelligible crosstalk in the demodulated output of the signal carrier (A_2) interfered from the first carrier (A_1) is given as follows

$$A_1^2 \left| \int_{-\infty}^{\infty} e^{-R_{\phi_1}(0) + R_{\phi_1}(x)} [\mathrm{Im}\{h_{11}(x)\}](1 - e^{j2\pi fx}) \, dx \right|^2$$

$$\cdot W_{\phi_1}(f) f^2 \left[\mathrm{Im}\left(\frac{M_1}{M_s}\right) \right]^2. \quad (3.3.1.1.28)$$

Using the relations

$$\mathrm{Im}\{h_{11}(x)\} = \frac{1}{(2j)} \left[\int_{-\infty}^{\infty} Y_{11}(y) e^{j2\pi yx} dy - \int_{-\infty}^{\infty} Y_{11}(y)^* \, e^{-j2\pi yx} dy \right]$$

$$(3.3.1.1.29)$$

where $Y_{11}(f)$ is the low pass analog transfer function of $h_{11}(t)$ and

$$W_{c_1}(f) = \int_{-\infty}^{\infty} e^{-R_{\phi_1}(0) + R_{\phi_1}(x) \pm j2\pi fx} \, dx \quad (3.3.1.1.30)$$

where $W_{c_1}(f)$ is the power spectrum of the A_1 FM signal without any filter distortion (ideal case), whose total power is unity and center frequency is shifted to zero. Then, Equation 3.3.1.1.26 becomes

$$\frac{A_1^2}{4} f^2 W_{\phi_1}(f) \left| \int_{-\infty}^{\infty} [Y_{11}(y) - Y_{11}(-y)^*][W_{c_1}(y) - W_{c_1}(y+f)] \, dy \right|^2$$

$$\cdot \left[\mathrm{Im}\left(\frac{M_1}{M_s}\right) \right]^2 \quad (-\infty < f < \infty). \quad (3.3.1.1.31)$$

The condition to be filled for the intelligible crosstalk to be zero is that the filter F_{11} must be symmetric, i.e.,

$$Y_{11}(f) = Y_{11}(-f)^*. \quad (3.3.1.1.32)$$

Note here that, although Equation 3.3.1.1.32 gives zero to Equation 3.3.1.1.31, the modulation transfer is not really zero but only becomes very small, since the result of Equation 3.3.1.1.31 is an approximation assuming that ϵ_1 is very small ($|\epsilon_1| << 1$).

Finally, the power spectrum of the intelligible crosstalk is given by

$$\frac{A_1^2}{4} \left[\mathrm{Im}\left\{\frac{M_1}{M_s}\right\} \right]^2 f^2 W_{\phi_1}(f) \left| \int_{-\infty}^{\infty} [Y_{11}(y) - Y_{11}(-y)^*][W_{c_1}(y) - W_{c_1}(y+f)] dy \right|^2$$

$$(-\infty < f < \infty). \quad (3.3.1.1.33)$$

For the evaluation of the integral of the above result, two approaches will be explained here.

(i) Power series expansion of filter transfer function.
  Assume that $Y_{11}(f)$ is expanded by a power series of f as in Equation 2.1.1.1.1,

$$Y_{11}(f) = \sum_{k=0}^{\infty} a_k f^k \qquad (3.3.1.1.34)$$

where the a_k's are complex numbers. Then,

$$Y_{11}(f) - Y_{11}(-f)^* = \sum_{k=0}^{\infty} [a_k - (-1)^k a_k^*] f^k \qquad (3.3.1.1.35)$$

representing

$$a_k = a_{kr} + j a_{ki} \qquad (3.3.1.1.36)$$

where a_{kr} and a_{ki} are respectively the real and imaginary parts of a_k. Obviously,

$$a_k - (-1)^k a_k^* = (2j) a_{ki} \qquad \text{for even } k$$

$$a_k - (-1)^k a_k^* = 2 a_{kr} \qquad \text{for odd } k. \qquad (3.3.1.1.37)$$

Thus,

$$Y_{11}(f) - Y_{11}(-f)^* = (2j) \sum_{k=0}^{\infty} a_{(2k)i} f^{2k} + 2 \sum_{k=0}^{\infty} a_{(2k+1)r} f^{2k+1}.$$

$$(3.3.1.1.38)$$

Substituting this result into Equation 3.3.1.1.33,

$$W_I(f) = \left[A_1 \operatorname{Im}\left(\frac{M_1}{M_s} \right) \right]^2 f^2 W_{\phi_1}(f) \left[\left\{ \sum_{\ell=1}^{\infty} b_{(2\ell)i} f^{2\ell} \right\}^2 \right.$$

$$\left. + \left\{ \sum_{\ell=0}^{\infty} b_{(2\ell+1)r} f^{2\ell+1} \right\}^2 \right] \qquad (3.3.1.1.39)$$

where

$$\sum_{k=\ell}^{\infty} a_{(2k)i} \; {}_{2k}C_{2k-2\ell} \; m_{2k-2\ell} = b_{(2\ell)i},$$

$$\sum_{k=\ell}^{\infty} a_{(2k+1)r} \; {}_{2k+1}C_{2\ell+1} \; m_{2k-2\ell} = b_{(2\ell+1)r} \qquad (3.3.1.1.40)$$

where

$$m_{2k} = \int_{-\infty}^{\infty} f^{2k} W_{c_1}(f)\, df$$

and

$$m_{2k+1} = \int_{-\infty}^{\infty} f^{2k+1} W_{c_1}(f)\, df = 0 \qquad (3.3.1.1.41)$$

since $W_{c_1}(f)$ is an even function of f.

From Equation 3.3.1.1.39, the $a_{1r}f$ term (a linear slope of the amplitude) and the $a_{2i}f^2$ term (a linear slope of group delay) give the intelligible crosstalk. Consider the simplest example,

$$Y_{11}(f) = a_0 + a_1 f + a_2 f^2. \qquad (3.3.1.1.42)$$

In this case,

$$b_{0i} = a_{0i}\ {}_0C_0\, m_0 + a_{2i}\ {}_2C_2\, m_2$$

$$= a_{0i} + a_{2i}\, m_2 = a_{2i}\, m_2 = a_{2i}\, \sigma^2,$$

$$b_{2i} = a_{2i}\ {}_2C_2\, m_0 = a_{2i},$$

$$b_{1r} = a_{1r}\ {}_1C_1\, m_0 = a_{1r} \qquad (3.3.1.1.43)$$

where $m_0 = 1$, $m_2 = \sigma^2$.

$$(\sigma = \text{r.m.s. frequency deviation of the } A_1 \text{ signal}). \qquad (3.3.1.1.44)$$

Because of the normalization for the filter amplitude and group delay explained in Section 2.1.1,

$$a_{0r} = 1 \text{ and } a_{0i} = 0. \qquad (3.3.1.1.45)$$

Thus, in this case, $W_I(f)$ of Equation 3.3.1.1.39 is given by

$$W_I(f) = \left[A_1 \operatorname{Im}\left\{ \frac{M_1}{M_s} \right\} \right]^2 f^2 W_{\phi_1}(f)\, [(a_{2i}f^2)^2 + (a_{1r}f)^2]. \qquad (3.3.1.1.46)$$

The moments m_{2k} defined by Equation 3.3.1.1.41 can be obtained as follows:

$$m_{2k} = \int_{-\infty}^{\infty} f^{2k} W_{c_1}(f)\, df$$

$$= \left[\frac{1}{(j2\pi)^{2k}} \frac{d^{2k}}{d\tau^{2k}} \int_{-\infty}^{\infty} W_{c_1}(f)\, e^{j2\pi f\tau}\, df \right]_{\tau=0}$$

$$= \left[\frac{(-1)^k}{(2\pi)^{2k}} \frac{d^{2k}}{d\tau^{2k}} e^{-R_{\phi_1}(0) + R_{\phi_1}(\tau)} \right]_{\tau=0}. \qquad (3.3.1.1.47)$$

If $e^{-R_{\phi_1}(0)\,+\,R_{\phi_1}(\tau)}$ is expanded by a power series of τ as

$$e^{-R_{\phi_1}(0)\,+\,R_{\phi_1}(\tau)} = \sum_{k=0}^{\infty} b_{2k}\,\tau^{2k} \qquad (3.3.1.1.48)$$

where the autocorrelation function $e^{-R_{\phi_1}(0)\,+\,R_{\phi_1}(\tau)}$ is an even function of τ. Then,

$$m_{2k} = \frac{(-1)^k}{(2\pi)^k}\,(2k)!\,b_{2k}. \qquad (3.3.1.1.49)$$

When the power series expansion of $R_{\phi_1}(\tau)$ is given as

$$R_{\phi_1}(\tau) = \sum_{m=0}^{\infty} C_{2m}\,\tau^{2m}. \qquad (3.3.1.1.50)$$

There exists a recurrence relation to obtain b_{2k} from the C_{2m}'s. Differentiate Equation 3.3.1.1.48 by τ,

$$R_{\phi_1}(\tau)'\,e^{-R_{\phi_1}(0)\,+\,R_{\phi_1}(\tau)}$$

$$= \sum_{k=0}^{\infty} (2k)\,b_{2k}\,\tau^{2k-1}$$

$$= \left[\sum_{l=0}^{\infty} (2l)\,C_{2l}\,\tau^{2l-1}\right]\left[\sum_{m=0}^{\infty} b_{2m}\,\tau^{2m}\right]$$

$$= \sum_{l=0}^{\infty}\sum_{m=0}^{\infty} (2l)\,C_{2l}\,b_{2m}\,\tau^{2(l+m)-1}. \qquad (3.3.1.1.51)$$

From the comparison between the right and left terms, the following relation exists

$$(2k)\,b_{2k} = \sum_{l=0}^{k} (2l)\,C_{2l}\,b_{2k-2l},$$

$$b_{2k} = \frac{1}{2k}\sum_{l=0}^{k} (2l)\,C_{2l}\,b_{2k-2l}$$

$$= \frac{1}{2k}[2C_2\,b_{2k-2} + 4C_4\,b_{2k-4} + \cdots + (2k)\,C_{2k}\,b_0]. \qquad (3.3.1.1.52)$$

Thus, b_{2k} can be obtained from $b_{2k-2}, b_{2k-4}, \ldots, b_2, b_0$ if $C_2, C_4, \ldots, C_{2k}$ are known.

The crosstalk ratio (N.P.R.) due to this intelligible crosstalk at channel f is given by

$$N.P.R. = \frac{\left(\dfrac{\sigma^2}{M}\right)}{W_I(f)\, G_p(f)\, \Delta f} \qquad (3.3.1.1.53)^\dagger$$

where $G_p(f)$ represents the pre-emphasis effect and σ and M are respectively the r.m.s. frequency deviation and the number of channels of the FDM/FM. Some practical examples are explained in Figure 3.3.1.1.2. The specification of the intelligible crosstalk ratio is 58 dB according to the CCITT recommendation.

(ii) Fourier series expansion of filter transfer function.
In some applications, it is more convenient to use the Fourier series expansion for the approximation of the filter transfer function (e.g., the case of unsymmetric ideal cutoff filters) as done in Section 2.1.1.1.

$$Y_{11}(f) = \sum_{k=-\infty}^{\infty} a_k\, e^{-j2\pi f \frac{k}{F_0}} \qquad (3.3.1.1.54)$$

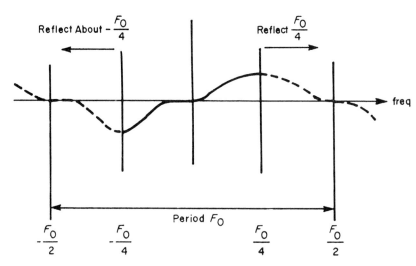

Figure 3.3.1.1.2 Fourier Series Representation of Filter Response

---

$^\dagger \Delta f$ is the voice channel bandwidth (4 kHz) as in Equation 2.1.5.25.

$$h_{11}(t) = \sum_{k=-\infty}^{\infty} a_k \, \delta\left(t - \frac{k}{F_0}\right). \tag{3.3.1.1.55}$$

In this case, it is convenient to use the result of Equation 3.3.1.1.28.
Thus,

$$\int_{-\infty}^{\infty} e^{-R_{\phi_1}(0) + R_{\phi_1}(x)} \left[\sum_{k=-\infty}^{\infty} [\text{Im}(a_k)] \delta\left(x - \frac{k}{F_0}\right) \right]$$

$$\cdot [1 - e^{j2\pi fx}] \, dx$$

$$= \sum_{k=-\infty}^{\infty} [\text{Im}(a_k)] \, e^{-R_{\phi_1}(0) + R_{\phi_1}\left(\frac{k}{F_0}\right)} [1 - e^{j\frac{2\pi}{F_0}kf}]$$

$$= \sum_{k=-\infty}^{\infty} [\text{Im}(a_k)] \, e^{-R_{\phi_1}(0) + R_{\phi_1}\left(\frac{k}{F_0}\right)} e^{j\pi\frac{k}{F_0}f} (-2j) \sin\left(\pi\frac{k}{F_0}f\right). \tag{3.3.1.1.56}$$

Then, Equation 3.3.1.1.28 becomes

$$A_1^2 \left| \sum_{k=-\infty}^{\infty} [\text{Im}(a_k)] \, e^{-R_{\phi_1}(0) + R_{\phi_1}\left(\frac{k}{F_0}\right)} \sin\left(\frac{\pi}{F_0}kf\right) \right|^2$$

$$\cdot W_{\phi_1}(f) f^2 \left[\text{Im}\left(\frac{M_1}{M_S}\right) \right]^2. \tag{3.3.1.1.57}$$

This is the approach used in [66]. Some practical examples are shown in Figures 3.3.1.1.2–3.3.1.1.6. This section will finish on an interesting case.

Consider a nonsymmetric ideal cutoff filter

$$Y_{11}(f) = 1 \qquad -f_2 \le f \le f_1 \qquad (f_1 \ne f_2)$$

$$= 0 \qquad \text{Elsewhere.} \tag{3.3.1.1.58}$$

Substituting this filter characteristic into Equation 3.3.1.1.31,

$$W_I(f) = \left(\frac{A_1^2}{4}\right) \left[\text{Im}\left(\frac{M_1}{M_S}\right) \right]^2 f^2 \, W_\phi(f) \left[-\frac{1}{2}\{I_{C_1}(f + f_2) \right.$$

$$\left. + I_{C_1}(f - f_2)\} + \frac{1}{2}\{I_{C_1}(f - f_1) + I_{C_1}(f + f_1)\} \right]^2 \tag{3.3.1.1.59}$$

where

$$I_{C_1}(f) = 2 \int_0^f W_{c_1}(x) \, dx \tag{3.3.1.1.60}$$

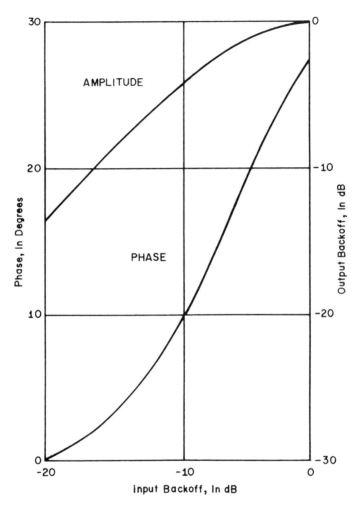

Figure 3.3.1.1.3   Laboratory TWT Characteristics

where, by the definition of $W_{c_1}(x)$, $I_{C_1}(0) = 0$ and $I_{C_1}(\infty) = 1$. $I_{C_1}(f)$ is the cumulative power spectrum distribution function. In many cases, it is difficult to evaluate the function $I_{C_1}(f)$ and then Equation 3.3.1.1.57 can be used, where the coefficients a_k's are given by

$$\mathrm{Im}(a_k) = \frac{\sin\left(\pi(f_1 - f_2)\dfrac{k}{F_0}\right)\,\sin\left(\pi(f_1 + f_2)\dfrac{k}{F_0}\right)}{\pi k}. \qquad (3.3.1.1.61)$$

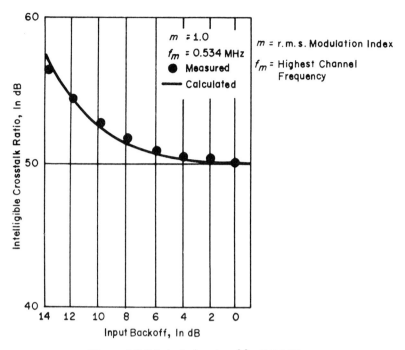

Figure 3.3.1.1.4 Laboratory Measurement

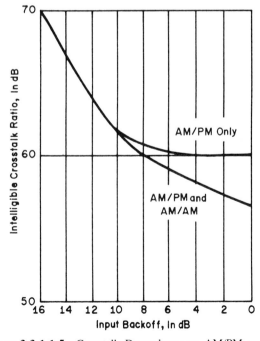

Figure 3.3.1.1.5 Crosstalk Dependence on AM/PM and AM/AM

217

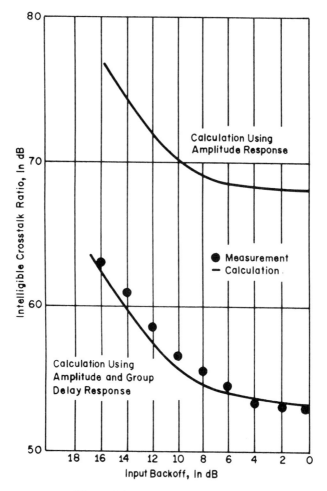

Figure 3.3.1.1.6   Group Delay Test

3.3.1.2   Double Nonlinear Device Cascaded Case

In the preceding Section, there is only one nonlinear device in the transmission chain (see Figure 3.3.1.1.1), which is probably a satellite TWTA or SSPA. In this case, a double nonlinear device cascaded case will be covered.

The notations of Figure 3.3.1.2.1 are explained as follows:

F_1 and F_2 : Pre-HPA filters.
F_{11} and F_{22} : Satellite input filters.

The satellite output and ground terminal receiver filters are ignored here, since they do not contribute to the intelligible crosstalks from the first signal (A_1) into

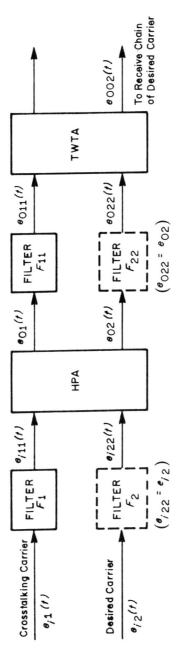

Figure 3.3.1.2.1 Crosstalk System Configuration

the second signal (A_2) as explained in Section 3.3.1.1. It is also assumed here that the second signal is not modulated at all (therefore, the filter is not needed), since this assumption does not change the analysis of this problem as seen from the analysis in Section 3.3.1.1. In this case, four intelligible crosstalks from the first signal (A_1) to the second signal (A_2) caused by different structures exist. Figure 3.3.1.2.2 explains these four components.

A physical interpretation of these four intelligible distortion components can be summarized as follows:

(a) The amplitude of the crosstalking carrier receives a small amount of amplitude modulation as it passes through the filter F_1. This amplitude fluctuation, which contains the intelligible component of the baseband signal of the crosstalking carrier, is transferred into the phase of the desired carrier due to the AM/PM conversion characteristics of the HPA when both carriers pass through the HPA. The first distortion component is due to this effect.

(b) The second distortion component (cross term) is due to the fact that the amplitude fluctuation described in (a) causes a small amount of amplitude fluctuation in the desired signal due to the HPA AM/AM characteristics. Subsequently, the resulting amplitude fluctuation is then transferred into the phase of the desired carrier due to the TWTA AM/PM characteristics as this carrier passes through the TWTA.

(c) Similarly, the third distortion component (cross term) is also due to the amplitude fluctuation described in (a). This amplitude fluctuation of the crosstalking carrier is suppressed by the HPA AM/AM characteristics as this carrier passes through the HPA. The resulting amplitude fluctuation is then transferred into the phase of the desired carrier due to the TWTA AM/PM characteristics when both carriers pass through the TWTA.

(d) The fourth distortion component is due to the filter F_{11} and to the TWTA. At the output of the filter F_{11}, the crosstalking carrier receives another amplitude fluctuation, which again is transferred into the phase of the desired carrier due to the TWTA AM/PM characteristics.

It is noted that the first three components are due to the filter F_1, HPA and TWTA while the last one is due to the filter F_{11} and TWTA. These terms will be added on a voltage basis. From results given later, the second distortion component appears to be negligible compared to the others since the transfer of the amplitude fluctuation (after the filter F_1) of the crosstalking carrier into the amplitude of the desired carrier by the HPA is fairly small. In addition, the third distortion component tends to be more suppressed by the amplitude nonlinearity of the HPA as the HPA operating point moves from the linear region to the saturation region.

Consider the system configuration as shown in Figure 3.3.1.2.1. Represent the crosstalking and desired carriers (at FM modulator outputs) respectively as

$$e_{i1}(t) = A_1 \, e^{j\omega_1 t + j\phi_1(t)} \qquad\qquad (3.3.1.2.1)$$

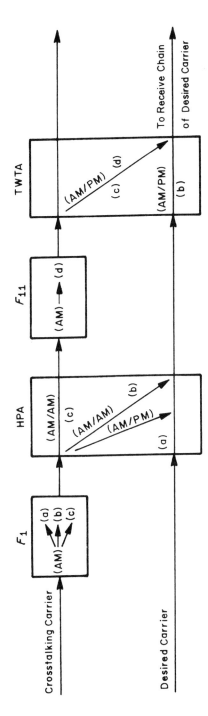

Figure 3.3.2.2 Example of Modulation Transfer from PSK Signal to FDM/FM Signal in Case of Large TWTA Backoff

and

$$e_{i2}(t) = A_2 \, e^{\, j\omega_2 t + j\phi_2(t)} \tag{3.3.1.2.2}$$

where A_1, ω_1, and $\phi_1(t)$ are the crosstalking carrier amplitude, angular frequency, and phase, and A_2, ω_2, and $\phi_2(t)$, the desired carrier amplitude, angular frequency, and phase. (Note that A_1 and A_2 are not functions of time.)

After F_1 and F_2, the two carriers can be represented as

$$e_{i11}(t) = A_1[1 + \varepsilon_1(t)] \, e^{\, j\omega_1 t + j\phi_1(t) + j\Delta_1(t)} \tag{3.3.1.2.3}$$

and

$$e_{i22}(t) = A_2 \, e^{\, j\omega_2 t + j\phi_2(t)}. \tag{3.3.1.2.4}$$

It is implicitly assumed here that the amplitude and group delay of F_1 at ω_1 are approximately at 0 dB attenuation and 0 second delay. This normalization assures the validity of the first order approximation, i.e., $|\varepsilon_1(t)| \ll 1$ and $|\Delta_1(t)| \ll 1$. The generality of the analysis is not affected by this normalization since the normalization in amplitude only changes the magnitude of the signal whereas the normalization in group delay (constant group delay difference) only shifts the signal in time without distortion. If the values of $\varepsilon_1(t)$ and $\Delta_1(t)$ in Equation 3.3.1.2.3 are not small (i.e., normalization in amplitude and group delay are not assumed), then the first order approximation theory normally used in practice is no longer applicable.

In general, when two FDM/FM carriers represented by Equations 3.3.1.2.3 and 3.3.1.2.4 pass through a nonlinear amplifier, the output of the crosstalking carrier, for example, can be expressed as $M(A_1, A_2) \exp[j\omega_1 t + \phi_1(t)]$, where M is a complex function of A_1 and A_2 and determined by the nonlinear characteristics of the device (see Section 3.2).

Therefore, at the HPA output, the crosstalking carrier is given by

$$e_{01}(t) = M_H[(A_1(1 + \varepsilon_1(t)), A_2] \, e^{\, j\omega_1 t + j\phi_1(t) + j\Delta_1(t)} \tag{3.3.1.2.5}$$

where M_H is a complex function of $A_1(1 + \varepsilon_1(t))$ and A_2.

Since, in addition to $|\varepsilon_1| \ll 1$, $(\partial M_H / \partial A_1) \leq 1$ (due to HPA AM/AM characteristics) and $(A_1 / M_H) \ll 1$, Equation 3.3.1.2.5 can be further simplified to

$$e_{01}(t) \approx |M_H(A_1, A_2)|$$

$$\cdot \left\{ 1 + \mathrm{Re}\left[\frac{\dfrac{\partial M_H(A_1, A_2)}{\partial A_1}}{M_H(A_1, A_2)} \right] A_1 \varepsilon_1(t) \right\}$$

$$\cdot \exp\left\{ j\omega_1 t + j\phi_1(t) + j\Delta_1(t) + j\angle M_H(A_1, A_2) \right.$$

$$+ j \, \text{Im} \left[\frac{\dfrac{\partial M_H(A_1, A_2)}{\partial A_1}}{M_H(A_1, A_2)} \right] A_1 \varepsilon_1(t) \right\} \qquad (3.3.1.2.6)$$

where $\angle$ denotes the angle of a complex number.

At the HPA output, the desired carrier is given by

$$e_{02}(t) = M_H(A_2, A_1(1 + \varepsilon_1(t))) \, e^{j\omega_2 t + j\phi_2(t)}. \qquad (3.3.1.2.7)$$

From the same approach as that used in the approximation of Equation 3.3.1.2.6,

$$e_{02}(t) \approx |M_H(A_2, A_1)|$$

$$\cdot \left\{ 1 + \text{Re} \left[\frac{\dfrac{\partial M_H(A_2, A_1)}{\partial A_1}}{M_H(A_2, A_1)} \right] A_1 \varepsilon_1(t) \right\}$$

$$\cdot \exp\left\{ j\omega_2 t + j\phi_2(t) + j\angle M_H(A_2, A_1) \right.$$

$$+ j \, \text{Im} \left[\frac{\dfrac{\partial M_H(A_2, A_1)}{\partial A_1}}{M_H(A_2, A_1)} \right] A_1 \varepsilon_1(t) \right\}. \qquad (3.3.1.2.8)$$

Due to the assumption of the transparency of F_{22} as explained earlier, the desired carrier at the TWTA input is

$$e_{022}(t) = e_{02}(t). \qquad (3.3.1.2.9)$$

The crosstalking carrier at the output of F_{11}, or at the TWTA input, can be represented by[†]

$$e_{011}(t) \approx |M_H(A_1, A_2)|$$

$$\cdot \left\{ 1 + \mathrm{Re} \left[\frac{\frac{\partial M_H(A_1, A_2)}{\partial A_1}}{M_H(A_1, A_2)} \right] A_1 \varepsilon_1(t) + \varepsilon_{11}(t) \right\}$$

$$\cdot \exp \left\{ j\omega_1 t + j\phi_1(t) + j\Delta_1(t) + j\angle M_H(A_1, A_2) \right.$$

$$+ j \, \mathrm{Im} \left[\frac{\frac{\partial M_H(A_1, A_2)}{\partial A_1}}{M_H(A_1, A_2)} \right] A_1 \varepsilon_1(t) + j\Delta_{11}(t) \right\} \qquad (3.3.1.2.10)$$

where $\varepsilon_{11}(t)$ and $\Delta_{11}(t)$ are respectively the amplitude and group delay distortions due to the filter F_{11} when the input is given by Equation 3.3.1.2.6. Since filter distortions are very small, $\varepsilon_{11}(t)$ and $\Delta_{11}(t)$ are almost equal to those distortions that would have appeared if the input to F_{11} is represented by the undistorted signal of Equation 3.3.1.2.1. The justification of this approximation is as follows. The difference between Equations 3.3.1.2.1 and 3.3.1.2.6 is small (first order). Represent e_{01} by $e_{01} = e_{i1} + \Delta$. When $e_{01}(t)$ passes through F_{11}, the distortions of $e_{01}(t)$ consist of two parts: the distortion of $e_{i1}(t)$ and the distortion of $\Delta(t)$. Since $\Delta(t)$ is much smaller than $e_{i1}(t)$ (first order effect), the distortion of $\Delta(t)$ is much smaller than that of $\Delta_{11}(t)$. The latter distortion becomes a second order effect with respect to $e_{i1}(t)$ and can be ignored.

Define

$$B_1 = M_H(A_1, A_2)$$

and

$$B_2 = M_H(A_2, A_1). \qquad (3.3.1.2.11)$$

[†]In practice, $e_{011}(t)$ is only proportional to the right-hand side of Equation 3.3.1.2.9. However, as the TWTA input backoff is properly set, the equality of Equation 3.3.1.2.9 can be assigned without losing any generality of this analysis.

Using Equation 3.3.1.2.11 in Equation 3.3.1.2.10, then

$$e_{011}(t) = |B_1|\left[1 + \mathrm{Re}\left(\frac{1}{B_1}\frac{\partial B_1}{\partial A_1}\right)A_1\,\varepsilon_1(t) + \varepsilon_{11}(t)\right]$$

$$\cdot \exp\left[j\omega_1 t + j\phi_1(t) + j\Delta_1(t) + j\angle B_1\right.$$

$$\left. + j\,\mathrm{Im}\left(\frac{1}{B_1}\frac{\partial B_1}{\partial A_1}\right)A_1\,\varepsilon_1(t) + j\Delta_{11}(t)\right]. \qquad (3.3.1.2.12)$$

Similarly, e_{022} becomes

$$e_{022}(t) = |B_2|\left[1 + \mathrm{Re}\left(\frac{1}{B_2}\frac{\partial B_2}{\partial A_1}\right)A_1\,\varepsilon_1(t)\right]$$

$$\cdot \exp\left[j\omega_2 t + j\phi_2(t) + j\angle B_2\right.$$

$$\left. + j\,\mathrm{Im}\left(\frac{1}{B_2}\frac{\partial B_2}{\partial A_1}\right)A_1\,\varepsilon_1(t)\right]. \qquad (3.3.1.2.13)$$

The two signals $e_{011}(t)$ and $e_{022}(t)$ are present at the TWTA input. At the TWTA output, the desired carrier, which is required in the evaluation of double intelligible crosstalk impairment, is given by

$$e_{002}(t) = M_T\left(|B_2|\left[1 + \mathrm{Re}\left(\frac{1}{B_2}\frac{\partial B_2}{\partial A_1}\right)A_1\,\varepsilon_1(t)\right], |B_1|\right.$$

$$\cdot\left[1 + \mathrm{Re}\left(\frac{1}{B_1}\frac{\partial B_1}{\partial A_1}\right)A_1\,\varepsilon_1(t) + \varepsilon_{11}(t)\right]\right)$$

$$\cdot \exp\left[j\omega_2 t + j\phi_2(t) + j\angle B_2 + j\,\mathrm{Im}\left(\frac{1}{B_2}\frac{\partial B_2}{\partial A_1}\right)A_1\,\varepsilon_1(t)\right]. $$
$$(3.3.1.2.14)$$

Expanding this in a Taylor series expansion with respect to ε_1 and ε_2, and taking only the first order terms, then

$$e_{002}(t) \approx \left\{M_T(|B_2|, |B_1|) + \frac{\partial M_T(|B_2|, |B_1|)}{\partial |B_2|}\,|B_2|A_1\,\varepsilon_1(t)\right.$$

$$\cdot \mathrm{Re}\left(\frac{1}{B_2}\frac{\partial B_2}{\partial A_1}\right) + \frac{\partial M_T(|B_2|, |B_1|)}{\partial |B_1|}\,|B_1|\left[A_1\,\varepsilon_1(t)\right.$$

$$\cdot \mathrm{Re}\left(\frac{1}{B_1}\frac{\partial B_1}{\partial A_1}\right) + \varepsilon_{11}(t)\left.\right]\right\}$$

$$\cdot \exp\left[j\omega_2 t + j\phi_2(t) + j\angle B_2 + j\,\mathrm{Im}\left(\frac{1}{B_2} \frac{\partial B_2}{\partial A_1} \right) A_1\,\varepsilon_1(t) \right].$$

$$(3.3.1.2.15)$$

(T of M_T implies TWTA).

From further simplifications (see Equation 3.3.1.2.6), the desired carrier at the TWTA output is given as

$$e_{002}(t) \approx \left| M_T(|B_2|, |B_1|) \right|$$

$$\cdot \left\{ 1 + \mathrm{Re}\left[\frac{\dfrac{\partial M_T(|B_2|, |B_1|)}{\partial |B_2|}}{M_T(|B_2|, |B_1|)} \right] |B_2| \right.$$

$$\cdot A_1\,\varepsilon_1(t)\,\mathrm{Re}\left(\frac{1}{B_2} \frac{\partial B_2}{\partial A_1} \right)$$

$$+ \mathrm{Re}\left[\frac{\dfrac{\partial M_T(|B_2|, |B_1|)}{\partial |B_1|}}{M_T(|B_2|, |B_1|)} \right] |B_1| \left[A_1\,\varepsilon_1(t) \right.$$

$$\cdot \mathrm{Re}\left(\frac{1}{B_1} \frac{\partial B_1}{\partial A_1} \right) + \varepsilon_{11}(t) \right] \right\} \cdot \exp\left\{ j\omega_2 t + j\phi_2(t) \right.$$

$$+ j\angle B_2 + j\,\mathrm{Im}\left(\frac{1}{B_2} \frac{\partial B_2}{\partial A_1} \right) A_1\,\varepsilon_1(t)$$

$$+ j\,\mathrm{Im}\left[\frac{\dfrac{\partial M_T(|B_2|, |B_1|)}{\partial |B_2|}}{M_T(|B_2|, |B_1|)} \right] \mathrm{Re}\left(\frac{1}{B_2} \frac{\partial B_2}{\partial A_1} \right) A_1 |B_2|\,\varepsilon_1(t)$$

$$+ j\,\mathrm{Im}\left[\frac{\dfrac{\partial M_T(|B_2|, |B_1|)}{\partial |B_1|}}{M_T(|B_2|, |B_1|)} \right] \mathrm{Re}\left(\frac{1}{B_1} \frac{\partial B_1}{\partial A_1} \right) A_1 |B_1|\,\varepsilon_1(t)$$

$$(3.3.1.2.16)$$

$$+ j\,\mathrm{Im}\left[\frac{\dfrac{\partial M_T(|B_2|, |B_1|)}{\partial |B_1|}}{M_T(|B_2|, |B_1|)} \right] |B_1|\,\varepsilon_{11}(t) \right\}.$$

In this result, the phase is important because the amplitude modulation is going to be eliminated by the hard-limiter before the FM discriminator. The fourth, fifth, sixth, and seventh terms in the phase of Equation 3.3.1.2.16 contain the intelligible crosstalk components.

Define

$$C_1 = M_T(|B_1|, |B_2|) \qquad (3.3.1.2.17)$$

$$C_2 = M_T(|B_2|, |B_1|). \qquad (3.3.1.2.18)$$

In Equation 3.3.1.2.16, the relevant phase component, $I(t)$, which contains the above four terms, can be expressed as

$$
\begin{aligned}
I(t) = \Bigg[&\mathrm{Im}\left(\frac{A_1}{B_2}\frac{\partial B_2}{\partial A_1}\right) + \mathrm{Im}\left(\frac{|B_2|}{C_2}\frac{\partial C_2}{\partial |B_2|}\right) \\
&\cdot \mathrm{Re}\left(\frac{A_1}{B_2}\frac{\partial B_2}{\partial A_1}\right) + \mathrm{Im}\left(\frac{|B_1|}{C_2}\frac{\partial C_2}{\partial |B_1|}\right) \\
&\cdot \mathrm{Re}\left(\frac{A_1}{B_1}\frac{\partial B_1}{\partial A_1}\right)\Bigg]\varepsilon_1(t) + \mathrm{Im}\left(\frac{|B_1|}{C_2}\frac{\partial C_2}{\partial |B_1|}\right)\varepsilon_{11}(t). \quad (3.3.1.2.19)
\end{aligned}
$$

The first term of the coefficient of $\varepsilon_1(t)$ corresponds to the intelligible crosstalk component in (a), the second term to that in (b), and the third term to that in (c). The coefficient of $\varepsilon_{11}(t)$ corresponds to the component described in (d). It is noted that the term $\mathrm{Re}[(A_1/B_2)(\partial B_2/\partial A_1)]$ represents the amplitude transfer from the amplitude fluctuation of the crosstalking carrier to the desired carrier amplitude due to the HPA, as mentioned in (b). Also, the term $\mathrm{Re}[(A_1/B_1)(\partial B_1/\partial A_1)]$ represents the suppression of the amplitude fluctuation of the crosstalking carrier due to the HPA as mentioned in (c).

Rewrite Equation 3.3.1.2.19 as

$$I(t) = (D_{N_1F} + D_{N_1S} + D_{N_1T})\varepsilon_1(t) + D_{N_2}\varepsilon_{11}(t) \qquad (3.3.1.2.20)^\dagger$$

or

$$I(t) = D_{N_1}\varepsilon_1(t) + D_{N_2}\varepsilon_{11}(t) \qquad (3.3.1.2.21)$$

where the terms D_{N_1F}, D_{N_1S}, and D_{N_1T} represent respectively the first, second, and third terms of the coefficient D_{N_1} of $\varepsilon_1(t)$, and D_{N_2} is the coefficient of $\varepsilon_{11}(t)$. It is observed that there will be some differences in propagation time among the distortion components included in $\varepsilon_1(t)$ and $\varepsilon_{11}(t)$ due to variations in the propagation time in various transmission path lengths. However, since the two carriers are generated at the same earth station and since the assumption that the maximum time difference is about a few nanoseconds is practically true, the four intelligible

---

$^\dagger D_{N_1F}$, D_{N_1S}, D_{N_1T} and D_{N_2} are similar to the coefficient k_T used in [65].

crosstalk components can be added on a voltage basis (the effect of the time difference at baseband frequencies is negligible for any voice channel since the top baseband frequency of the desired carrier is at most a few megahertz).

At the output of the FM discriminator, in addition to the desired carrier baseband signal, $1/2\pi\, d\phi_2(t)/dt$, there will be intelligible crosstalk components included in $I(t)$.

The phase component, $I(t)$, includes the direct current component, unintelligible noise components, and intelligible crosstalk components. In order to separate the last components from the others, the autocorrelation function of $I(t)$ is obtained. Then the power spectrum of intelligible crosstalk components after FM demodulation can be evaluated by Fourier transformation.

The crosstalking carrier at the F_1 output, $e_{i11}(t)$, can be expressed as

$$e_{i11}(t) = A_1\, e^{j\omega_1 t}\, [e^{j\phi_1(t)} \circledast h_1(t)] \tag{3.3.1.2.22}$$

where $\circledast$ denotes the convolution operation, and $h_1(t)$, the equivalent low-pass impulse response of F_1, is in general complex.

Under the assumption of a first-order theory, Equation 3.3.1.2.22 yields

$$e^{-j\phi_1(t)}\, [e^{j\phi_1(t)} \circledast h_1(t)] = [1 + \varepsilon_1(t)]e^{j\Delta_1(t)}$$

$$\approx [1 + \varepsilon_1(t)] + j\Delta_1(t). \tag{3.3.1.2.23}$$

Therefore,

$$\varepsilon_1(t) = \mathrm{Re}\{e^{-j\phi_1(t)}\, [e^{j\phi_1(t)} \circledast h_1(t)] - 1\}. \tag{3.3.1.2.24}$$

In a way similar to Equation 3.3.1.2.24, from Equation 3.3.1.2.21,

$$I(t) = \mathrm{Re}\left\{\int_{-\infty}^{\infty} [D_{N_1} h_1(x) + D_{N_2} h_{11}(x)]\, e^{-j\phi_1(t) + j\phi_1(t-x)}\, dx \right.$$

$$\left. - (D_{N_1} + D_{N_2}) \right\} \tag{3.3.1.2.25}$$

where $h_{11}(t)$, the equivalent low-pass impulse response of F_{11} is also complex. The term $(D_{N_1} + D_{N_2})$ will be dropped in this result for the convenience of the analysis since it eventually gives only the direct current component.

Let

$$h(t) = D_{N_1} h_1(t) + D_{N_2} h_{11}(t) \tag{3.3.1.2.26}$$

then

$$I(t) = \mathrm{Re}\left[\int_{-\infty}^{\infty} h(x)\, e^{-j\phi_1(t) + j\phi_1(t-x)}\, dx \right]. \tag{3.3.1.2.27}$$

Using the formula

$$\text{Re}(a)\ \text{Re}(b) = \frac{1}{2}\text{Re}(ab^*) + \frac{1}{2}\text{Re}(ab) \qquad (3.3.1.2.28)$$

where

$$a(t) = \int_{-\infty}^{\infty} h(x)\ e^{-j\phi_1(t)\ +\ j\phi_1(t-x)}\ dx \qquad (3.3.1.2.29)$$

$$b(t + \tau) = \int_{-\infty}^{\infty} h(y)\ e^{-j\phi_1(t+\tau)\ +\ j\phi_1(t+\tau-y)}\ dy \qquad (3.3.1.2.30)$$

and the notation a^*, for example, denotes the complex conjugate of a, the autocorrelation of $I(t)$ is given by

$$\overline{I(t)I(t + \tau)} = \frac{1}{4}\overline{a(t)\,b^*(t + \tau)} + \frac{1}{4}\overline{a^*(t)\,b(t + \tau)}$$

$$+ \frac{1}{4}\overline{a(t)\,b(t + \tau)} + \frac{1}{4}\overline{a^*(t)\,b^*(t + \tau)}. \qquad (3.3.1.2.31)$$

Thus, in a way similar to Equation 3.3.1.1.31, the power spectrum of the intelligible crosstalk components after an FM demodulation is (considering only positive frequency)

$$\frac{1}{2}f^2 W_{\phi_1}(f) \left| \int_{-\infty}^{\infty} [W_{C_1}(x) - W_{C_1}(f + x)] \right.$$

$$\left. \cdot [Y(x) - Y^*(-x)]\ dx \right|^2, \qquad (0 \le f < \infty) \quad (3.3.1.2.32)^\dagger$$

where

$$Y(f) = D_{N_1}Y_{C+}^{(1)}(f) + D_{N_2}Y_{C+}^{(11)}(f) \qquad (3.3.1.2.33)$$

where $Y_{C+}^{(1)}(f)$ and $Y_{C+}^{(11)}(f)$ are respectively the transfer functions of the equivalent low-pass filters of F_1 and F_{11}. In order to evaluate this result, the same approach as that explained in Section 3.3.1.1 can be used.

When the HPA and TWTA are both operated in large backoff areas, their amplitude (AM/AM) characteristics can be assumed to be linear and their phase change (AM/PM) characteristics to be proportional to the input power. Therefore,

---

†The factor A_1^2 of Equation 3.3.1.1.31 does not appear in this case, since it is included in $Y(x)$ here.

$$g_H(A) = k_H A$$

$$f_H(A) \overset{\cdot}{=} \gamma_H A^2$$

$$g_T(A) = k_T A$$

$$f_T(A) = \gamma_T A^2 \qquad (3.3.1.2.34)$$

where k_H, k_T, γ_H, and γ_T are the proportional constants.

Therefore, when the inputs to the HPA are represented in the forms of Equations 3.3.1.2.1 and 3.3.1.2.2, the complex output amplitudes of the crosstalking and desired carriers can, after some manipulations, be shown to be respectively (in large backoff regions, the higher order terms are ignored here)

$$B_1 = k_H A_1 + j k_H \gamma_H (A_1^3 + 2 A_1 A_2^2)$$

and

$$B_2 = k_H A_2 + j k_H \gamma_H (A_2^3 + 2 A_2 A_1^2). \qquad (3.3.1.2.35)$$

Similarly, at the TWTA output, the amplitudes are

$$C_1 = k_T |B_1| + j k_T \gamma_T (|B_1|^3 + 2|B_1||B_2|^2)$$

and

$$C_2 = k_T |B_2| + j k_T \gamma_T (|B_2|^3 + 2|B_2||B_1|^2). \qquad (3.3.1.2.36)$$

Using the above results of Equation 3.3.1.2.19, the relevant phase component, $I(t)$, which includes the intelligible crosstalk components, can be approximated as (higher order terms ignored)

$$I(t) \simeq (4\gamma_H A_1^2 + 4\gamma_T |B_1|^2)\varepsilon_1(t) + 4\gamma_T |B_1|^2 \varepsilon_{11}(t). \qquad (3.3.1.2.37)$$

As seen from Equation 3.3.1.2.37, the third cross term, $4\gamma_T |B_1|^2 \varepsilon_1(t)$ cannot be ignored compared with either the first or the fourth term. The second cross terms is negligible (the order of the terms here refers to Equation 3.3.1.2.19). In particular, this result indicates that it would be much simpler to reduce the intelligible crosstalk impairment by improving the amplitude and group delay responses of the filters than the HPA and TWTA nonlinear characteristics.

HPA and TWTA Operated in Any Backoff Regions

In this case, the four distortion terms will be evaluated by means of the expressions of Equations 3.3.1.2.32 and 3.3.1.2.33 and the power series expansions of $Y_{C+}^{(1)}(f)$ and $Y_{C+}^{(11)}(f)$.

Using the Bessel expansion of Equation 3.3.1.1.11, it follows that

$$B_1 = \sum_{s=1}^{L_H} b_s^{(H)} J_1(s\alpha_H A_1) J_0(s\alpha_H A_2)$$

$$B_2 = \sum_{s=1}^{L_H} b_s^{(H)} J_1(s\alpha_H A_2) J_0(s\alpha_H A_1)$$

$$C_1 = \sum_{s=1}^{L_T} b_s^{(T)} J_1(s\alpha_T |B_1|) J_0(s\alpha_T |B_2|)$$

and

$$C_2 = \sum_{s=1}^{L_T} b_s^{(T)} J_1(s\alpha_T |B_2|) J_0(s\alpha_T |B_1|) \qquad (3.3.1.2.38)$$

where J_n is defined as a Bessel function of the first kind of order n.

Differentiations of B_1, B_2, and C_2 are required in Equation 3.3.1.2.19. Therefore, in this case,

$$\frac{\partial B_1}{\partial A_1} = \frac{1}{2} \sum_{s=1}^{L_H} s\alpha_H b_s^{(H)} [J_0(s\alpha_H A_1) - J_2(s\alpha_H A_1)] J_0(s\alpha_H A_2)$$

$$\frac{\partial B_2}{\partial A_1} = -\sum_{s=1}^{L_H} s\alpha_H b_s^{(H)} J_1(s\alpha_H A_1) J_1(s\alpha_H A_2)$$

$$\frac{\partial C_2}{\partial |B_1|} = -\sum_{s=1}^{L_T} s\alpha_T b_s^{(T)} J_1(s\alpha_T |B_1|) J_1(s\alpha_T |B_2|)$$

and

$$\frac{\partial C_2}{\partial |B_2|} = \frac{1}{2} \sum_{s=1}^{L_T} s\alpha_T b_s^{(T)} [J_0(s\alpha_T |B_2|)$$

$$- J_2(s\alpha_T |B_2|)] J_0(s\alpha_T |B_1|). \qquad (3.3.1.2.39)$$

Therefore, the coefficients D_{N_1} and D_{N_2} can be obtained using these results. Also, assume that

$$Y_{C+}^{(1)}(f) = \sum_{n=0}^{L} a_n^{(1)} f^n$$

and that

$$Y_{C+}^{(11)}(f) = \sum_{n=0}^{L} a_n^{(11)} f^n \qquad (3.3.1.2.40)$$

where L is an integer. The coefficients $a_k^{(1)}$ and $a_k^{(11)}$ are, in general, complex. Then, $Y(f)$ in Equation 3.3.1.2.33 becomes

$$Y(f) = \sum_{n=0}^{L} (D_{N_1} a_n^{(1)} + D_{N_2} a_n^{(11)}) f^n. \qquad (3.3.1.2.41)$$

Also, the integral in Equation 3.3.1.2.32 can be computed using the moments of $W_{C_1}(x)$ given in Section 3.3.1.1. Consequently, the N.P.R. (f) can be readily evaluated.

The analytical results given in this Section can be implemented in a computer program to facilitate evaluations of intelligible crosstalk impairment in a double cascaded nonlinearities environment. Two examples will be considered. In the first example, the filters F_1 and F_{11} will be assumed to have identical transfer functions. In the second example, F_1 will be improved over F_{11} (i.e., more severely specified than F_{11}). These examples are intended to show the effects of improving the amplitude and group delay characteristics of the transmit side (i.e., filter F_1) on the N.P.R.

The HPA and TWTA nonlinear characteristics used are those of the Hughes Models 876H 700W TWT and 1244H 8.5W TWT (Fig. 3.3.1.2.3) respectively. The two equal-amplitude FDM/FM carriers accessing both the HPA and TWTA (transponder bandwidth = 77 MHz) are assumed to have identical transmission parameters: number of channels = 612, rms multichannel deviation = 4878 KHz, top baseband frequency = 2540 KHz, bottom baseband frequency = 12 KHz, bandwidth = 36 MHz, and standard CCIR pre-emphasis factors. The N.P.R. will be computed at the top baseband frequency slot of the desired carrier at various HPA and TWTA input backoffs.

Example 1: Identical F_1 *and* F_{11}
In this example, it is assumed that F_1 and F_{11} have identical transfer functions. Figure 3.3.1.2.4 shows the amplitude and group delay responses in which the slope of the amplitude in the carrier bandwidth is 1 dB in 36 MHz, and that of the group delay, 4 ns in 36 MHz. It should be noted here that the symmetric portions in both amplitude and group delay responses do not contribute to the intelligible crosstalk impairment.

Figure 3.3.1.2.5 shows the calculated N.P.R. at various HPA and TWTA input backoffs. From these numerical results, it can be seen that degradations in the N.P.R. are controlled by the AM/PM characteristics of the HPA. However, the N.P.R.'s are found not to be sensitive to changes at the HPA operating point. Also, in the TWTA input backoff range of −6 to −14 dB, the N.P.R.'s obtained at a HPA input backoff of −10 dB are much worse than those at a backoff of −50 dB (equivalent to the case with F_1 and F_{11} linearly cascaded, and with no HPA). This means that because of HPA nonlinearities, the amplitude and group delay responses of F_1 must be much more severely specified than those of F_{11} so that the effects of F_1 are negligible.

Table 3.3.1.2.1 shows the values of D_{N_2}, D_{N_1F}, D_{N_1S}, D_{N_1T}, and D_{N_1} at a HPA input backoff of −10 dB and TWTA input backoff range of −6 to −14 dB. It can be seen that component (a), which corresponds to D_{N_1F} and is described in this Section, tends to dominate over all the other components, namely, (b), (c), and (d). Also, in any backoff areas of TWTA shown in Table 1, cross term

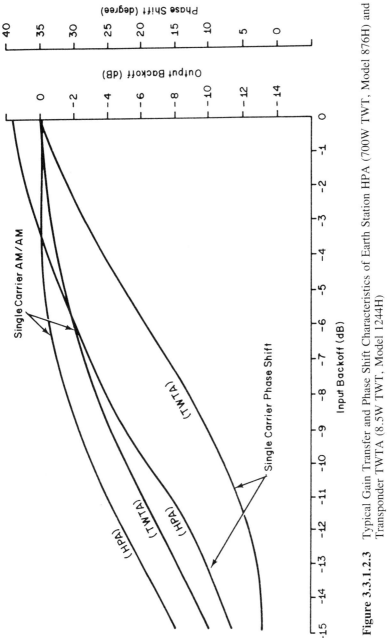

Figure 3.3.1.2.3 Typical Gain Transfer and Phase Shift Characteristics of Earth Station HPA (700W TWT, Model 876H) and Transponder TWTA (8.5W TWT, Model 1244H)

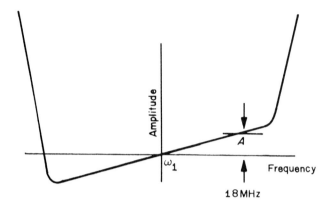

Figure 3.3.1.2.4(a)   Filter Amplitude Response

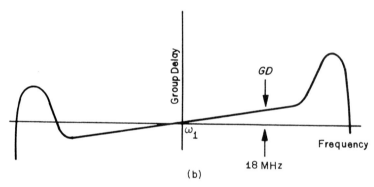

(b)

Notes:

1. $A = 0.5\,dB$ for F_1 (Example 1) and F_{11} (Examples 1 and 2)
    $A = 0.15\,dB$ for F_1 (Example 2)

2. $GD = 2\,ns$ for F_1 (Example 1) and F_{11} (Examples 1 and 2)
    $GD = 0.5\,ns$ for F_1 (Example 2)

Figure 3.3.1.2.4(b)   Filter Group Delay Response

(b) is small and negative, and cross term (c) is close to component (d) except that there is a suppression effect (which becomes larger when the HPA operating point moves to the saturation region) due to the HPA AM/AM characteristics. Therefore, it is preferable that the distortion effects of F_1 could be ignored since they can be controlled at the transmit earth station.

Example 2: F₁ *Better than* F₁₁
In this example, the responses of F_1 will be improved (e.g., slopes of the amplitude and group delay responses of 0.3 dB and 1 ns in 36 MHz respectively,

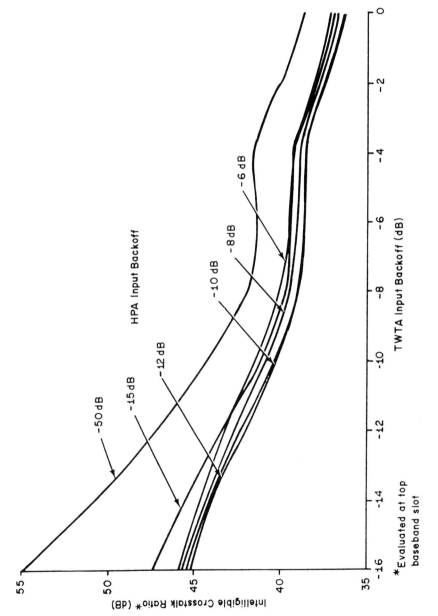

Figure 3.3.1.2.5   Intelligible Crosstalk Ratio versus HPA and TWTA Input Backoffs (Example 1)

Table 3.3.1.2.1

Computed Values of D_{N_1F}, D_{N_1S}, D_{N_1T}, D_{N_1}, and D_{N_2}
(Example 1)

		HPA Input Backoff $= -10$ dB				
		D_{N_1F} [Term (a)]	D_{N_1S} [Cross Term (b)]	D_{N_1T} [Cross Term (c)]	D_{N_1} [Total (a), (b), and (c)]	D_{N_2} [Term (d)]
TWTA Input Backoff (dB)	-6	0.3200	-0.0094	0.2960	0.6066	0.3420
	-8	0.3200	-0.0194	0.2830	0.5836	0.3270
	-10	0.3200	-0.0190	0.2220	0.5230	0.2560
	-12	0.3200	-0.0143	0.1540	0.4597	0.1780
	-14	0.3200	-0.0097	0.1000	0.4103	0.1160

as shown in Figure 3.3.1.2.4). Figure 3.3.1.2.6 shows the calculated N.P.R.'s
for the same HPA and TWTA input backoffs. The HPA and TWTA are found
to have almost the same effects on the N.P.R. as the case in which there is no
HPA. Comparison of Figures 3.3.1.2.5 and 3.3.1.2.6 shows that the effects of
F_1 are now smaller than those of the previous example and are almost negligible.
Also, the N.P.R.'s are much better than those of the previous example.

The above examples clearly indicate that in order to control crosstalk impairment effects in satellite channels, in which two carriers access both the HPA
and the TWTA, the filter characteristics of F_1 at the transmit side must be more
severely specified than F_{11}.

As explained in Equation 3.3.1.1.32, if $Y(f)$ defined by Equation 3.3.1.2.33
is symmetric around zero frequency (the carrier frequency f_0), by choosing
$Y_{C+}^{(1)}(f)$ properly, ($Y_{C+}^{(11)}(f)$ cannot be changed because it is located in the satellite), the intelligible crosstalk component given by Equation 3.3.1.2.32 becomes very small. This is an equalization for the intelligible crosstalk by designing
the pre-HPA filter properly. From Equation 3.3.1.2.33, for an arbitrary symmetric filter $Y(f)$, if $Y_{C+}^{(1)}(f)$ is chosen as

$$Y_{C+}^{(1)}(f) = \frac{1}{D_{N_1}}[Y(f) - D_{N_2}Y_{C+}^{(11)}(f)] \qquad (3.3.1.2.42)$$

in the passband of the FDM/FM signal, the equalization becomes possible.
Because of the nonlinearity of the two devices, the values of D_{N_1} and D_{N_2} are
not equal to unity. Although $Y(f)$ can be arbitrary as long as it is symmetric,
it should be chosen so that the design of $Y_{C+}^{(1)}(f)$ becomes simpler. Note here
that the equalization of Equation 3.3.1.1.42 is only possible for fixed backoffs

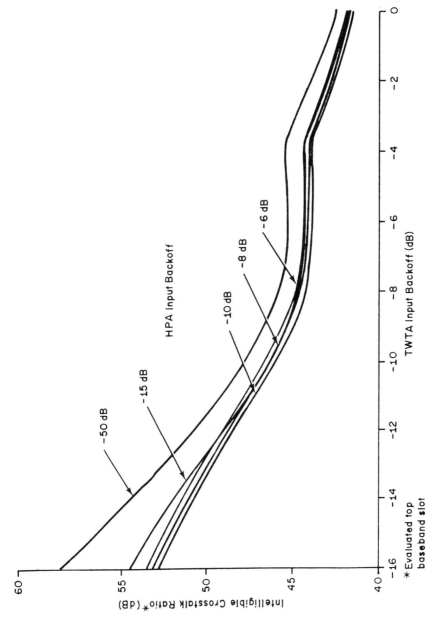

Figure 3.3.1.2.6 Intelligible Crosstalk Ratio versus HPA and TWTA Input Backoffs (Example 2)

of two nonlinear devices. However, it can be shown that the determination of the equalization due to the variations of the backoffs is not so large so that a still large amount of intelligible crosstalk reduction is possible for fairly large variations of the backoffs.

3.3.2   Modulation Transfer from Digital Carriers to FDM/FM Carriers

As explained in Section 4.3 of Volume I, the envelope of the PSK signal fluctuates after the bandwidth limitation of the pulse shaping filter, or IF filter. Because of this envelope fluctuation of the PSK signal, if a FDM/FM signal passes through a nonlinear device (which has a AM/PM nonlinearity) with this PSK signal, the FDM/FM signal receives a disturbance. This disturbance consists of line spectra and of a continuous spectrum in the demodulated baseband of the FDM/FM signal. The analysis is rather sophisticated in this case because it involves a nonlinear random process. Let us start with a simple case before a general approach is shown, in order for the readers to have a concrete example. Let us assume that a QPSK signal and a FDM/FM signal passes through a nonlinear device with a large backoff, where the amplitude is linear and the phase is proportional to the input power.

One of the inputs to the nonlinear device is given, from Equation 2.3.2.5, by

$$e_{i1}(t) = A_1 e^{j\omega_1 t + j\theta} \sum_{k=-\infty}^{\infty} s(t - kT) e^{j\phi k}$$

$$= B(t) e^{j\omega_1 t + j\theta + j\lambda(t)} \tag{3.3.2.1}$$

where $s(t)$ is given by Equation 2.3.2.6. In it, $h_1(t)$ is the low pass analog impulse response of the filter F_1. Another input is the FDM/FM signal,

$$e_{i2}(t) = A_2 e^{j\omega_2 t + j\phi(t)}. \tag{3.3.2.2}$$

Then, the FDM/FM signal at the output of the nonlinear device is

$$e_{02}^{(0)}(t) = M(0, 1; B(t), A_2) e^{j\omega_0 t + j\phi(t)} \tag{3.3.2.3}$$

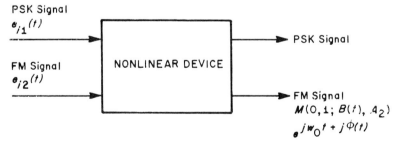

Figure 3.3.2.1   Model for Modulation Transfer from PSK Signal to FM Signal

where

$$M(0, 1; B, A_2) = \int_0^\infty \int_0^\infty \gamma J_1(A_2\gamma) J_0(B(t)\gamma) J_1(\gamma\rho) \, \rho g(\rho) e^{jf(\rho)} \, d\gamma \, d\rho.$$

$$(3.3.2.4)$$

Since $g(\rho)$ and $f(\rho)$ are here given by

$$g(\rho) = g_0\rho, f(\rho) = \beta\rho^2, \tag{3.3.2.5}$$

$$g(\rho)e^{jf(\rho)} \simeq g_0\rho(1 + j\beta\rho^2) = g_0\rho + jg_0\beta\rho^3 \tag{3.3.2.6}$$

(see Equations 3.2.9.2 and 3.2.11.1.23). Then $M(0, 1; B, A_2)$ is given by

$$\begin{aligned} M(0, 1; B, A_2) &= \{g_0A_2 + jg_0\beta(A_2^3 + 2B^2A_2)\} \\ &= g_0A_2\{1 + j\beta(A_2^2 + 2B^2)\} \\ &\simeq g_0A_2 e^{j\beta(A_2^2 + 2B^2)}. \end{aligned} \tag{3.3.2.7}$$

Thus,

$$e_{02}^{(0)}(t) \simeq g_0A_2 e^{j\beta A_2^2} e^{j\omega_0 t + j\phi(t) + j2\beta[B(t)]^2}. \tag{3.3.2.8}$$

In this, the modulation transfer from the QPSK signal to the FDM/FM signal, after the FM demodulator, is

$$\frac{1}{2\pi} \frac{d}{dt} \{[B(t)]^2\}(2\beta). \tag{3.3.2.9}$$

The power spectrum of this component is that of $(2\beta)[B(t)]^2$ multiplied by f^2. Therefore, the power spectrum of $(2\beta)[B(t)]^2$ will be obtained in the following. From Equation 3.3.2.1, $B(t)$ is given by,

$$B(t) = A_1 \left| \sum_{k=-\infty}^{\infty} s(t - kT) e^{j\phi_k} \right|. \tag{3.3.2.10}$$

Thus,

$$\begin{aligned} (2\beta)[B(t)]^2 &= (2\beta)A_1^2 \left| \sum_{k=-\infty}^{\infty} s(t - kT) e^{j\phi_k} \right|^2 \\ &= (2\beta)A_1^2 \sum_{k_1=-\infty}^{\infty} \sum_{k_2=-\infty}^{\infty} s(t - k_1 T) s(t - k_2 T)^* \, e^{j\phi_{k_1} - j\phi_{k_2}}. \end{aligned}$$

$$(3.3.2.11)$$

In order to find the autocorrelation function of this result, rewrite Equation 3.3.2.11 as follows:

$$\sum_{k_1=-\infty}^{\infty}\sum_{k_2=-\infty}^{\infty} s(t-k_1T)s(t-k_2T)^* e^{j\phi_{k_1}-j\phi_{k_2}} = \sum_{k_1=-\infty}^{\infty} |s(t-k_1T)|^2$$

$$+ \sum_{k_1=-\infty}^{\infty} s(t-k_1T)s(t-(k_1-1)T)^* e^{j\phi_{k_1}-j\phi_{k_1-1}}$$

$$+ \sum_{k_1=-\infty}^{\infty} s(t-k_1T)s(t-(k_1+1)T)^* e^{j\phi_{k_1}-j\phi_{k_1+1}}$$

$$+ \sum_{k_1=-\infty}^{\infty} s(t-k_1T)s(t-(k_1-2)T)^* e^{j\phi_{k_1}-j\phi_{k_1-2}}$$

$$+ \sum_{k_1=-\infty}^{\infty} s(t-k_1T)s(t-(k_1+2)T)^* e^{j\phi_{k_1}-j\phi_{k_1+2}}.$$

$$\cdot$$
$$\cdot$$
$$\cdot$$

$$(3.3.2.12)$$

Then,

$$\sum_{k_1=-\infty}^{\infty}\sum_{k_2=-\infty}^{\infty} s(t+\tau-k_1T)s(t+\tau-k_2T) e^{j\phi_{k_1}-j\phi_{k_2}}$$

is obtained by replacing t in Equation 3.3.2.12 by $t+\tau$. Multiplying Equations 3.3.2.12 by this result and taking the average on ϕ_k,

$$\text{Average } [B(t)B(t+\tau)] = \left[\sum_{k_1=-\infty}^{\infty} |s(t-k_1T)|^2\right]\left[\sum_{k_2=-\infty}^{\infty} |s(t+\tau-k_2T)|^2\right]$$

$$+ \sum_{k_1=-\infty}^{\infty} [s(t-k_1T)s(t-(k_1-1)T)^*][s(t+\tau-k_1T)s(t+\tau-(k_1-1)T)^*]^*$$

$$+ \sum_{k_1=-\infty}^{\infty} [s(t-k_1T)s(t-(k_1+1)T)^*][s(t+\tau-k_1T)s(t+\tau-(k_1+1)T)^*]^*$$

$$+ \sum_{k_1=-\infty}^{\infty} [s(t-k_1T)s(t-(k_1-2)T)^*][s(t+\tau-k_1T)s(t+\tau-(k_1-2)T)^*]^*$$

$$+ \sum_{k_1 = -\infty}^{\infty} [s(t - k_1 T) s(t - (k_1 + 2)T)^*][s(t + \tau - k_1 T) s(t + \tau - (k_1 + 2)T)^*]^*$$

$$\vdots$$

$$= \left[\sum_{k_1 = -\infty}^{\infty} |s(t - k_1 T)|^2 \right] \left[\sum_{k_1 = -\infty}^{\infty} |s(t + \tau - k_1 T)|^2 \right]$$

$$+ 2\,\mathrm{Re} \left\{ \sum_{k_1 = -\infty}^{\infty} [s(t - k_1 T) s(t - (k_1 - 1)T)^*] \right.$$

$$\left. \cdot [s(t + \tau - k_1 T) s(t + \tau - (k_1 - 1)T)^*]^* \right\}$$

$$+ 2\,\mathrm{Re} \left\{ \sum_{k_1 = -\infty}^{\infty} [s(t - k_1 T) s(t - (k_1 - 2)T)^*] \right.$$

$$\left. \cdot [s(t + \tau - k_1 T) s(t + \tau - (k_1 - 2)T)^*]^* \right\}$$

$$\vdots$$

$$(3.3.2.13)$$

The first term of this gives the line spectra, since

$$\sum_{k_1 = -\infty}^{\infty} |s(t - k_1 T)|^2$$

is a periodic function of T. Using Equation 2.5.19 of Volume I,

$$\sum_{k_1 = -\infty}^{\infty} |s(t - k_1 T)|^2 = \sum_{k_1 = -\infty}^{\infty} Y_s^{(L)} \left(\frac{k_1}{T} \right) e^{j2\pi \frac{t}{T} k_1} \qquad (3.3.2.14)$$

where

$$Y_s^{(L)}(f) = \frac{1}{T} \int_{-\infty}^{\infty} |s(t)|^2 e^{-j2\pi f t} \, dt. \qquad (3.3.2.15)$$

Thus, the line spectra components are given by

$$(2\beta)^2 A_1^4 \sum_{k=-\infty}^{\infty} \left| Y_s^{(L)} \left(\frac{k}{T} \right) \right|^2 \delta\left(f - \frac{k}{T} \right) \left(\frac{k}{T} \right)^2. \qquad (3.3.2.16)$$

The second, third and following terms give the continuous spectrum,

$$\frac{2}{T} \left| \int_{-\infty}^{\infty} s(t) s(t+T)^* e^{-j2\pi ft} dt \right|^2$$

$$+ \frac{2}{T} \left| \int_{-\infty}^{\infty} s(t) s(t+2T)^* e^{-j2\pi ft} dt \right|^2 + \cdots$$

$$= \sum_{k=1}^{\infty} \frac{2}{T} \left| \int_{-\infty}^{\infty} Y_s^{(c)}(x) Y_s^{(c)}(x-f)^* e^{-j2\pi(kT)x} dx \right|^2 \qquad (3.3.2.17)$$

where

$$Y_s^{(c)}(f) = \int_{-\infty}^{\infty} s(t) e^{-j2\pi ft} dt. \qquad (3.3.2.18)$$

Thus, the power spectrum of the modulation transfer is given by

$$(2\beta)^2 A_1^4 \sum_{k=-\infty}^{\infty} \left(\frac{k}{T} \right)^2 \left| Y_s^{(L)} \left(\frac{k}{T} \right) \right|^2 \delta\left(f - \frac{k}{T} \right)$$

$$+ (2\beta)^2 A_1^4 \frac{2f^2}{T} \sum_{k_1=1}^{\infty} \left| \int_{-\infty}^{\infty} Y_s^{(c)}(x) Y_s^{(c)}(x-f) e^{-j2\pi(kT)x} dx \right|^2.$$

$$(3.3.2.19)$$

For example, the overlapped raised cosine will be assumed to offer more elements of explanation. The overlapped raised cosine can be easily achieved when F_1 is a Bessel filter with an attenuation pole and BT = 1.2, and when the input signal is the window function given by

$$V(t) = 1 \qquad |t| < \frac{T}{2}$$

$$= 0 \qquad |t| \geq \frac{T}{2}. \qquad (3.3.2.20)^\dagger$$

[†] The output of this filter for the input of this square wave is approximately very close to the wave form of Equation 3.3.2.21 (although not exactly the same).

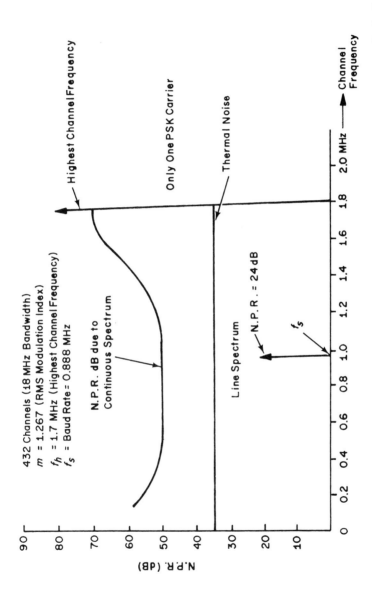

Figure 3.3.2.2 Example of Modulation Transfer from PSK Signal to FDM/FM Signal in Case of Large TWTA Backoff

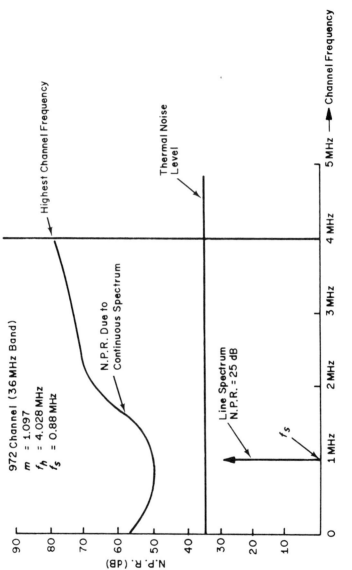

Figure Figure 3.3.2.3 Example of Modulation Transfer from PSK to FDM/FM in Case of Large TWTA Backoff

Then,

$$s(t) \simeq \cos^2\left(\frac{\pi}{2T}t\right), \qquad |t| \leq T$$

$$\simeq 0, \qquad\qquad\qquad \text{Elsewhere.} \qquad (3.3.2.21)$$

Then,

$$Y_s^{(L)}(f) = \frac{3}{4}\frac{\sin(2\pi fT)}{(2\pi fT)} + \frac{1}{2}\frac{\sin\left\{2\pi\left(f - \frac{1}{2T}\right)T\right\}}{2\pi\left(f - \frac{1}{2T}\right)T}$$

$$+ \frac{1}{2}\frac{\sin\left\{2\pi\left(f + \frac{1}{2T}\right)T\right\}}{2\pi\left(f + \frac{1}{2T}\right)T} + \frac{1}{8}\frac{\sin\left\{2\pi\left(f - \frac{1}{T}\right)T\right\}}{2\pi\left(f - \frac{1}{T}\right)T}$$

$$+ \frac{1}{8}\frac{\sin\left\{2\pi\left(f + \frac{1}{T}\right)T\right\}}{2\pi\left(f + \frac{1}{T}\right)T} \qquad (3.3.2.22)$$

where

$$\left|Y_s^{(L)}(0)\right|^2 = \frac{9}{16}$$

$$\left|Y_s^{(L)}\left(\pm\frac{1}{T}\right)\right|^2 = \frac{1}{64}$$

$$\left|Y_s^{(L)}\left(\pm\frac{k}{T}\right)\right|^2 = 0, \qquad k \geq 2. \qquad (3.3.2.23)$$

For the continuous spectrum, only the first term of Equation 3.3.2.17 is not zero, which is given by

$$\left| \int_{-\infty}^{\infty} s(t)s(t+T)^* e^{-j2\pi ft} \, dt \right|^2$$

$$= \left| \int_{-\infty}^{\infty} Y_s^{(c)}(x) Y_s^{(c)}(x-f)^* \, e^{-j2\pi(kT)x} \, dx \right|^2$$

$$= \left[\frac{T}{8} \frac{\sin(\pi fT)}{\pi fT} + \frac{T}{16} \frac{\sin\left\{ \pi\left(f - \dfrac{1}{T}\right)T \right\}}{\pi\left(f - \dfrac{1}{T}\right)T} \right.$$

$$\left. + \frac{T}{16} \frac{\sin\left\{ \pi\left(f + \dfrac{1}{T}\right)T \right\}}{\pi\left(f + \dfrac{1}{T}\right)T} \right]^2 . \qquad (3.3.2.24)$$

Substituting these results into Equation 3.3.2.19, the power spectrum of the modulation transfer can be obtained. Figures 3.3.2.2 and 3.3.2.3 show practical examples of modulation transfers.

The above case can be applied only to large backoff areas. A general approach applicable to any backoff areas will be explained in the following. Suppose that $e_{i1}(t)$ in the ℓ-th symbol interval $(\ell T - T/2, \ell T + T/2)$ is given by

$$e_{i1} = A_1 e^{j\omega_1 t + j\theta} \sum_{k=\ell-n_1}^{\ell+n_2} s(t - kT) e^{j\phi_k}. \qquad (3.3.2.25)$$

It is here assumed that the effects of the intersymbol interferences are finite, i.e., the pulse $s(t)$ is confined to $(-n_1 T - T/2, n_2 T + T/2)$. This assumption is not rigorous in practical examples but constitutes a good approximation in most cases, since $s(t)$ attenuates exponentially with time in negative and positive values of t for physically realizable filters.

Thus, define the function

$$E(t - \ell T; \Phi_\ell) = \sum_{k=\ell-n_1}^{\ell+n_2} s(t - kT) e^{j\phi_k}, \quad \left(\ell T - \frac{T}{2} \le t \le \ell T + \frac{T}{2} \right)$$

$$= 0, \quad t \in \text{Elsewhere}.$$

$$(3.3.2.26)$$

Using this function, Equation 3.3.2.1 becomes

$$e_{i1} = A_1 e^{j\omega_1 t + j\theta} \sum_{\ell=-\infty}^{\infty} E(t - \ell T; \Phi_\ell)$$

$$= B(t) e^{j\omega_1 t + j\lambda + j\theta} \qquad (3.3.2.27)$$

Now, $E(t; \Phi_\ell)$ is correlated with $E(t; \Phi_{\ell-n_1-n_2+1})$, $E(t; \Phi_{\ell-n_1-n_2+2})$, $\cdots$, $E(t; \Phi_{\ell+n_1+n_2-2})$, $E(t; \Phi_{\ell+n_1+n_2-1})$, while all the ϕ_k's are mutually interdependent. Using this $E(t; \Phi_\ell)$, the input of the FM demodulator is given from Equation 3.3.2.3, by,

$$e_{02}^{(0)}(t) = |M(0, 1; A_2, B(t))| e^{j\omega_2 t + j\phi(t) + j\angle M}. \qquad (3.3.2.28)$$

Thus, the demodulated modulation transfer is given by

$$\frac{1}{2\pi} \frac{d}{dt} \{\angle M(0, 1; A_2, B(t))\} = \frac{1}{2\pi} \frac{d}{dt} \text{Im}\{\ln[M(0, 1; B(t), A_2)]\}. \qquad (3.3.2.29)$$

The power spectrum of this function must be obtained, which is that of

$$\text{Im}\{\ln[M(0, 1; B, A_2)]\} = I(t). \qquad (3.3.2.30)$$

$I(t)$ in the time interval $(kT - 1/2\, T,\ kT + T/2)$ is

$$I(t) = I(t - kT; \Phi_k)$$

$$= \text{Im}\{\ln[M(0, 1; A_1|E(t - kT; \Phi_k)|, A_2)]\}\, V(t - kT) \qquad (3.3.2.31)$$

where $V(t)$ is defined by Equation 3.3.2.20.

The autocorrelation function of Equation 3.3.2.30 is given by

$$\underset{\Phi}{E}\{I(t)\, I(t+\tau)\} = \sum_{k=-\infty}^{\infty} R_k(\tau - kT) \qquad (3.3.2.32)^\dagger$$

where

$$R_k(\tau) = \underset{\Phi_0, \Phi_k}{E} \left[\frac{1}{T} \int_{-\frac{T}{2}}^{\frac{T}{2}} I(t; \Phi_0)\, I(t+\tau; \Phi_k)\, dt \right] \qquad (k \neq 0)$$

$$R_0(\tau) = \underset{\Phi_0}{E} \left[\frac{1}{T} \int_{-\frac{T}{2}}^{\frac{T}{2}} I(t; \Phi_0)\, I(t+\tau, \Phi_0)\, dt \right]. \qquad (3.3.2.33)$$

$\dagger$ See Section 2.11 of Volume I for the results.

Define

$$R_\infty(\tau) = \frac{1}{T} \int_{-\frac{T}{2}}^{\frac{T}{2}} E_{\Phi_0} \{I(t; \Phi_0)\} \, E_{\Phi_0} \{I(t+\tau; \Phi_0)\} dt. \qquad (3.3.2.34)$$

Then, Equation 3.3.2.32 becomes

$$E_\Phi [I(t)I(t+\tau)] = \sum_{k=-\infty}^{\infty} [R_k(\tau - kT) - R_\infty(\tau - kT)] + \sum_{k=-\infty}^{\infty} R_\infty(\tau - kT).$$

$$(3.3.2.35)$$

Since I_0 and I_k become independent when $k \to \infty$,

$$\underset{k \to \infty}{\text{Lim}} [R_k(\tau - kT) - R_\infty(\tau - kT)] = 0. \qquad (3.3.2.36)$$

Therefore, the first and second terms of Equation 3.3.2.35 are, respectively, the continuous spectrum and line spectrum.

(i) Line Spectra

The autocorrelation function of the line spectra are given by

$$\sum_{k=-\infty}^{\infty} R_\infty(\tau - kT). \qquad (3.3.2.37)$$

From Equation 3.3.2.34, the power spectra of the line spectra are given as follows. Using the Fourier transform

$$\int_{-\frac{T}{2}}^{\frac{T}{2}} E_{\Phi_0} \{I(t; \Phi_0)\} e^{-j2\pi ft} \, dt = \epsilon(f) \qquad (3.3.2.38)$$

$$W^{(L)}(f) = \frac{1}{T} \sum_{k=-\infty}^{\infty} \left| \epsilon\left(\frac{k}{T}\right) \right|^2 \delta\left(f - \frac{k}{T}\right) \qquad (-\infty < f < \infty). \qquad (3.3.2.39)$$

(ii) Continuous Spectrum

The continuous spectrum portion of $I(t)$ is done by Fourier transforming the first term of Equation 3.3.2.35

$$\sum_{k=-\infty}^{\infty} e^{j2\pi kTf} \int_{-\infty}^{\infty} [R_k(\tau) - R_\infty(\tau)] e^{j2\pi f\tau} \, d\tau$$

$$= \sum_{k=-n_1}^{n_2} e^{j2\pi fkT} \int_{-\infty}^{\infty} [R_k(\tau) - R_\infty(\tau)] e^{j2\pi f\tau} \, d\tau \qquad (3.3.2.40)$$

since, from Equation 3.3.2.26,

$$R_k(\tau) = R_\infty(\tau) \qquad \text{for } k > n_2 \text{ and } k < -n_1. \qquad (3.3.2.41)$$

Defining

$$W_{\Phi_\ell}(f) = \int_{-\frac{T}{2}}^{\frac{T}{2}} I(t;\, \Phi_\ell)e^{-j2\pi ft}\, dt$$

$$= \int_{-\frac{T}{2}}^{\frac{T}{2}} \mathrm{Im}\{\ln[M(0,\, 1;\, A_1|E(t;\, \Phi_\ell)|,\, A_2)]\}e^{-j2\pi ft}\, dt. \quad (3.3.2.42)$$

The continuous spectrum is finally given by

$$\frac{1}{T} \sum_{k=-(n_1+n_2)}^{(n_1+n_2)} e^{j2\pi fTk}\, [\underset{\Phi_0,\Phi_k}{E}\, \{W_{\Phi_0}(f)\, W_{\Phi_k}(-f)\} - \underset{\Phi_0}{|E}\, \{W_{\Phi_0}(f)\}|^2].$$

$$(3.3.2.43)$$

Figures 3.3.2.4–3.3.2.8 show the practical examples calculated according to the above analytical results. Some results are compared with measured data, which show good congruence. All these analyses and calculated results lead one to conclude that the baseband channel of the FDM/FM, whose frequencies are equal to the symbol rates of the digital carriers, cannot be used because of large tonal interferences. In addition to these tonal interferences, if the power levels of the digital carriers are larger than that of FDM/FM carriers, the continuous power spectra cannot be ignored. See Reference [70] for detailed analyses and results.

In the above analysis, modulation transfers only due to the bandwidth limitation of the PSK signal are considered. There is another important modulation transfer from PSK signals to FDM/FM signals, which is produced by the burst mode of the PSK signals, when the PSK signals are in the TDMA (time division multiple access). For simplicity's sake, it is also assumed here that only one FDM/FM signal and one TDMA signal (QPSK) pass through the nonlinear device.

In practice, the TDMA/PSK signals receive two types of envelope changes, i.e., one due to filters and the other, due to the TDMA burst mode. Again, to avoid complexity, the envelope change due to the TDMA burst mode is considered, and the envelope change due to filters is ignored in the following. However, a combined general case will be discussed later. Now, $e_{i1}(t)$ of Equation 3.3.2.1 becomes

$$e_{i1} = A_1\left[\sum_{k=-\infty}^{\infty} V_F(t - k\, T_F - t_0)\right]$$

$$\cdot \left[\sum_{\ell=-\infty}^{\infty} V(t - \ell T)e^{j\phi_\ell}\right] \quad (3.3.2.44)$$

where $V(t)$ is defined by Equation 3.3.2.20 and $V_F(t)$ is the burst function in a frame (t_0 is an initial time setting), and T_F is the frame period.

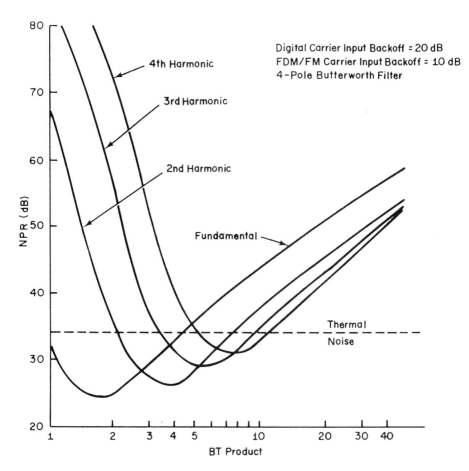

Figure 3.3.2.4 N.P.R. in 972-Channel Carrier Due to Discrete Spectrum of Modulation Transfer Noise from 1.765 Mbit/s QPSK Carrier versus *BT* Product. Digital Carrier Input Backoff: 20 dB. FDM/FM Carrier Input Backoff: 10 dB. Four-Pole Butterworth Filter

$$V_F(t) = 1 \qquad \text{when the TDMA signal appears}$$

and

$$= 0 \qquad \text{when the TDMA signal disappears.} \qquad (3.3.2.45)$$

In this case, $B(t)$ of Equation 3.3.2.1 is given by

$$B(t) = A_1 \sum_{k=-\infty}^{\infty} V_F(t - kT_F). \qquad (3.3.2.46)$$

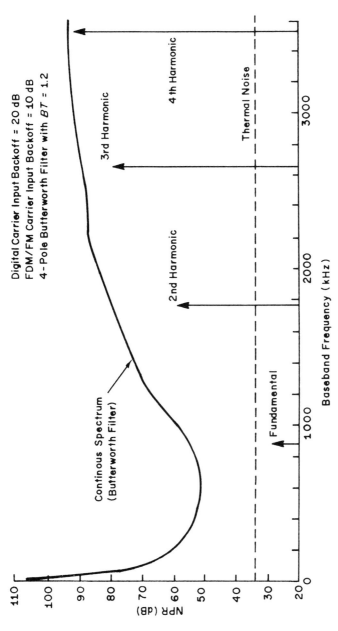

Figure 3.3.2.5 Continuous and Discrete Spectra N.P.R.'s in 972-Channel Carrier Due to 1.765 Mbit/s QPSK Carrier. Digital Carrier Input Backoff: 20 dB. FDM/FM Carrier Input Backoff: 10 dB. Four-Pole Butterworth Filter with $BT = 1.2$

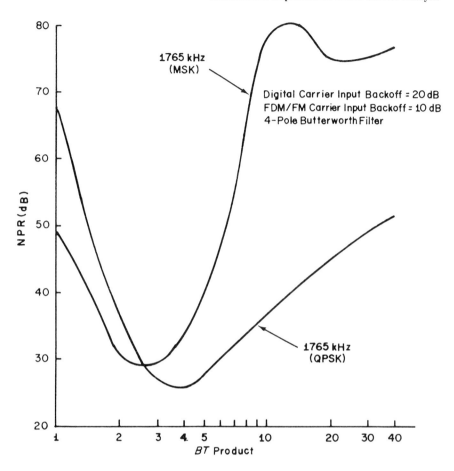

Figure 3.3.2.6   N.P.R. Corresponding to 1765 kHz Component in 972-Channel
Carrier Due to 1.765 Mbit/s QPSK and MSK Carriers versus
BT product. Digital Carrier Input Backoff: 20 dB. FDM/FM
Carrier Input Backoff: 10 dB. Four-Pole Butterworth Filter

Therefore, the function $I(t)$ of Equation 3.3.2.30 is not a random function but
a deterministic periodic function of t whose period is T_F. Therefore, $I(t)$ can be
expanded by a Fourier series as

$$I(t) = \sum_{k=-\infty}^{\infty} a_k \, e^{j2\pi \frac{k}{T_F} t} \qquad (3.3.2.47)$$

where

$$a_k = \frac{1}{T_F} \int_0^{T_F} I(t) e^{-j2\pi \frac{k}{T_F} t} \, dt. \qquad (3.3.2.48)$$

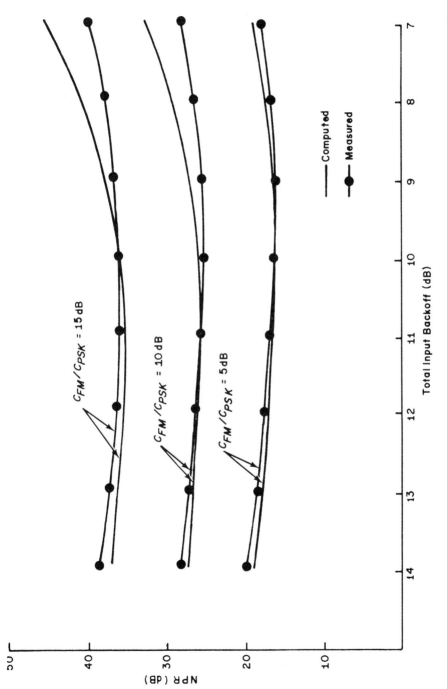

Figure 3.3.2.7 Fundamental Component N.P.R. in 312-Channel Carrier Due to 1.248 Mbit/s QPSK Carrier versus Total Input Backoff. Comparison between Measured and Computed Results (Preemphasis not Included)

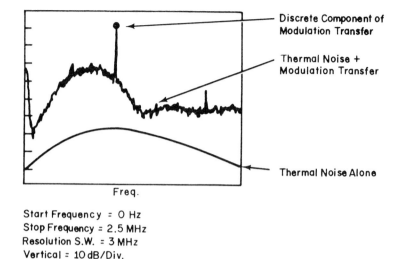

Start Frequency = O Hz
Stop Frequency = 2.5 MHz
Resolution S.W. = 3 MHz
Vertical = 10 dB/Div.

Figure 3.3.2.8   Received Baseband of 972-Channel Carrier. Digital Carrier
Modulated. Frequency Span = 2.5 MHz

Using this expansion, the power spectra of the line components of the demodulated modulation transfer are given by

$$W_I(f) = \sum_{k=-\infty}^{\infty} f^2 \, |a_k|^2 \, \delta\left(f - \frac{k}{T_F}\right)$$

$$= \sum_{k=-\infty}^{\infty} |a_k|^2 \left(\frac{k}{T_F}\right)^2 \delta\left(f - \frac{k}{T_F}\right) \qquad (-\infty < f < \infty). \quad (3.3.2.49)$$

Note here that the frame rate of the TDMA signal $(1/T_F)$ is usually much
lower than the symbol rate of the PSK $(1/T)$ $(1/T_F$ is around the order of 500 Hz).
In order to give readers some practical feeling, let us evaluate one of the simplest
cases of $V_F(t)$ (which occurs practically at HPA) as shown in Figure 3.3.2.10.
In this case,

$$a_k = \frac{1}{T_F} \text{Im}\{\ln[M(0, 1; A_1, A_2)]\} \int_0^{\Delta T_F} e^{-j2\pi \frac{k}{T_F} t} \, dt$$

$$= \left(\frac{\Delta T_F}{T_F}\right) \left[\frac{\sin\left(\pi \frac{k}{T_F} \Delta T_F\right)}{\left(\pi \frac{k}{T_F} \Delta T_F\right)}\right] e^{-j\pi \frac{k}{T_F} \Delta T_F} \text{Im}\{\ln[M(0, 1; A_1, A_2)]\}.$$

$$(3.3.3.2.50)$$

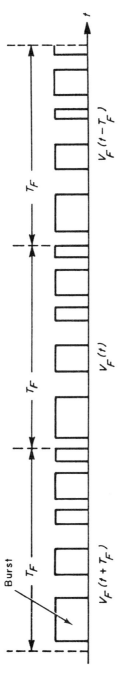

Figure 3.3.2.9 Example of Frame Window Function

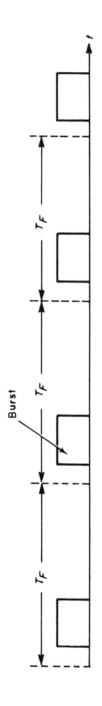

Figure 3.3.2.10 Frame Window Function of Only One Burst per Frame

Therefore,

$$
|a_k|^2 = \left(\frac{\Delta T_F}{T_F}\right)^2 \left[\frac{\sin\left(\pi \dfrac{k}{T_F} \Delta T_F\right)}{\left(\pi \dfrac{k}{T_F} \Delta T_F\right)}\right]^2 [\mathrm{Im}\{\ln M(0,\ 1;\ A_1,\ A_2)\}]^2.
$$

(3.3.2.51)

Thus,

$$
W_l(f) = \left(\frac{\Delta T_F}{T_F}\right)^2 [\mathrm{Im}\{\ln M(0,\ 1;\ A_1,\ A_2)\}]^2
$$

$$
\cdot \sum_{k=-\infty}^{\infty} \left\{\frac{\sin\left(\pi k \dfrac{\Delta T_F}{T_F}\right)}{\left(\pi k \dfrac{\Delta T_F}{T_F}\right)}\right\}^2 \left(\frac{k}{T_F}\right)^2 \delta\left(f - \frac{k}{T_F}\right) \qquad (-\infty < f < \infty).
$$

(3.3.2.52)

As seen from this result, the line spectrum at $f = k/T_F$ does not decrease when k increases, i.e., it is just oscillating with k. Figures 3.3.2.11–3.3.2.13 show the numerical examples for these cases. As can be easily seen from Equation 3.3.2.4, the cases in which there is more than one FDM/FM carrier, can be easily handled by just extending Equation 3.3.2.4 into

$$
M(0,\ 0,\ \ldots,\ \overset{\ell\text{th}}{1},\ \ldots,\ 0,\ 0;\ B(t),\ A_2,\ A_3,\ \ldots,\ A_{n-1})
$$

$$
= \int_0^\infty \int_0^\infty \gamma J_1(A_\ell \gamma)\, J_0(B(t)\gamma) \prod_{\substack{p=2 \\ (p \neq \ell)}}^{n-1} J_0(A_p \gamma)
$$

$$
\cdot J_1(\rho \gamma)\rho g(p)e^{jf(\rho)}\, d\rho\, d\gamma
$$

(3.3.2.53)

as far as there is only one PSK signal, where the ℓ-th carrier is considered as the FDM/FM signal to be demodulated. In this case, the approaches to obtain the line spectra and continuous spectrum due to the filter bandwidth limitation of the PSK signal $(B(t))$, and the line spectra due to the TDMA burst mode are exactly the same as above (only one FDM/FM and one PSK). However, if there is more than one PSK signal, the above approaches cannot be used in general, unless the ratio between the symbol rates of two PSK signals is rational. Even if the symbol rate ratio is a rational number, this approach is extremely complicated, although the above analysis can be applied.

Therefore, a different approach must be applied. This book only shows a guideline for this general case and readers are recommended to read Reference

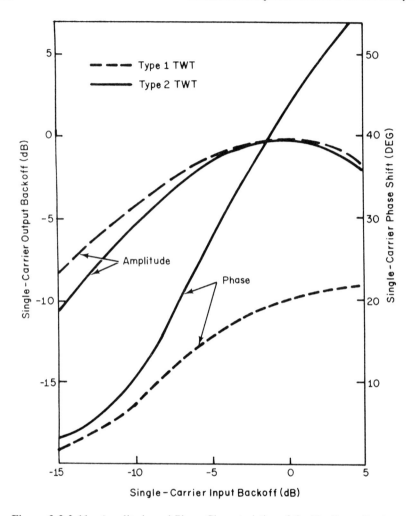

Figure 3.3.2.11 Amplitude and Phase Characteristics of the Nonlinear Devices

[71] for a more detailed analysis. If the symbol rates of two PSK signals are different, the general formula of Equation 3.3.2.32 cannot be used, unless the ratio between two symbols is a rational number. In case where T_2 and T_1 (respectively, the symbol periods of two PSK signals) have a rational ratio, take the least common multiple of T_1 and T_2, i.e.,

$$T = q_1 T_1, \ T = q_2 T_2 \qquad (3.3.2.54)$$

where q_1 and q_2 are the integers which give T the smallest possible value. Then, the general formula of Equation 3.3.2.32 is still applicable, except for the fact that the random variable Φ_0, Φ_k becomes complicated.

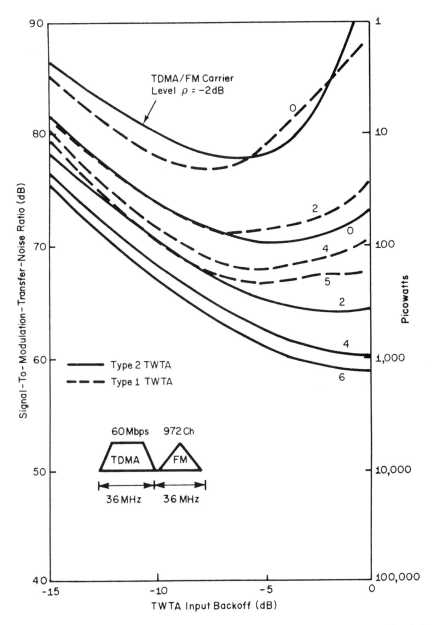

Figure 3.3.2.12 SNR versus TWTA Input Backoff (one TDMA and one FM Carrier)

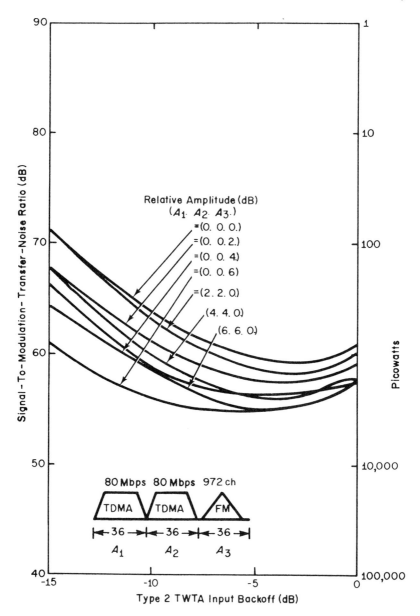

Figure 3.3.2.13   SNR versus TWTA Input Backoff (two TDMA and one FM
                        Carriers)

When the ratio between T_1 and T_2 is not a rational number, the following approach can be used. Let us assume that there are n_1 FDM/FM signals and n_2 PSK signals. Then $I(t)$ of Equation 3.3.2.30 is now given by

$$I(t) = \text{Im} \log[M(1, 0, \ldots, 0; A_1, A_2, \ldots, A_{n_1}, B_1, B_2, \ldots, B_{n_2})]$$

(3.3.2.55)

where

$$M(1, 0, \ldots, 0; A_1, A_2, \ldots, A_{n_1}, B_1, B_2, \ldots, B_{n_2})$$

$$= \int_0^\infty \int_0^\infty \gamma J_1(A_1\gamma)\left[\prod_{p=2}^{n_1} J_0(A_p\gamma)\right]\left[\prod_{q=1}^{n_2} J_0(B_q\gamma)\right]$$

$$\cdot J_1(\gamma\rho)\rho g(\rho)e^{jf(\rho)}\,d\rho.$$

(3.3.2.56)

For analytical convenience, the A_1-carrier here is assumed to be the FDM/FM signal to be demodulated. Other cases can be handled in the same way.

Assume that Equation 3.3.2.56 is expanded by a power series of $B_1, B_2, \ldots, B_{n_2}$ as

$$I(t) = \sum_{\ell_1=0}^\infty \sum_{\ell_2=0}^\infty \cdots \sum_{\ell_{n_2}=0}^\infty C_{\ell_1,\ell_2,\ldots,\ell_{n_2}} B_1^{\ell_1} B_2^{\ell_2} \cdots B_{n_2}^{l_{n_2}} \quad (3.3.2.57)$$

where $C_{\ell_1,\ell_2,\ldots,\ell_{n_2}}$ is a function of the nonlinear characteristics $g(\rho)$, $f(\rho)$, and $A_1, A_2, \ldots, A_{n_1}$.

As explained in Reference [70], the line spectra components are given by the average of $I(t)$ on all the random variables in $B_1, B_2, \ldots, B_{n_2}$, i.e.,

$$E\{I(t)\} = \sum_{\ell_1=0}^\infty \sum_{\ell_2=0}^\infty \cdots \sum_{\ell_{n_2}=0}^\infty C_{\ell_1,\ell_2,\ldots,\ell_{n_2}} \prod_{k=1}^{n_2} E\{B_k^{\ell_k}\} \quad (3.3.2.58)$$

where average $\{B_k^{\ell_k}\}$ is obviously a periodic function of t and can be expanded by a Fourier series whose period is the symbol period T_k of the k-th PKS signal. Therefore, the line spectra contained in Average $\{I(t)\}$ are at the frequencies of

$$\frac{m_1}{T_1} + \frac{m_2}{T_2} + \cdots + \frac{m_{n_2}}{T_{n_2}} \quad (3.3.2.59)$$

where all the m_k's take zero and negative and positive integers.

Approaches to obtain the continuous spectrum of $I(t)$ is unknown to the author at this moment, although the effects of the continuous spectrum are not negligible at all.

3.3.3   Modulation Transfer From Digital Carriers to Digital Carriers

When a number of digital carriers pass through a nonlinear device, a degradation of each carrier occurs due to the intermodulation products, adjacent channel interferences and modulation transfers. In this Section, only the modulation transfers are analyzed (the other signal degradations are explained in the other Sections). Detailed analyses will not be done, since the effects of the modulation transfer from PSK signals to PSK signals are not well known yet. Therefore, after some simple explanations on this subject, only key points will be listed for readers. The complete solutions of this Section belong to future studies.

To begin with, consider only two PSK input signals as

$$e_i(t) = A_1(t)\, e^{j(\omega_0 + \omega_1)t + j\phi_1(t)}$$

$$+ A_2(t)\, e^{j(\omega_0 + \omega_2)t + j\phi_2(t)} \qquad (3.3.3.1)^\dagger$$

where the first term is a filtered PSK signal, which is considered as an interferer and the second is another PSK signal, which is considered as the main signal. The symbol rates of these two PSK signals are not necessarily the same here. The signal of the A_2-carrier at the output of the nonlinear device is given by

$$M(0,\, 1;\, A_1(t),\, A_2(t))\, e^{j(\omega_0 + \omega_2)t + j\phi_2(t)} \qquad (3.3.3.2)$$

where

$M(0,\, 1;\, A_1(t),\, A_2(t))$

$$= \int_0^\infty \int_0^\infty \gamma J_0(A_1(t)\gamma)\, J_1(A_2(t)\gamma)\, J_1(\gamma\rho)\rho g(\rho)\, e^{jf(\rho)}\, d\gamma\, d\rho. \qquad (3.3.3.3)$$

Equation 3.3.3.2 can be rewritten as

$$\left| M(0,\, 1;\, A_1(t),\, A_2(t)) \right| e^{j(\omega_0 + \omega_1)t + j\phi_2(t)}\, e^{j\angle M(0,\, 1;\, A_1(t),\, A_2(t))} \qquad (3.3.3.4)$$

where

$$\angle\, M(0,\, 1;\, A_1(t),\, A_2(t)) = \mathrm{Im}\{\ln[M(0,\, 1;\, A_1(t),\, A_2(t))]\}. \qquad (3.3.3.5)$$

As seen from these two results, the amplitude and phase of the A_2-carrier are respectively function of $A_1(t)$ which variates with the symbol rate of the A_1-carrier. Figure 3.3.3.1 shows the change of the amplitude and phase of the A_2-carrier when the A_1-carrier appears and disappears at various backoffs. From this Figure, it is clear that the following things occurs:

(i) In the areas of small backoffs, a fairly large amount of the phase change of the A_2-carrier appears when the A_1-carrier appears and disappears. This

---

$^\dagger A_1(t)$ and $A_2(t)$ undergo large changes with t because of the pulse shaping filters, as explained in Section 2.1.3.

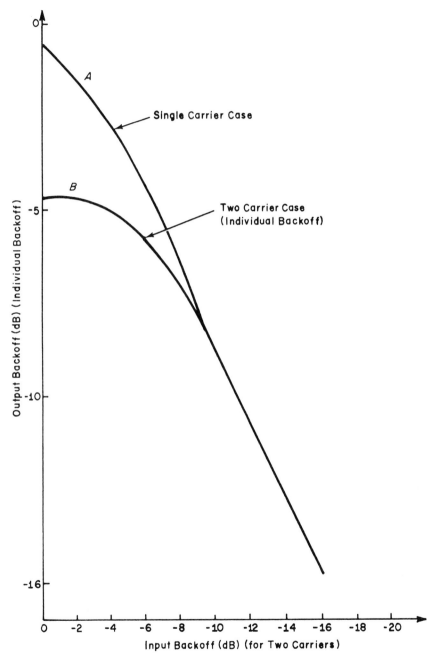

Figure 3.3.3.1(a) Input Backoff versus Output Backoff for Single Carrier Case and Two Carrier Case

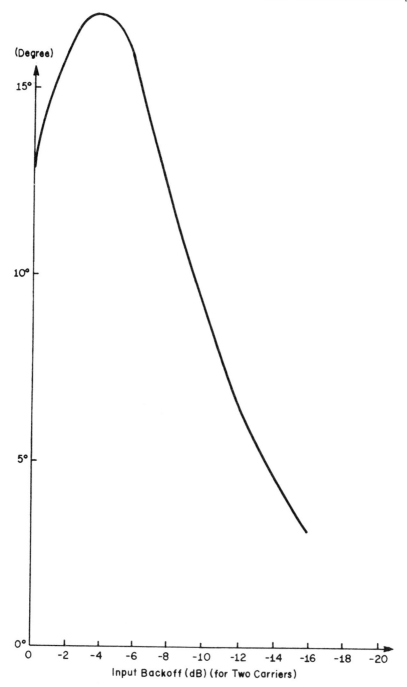

Figure 3.3.3.1(b)   Phase Difference Between Single Carrier Case and Two Carrier Case

results in the degradation of the error probabilities of the A_2-carrier if the amplitude of the A_2-carrier is not strengthened when the A_1-carrier disappears. However, because of the strengthened amplitude produced when the A_1-carrier disappears, the error probability degradation due to the phase change is cancelled. This effect is dependent upon the relative positions of two symbol periods.

(ii) In large backoff areas, the amplitude change of the A_2-carrier is almost zero when the A_1-carrier appears and disappears but the phase of the A_2-carrier changes because of the change of the A_1-carrier envelope. Since there is no amplitude fluctuation of the A_2-carrier and only the phase fluctuates, the degradation of the error probabilities of the A_2-carrier certainly occurs. However, it may happen that the demodulation filter at the ground terminal reduces this change of phase.

Thus, the degradation of the phase may be small (as shown by some measurements). It is a fact that many things are still unknown in this area. This effect is also dependent on the relative position of two PSK symbol periods as shown in Figure 3.3.3.2. If there are more than two carriers, the degradation of the PSK signals decreases because of the larger back off being used (the more numerous the carriers, the more backoff is needed compared with a two carrier case because of the intermodulation products).

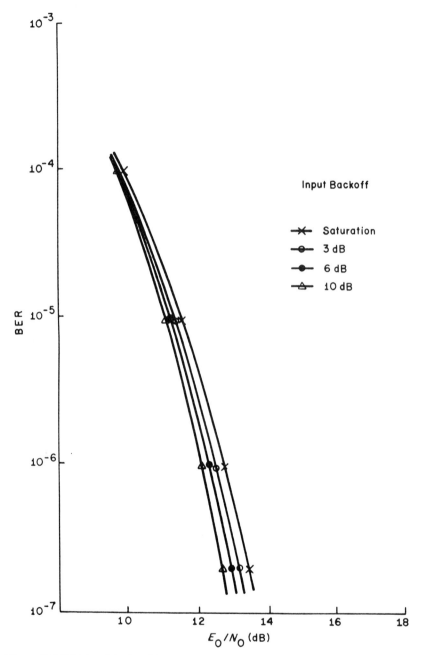

Figure 3.3.3.2(a)   Calculated BER versus E_b/N_0 at Various Total TWTA Input
                         Backoffs. Two Equal-Level 2.731 Mbit/s QPSK Carriers (Two-
                         Carrier Case). Nonsynchronous Data, 1 Bit Delay. E_b Refers to
                         Unmodulated Power

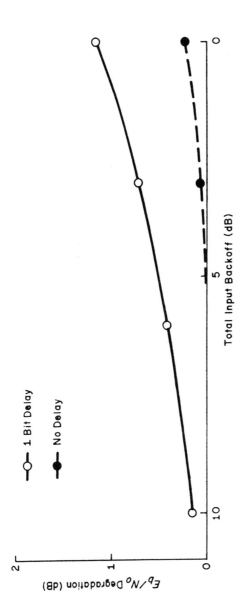

Figure 3.3.3.2(b) Calculated Degradation in E_b/N_0 due to Modulation Transfer Noise Effect at BER $= 10^{-6}$ versus Total TWTA Input Backoff. Degradation Obtained from Comparison of BER Performance between Single-Carrier Case and Two-Carrier Case (Two Equal-Level Carriers). E_b Refers to Unmodulated Power

3.4   EXERCISES

1. Prove that k of Equation 3.1.43 must be an odd positive integer.

2. Prove Equations 3.1.44 and 3.1.45.

3. Derive the result of Equation 3.2.2.5.

4. Derive Equation 3.2.4.3.

5. Derive Equation 3.2.6.19 from Equations 3.2.6.17 and 3.2.6.18.

6. Prove the result of Equation 3.2.6.28.

7. Prove the result of Equation 3.2.6.27 from Equation 3.2.6.24.

8. Prove Equation 3.2.6.37.

9. Prove the result of Equation 3.2.7.7.

10. Prove Equation 3.2.8.23 from 3.2.8.21.

11. Prove Equation 3.2.8.27 from Equation 3.2.8.24.

12. Derive the results of Equations 3.2.11.1.6 and 3.2.11.1.7 by yourself.

13. Derive Equation 3.3.1.1.40.

14. Derive the result of Equation 3.3.1.2.19 by yourself following the previous derivations.

15. Derive Equation 3.3.2.17 using Equation 3.3.2.18.

16. Derive Equations 3.3.2.22, 3.3.2.23, and 3.3.2.24 from Equation 3.3.2.21.

Chapter 4

MULTIPLE ACCESS AND TRANSMISSION SYSTEMS OPTIMIZATION

4.0 INTRODUCTION

Since multiple access and transmission systems optimization is especially important in satellite communications, where the transmitting power is limited and it is very important to utilize the available satellite power efficiently, this chapter concentrates on these areas only.

4.1 MULTIPLE ACCESS AND TRANSMISSION SYSTEMS OPTIMIZATION

Suppose there are traffic demands to be transmitted from a number of ground terminals to a number of ground terminals.

As seen from Figure 4.1.1, for example, assume that many traffics (voices, data, TV signals, etc.) from A, B, C, D, and E stations must be sent to A′, B′, C′, D′, E′ and F stations. As explained in preceding sections, there are many ways of transmitting these signals, e.g., voices, data, TV signals, etc. For example, a single voice can be transmitted by SCPC/PSK or SCPC/FM signals (usually companded). Data can be transmitted by PSK, DPSK, MSK, etc. Combined voices (FDM) can be transmitted by FDM/FM or PSK, DPSK, MSK, FSK, etc. All these are approaches of modulations. However, when all these modulated carriers transmitted from A, B, C, D and E stations go through a transponder, there are essentially three ways of utilizing it, frequency division multiple access (FDMA), time division multiple access (TDMA) and coded multiple access (CMA).

These access technologies will be explained in the following:

(i) Frequency division multiple access

In this case, all these modulated carriers which all use different carrier frequencies are amplified by the transponder. Since a number of modulated carriers share an amplifier together, the intermodulation products and modulation transfers are produced in addition to the other types of transmission impairments

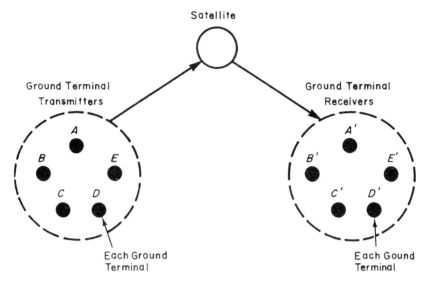

Figure 4.1.1 Satellite Communication Multiple Access Techniques

(e.g., filter distortions, thermal noise, interferences from other communication systems).

Thus, the transponder output power must be reduced (increase the backoff of the transponder) to reduce these effects, so as to operate the transponder amplifier in a more linear region.

(ii) Time division multiple access

In this case, as explained in Section 2.3.6, each carrier transmitted from the A, B, C, D and E stations uses the transponder at different times so that it can be better utilized, since no intermodulation product or modulation transfer is

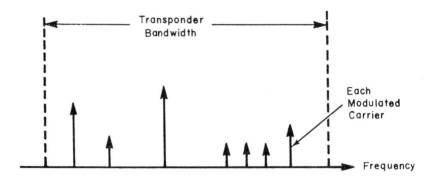

Figure 4.1.2 Transponder Loading by Frequency Division Multiple Access

produced in this case. Thus, each carrier utilizes the transponder by means of time division. Although it is efficient from the point of view of transponder power utilization, the ground station antennas or HPA become larger and the modems become more expensive because of a higher bit utilization.

(iii) Coded multiple access

In this case, each transmitter modulates its carriers so that each receiver separates the information it needs by means of codings (or patterns), i.e., the time division multiple access or frequency division access is not used to separate the information it needs. For example, spread spectrum technologies belong to this category. One example of the spread spectrum modulations commonly used is the double PSK modulation. In this case, the baseband PCM signal modulates the carrier first (for example, 32 kbits/sec BPSK which is the regular SCPC/PSK signal) and then, this BPSK signal is modulated again, which is a repetition of a same bit pattern (e.g., 5 Mbits/sec). Thus, the final signal of this case can be represented by

$$e(t) = A \sin(\omega_0 t + \phi_1(t) + \phi_2(t) + \theta) \tag{4.1.1}$$

where $\phi_1(t)$ is the information bit stream to be transmitted and $\phi_2(t)$ is a much higher bit stream which is independent from ϕ_1 and a periodic function of a same pattern. In this example, the bandwidth required for a regular BPSK signal (32 kbits/sec) is about 32 kHz $\times$ 1.1 = 35.2 kHz, and the spread spectrum double modulation needs a 5 MHz $\times$ 1.1 = 5.5 MHz bandwidth.

Therefore, if the demodulator demodulates this signal $e(t)$ at the receiver through a conventional BPSK demodulator, the required carrier must be

$$10 \log(5.5 \text{ MHz}/35.2 \text{ kHz}) = 21.9 \text{ dB}$$

time greater than that of the conventional BPSK of 32 kbits/sec transmission. This is very inconvenient from the transmission point of view. Therefore, the transmitting power is taken to be the same as that of the conventional BPSK (32 kbits/sec) transmission. The carrier-to-noise-power ratio for the conventional BPSK is about (C/N) = 12 dB (considering all the practical margins) and therefore (C/N) of the spread spectrum transmission is

$$(\text{C/N}) = 12 \text{ dB} - 21.9 \text{ dB} = -9.9 \text{ dB}$$

at the receiver. At the receiver side of this case, the following signal is generated as

$$e_1(t) = B \sin(\omega_1 t + \phi_2(t - \epsilon) + \lambda) \tag{4.1.2}$$

since $\phi_2(t)$ is the known bit stream. The elimination of $\phi_2(t)$ can be done by the following feedback system. First, make the product between $e(t)$ and $e_1(t)$ as

$$e_1(t) e(t) = \frac{AB}{2} \cos\{(\omega_0 - \omega_1)t + \phi_1(t) + \phi_2(t) - \phi_2(t - \epsilon) + \theta - \lambda\}$$

$$+ \frac{AB}{2} \cos\{(\omega_0 + \omega_1)t + \phi_1(t) + \phi_2(t) + \phi_2(t - \epsilon) + \theta + \lambda\}.$$

$$(4.1.3)$$

Then, the zonal filter picks up the first term of this result ($\omega_0 - \omega_1$ component) only. This component goes through the bandpass filter whose bandwidth is approximately 32 kHz $\times$ 1.1 = 35.2 kHz. If ϵ is not zero, a high bit rate modulation (5 Mbits/sec) still exists, since $\phi_2(t) - \phi_2(t - \epsilon) \neq 0$.

Thus, the output of this filter is reduced, since the spectrum spectrum is spread much more than that of 35.2 kHz.

The feedback system adjusts ϵ so that the filter output becomes maximum. This is the first demodulation scheme to obtain the original information bit stream signal (32 kbits/sec).

After this demodulation, (C/N) can be improved from -9.9 dB to $+12$ dB. This spread spectrum has the following merits:

(i) Since the power spectrum is much more spread than the original PSK, the interference to other signals whose bandwidth is smaller than 5 MHz improves.

(ii) This system is very strong against spiky power spectrum interferences (the bandwidth of the interferences must be much narrower than 5 MHz for this example) (the best example is an unmodulated carrier interference), since, in the first demodulation process, the interference receives the second higher bit rate modulation (5 Mbits/sec) and therefore, the power spectrum of the interference becomes much more spread than the original bit modulation (32 kbits/sec). Then, the second narrower bit filter (32 $\times$ 1.1 kHz) picks up only a very small portion of it.

If the interference is an unmodulated carrier (a tone), the carrier-to-interference-power ratio is approximately improved by

$$10 \log(5 \text{ MHz}/36 \text{ kHz}) = 21.9 \text{ db}.$$

In this system, a special bit stream is used to distinguish this signal from the other signals and therefore, this signal can be superposed on the other signals in the same frequency band which can be in a same type or in a different type of modulations and whose power can be even larger than this signal power.

This spread spectrum signal cannot have any gain over the white noise or the interferences whose power spectra are equally or more spread than that of this signal $e(t)$.

Thus, when the ground stations A, B, C, D, E transmit all kinds of traffics, in order to bring the overall cost down and, at the same time, in order to obtain a good quality of transmission, the following factors must be considered.

(i)   What kind of modulation scheme should be chosen for each traffic from each station?
(ii) What kind of multiple access should be used?
(iii) The power and carrier frequencies must be chosen carefully, especially in the FDMA case.
(iv) The efficient utilization of satellite transponder (maximum channel capacity) must be achieved by using the optimum multiple access and modulation.
(v)   The cost of earth station equipments including the antenna, amplifiers, mixers, modems, etc.
(vi) The operational and maintenance easiness, flexibility, etc., must be considered.

The outline of all the above factors has usually been done through engineers' experiences, intuititions and simple calculations, since such an overall optimization is almost impossible to achieve at this time. Only theoretically interesting local optimization has been done in satellite communications.

These local optimization approaches will be explained in the following.

In the INTELSAT FDMA/FM system optimization, there is a software called "STRIP." This software optimizes the carrier power of each FDM/FM signal in a transponder, considering (a) thermal noise, (b) intermodulation products, (c) cochannel interferences coming from the frequency reused transponders (separated by cross polarizations or antenna coverages of satellites).

In case of Figure 4.1.3, four transponders are in the same frequency band and are separated by the cross polarization or antenna coverage. In INTELSAT, for example, each transponder carries 30/40 FDM/FM carriers. The optimization (highest channel capacities or transmission qualities) must be done by changing the power of each carrier considering items (a), (b) and (c). The optimization parameters are here each carrier power and transponder backoff (how much power the transponder utilized in total). If the power of one carrier is increased, the interference into the other carriers on the same frequency band is increased, and the intermodulated product power of the same transponder is increased. The most computer time consuming task comes from the analysis of intermodulation products in this case.

The other problems are minor, since the power spectrum of FDM/FM signals is approximated by Gaussian shapes (see Section 5.3 of Volume I). The algorithm of this case consists of making the worst FM carrier performance better by changing each carrier level considering factors (a), (b) and (c).

Up to recently, the STRIP was limited to the case where all the transponder carriers are FDM/FM. However, just recently, a more general case considering the case where FDM/FM and PSK carriers are mixed in transponders has been completed. But, the optimization is only limited to the extent that only each carrier power can be changed in the optimization process considering factors (a), (b) and (c), which are merely a very small portion of items (i), . . . (vi),

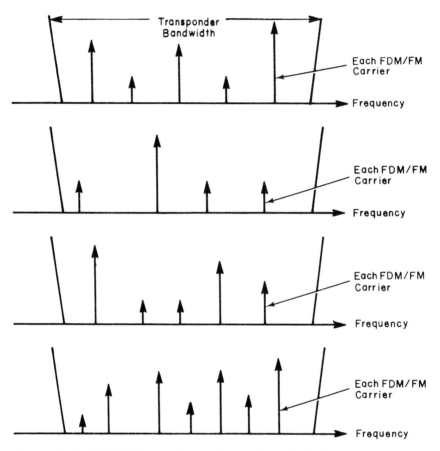

Figure 4.1.3 FDM/FM Carrier Transponder Loading with Cochannel Interferences

to be considered ideally. At present, even the location of each carrier frequency
cannot be optimized in STRIP.

Recently, in KDD laboratories, a software which optimizes only the location
of each carrier (and not both power and location at the same time), has been
developed.

All the other factors have only been considered through engineers' rough and
simple calculations, experiences and intuitions.

Chapter 5

INTERFERENCE ANALYSIS

5.0 INTRODUCTION

This Chapter analyzes interferences between various signals (FDM/FM, SCPC/FM, TV/FM, SCPC/PSK, continuous mode PSK, TDMA/PSK . . .) exploring thirty-six combinations. The continuous mode PSK is defined by a PSK signal whose symbol rate is higher than 32 k bauds (mostly higher than 200 k bauds) and which is not in a burst mode.

In most of the analysis in this Chapter, the power spectra shown in Chapter V of Volume I can be used here but, in some cases, time domain analysis is required in cases where the power spectrum analysis loses its significance because of filter transients. Note here that a particular combination of interferences requires particular precautions, e.g., the interference from FDM/FM into SCPC/PSK is different from the interference from SCPC/FM into SCPC/PSK.

This is why thirty-six combinations are analyzed here. This Chapter is written mainly (but not exclusively) with satellite communication transmissions in mind.

5.1 INTERFERENCE EFFECTS ON FDM/FM SIGNALS

In normal cases, the power spectrum analysis is enough to evaluate the N.P.R. values. The demodulated interference power spectrum is given by

$$\frac{f^2}{2C} I_N(f) \ (-\infty < f < \infty) \tag{5.1.1}$$

where $I_N(f)$ is given by Equation 2.1.5.49,[†] i.e., by the convolution of the interference and of the r.f. signal power spectra. Therefore, the N.P.R. (noise power ratio) at channel frequency is given by

$$\frac{\frac{\sigma^2}{(f_h - f_\ell)} G_p(f) \, \Delta f}{\Delta f \frac{f^2}{2C} [I(f) + I(-f)]} = \frac{C}{\left\{ \frac{I(f) + I(-f)}{2} \right\}}$$

[†]In this case, $W_N(f)$ of Equation 2.1.5.49 becomes an interference power spectrum instead of the power spectrum of the noise.

$$\cdot \frac{\sigma^2}{f^2(f_h - f_\ell)} G_p(f) \qquad (5.1.2)$$

where σ, f_h, f_ℓ, C and $G_p(f)$ are respectively the r.m.s. frequency deviation, highest channel frequency, and lowest channel frequency, and carrier power and pre-emphasis gain of the desired FDM/FM signal. Δf is a 4 KHz bandwidth for a voice signal. The functions $I(f)$ will be changed according to the interference signals.

5.1.1   From FDM/FM Into FDM/FM

In this case, both signal and interference are FDM/FM signals.

As analyzed in Section 5.3 of Volume I, the power spectrum of the FDM/FM signal consists of two portions, the residual carrier component, and the continuous spectrum due to the modulation. In most satellite communication cases, the power spectrum of the FDMA/FM signal can be approximated by a Gaussian shape especially in the frequency area around the carrier where the power is the most concentrated and the effects are the largest (see Section 5.3 of Volume I). But, in some cases where the modulation index is small and the lowest channel frequency is not low, the Gaussian approximation is not valid anymore (see Section 5.3 of Volume I). In such a case, the power spectrum of the FDM/FM must be calculated by the approaches described in Section 5.3 of Volume I.

Also, when the number of channels decreases, the energy dispersal signal is added to the baseband signal modulation. As explained in Section 5.3 of Volume I, the power spectrum of the FDM/FM signal can be written if there are more than 60 channels, as

$$C\, e^{-R_\phi(0)}\, \delta(f - f_0) + W_{cc}(f - f_0) \qquad (0 < f) \qquad (5.1.1.1)$$

where C is the FM signal power and $R_\phi(0)$ is the autocorrelation function of the modulating phase (therefore, $R_\phi(0)$ is the power of the phase). $W_{cc}(f - f_0)$ is the continuous portion.

Thus, represent the power spectra of the desired FDM/FM signals and of the interference FDM/FM signals respectively, by

$$C_s e^{-R_{\phi_s}(0)} \delta(f - f_{0s}) + W_{ccs}(f - f_{0s}) \qquad (5.1.1.2)$$

and

$$C_I e^{-R_{\phi_I}(0)} \delta(f - f_{0I}) + W_{ccI}(f - f_{0I}). \qquad (5.1.1.3)$$

Therefore, the function $I_N(f)$ is given by

$$I_N(f) = \frac{1}{C_s} \int_{-\infty}^{\infty} [C_s e^{-R_{\phi_s}(0)} \delta(x) + W_{ccs}(x)]$$

$$\cdot \, [C_1 e^{-R_{\phi_I}(0)} \, \delta(f - f_{0I} + f_{0s} - x)$$

$$+ \, W_{ccI}(f - f_{0I} + f_{0s} - x)] \, dx$$

$$= C_I e^{-R_{\phi_I}(0) - R_{\phi_s}(0)} \, \delta(f - f_{0I} + f_{0s})$$

$$+ \, e^{-R_{\phi_s}(0)} \, W_{ccI}(f - f_{0I} + f_{0s})$$

$$+ \, \frac{C_I}{C_s} e^{-R_{\phi_I}(0)} \, W_{ccs}(f - f_{0I} + f_{0s})$$

$$+ \, \frac{1}{C_s} \int_{-\infty}^{\infty} W_{ccs}(x) \, W_{ccI}(f - f_{0I} + f_{0s} - x) \, dx \qquad (-\infty < f < \infty)$$

$$(5.1.1.4)$$

where the first term is the line spectrum and the other terms are continuous spectra. In other terms, if neither the residual carrier power of the interference nor the signal are negligible, then a line spectrum appears in the demodulated baseband interference, which is located at the frequency $|f_{0I} - f_{0s}|$.

Since the line components (tones) or intelligible crosstalks are much more harmful than noise-like interferences, one must be cautious with the analysis. If one of the residual carrier powers is negligible, i.e., the value of $e^{-R_{\phi_s}(0)}$ or $e^{-R_{\phi_I}(0)}$ is very small, as in normal cases of satellite communications and if two continuous components exist as seen from Equation 5.1.1.4, then

If $e^{-R_{\phi_s}(0)} \simeq 0$,

$$I_N(f) = \frac{C_I}{C_s} e^{-R_{\phi_I}(0)} \, W_{ccs}(f - f_{cI} + f_{0s})$$

$$+ \, \frac{1}{C_S} \int_{-\infty}^{\infty} W_{ccs}(x) W_{ccI}(f - f_{0I} + f_{0s} - y) \, dx \qquad (5.1.1.5)$$

If $e^{-R_{\phi_I}(0)} \simeq 0$,

$$I_N(f) \simeq e^{-R_{\phi_s}(0)} \, W_{ccI}(f - f_{0I} + f_{0s})$$

$$+ \, \frac{1}{C_s} \int_{-\infty}^{\infty} W_{ccs}(x) W_{ccI}(f - f_{0I} + f_{0s} - x) \, dx \qquad (5.1.1.6)$$

If $e^{-R_{\phi_I}(0)} \simeq 0$ and $e^{-R_{\phi_s}(0)} \simeq 0$,

$$I_N(f) = \frac{1}{C_s} \int_{-\infty}^{\infty} W_{ccs}(x) \, W_{ccI}(f - f_{0I} + f_{0s} - x) \, dx. \qquad (5.1.1.7)$$

The conditions for $e^{-R_{\phi_s}(0)} \simeq 0$ or for $e^{-R_{\phi_I}(0)} \simeq 0$, are obviously seen from Equation 5.1.2.6 of Volume I, as mentioned in this Section. In most cases in satellite communications, the residual carrier power of the FDM/FM signal is negligible and the Gaussian approximation for the power spectrum is valid. Therefore, in this case,

$$I_N(f) \simeq C_I \int_{-\infty}^{\infty} \frac{e^{-\frac{1}{2}\frac{x^2}{\sigma_s^2}}}{\sqrt{2\pi}\,\sigma_s} \; \frac{e^{-\frac{1}{2}\frac{(f-f_{0I}+f_{0s}-x)^2}{\sigma_I^2}}}{\sqrt{2\pi}\,\sigma_I}\, dx$$

$$= C_I \frac{e^{-\frac{(f-f_{0I}+f_{0s})^2}{2(\sigma_s^2+\sigma_I^2)}}}{\sqrt{2\pi}\,\sqrt{\sigma_s^2+\sigma_I^2}} \, . \tag{5.1.1.8}$$

When the number of channels is reduced and the energy dispersal becomes a dominant modulating signal, the power spectrum of the FDM/FM signal can be approximated by a rectangular shape whose width is f_d (peak-to-peak deviation) (see Section 5.2 of Volume I).

In this case, it is simpler to evaluate $I_N(f)$.

5.1.2   From SCPC/FM Into FDM/FM

As shown in Section 5.4 of Volume I, the power spectrum of the SCPC/FM signal is very spiky around carrier frequency f_0 (most of the energy is within 4 KHz around f_0). On the other hand, the power spectrum of the FDM/FM signal is much wider than that of the SCPC/FM signal (the 12 channel FDM/FM signal occupies 1.25 MHz bandwidth and the SCPC/FM signal, only 25 KHz). Therefore, $I_N(f)$ of Equation 5.1.1.4 can be approximated as[†]

$$I_N(f) \simeq C_I e^{-R_{\phi_I}(0)-R_{\phi_s}(0)}\, \delta(f-f_{0I}+f_{0s})$$

$$+ \; e^{-R_{\phi_s}(0)}\, W_{ccI}(f-f_{0I}+f_{0s})$$

$$+ \; \frac{C_I}{C_s}\, e^{-R_{\phi_I}(0)}\, W_{ccs}(f-f_{0I}+f_{0s})$$

$$+ \; \frac{C_I}{C_s}\, (1-e^{-R_{\phi_I}(0)})\, W_{ccs}(f-f_{0I}+f_{0s}). \tag{5.1.2.1}$$

In normal cases of satellite communications, $e^{-R_{\phi_s}(0)} \simeq 0$.
In such cases,

$$I_N(f) \simeq \frac{C_I}{C_s}\, e^{-R_{\phi_I}(0)}\, W_{ccs}(f-f_{0I}+f_{0s})$$

[†]The power spectrum of SCPC/FM does not have a Gaussian shape in distribution, but let $C_I e^{-R_{\phi_I}}$ represent the residual carrier power of the SCPC/FM for notation convenience.

$$+ \frac{C_I}{C_s} (1 - e^{-R_{\Phi_I}(0)}) \, W_{ccs}(f - f_{0I} + f_{0s}).$$

This is equal to

$$I_N(f) \simeq \frac{C_I}{C_s} W_{ccs}(f - f_{0I} + f_{0s}) \qquad (-\infty < f < \infty). \qquad (5.1.2.2)$$

Thus, the power spectrum of the demodulated interference is proportional to the r.f. signal power spectrum.

Since a large number of SCPC/FM signals, which are all equally spaced in frequency and are almost equal in power level, usually occupy a transponder, the total demodulated interference power spectrum is, from rewriting Equations 5.1.2.1 and 5.1.2.2 as $I(f - f_{0I} + f_{0s})$,

$$W_I(f) = \sum_{k=-M_1}^{M_2} I(f - f_{0I} + f_{0s} - k\Delta f) \qquad (5.1.2.3)$$

where Δf is the frequency spacing of each SCPC/FM and $(M_1 + M_2 + 1)$ is the number of these interferences. Since the value of Δf is much smaller than the bandwidth of the FDM/FM signal, the accumulation of these small SCPC/FM signal effects cannot be ignored sometimes, although each SCPC/FM power can be.

5.1.3 From TV/FM Into FDM/FM

As seen from the explanation of Section 5.5 of Volume I, the power spectrum of a TV/FM signal is very non-stationary and changes very much from time to time depending on programs. Therefore, it is hard to describe the effects on FDM/FM signals in general.

The effects of modulated TV/FM signals without energy dispersal will be analyzed first and then, the case where the energy dispersal dominates the modulation with a weak signal modulation will be discussed.

Since the video baseband signal contains the line spectra, the power spectrum of a TV/FM signal is very spiky as seen from Figure 5.5.3 of Volume I. However, the demodulated TV interference power spectrum becomes much smoother because of the convolution of Equation 5.1.1.4, depending on how much the power spectrum spread of the FDM/FM signal is. The larger the size of the FDM/FM signal, the smoother it is. Figure 5.1.3.1 of Volume II shows the convolution of the TV/FM power spectrum of Figure 5.5.3 of Volume I, and a typical FDM/FM signal, where one can see that all the sharp spikes of Figure 5.5.3 of Volume I disappear because of the convolution with the Gaussian type power spectrum.

Next, take the case where video modulation is very weak and only the energy dispersal dominates the modulation. If there is only energy dispersal, the power spectrum consists of many small line spectra whose space is equal to the energy

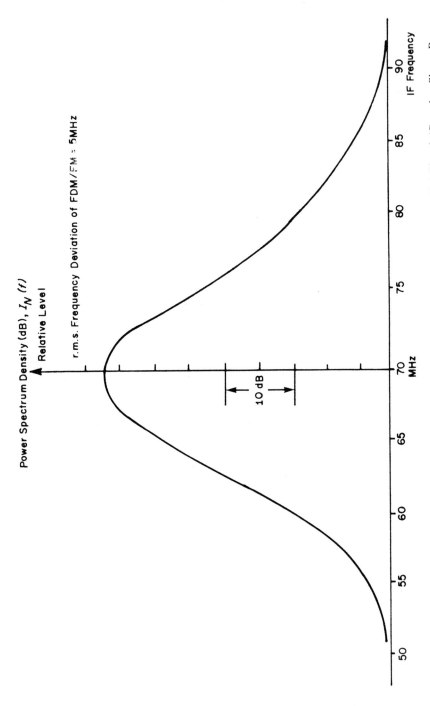

5.1.3.1 Result of Convolution Between FM Video Spectrum (Color Bar Test Signal) and FDM/FM Signal (Gaussian Shape Power Spectrum)

dispersal sweep rate (e.g., 30 Hz and about 15 KHz respectively) for the frame and line rate energy dispersals and the envelope of these line spectra is shown in Figure 5.5.4 of Volume I where the width of the rectangular shape is the peak-to-peak dispersal frequency deviation (usually 2 MHz).

On the other hand, the filter bandwidth of the FDM/FM signal is at least 1 MHz. Therefore, when the TV signal instantaneous frequency is swept slowly (30 Hz or 15 KHz) (as in the shape of Figure 5.2.1 of Volume I), ± 1 MHz compared with a 1 MHz FDM/FM bandwidth and when the frequency distance between the TV/FM and the FDM/FM signals is close (i.e., co-channeled), the time response of the FDM/FM IF filter for this TV/FM signal is shown in Figure 5.1.3.2, where T_e is the energy dispersal periodic period (see Figure 5.2.1 of Volume I), B_{FDM} is the IF filter bandwidth of the FDM/FM signal, f_d is the peak-to-peak deviation of the TV/FM signal, and A_{TV} is the amplitude of the TV/FM signal. In case $B_{FDM}/f_d > 1$, the TV/FM signal (modulated only by the energy dispersal signal) passes through this IF filter without any distortion. When the FDM/FM IF filter is not large enough to make a response of this type (Figure 5.1.3.2), the time response becomes completely different as shown in this Section with respect to TV/FM interference into SCPC/FM (with line rate energy dispersal). Therefore, the TV/FM signal interferes with the FDM/FM signal with its full power for a percentage of the time B_{FDM}/f_d as shown in Figure 5.1.3.2. Thus, in this time period $T_e B_{FDM}/f_d$, the threshold deterioration of the FDM/FM signal must be considered, since the TV/FM signal occupies at least half the transponder and the FDM/FM signal may occupy a small portion of the transponder power. In this case, the isolation effect (the isolation due to cross polarization, satellite orbital spacing, etc.) will be very much reduced. However, in the above threshold area, the time domain analysis is not required and the function $I_N(f)$ as shown in Figure 5.1.3.1 is only necessary to evaluate the N.P.R. value.

5.1.4   From SCPC/PSK Into FDM/FM

The power spectrum of SCPC/PSK is given by Equation 5.6.1.5 of Volume I, i.e.,

$$W_I(f) = C_I T_I \left[\frac{\sin\{\pi T_I(f - f_{0I})\}}{\pi T_I(f - f_{0I})} \right]^2 \left| Y_I(f - f_0) \right|^2 \qquad (5.1.4.1)$$

where C_I, T_I, f_{0I} and $Y_I(f - f_0)$ represent respectively the carrier power, symbol period, carrier frequency and transfer function of the transmitter filters of the interference signal which cuts off all the sidelobes as explained in Section 2.3. In the present SCPC/PSK signal, the symbol rate $(T_I)^{-1}$ is 32 K bauds which is much smaller than the FDM/FM spectrum bandwidth. Thus, the function $I_N(f)$ is given by

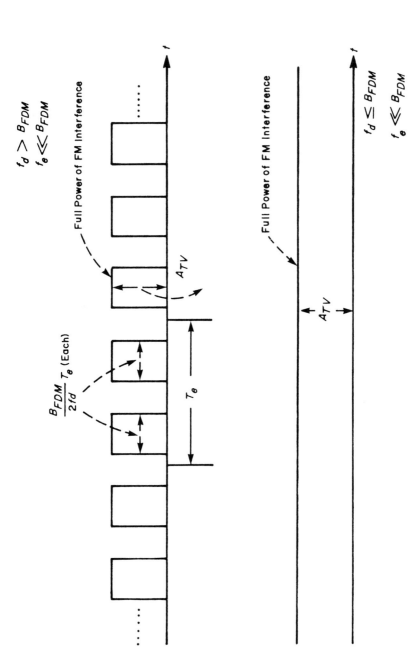

5.1.3.2   Output Wave Form of FDM/FM Demodulator Filter (Envelope) for Energy Dispersed FM Signal Input

$$I_N(f) = \frac{1}{C_s} \int_{-\infty}^{\infty} W_I(x - f_{0I} + f_{0s}) \, [C_s e^{-R_{\phi_s}(0)}$$

$$\cdot \, \delta(f - x) + W_{ccs}(f - x)] \, dx$$

$$= e^{-R_{\phi_s}(0)} \, W_I(f - f_{0I} + f_{0s})$$

$$+ \frac{1}{C_s} \int_{-\infty}^{\infty} W_I(x - f_{0I} + f_{0s}) \, W_{ccs}(f - x) \, dx$$

$$\simeq e^{-R_{\phi_s}(0)} \, W_I(f - f_{0I} + f_{0s})$$

$$+ \frac{C_I}{C_s} \, W_{ccs}(f - f_{0I} + f_{0s}). \tag{5.1.4.2}$$

As explained in the preceding sections, in most satellite communications, the residual carrier power is negligible. In this case,

$$I_N(f) \simeq \frac{C_I}{C_s} \, W_{ccs}(f - f_{0I} + f_{0s}). \tag{5.1.4.3}$$

Since the SCPC/PSK signals appear as a large group with equally spaced frequency and with equal power (approximately), the total effect of the SCPC/PSK on the FDM/FM signal is given by

$$\sum_{k=-M_1}^{M_2} I_N(f - k\Delta f) \tag{5.1.4.4}$$

where Δf is the carrier spacing of the SCPC/PSK signal and the total number of SCPC/PSK signals is $(M_1 + M_2 + 1)$. Usually, Δf is much smaller than the power spectrum of the FDM/FM signal bandwidth and therefore one has to consider the effect of a number of SCPC/PSK interferences. In the case where energy dispersal modulation dominates, Equation 5.1.4.3 can be used and $W_{ccs}(f)$ can be assumed to be a rectangular shape as shown in Figure 5.5.4 of Volume I.

5.1.5 From Continuous Mode PSK Into FDM/FM Signal

The power spectrum of the continuous mode PSK signal is given by the same representation as Equation 5.1.4.1. However, the interference power spectrum bandwidth is much wider than that of the SCPC/PSK and is comparable to that of the FDM/FM signal or can be even larger than that. Therefore, $I_N(f)$ is given by

$$I_N(f) = e^{-R_{\phi_s}(0)W_I(f - f_{0I} + f_{0s})}$$

$$+ \frac{1}{C_s} \int_{-\infty}^{\infty} W_I(x - f_{0I} + f_{0s}) W_{ccs}(f - x) \, dx$$

$$
\begin{aligned}
=: \; e^{-R_{\phi_s}(0)} \, C_I T_I &\left[\frac{\sin\{\pi T_I(f - f_{0I} + f_{0s})\}}{\{\pi T_I(f - f_{0I} + f_{0s})\}} \right]^2 \\
+ \; C_I &\int_{-T_I}^{T_I} \left[1 - \frac{|\tau|}{T_I} \right] [e^{-R_{\phi_s}(0) + R_\phi(\tau)} - e^{-R_\phi(0)}] \\
&\cdot e^{j2\pi(f - f_{0I} + f_{0s})\tau} \, d\tau \, .
\end{aligned}
\tag{5.1.5.1}
$$

As repeatedly mentioned in the preceding sections of this Chapter, in most cases of satellite communications, $\exp[-R_\phi(0)] \simeq 0$ and the power spectrum can be approximated as a Gaussian shape. Then,

$$
\begin{aligned}
I_N(f) \simeq C_I &\int_{-T_I}^{T_I} \left[1 - \frac{|\tau|}{T_I} \right] e^{-\frac{(2\pi\sigma)^2}{2}\tau^2} \\
&\cdot e^{j2\pi(f - f_{0I} + f_{0s})\tau} \, d\tau \, .
\end{aligned}
\tag{5.1.5.2}
$$

In Equations 5.1.5.1 and 5.1.5.2, the effect of the PSK signal transmitter filters is ignored. However, the sidelobe power spectrum is much smaller (-13.5 dB down) than the main lobe which is a good approximation in most cases.

If there is a number of interferences of this type, the addition of Equation 5.1.4.4 must be done. If the energy dispersal dominates the FDM/FM modulation,

$$
\begin{aligned}
I_N(f) &= \frac{C_I T_I}{f_d} \int_{f - f_{0I} + f_{0s} - f_d/2}^{f - f_{0I} + f_{0s} + f_d/2} \left[\frac{\sin(\pi T_I y)}{(\pi T_I y)} \right]^2 dy \\
&= \frac{C_I}{f_d} \frac{1}{\pi} \int_{\pi T_I(f - f_{0I} + f_{0s} - f_d/2)}^{\pi T_I(f - f_{0I} + f_{0s} + f_d/2)} \left(\frac{\sin x}{x} \right)^2 dx \, .
\end{aligned}
\tag{5.1.5.3}
$$

5.1.6   From TDMA/PSK Signal Into FDM/FM Signal

The difference between the continuous mode PSK and the TDMA/PSK signals, from the interference point of view, is that the former always exists as a source of interference and the latter disappears periodically because of the burst mode of the TDMA.

Represent the TDMA interference by

$$
\begin{aligned}
I(t) &= V_B(t) e_I(t) e^{j\omega_I t} \\
&= V_B(t) A_I e^{j\omega_I t + j\phi_I(t)}
\end{aligned}
\tag{5.1.6.1}
$$

where $e_I(t)$ is the continuous PSK signal and $V_B(t)$ is the burst mode envelope of the TDMA signal which is a periodic function of the frame rate (e.g., 500 Hz).

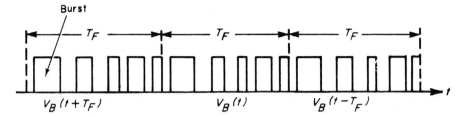

Figure 5.1.6.1   Example of Frame Window Function

$$V_B(t) = 1 \text{ when a burst appears}$$

$$= 0 \text{ when no burst appears.} \qquad (5.1.6.2)$$

Represent also the FDM/FM signal by

$$e_s(t) = A_s e^{j\omega_s t + j\phi_s(t) + j\theta_s}. \qquad (5.1.6.3)$$

Then, from Equation 2.1.5.6, the demodulated interference (before the channel filters) is given by

$$\frac{1}{2\pi} \frac{d}{dt} \text{Im} \left\{ \frac{I(t)}{A_s} e^{-j\phi_s(t) - j\theta_s - j\omega_s t} \right\}$$

$$= \frac{1}{2\pi} \frac{d}{dt} \text{Im} \left\{ \frac{V_B(t)}{A_s} e_I(t) e^{-j\phi_s(t) - j\theta_s - j(\omega_s - \omega_I)t} \right\} \qquad (5.1.6.4)$$

As seen from this result, the demodulated interference (before channel filters) disappears when there is no burst. Now, let us see the output of a channel filter of the FDM/FM signal for the input of Equation 5.1.6.4. The problem is whether this coming on and off of the interference in Equation 5.1.6.4 still holds after channel filters or not (channel filters mean that each voice band filter should pick up each voice after the FDM/FM demodulation. See Section 3.1.4 of Volume I.)

The impulse response of a channel filter can be represented by

$$e^{j2\pi f_{ch} t} h(t) \qquad (5.1.6.5)$$

where f_{ch} is the lower edge band frequency allocated for this channel and $h(t)$ is the voice bandpass filter (about 300 Hz/3000 Hz). The rough time width of $h(t)$ is 1/3000 sec.

On the other hand, the frame time length T_F is variable, roughly from 1/500 to 1/2000 sec depending on the TDMA system design.

If the impulse response of Equation 5.1.6.5 convolves with Equation 5.1.6.4 (see Figure 5.1.6.1), two cases may occur:

(a) If the frame period is very long and each burst is longer than the width of $h(t)$ (1/3000 sec), the demodulated TDMA interference (after the channel

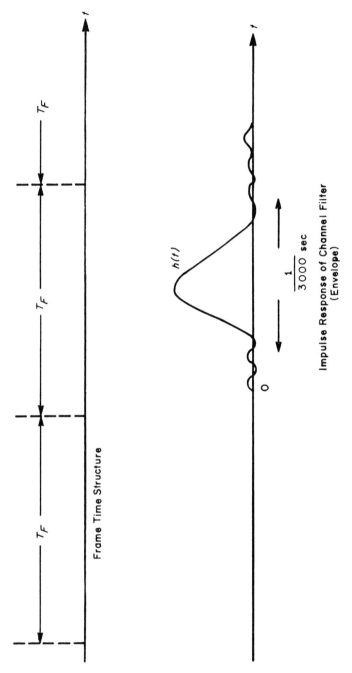

Figure 5.1.6.2   Channel Filter Output of FDM/FM for TDMA Interference Input

filter) appears and disappears, although the amount may be small depending on the values of ϕ_I and $(\omega_s - \omega_I)$.

(b) If each burst is not long enough or if each burst is short, then the bursts distorted by the channel filter eliminate the on-off effect of the TDMA signal.

In the following, the average power of the demodulated interference at each channel will be evaluated. The power spectrum of $I(t)$ is the convolution of the power spectra of $e_I(t)e^{j\omega_I t}$ and $V_B(t)$. The former is given by Equation 5.6.1.5 of Volume I and the latter is given by

$$W_B(f) = \sum_{k=-\infty}^{\infty} |a_k|^2 \, \delta\left(f - \frac{k}{T_F}\right) \tag{5.1.6.6}$$

where

$$a_k = \frac{1}{T_F} \int_0^{T_F} V_B(t) e^{-j2\pi \frac{k}{T_F} t} \, dt. \tag{5.1.6.7}$$

The frame rate $1/T_F$ is much smaller than the TDMA/PSK symbol rate (e.g., $1/T_F = 500$ Hz and $1/T_I = 60$ MHz in INTELSAT case). Therefore, if $W_B(f)$ and $W_I(f)$ are convolved, $W_B(f)$ can be considered as a δ-function (instead of the sum of many δ-functions, as shown by Equation 5.1.6.6). Note here that

$$\int_{-\infty}^{\infty} W_B(f) df = P_B = \sum_{k=-\infty}^{\infty} |a_k|^2$$

$$= \frac{1}{T_F} \int_0^{T_F} [V_B(t)]^2 dt \tag{5.1.6.8}$$

where P_B is the percentage of time the bursts are appearing. Therefore, the power spectrum of the TDMA/PSK is given by

$$W_I(f) = \int_{-\infty}^{\infty} W_B(f-x) \, C_I T_I \left[\frac{\sin\{\pi(x - f_{0I}) T_I\}}{\{\pi(x - f_{0I}) T_I\}}\right]^2$$

$$|Y_1(x - f_{0I})|^2 \, dx \simeq P_B C_I T_I \left[\frac{\sin\{\pi(f - f_{0I}) T_I\}}{\{\pi(f - f_{0I}) T_I\}}\right]^2$$

$$\cdot |Y_I(f - f_{0I})|^2 \tag{5.1.6.9}$$

where $Y_I(f - f_{0I})$ has the same definition as Equation 5.1.4.1 and C_I is the power of the TDMA/PSK signal, assuming that all the bursts have equal power and that the transponder is completely filled up (same as for the continuous PSK case). Then, the analytical result of Sections 5.1.4 and 5.1.5 can be used. The only difference is that the TDMA/PSK power spectrum is approximately uniformly reduced by the factor P_B from the power spectrum of the continuous mode PSK signal.

5.2   INTERFERENCE EFFECTS ON SCPC/FM SIGNALS

The power spectrum bandwidth of SCPC/FM signal is much narrower than that of FDM/FM, TV/FM, SCPC/PSK, continuous mode PSK and TDMA/PSK signals. The interference effects of SCPC/FM on SCPC/FM signals belong to a different case, since both signal and interference have the same power spectrum or a similar one.

The interference effects of the former four signals (except for the TV/FM signal) on the SCPC/FM signal are stationary, since the convolved results of these signal power spectra with the SCPC signal are unchanged, although the power spectrum of the SCPC/FM signal is non-stationary.

5.2.1   From FDM/FM Into SCPC/FM

To obtain function $I_N(f)$, the representation of Equation 5.1.1.4 can be used, where $C_s e^{-R_{\phi_s}(0)}\,\delta(f)$, $W_{ccs}(f)$, $C_I e^{-R_{\phi_I}(0)}\delta(f)$ and $W_{ccI}(f)$ are respectively the residual carrier power and the continuous power spectrum of the SCPC signal (see Section 5.4 of Volume I) and the residual carrier power of the FDM/FM signal (see Section 5.3 of Volume I). The power spectrum of the FDM/FM signal is much wider than that of the SCPC/FM and therefore,

$$
\begin{aligned}
I_N(f) &\simeq C_I e^{-R_{\phi_I}(0)-R_{\phi_s}(0)}\,\delta(f-f_{0I}+f_{0s}) \\
&\quad + e^{-R_{\phi_s}(0)}\,W_{ccI}(f-f_{0I}+f_{0s}) \\
&\quad + \frac{C_I}{C_s}\,e^{-R_{\phi_I}(0)}\,W_{ccs}(f-f_{0I}+f_{0s}) \\
&\quad + \frac{1}{C_s}\,[C_s - C_s e^{-R_{\phi_s}(0)}]\,W_{ccI}(f-f_{0I}+f_{0s}) \\
&\simeq \frac{C_I}{C_s}\,e^{-R_{\phi_I}(0)}\,W_{ccs}(f-f_{0I}+f_{0s}) \\
&\quad + C_I\,e^{-R_{\phi_I}(0)-R_{\phi_s}(0)}\,\delta(f-f_{0I}+f_{0s}) \\
&\quad + W_{ccI}(f-f_{0I}+f_{0s})
\end{aligned}
$$

(5.2.1.1)[†]

where $e^{-R_{\phi_s}(0)}$ and $W_{ccs}(f-f_{0I}+f_{0s})$ change from time to time in a non-stationary way. However, these two components (the power spectrum of SCPC) are important or not depending on the values of $(f_{0I}-f_{0s})$, i.e.,

(a) If $|f_{0I} - f_{0s}| \geq 8$ KHz, then the line spectrum will be filtered away and if

---

[†]The line spectrum component cannot be ignored in some cases, although it is very small, since it creates a tonal interference.

$|f_{0I} - f_{0s}| < 4$ KHz, then it gives the SCPC/FM signal a tonal interference (after demodulation).

(b) $|f_{0I} - f_{0s}| \geq 8$ KHz, the effect of $W_{ccs}(f)$ is negligible since the power spectrum of the SCPC is concentrated within 4 KHz. If $|f_{0I} - f_{0s}| < 8$ KHz, this effect must be considered.

The last term of Equation 5.2.1.1 always exists and, when the energy dispersal only is applied in the FDM/FM signal, tonal interferences appear in the baseband signal of the SCPC/FM. If energy dispersal is not applied and the interference residual carrier power is very small,

$$I_N(f) \simeq W_{ccI}(f - f_{0I} + f_{0s})$$

$$\simeq C_I \frac{1}{\sqrt{2\pi}\,\sigma_I} e^{-\frac{(f - f_{0I} + f_{0s})^2}{2\sigma_I^2}}. \tag{5.2.1.2}$$

In this SCPC/FM signal case, the total demodulated interference power in the voice band must be evaluated.

$$\frac{1}{2C_s} \int_{-\infty}^{\infty} f^2 I_N(f) \, |Y_V(f)|^2 df \tag{5.2.1.3}$$

where $Y_V(f)$ is the bandpass filter of the voice signal.

5.2.2 From TV/FM Into SCPC/FM

In this case, two types of analyses must be done: one is the power spectrum analysis which is necessary for the above threshold analysis, and the other is the threshold analysis in which time domain analysis is required. The power spectrum analysis is first described and then, time domain analysis will be shown.

In the former case, the result of Equation 5.1.1.4 is still applicable. The first term of Equation 5.1.1.4 appears only when the residual carriers of both signal and interference exist, the second term exists when the residual carrier of the signal (SCPC/FM) exists, the third term exists when the residual carrier of the interference (TV/FM) exists. Although the convolution of the last term is smoother than the continuous power spectrum of the TV/FM signal ($W_{ccI}(f - f_{0I} + f_{0s})$), it is not clear whether the following approximation can be done or not

$$\frac{1}{C_s} \int_{-\infty}^{\infty} W_{ccs}(x) \, W_{ccI}(f - f_{0I} + f_{0s} - x) \, dx$$

$$\simeq (1 - e^{-R_{\phi_s}(0)}) \, W_{ccI}(f - f_{0I} + f_{0s}) \tag{5.2.2.1}^\dagger$$

---

†It is assumed in this approximation that W_{ccI} is much more widely spread than W_{ccs}, which is true in most practical cases. For the convenience of the notation, $c_s e^{-R_{\phi_s}(0)}$ is represented as the signal residual carrier power, although it is no mathematically correct.

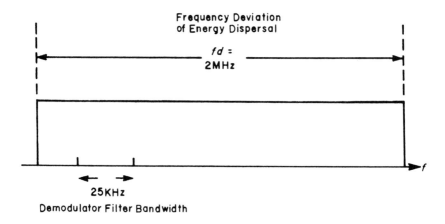

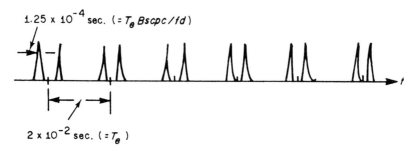

Figure 5.2.2.1   SCPC/FM Demodulator Filter Output for Energy Dispersal FM Signal Input (Frame Rate Energy Dispersal Case)

since both power spectra are spiky in fine structures. In this case, the integral of Equation 5.2.1.3 must be evaluated.

In order to evaluate the threshold characteristics of the TV/FM interference effects on the SCPC/FM, time domain analysis must be done as follows. When the baseband signal of the TV/FM modulation becomes weak and energy dispersal dominates the modulation, the deterioration of the SCPC/FM threshold characteristic becomes serious in the case of frame rate energy dispersal (of TV/FM). As explained in Section 5.1.3, if the IF filter bandwidth of the signal (SCPC/FM, 25 KHz) is much larger than the energy dispersal rate, in the same percentage of time (See Figure 5.1.3.2), the TV/FM signal interferes with the SCPC/FM signal with full power in a pulse shape. Therefore, if the TV/FM signal is modulated by the frame rate energy dispersal, since the ratio between the SCPC/FM IF bandwidth and frame rate is $25 \times 10^3/50 = 500$, the TV/FM interference repeatedly hits the SCPC/FM signal with full power as an impulse whose frequency is 50 Hz and pulse width is $T_e B_{scpc}/2f_d = (1/(2 \times 50 \text{ Hz})) \times 25 \times 10^3 \text{ Hz} \times (2 \times 10^6)^{-1} = 1.25 \times 10^{-4}$ sec.

Assuming that the SCPC carrier is located around the TV/FM carrier, the approximation for a_k of Equation 5.2.14 of Volume I is used to obtain

$$A e^{j\omega_I t} \sum_{k=-250}^{250} a_k e^{-j\frac{2\pi}{T_e}kt}$$

$$\simeq A e^{j\omega_I t} \sum_{k=-250}^{250} \sqrt{\frac{2}{m}} \cos\left[\left(\frac{m}{8} + \frac{k}{2} - \frac{1}{4}\pi\right)\right]$$

$$\cdot e^{-j\frac{2\pi}{T_e}kt} = A e^{j\omega_I t} E(t)$$

$$= A e^{j\omega_I t} \frac{1}{\sqrt{2m}} \left[e^{j\left(\frac{m}{8} - \frac{1}{4}\right)\pi} \frac{\sin\left(\pi\left(\frac{t}{T_e} - \frac{1}{4}\right)(501)\right)}{\sin\left(\pi\left(\frac{t}{T_e} - \frac{1}{4}\right)\right)} \right.$$

$$\left. + e^{-j\left(\frac{m}{8} - \frac{1}{4}\right)\pi} \frac{\sin\left(\pi\left(\frac{t}{T_e} + \frac{1}{4}\right)(501)\right)}{\sin\left(\pi\left(\frac{t}{T_e} + \frac{1}{4}\right)\right)} \right]. \qquad (5.2.2.2)$$

Figure 5.2.2.2 shows the plot of $|E(t)|$ where

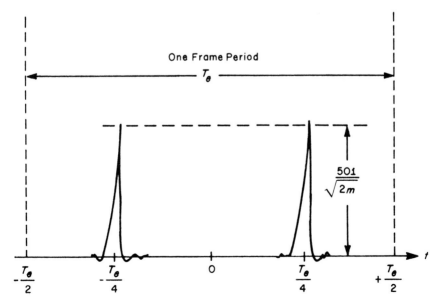

Figure 5.2.2.2 Wave Form Shape of Function $E(t)$ (Frame Rate Energy Dispersal Case)

$$m = f_d/f_e. \qquad (5.2.2.3)$$

The power of each SCPC/FM is the transponder output backoff -6 dB $-$ 26 dB $= -32$ dB (with 400 carriers), while the TV/FM carrier power is 0 dB or -4.0 dB input backoff, depending on whether there is one or two carriers per transponder.[†] Thus, one can imagine that the TV/FM interference hits the SCPC/FM signal very hard. In order not to have any threshold deterioration during this pulse period, the isolation between the TV/FM and SCPC/FM must be 43 dB or more.

On the other hand, if the line rate energy dispersal is used for a TV/FM signal (15 KHz rate), only two line components of the power spectra (see Figure 5.2.2.3) fall at most in the IF filter of the SCPC/FM signal (25 KHz bandwidth).

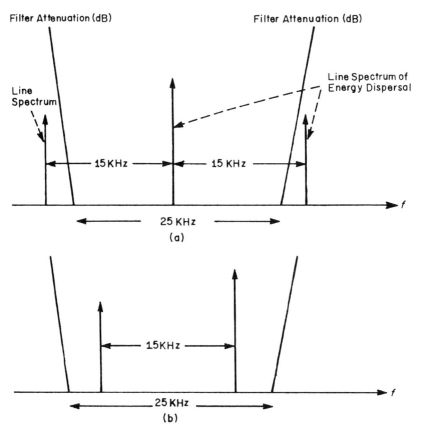

Figure 5.2.2.3   15 KHz FM Energy Dispersal Interferences into SCPC Signal

---

[†]In order to obtain the level difference between the SCPC/FM and TV/FM signals at the SCPC/ FM demodulator, factors such as antenna isolation, polarization isolation, etc. must be considered, in addition to the above backoff level difference.

Therefore, there is no such problem of threshold deterioration. Figure 5.2.2.4 shows the combined time function of these two line spectra (sinusoidal waves).

The total power of these 501 line spectra (Equation 5.2.2.2) is

$$\frac{A^2}{2} \frac{(501)}{m} \tag{5.2.2.4}$$

while the instantaneous peak power of Equation 5.2.2.2, which occurs when $t = T_e/4 + kT_e/2$, is

$$\frac{A^2}{2} \frac{2(250)^2}{m} \tag{5.2.2.5}$$

where

$$m = \frac{2 \times 10^6 \text{ Hz}}{50 \text{ Hz}} = 4 \times 10^4.$$

Thus, the peak power is 24.0 dB larger than the average power. On the other hand, in a line rate energy dispersal case, the total power is

$$\frac{A^2}{2} \frac{2}{m} \tag{5.2.2.6}$$

where

$$m = \frac{2 \times 10^6 \text{ Hz}}{15.7 \times 10^3 \text{ Hz}} = 127.4. \tag{5.2.2.7}$$

Thus, from Equations 5.2.2.4 and 5.2.2.6, the average power of the frame and line rates is about the same.

The peak power of the line rate case is only 3 dB larger than that of the average power. This is the reason why the frame rate energy dispersal of the

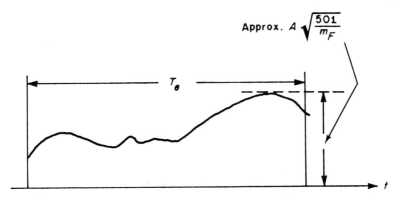

Figure 5.2.2.4 Output Wave Form of SCPC Demodulator Filter for Energy Dispersal FM Signal Input (Line Rate Energy Dispersal Case)

TV/FM interference is much more harmful to the SCPC/FM signal threshold characteristics.

5.2.3   From SCPC/FM Into SCPC/FM

The results of Equations 5.1.1.4 and 5.2.1.3 can be used. The demodulated interference power spectrum $(1/2C_s)f^2 I_N(f)$ varies quickly from time to time because of the non-stationary nature of the voice signals (interference and signal). The locations of the interfering SCPC/FM signals relative to the desired SCPC/FM signal should be far enough from one another so that

(a) The line spectrum (the first term of Equation 5.1.1.4) should not be within the signal baseband, i.e., $|f_{0I} - f_{0s}| > 4$ KHz, since the effect of the tonal interference is very severe.
(b) If possible, $|f_{0I} - f_{0s}| > 8$ KHz should be maintained, since the effects of the second and the third terms of Equation 5.1.1.4 become very small in this case (see Figures 5.4.1 and 5.4.2 of Volume I).
(c) Since the convolution of the two continuous spectra of the SCPC/FM interference and signal has a wider distribution than that of each spectrum, a separation of $|f_{0i} - f_{0s}| > 12$ KHz makes the interference effects much smaller.

5.2.4   From SCPC/PSK Into SCPC/FM

Since the main lobe of the SCPC/PSK signal usually has the frequency width of the symbol rate (normally 32 KHz) and the power spectrum of the SCPC/FM is concentrated within ± 4 KHz around carrier frequency, function $I_N(f)$ can be approximated as

$$I_N(f) \simeq C_I T_I \left[\frac{\sin\{\pi(f - f_{0I} + f_{0s})\} T_I}{\pi(f - f_{0I} + f_{0s}) T_I} \right]^2$$
$$\cdot |Y_I(f - f_{0I} + f_{0s})|^2 \qquad (-\infty < f < \infty) \qquad (5.2.4.1)$$

where $Y_I(f - f_{0I})$ is the transfer function of the SCPC/PSK signal transmitter IF filter. If the SCPC/FM signal can be located at midpoint between two SCPC/PSK interferences, the effects of the interference can be minimized. The demodulated interference noise power is given by

$$(C_I T_I) \int_{-\infty}^{\infty} \left[\frac{\sin\{\pi(f - f_{0I} + f_{0s}) T_I\}}{\pi(f - f_{0I} + f_{0s}) T_I} \right]^2 |Y_I(f - f_{0I} + f_{0s})|^2$$
$$\cdot |Y_s(f)|^2 f^2 \, df \qquad (5.2.4.2)$$

where $Y_s(f)$ is the low pass filter of the SCPC/FM baseband signal.

5.2.5   From Continuous Mode PSK Signal Into SCPC/FM Signal

This case is essentially the same as that of Section 5.2.4. However, the symbol rate of the continuous PSK signal is much larger than the bandwidths of $Y_s(f)$ and of the SCPC/FM power spectrum (e.g., 100 Kbauds or larger) and the average power of the demodulated interference of Equation 5.2.4.2 can be further approximated by

$$(C_I T_I) \left[\frac{\sin\{\pi(f_{0I} - f_{0s})T_I\}}{\pi(f_{0I} - f_{0s})T_I} \right]^2 |Y_I(f_{0I} - f_{0s})|^2 \left(\frac{2B_v^3}{3} \right) \qquad (5.2.5.1)$$

where B_v is the voice bandwidth (3 KHz).

5.2.6   From TDMA/PSK Into SCPC/FM Signals

In a way similar to the explanations in Section 5.1.6, the TDMA burst mode effect may cause a burst interference change depending on the burst lengths in relation to the voice signal bandwidth (4 KHz). The average interference power is given by Equation 5.2.5.1 multiplied by P_B (defined by Equation 5.1.6.7), i.e.,

$$P_B(C_I T_I) \left[\frac{\sin\{\pi T_I(f_{0I} - f_{0s})\}}{\{\pi T_I(f_{0I} - f_{0s})\}} \right]^2 |Y_I(f_{0I} - f_{0s})|^2 \left(\frac{2B_v^3}{3} \right) . \qquad (5.2.6.1)$$

5.3   INTERFERENCE EFFECTS ON TV/FM SIGNALS

From the explanations in Section 5.1 and 5.2, it is not necessary to describe the demodulated interference power spectrum in detail, since function $I_N(f)$ only varies in magnitude and the distribution shape is unchanged even if the interference and the signal have exchanged their position. Therefore, in the following, only important factors will be pointed out, which are particularly important with a TV/FM signal.

In this case, two quantities must be evaluated as the demodulated noise power.

(i)   For the video baseband signal,

$$\frac{1}{C_s} \int_0^{6.2 \text{ MHz}} f^2 I_N(f) G_p(f) W_e(f) \, df \qquad (5.3.1)$$

where C_s is the TV/FM carrier power, $G_p(f)$ is the pre-emphasis effect and $W_e(f)$ is the weighting factor for the different frequency components (i.e., the effects of the different frequency components of the interference on the baseband video signal) (this function should be determined according to people's subjective intuitions) and

(ii)   the power of the interference in the baseband falling in the audio FM signal passband, where the interference spectrum can be assumed to be flat in this small bandwidth of the audio FM passband. The interference power on the audio FM signal is

$$\frac{1}{C_s} f_a^2 I_N(f_a) G_p(f_a) \Delta_a f \qquad (5.3.2)$$

where f_a is the carrier frequency of the audio FM signal in the video baseband and $\Delta_a f$ is the bandwidth of this FM signal.

5.3.1   From FDM/FM Into TV/FM

The function $I_N(f)$ is smoothed very much by the FDM/FM power spectrum as seen from Figure 5.1.3.1, although the TV/FM power spectrum is spiky and unsmoothed. Unless there are line spectrum components (tonal interferences), the demodulated interference should be noise-like.

5.3.2   From SCPC/FM Into TV/FM

The convolution of the SCPC/FM power spectrum with the TV/FM power spectrum results in one which is similar to the TV/FM power spectrum, but a little smoothed and spread.

The SCPC/FM interference usually interferes with the TV/FM as a large group and the effect of each SCPC/FM signal must be added to obtain the total effects with the weighting function $W_e(f)$.

5.3.3   From TV/FM Into TV/FM

As explained in the preceding sections, the power spectrum of the TV/FM signal is very non-stationary and varies from time to time. However, the average power spectrum has a Gaussian shape as reported in [22] and the convolution to obtain $I_N(f)$ is easy to achieve, since the convolution of two Gaussian shapes is a Gaussian shape. A rough estimation of interference effects may probably be done with reasonable simplicity by using this approach.

5.3.4   From SCPC/PSK Into TV/FM

The TV/FM power spectrum becomes very much smoothed after the convolution with the SCPC/PSK power spectrum whose width is about 32 KHz, although the rough shape of the function of $I_N(f)$ is similar to that of the TV/FM. Since the average power spectrum of the TV/FM signal can be in a Gaussian shape [22], $I_N(f)$ due to a SCPC/PSK is given by

$$I_N(f) \simeq C_I T_I e^{-R_{\phi_s}(0)} \left[\frac{\sin\{\pi T_I(f - f_{0I} + f_{0s})\}}{\pi T_I(f - f_{0I} + f_{0s})} \right]^2$$

$$+ C_I T_I (1 - e^{-R_{\phi_s}(0)}) \int_{-\infty}^{\infty} \left[\frac{\sin(\pi x T_I)}{\pi x T_I} \right]^2 \frac{1}{\sqrt{2\pi}\sigma_s}$$

$$\cdot\ e^{-\dfrac{(f - f_{0I} + f_{0s} - x)^2}{2\,\sigma_s^2}}\ |Y_I(x)|^2\ dx. \tag{5.3.4.1}^\dagger$$

Since the SCPC/PSK interferences come as a group, the total effects are a sum of these $I_N(f)$ as in Equation 5.1.2.3.

5.3.5 From Continuous Mode PSK Into TV/FM

The symbol rates of the continuous mode PSK signals are usually ·much larger than that of the SCPC/PSK signals (about 200 K bauds/60 M bauds) and the function $I_N(f)$ becomes much more smoothed than that of the SCPC/PSK case. In some cases (large baud rates), $I_N(f)$ becomes completely different from the case of a TV/FM signal (it becomes much flatter). The results of Equation 5.3.4.1 can still be applied and the sum of $I_N(f)$ for other PSK signals must also be done if needed.

5.3.6 From TDMA/PSK Into TV/FM

In most TDMA/PSK cases presently used, the TDMA/PSK symbol rates are larger than that of the TV/FM signal power spectrum bandwidth. Therefore, the function $I_N(f)$ has a shape similar to the power spectrum of the PSK multiplied by $|Y_I(f)|^2$. The representation of Equation 5.3.4.1 is also applicable with the multiplication of P_B defined by Equation 5.1.6.8. In this case, the TV/FM signal filter bandwidth is wide enough to obtain the interference appearing and disappearing in the demodulated TV baseband (due to the TDMA/PSK burst mode).

5.4 INTERFERENCE ON SCPC/PSK

For PSK signals, the demodulated noise power is not directly important. The direct measure of the PSK signal is the error probabilities in the demodulated bit sequences. If the interferences (or noise) are Gaussian, the total power falling in the receiving IF filter is only important in single sampling detection cases. In other detection cases (e.g., integrated and dumped detection cases), the power spectrum of the interference matters, even in Gaussian interference cases.

There are three practical approaches being used to evaluate the error probabilities of PSK signals.

(a) If there are not many interferences and if they are all in the passband of the PSK signal filters (i.e., if they are not distorted), then, the interference effects are not Gaussian at all, since the interference signals are peak-limited. This case is called "co-channel interferences."

(b) If there are more than five interferences and if none of them dominates the others, the total power of the interferences only needs to be evaluated in

---

†The residual carrier power of the TV/FM signal is represented by $C_s \exp[-R_{\phi_s}(0)]$ for notational convenience, although the baseband signal of TV/FM (TV signal) does not have a Gaussian probability function.

most cases, since the sum of these interferences can be approximated as a Gaussian process.

(c) If the power spectrum of the interference is much wider than that of the signal (the interference will be very much distorted by the signal filters), then, the total power of the interference falling in the signal filters is usually used to evaluate the error probabilities as an approximation, assuming this filtered interference is a Gaussian process, although this approximation in some cases is not accurate.

Since cases (b) and (c) are only a matter of integrating the interference power spectrum multiplied by the signal filter transfer functions, case (a) will be analyzed here. The SCPC/PSK signals are usually operated in linear regions of the non-linear devices (e.g., HPA and TWTA) and, therefore, a linear channel is assumed here. The non-linear channel case will be analyzed in the Section handling the case of the interferences on the TDMA or on the continuous mode PSK signal. The SCPC/PSK and SCPC/FM interference cases belong to (a) and the other cases (FDM/FM, TV/FM, continuous mode PSK and TDMA/PSK interference cases) belong to (c). In the following, the case (a) is analyzed.

As an illustration of a general case, the M-ary PSK case will be analyzed here.

Let us represent the input to the demodulator by

$$e_i(t) = A e^{j\omega_c t + j\theta} + N(t) e^{j\omega_c t}$$

$$+ \sum_{l=1}^{H} B_l e^{j\omega_l t + j\phi_l + j\lambda_l} \qquad (5.4.1)$$

where it is assumed that A and B_l are all constants. θ and λ_l are uniformly distributed in $(0, 2\pi)$.

$$N(t) = N_c(t) + jN_s(t) \qquad (5.4.2)$$

A = amplitude of the desired signal
ω_c = angular carrier frequency of the desired signal
θ = modulating angle of the desired signal
N_c = in-phase component of noise
N_s = quadrature component of noise
B_l = amplitude of the l-th carrier
ω_l = angular frequency of the l-th carrier
ϕ_l = modulating angle of the l-th carrier
λ_l = random phase of the l-th carrier
H = number of cochannel interferences

If it is assumed that θ is equally likely to be any of the M phases, the probability with which the received signal point P falls outside the decision cone D in Figure

5.4.2 represents the desired error probability. According to the analysis given in Section 2.3, the probability with which P falls inside D is

$$P_D = (2\pi\sigma_n^2)^{-1} \underset{\alpha,\beta}{E} \left[\int_0^\infty \int_0^{\Gamma x} \exp\left\{ -\frac{1}{2\sigma_n^2} \right.\right.$$

$$\left.\left. \cdot \left[(x - \alpha_0 - \alpha)^2 + (y - \beta_0 - \beta)^2\right] \right\} \right] dx\, dy \qquad (5.4.3)$$

where

$$\sigma_n^2 = \text{power of } N_s(t) \text{ or } N_c(t) \text{ (r.f. noise power)}$$

$$\alpha_0 = A\cos\left(\frac{\pi}{M}\right)$$

$$\beta_0 = A\sin\left(\frac{\pi}{M}\right)$$

$$\Gamma = \tan\left(\frac{2\pi}{M}\right)$$

$$\alpha = \sum_{l=1}^H B_l \cos[(\omega_l - \omega_c)t + \phi_l + \lambda_l]$$

$$\beta = \sum_{l=1}^H B_l \sin[(\omega_l - \omega_c)t + \phi_l + \lambda_l]$$

$$\underset{\alpha,\beta}{E} = \text{averaging with respect to } \alpha \text{ and } \beta.$$

Rewriting Equation 5.4.3 in terms of the characteristic function Φ_0 of the cochannel interference yields

$$P_D = (2\pi)^{-2} \int_{-\infty}^\infty \int_{-\infty}^\infty \int_0^\infty \int_0^{\Gamma x} e^{-j(x-\alpha_0)u - j(y-\beta_0)v}$$

$$\cdot \exp\left[-\frac{1}{2\sigma_n^2}(u^2 + v^2)\right] \Phi_0(u,v)\, du\, dv\, dx\, dy \qquad (5.4.4)$$

where

$$\Phi_0(u,v) = \underset{\alpha,\beta}{E}\{e^{ju\alpha + jv\beta}\}. \qquad (5.4.5)$$

If it is assumed that the random phases of the cochannel interference ϕ_0 are not interdependent and are uniformly distributed in $(0, 2\pi)$, then $\Phi_0(u,v)$ can be expressed as

$$\Phi_0(u,v) = \prod_{l=1}^H J_0(B_l\sqrt{u^2 + v^2}). \qquad (5.4.6)$$

In order to evaluate the integral of Equation 5.4.4, the power series expansion approach of $\Phi_0(u,v)$ is used here as in Section 2.6 of Volume I.

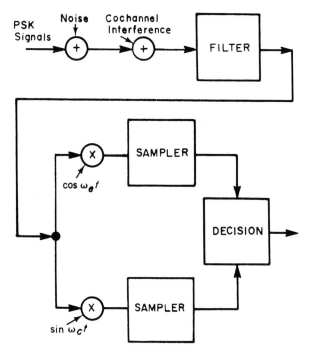

Figure 5.4.1   Receiving Scheme of PSK Systems

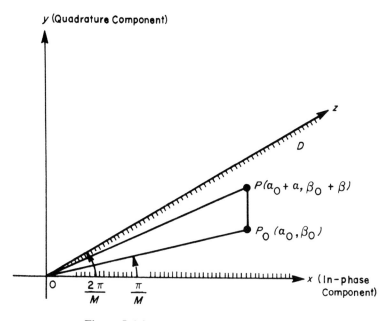

Figure 5.4.2   Signal Space of PSK Systems

To achieve faster convergence in the evaluation of error probabilities via the power series expansion method, define

$$\sigma^2 = \sigma_n^2 + \frac{\Delta}{2} \sum_{i=0}^{H} B_i^2. \tag{5.4.7}$$

Hence, σ^2 can be interpreted as the sum of the RF noise power and a part of the RF cochannel interference power (with the fraction Δ). With this definition, Equation 5.4.4 can be modified as follows:

$$P_D = (2\pi)^{-2} \int_{-\infty}^{\infty} \int_{-\infty}^{\infty} \int_{0}^{\infty} \int_{0}^{\Gamma x} e^{-\frac{1}{2}(u^2 + v^2)}$$

$$\cdot\, e^{-j(x - \alpha_1)u - j(y - \beta_1)v}\, \Phi_1(u, v)\, e^{\lambda^2/2(u^2 + v^2)}\, du\, dv\, dx\, dy \tag{5.4.8}$$

where

$$\alpha_1 = \frac{\alpha_0}{\sigma} = \frac{A}{\sigma} \cos\left(\frac{\pi}{M}\right) = \frac{A \cos(\pi/M)}{\sqrt{\sigma_n^2 + \dfrac{\Delta}{2} \sum_{l=1}^{H} B_l^2}} \tag{5.4.9a}$$

$$\beta_1 = \frac{\beta_0}{\sigma} = \frac{A}{\sigma} \sin\left(\frac{\pi}{M}\right) = \frac{A \sin(\pi/M)}{\sqrt{\sigma_n^2 + \dfrac{\Delta}{2} \sum_{l=1}^{H} B_l^2}} \tag{5.4.9b}$$

$$\lambda^2 = \frac{\dfrac{\Delta}{2} \sum_{l=1}^{H} B_l^2}{\sigma^2} = \frac{\dfrac{\Delta}{2} \sum_{l=1}^{H} B_l^2}{\sigma_n^2 + \dfrac{\Delta}{2} \sum_{l=1}^{H} B_l^2} \tag{5.4.9c}$$

$$\phi_1(u, v) = \prod_{l=1}^{H} J_0\left(\frac{B_l}{\sigma} \sqrt{u^2 + v^2}\right). \tag{5.4.10}$$

Now expand

$$\Phi_1(u, v)\, e^{\frac{\lambda^2}{2}(u^2 + v^2)}$$

into a power series:

$$\phi_1(u, v)\, e^{(\lambda^2/2)(u^2 + v^2)} = \sum_{m=0}^{\infty} \sum_{n=0}^{\infty} b_{2m, 2n}\, u^{2m} v^{2n}. \tag{5.4.11}$$

Define the Hermite functions $\Phi_n(x)$ as

$$\phi_n(x) = (2\pi)^{-1/2} H_n(x) \exp\left(\frac{-x^2}{2}\right) \tag{5.4.12}$$

for $n = 0, 1, 2, \ldots$, where $H_n(x)$ is the Hermite polynomial of degree n. These Hermite functions admit the following recurrence relationships:

$$\phi_n'(x) = -\phi_{n+1}(x)$$

$$\phi_{n+1}(x) = x\phi_n(x) - n\phi_{n-1}(x) \qquad (5.4.13)$$

where the prime denotes the differentiation with respect to x and

$$\phi_{-1}(x) \equiv (2\pi)^{-1/2} \int_x^\infty \exp\left(\frac{-t^2}{2}\right) dt \equiv \frac{1}{2} \operatorname{erfc}\left(\frac{x}{\sqrt{2}}\right). \qquad (5.4.14)^\dagger$$

Hence, substitution of equations 5.4.11–5.4.14 into Equation 5.4.8 yields

$$P_D = \int_0^\infty \int_0^{\Gamma x} \phi_0(x - \alpha_1)\,\phi_0(y - \beta_1)\,dy\,dx$$

$$+ \sum_{m,n}{}' (-1)^{m+n} b_{2m,2n}[\phi_{2m-1}(-\alpha_1)\,\phi_{2n-1}(-\beta_1)$$

$$- I_{2m,2n-1}(\alpha_1,\beta_1)] \qquad (5.4.15)$$

where the prime after the Σ denotes the exclusion of the term with $m = n = 0$, where $b_{0,0} = 1$, as can easily be seen from Equations 5.4.10 and 5.4.11 and where

$$I_{m,n}(\alpha_1,\beta_1) \equiv \int_0^\infty \phi_m(x - \alpha_1)\,\phi_n(\Gamma x - \beta_1)\,dx. \qquad (5.4.16)$$

The quantity in Equation 5.4.16 can be evaluated by using the recurrence method. The recurrence relationships for computing $I_{m,n}(\alpha_1,\beta_1)$ have been derived in Reference [77] and are as follows:

$$I_{m,n}(\alpha_1,\beta_1) = \phi_{m-1}(-\alpha_1)\,\phi_l(-\beta_1) - \Gamma I_{m-1,n+1}(\alpha_1,\beta_1) \qquad (5.4.17)$$

where

$$I_{0,n}(\alpha_1,\beta_1) = \sum_{l=0}^n {}_nC_l\,\phi_l\left(\alpha_1\sin\frac{2\pi}{M} - \beta_1\cos\frac{2\pi}{M}\right)$$

$$\cdot \left(\cos\frac{2\pi}{M}\right)^{l+1}\left[\delta_{n,l} - \phi_{n-l-1}\left(\alpha_1\cos\frac{2\pi}{M}\right.\right.$$

$$\left.\left. + \beta_1\sin\frac{2\pi}{M}\right)\left(-\sin\frac{2\pi}{M}\right)^{n-1}\right] \qquad (5.4.18)$$

in which

$$\delta_{n,l} = 1 \quad \text{if } n = l$$

$$= 0 \quad \text{if } n \neq l.$$

$\dagger$The definition of this error function, erfc(x) is different from the one defined in proceding sections (e.g., see Section 2.2 of Volume I).

If $M = 4$, then the term $I_{2m, 2n-1}(\alpha_1, \beta_1)$ in Equation 5.4.15 should be set equal to zero and computation of any $I_{m,n}(\alpha_1, \beta_1)$ is unnecessary.

Computation of the coefficients $b_{2m, 2n}$ is slightly different from the computation in [41]. The new computational procedure will be provided in the next part so that the Σ' term in Equation 5.4.15 can be evaluated. The first term in Equation 5.4.15 can be computed by direct integration or by the following approximation derived in Reference [41].

$$\int_0^\infty \int_0^{\Gamma x} \phi_0(x - \alpha_1) \phi_0(y - \beta_1) \, dy \, dx$$

$$= \frac{1}{2} \text{erfc}[2^{-1/2} C \cos \theta_2] + \frac{1}{2} \text{erfc}[-2^{-1/2} C \cos \theta_1]$$

$$+ \exp\left(-\frac{1}{2}C^2\right)\left\{(4\pi d)^{-1}C^2 \sin(\theta_1 - \theta_2) \cos(\theta_1 + \theta_2)\right.$$

$$- (2Md)^{-1}C^2 + (4\pi d)^{-1}C[\cos \theta_2(2d + C^2 \sin^2 \theta_2)^{1/2}$$

$$- \cos \theta_1(2d + C^2 \sin^2 \theta_1)^{1/2}] + (4\pi d)^{-1}(C^2 + 2d)$$

$$\left. \cdot \left[\sin^{-1}\left\{\frac{C \cos \theta_2}{(C^2 + 2d)^{1/2}}\right\} - \sin^{-1}\left\{\frac{C \cos \theta_1}{(C^2 + 2d)^{1/2}}\right\}\right]\right\}$$

where $2 \geq d \geq 4/\pi$, and

$$C \equiv (\alpha_1^2 + \beta_1^2)^{1/2} \qquad\qquad \theta_1 = \frac{\pi}{M} + \frac{2\pi}{M} - \theta_0$$

$$\theta_0 = \tan^{-1}\left(\frac{\beta_1}{\alpha_1}\right) \qquad\qquad \theta_2 = \frac{\pi}{2} - \theta_0. \qquad (5.4.19)$$

Therefore, the error probability

$$P_e \equiv 1 - P_D \qquad\qquad (5.4.20)$$

can be numerically computed from Equations 5.4.20 and 5.4.15.

Recurrence Relationship for $b_{2m, 2n}$

Denote the total RF-interference-to-RF-noise power ratio as k, and define L as the ratio of the carrier power to the sum of the RF noise power and the total RF interference power. In other terms,

$$k = \sum_{l=1}^{H} \frac{B_l^2}{2\sigma_n^2}$$

$$L \equiv \frac{A^2}{2\left(\sigma_n^2 + \dfrac{1}{2}\displaystyle\sum_{l=1}^{H} B_l^2\right)} = \frac{C/N}{1 + k}. \qquad (5.4.21)$$

Then, Equation 5.4.9 can be rewritten as

$$\alpha_1 = \left[\frac{2L(1 + k)}{1 + \Delta k} \right]^{1/2} \cos\left(\frac{\pi}{M}\right)$$

$$\beta_1 = \left[\frac{2L(1 + k)}{1 + \Delta k} \right]^{1/2} \sin\left(\frac{\pi}{M}\right)$$

$$\lambda^2 = \frac{\Delta k}{1 + \Delta k}. \tag{5.4.22}$$

Assuming all interferences are equal,

$$B = B_1 = B_2 = \cdots = B_H. \tag{5.4.23}$$

Thus, Equations 5.4.10 and 5.4.11 indicate that

$$\Phi_1(u, v) \exp\left(\frac{1}{2} \lambda^2(u^2 + v^2)\right)$$

$$= \left[J_0\left\{ \left[\frac{2k}{H(1 + \Delta k)} \right]^{1/2} [u^2 + v^2]^{1/2} \right\} \right]^H$$

$$\cdot \exp\left[\frac{1}{2} \lambda^2(u^2 + v^2) \right]$$

$$= \sum_{m,n} b_{2m, 2n} u^{2m} v^{2n}. \tag{5.4.24}$$

Two methods can be employed to obtain $b_{2m, 2n}$: the recurrence method and the convolution method.

Recurrence Method

Define

$$\gamma = (u^2 + v^2)^{1/2}$$

and

$$J_0\left\{ \left[\frac{2k}{H(1 + \Delta k)} \right]^{1/2} \gamma \right\} = \sum_{m=0}^{\infty} C_{2m} \gamma^{2m} \tag{5.4.25}$$

where

$$C_{2m} = (-1)^m (2^m m!)^{-2} \left[\frac{2k}{H(1 + \Delta k)} \right]^m. \tag{5.4.26}$$

Then, Equation 5.4.24 can be put into the following form:

$$\Phi_1(u, v) \exp\left[\frac{1}{2} \lambda^2(u^2 + v^2) \right]$$

$$= \left[J_0 \left\{ \left[\frac{2k}{H(1 + \Delta k)} \right]^{1/2} \gamma \right\} \right]^H \exp\left(\frac{1}{2} \lambda^2 \gamma^2 \right)$$

$$\equiv \sum_{m=0}^{\infty} d_{2m} \gamma^{2m}. \tag{5.4.27}$$

Since $\exp[(1/2)\lambda^2\gamma^2]$ can be expanded into power series

$$\exp\left(\frac{1}{2} \lambda^2 \gamma^2 \right) = \sum_{l=0}^{\infty} \frac{1}{l!} \left(\frac{1}{2} \lambda^2 \right)^l \gamma^{2l} \tag{5.4.28}$$

the coefficients d_{2m} can be obtained by comparing the coefficients of γ^{2m} on both sides of Equation 5.4.27 after substituting Equation 5.4.25 into 5.4.27. Hence, for $i \neq 0$,

$$d_{2i} = \frac{1}{2i} \sum_{p=0}^{i-1} [2H(i - p) C_{2i-2p} + \lambda^2 C_{2i-2p-2} - (2p) C_{2i-2p}] d_{2p}$$

$$d_0 = 1. \tag{5.4.29}$$

Now, Equation 5.4.27 can be written as

$$\Phi_1(u, v) \exp\left[\frac{1}{2} \lambda^2 (u^2 + v^2) \right] = \sum_{m=0}^{\infty} d_{2m} \gamma^{2m}$$

$$= \sum_{p=0}^{\infty} d_{2p} (u^2 + v^2)^p$$

$$= \sum_{m,n} b_{2m,2n} u^{2m} v^{2n}. \tag{5.4.30}$$

Using binomial expansion on $(u^2 + v^2)^p$ in Equation 5.4.30 and comparing coefficients yields

$$b_{2m,2n} = d_{2(m+n)} \frac{(m + n)!}{m!n!}. \tag{5.4.31}$$

Convolution Method

From Equations 5.4.23, 5.4.24 and 5.4.26, it is obvious that d_{2m} can be computed by convolving C_{2m} H times and then convolving with the coefficients in Equation 5.4.28. That is,

$$C_{2k}^{(1)} = \sum_{m=0}^{k} C_{2m} C_{2k-2m}$$

$$C_{2k}^{(2)} = \sum_{m=0}^{k} C_{2m} C_{2k-2m}^{(1)}$$

$$C_{2k}^{(H-1)} = \sum_{m=0}^{k} C_{2m} \, C_{2k-2m}^{(H-2)}$$

$$d_{2i} = \sum_{m=0}^{i} C_{2i-2m}^{(H-1)} (\lambda^2/2)^m \, \frac{1}{m!} \, . \tag{5.4.32}$$

Computational Procedure

The following is a modified computational procedure which is implemented on COMSAT's computer to determine the effects of Gaussian noise and up to four equal-strength cochannel interferences on the error probabilities of 4-, 8-, and 16-phase PSK systems:

(a) Decide the values of M, H, k, L and Δ. (To choose Δ, see Reference [41]).
(b) Compute α_1, β_1, and λ^2.
(c) Compute $1 - \int_0^\infty \int_0^{\Gamma x} \phi_0(x - \alpha_1) \, \phi_0(y - \beta_1) \, dy \, dx$ from Equation 5.4.19.
(d) Compute $b_{2m,2n}$ from Equations 5.4.24, 5.4.29 and 5.4.30 or from Equations 5.4.31 and 5.4.32.
(e) Compute $\Phi_n(-\alpha_1)$ and $\Phi_n(-\beta_1)$ from the recurrence relationship in Equation 5.4.13.
(f) Compute $I_{m,n}(\alpha_1, \beta_1)$ from Equation 5.4.17, if $M > 4$. (If $M = 4$, this computation is unnecessary.)
(g) Compute $P_e = 1 - P_D$ from Equation 5.4.15.
(h) If the convergence in the computation of Equation 5.4.15 is not fast enough, adjust the value of Δ to obtain a faster convergence (see Reference [41]).

Numerical Results and Discussion

Figures 5.4.3–5.4.5 show the numerical results for one, two, three, and four cochannel interferences in respectively 4-, 8-, and 16-phase PSK systems. In all the figures, the vertical axes represent the error probabilities, the horizontal axes represent L in dB, and the parameters represent k in dB. Since k, as defined in Equation 5.4.21, is the total RF-interference-to-RF-noise power ratio, the two extremes with $k = +\infty$ dB and $-\infty$ dB correspond to respectively noise-free and interference-free situations. Thus, the curves associated with $k = -\infty$ dB in all the figures should be identical to those error probabilities resulting from Gaussian noise alone. Consequently, the curves with $k = -\infty$ dB in Figure 5.4.3 are identical to the curves with $k = -\infty$ in Figures 5.4.4 and 5.4.5.

On the other hand, for the noise-free cases in which $k = +\infty$ dB, the error probabilities are always equal to zero for L above certain thresholds, since the amplitudes of these interferences are bounded. In this case, when the carrier-to-total-interference power ratio exceeds a certain threshold, the received signal will always lie in the correct decision region and hence, the error probability will be zero. These thresholds are determined by the number of cochannel

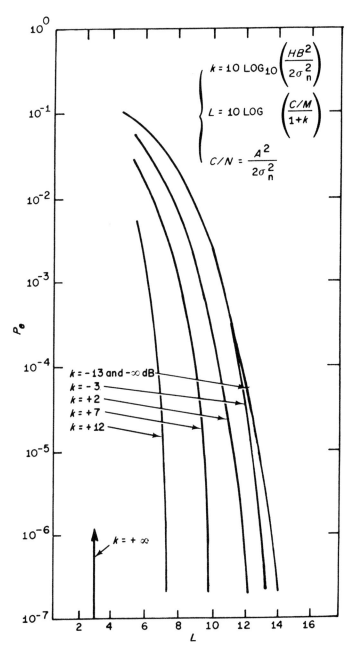

Figure 5.4.3(a) Error Probabilities of 4-Phase PSK in the Presence of Gaussian Noise and One Cochannel Interference ($H = 1$, 4_ϕ)

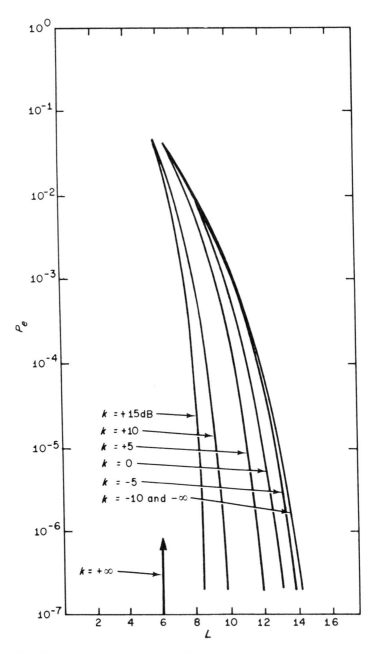

Figure 5.4.3(b) Error Probabilities of 4-Phase PSK in the Presence of Gaussian Noise and Two Cochannel Interferences ($H = 2, 4_\phi$)

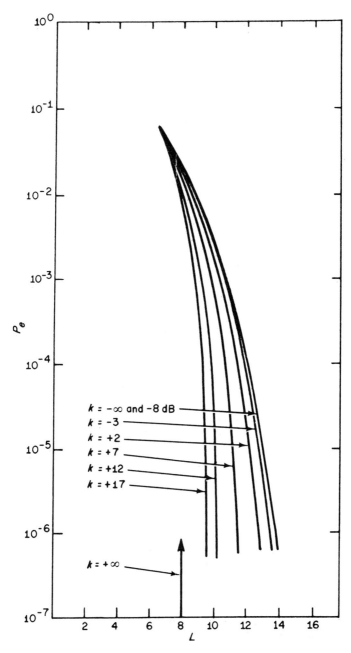

Figure 5.4.3(c) Error Probabilities of 4-Phase PSK in the Presence of Gaussian Noise and Three Cochannel Interferences ($H = 3$, 4_ϕ)

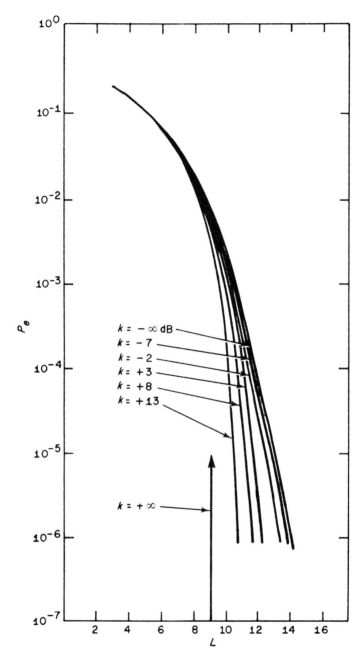

Figure 5.4.3(d) Error Probabilities of 4-Phase PSK in the Presence of Gaussian Noise and Four Cochannel Interferences ($H = 4$, 4_ϕ)

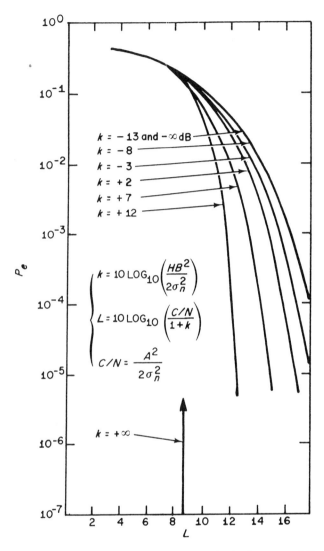

Figure 5.4.4(a) Error Probabilities of 8-Phase PSK in the Presence of Gaussian Noise and One Cochannel Interference ($H = 1, 8_\phi$)

interferences for a given M-ary PSK system. For instance, it can be seen from Figure 5.2.4.3 that, for the 4-phase PSK system, the thresholds are 3, 6, 8 and 9 dB, respectively, as a result of one, two, three, and four cochannel interferences.

Also, from these sets of Figures, it can be deduced that, for a fixed number of phases, M, a fixed interference-to-noise power ratio, k, and a fixed carrier-

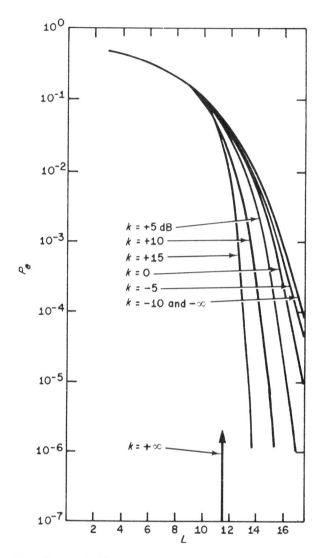

Figure 5.4.4(b) Error Probabilities of 8-Phase PSK in the Presence of Gaussian Noise and Two Cochannel Interferences ($H = 2$, 8_ϕ)

to-total-interference-and-noise power ratio, L, the error probability increases as the number of interferences, H, increases. This is quite reasonable. That is, as H increases to $+\infty$, the statistics of the sum of these independent H interferences becomes closer to being Gaussian. Thus, the error probability should approach that caused by Gaussian noise with the same amount of power.

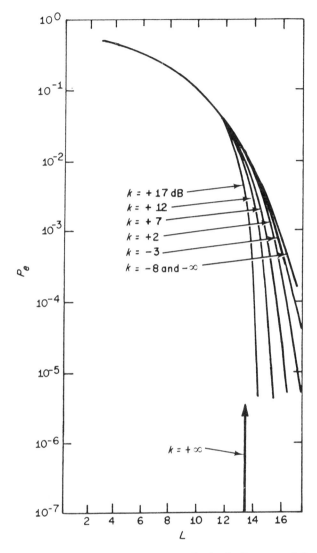

Figure 5.4.4(c)   Error Probabilities of 8-Phase PSK in the Presence of Gaussian Noise and Three Cochannel Interferences ($H = 3, 8_\phi$)

5.4.1   From FDM/FM Into SCPC/PSK

This case corresponds to Item (c) of Section 5.4 where the power spectrum of the FDM/FM interference is much wider than that of the SCPC/PSK signal. Assuming that the power spectrum of the FDM/FM signal is represented by

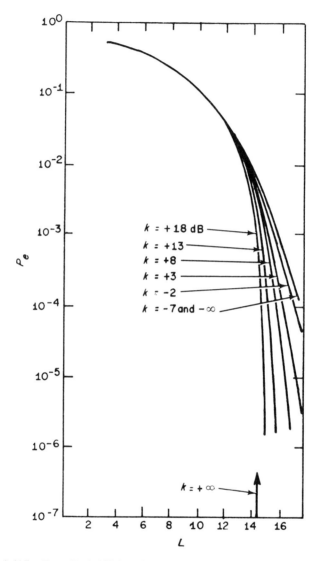

Figure 5.4.4(d) Error Probabilities of 8-Phase PSK in the Presence of Gaussian Noise and Four Cochannel Interferences ($H = 4$, 8_ϕ)

Equation 5.1.1.3 which is obtained in Section 5.3 of Volume I, the power falling in the passband of SCPC/PSK signal is

$$I = \int_{-\infty}^{\infty} [C_I e^{-R_{\phi_I}(0)} \delta(f - f_{0I}) + W_{ccI}(f - f_{0I})] \, |Y_s(f - f_{0s})|^2 \, df. \quad (5.4.1.1)$$

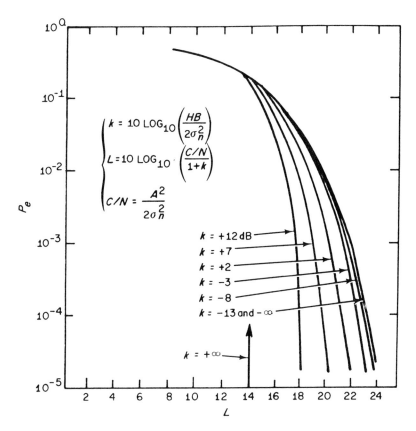

Figure 5.4.5(a)   Error Probabilities of 16-Phase PSK in the Presence of Gaussian Noise and One Cochannel Interference ($H = 1$, 16_ϕ)

This is further simplified into

$$\int_{-\infty}^{\infty} [C_I e^{-R_{\phi_I}(0)} \delta(f-f_{0I}+f_{0s}) + W_{ccI}(f-f_{0I}+f_{0s})] |Y_s(f)|^2 \, df$$

$$= C_I e^{-R_{\phi_I}(0)} |Y_s(f_{0I}-f_{0s})|^2$$

$$+ \int_{-\infty}^{\infty} W_{ccI}(f-f_{0I}+f_{0s})|Y_s(f)|^2 \, df$$

$$\simeq C_I e^{-R_{\phi_I}(0)} |Y_s(f_{0I}-f_{0s})|^2$$

$$+ B_s W_{ccI}(f_{0I}-f_{0s}) \tag{5.4.1.2}$$

where B_s is the bandwidth of the filter $Y_s(f)$. If the power spectrum of the FDM/FM signal can be approximated by a Gaussian shape, then $e^{-R_I(0)}$ becomes very small and

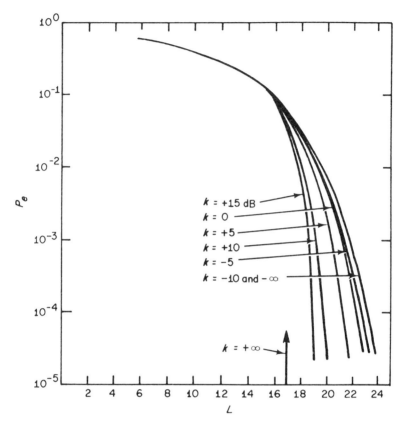

Figure 5.4.5(b)   Error Probabilities of 16-Phase PSK in the Presence of Gaussian Noise and Two Cochannel Interferences ($H = 2$, 16_ϕ)

$$I \simeq B_s \frac{C_I}{\sqrt{2\pi}\,\sigma_I}\, e^{-\frac{(f_{0I}-f_{0s})^2}{2\sigma_I^2}}.$$
(5.4.1.3)

If the first term of Equation 5.4.1.2 is not small (if $R_{\phi_I}(0)$ is not large enough or if $|Y(f_{0I} - f_{0s})|^2$ is not small enough), since this is a tonal component, the analysis of Section 5.4 must be applied (and the second term of Equation 5.4.1.2 is approximated as a thermal noise).

5.4.2   From SCPC/FM Into SCPC/PSK

Since the bandwidth of the SCPC/PSK signal is about 38 KHz and the frequency separation of the SCPC/FM signals is 25 KHz (e.g.), there are one or two SCPC/FM signals falling in the passband of the SCPC/PSK signal depending on the carrier locations. The analysis shown in Section 5.4 can be applied for this case.

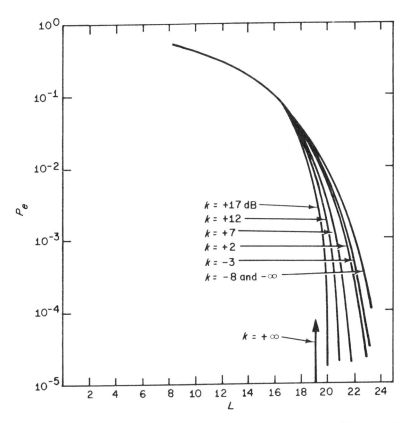

Figure 5.4.5(c)   Error Probabilities of 16-Phase PSK in the Presence of Gaussian Noise and Three Cochannel Interferences ($H = 3$, 16_ϕ)

Since the SCPC/PSK is mostly QPSK or BPSK at present, Figure 5.4.3(a) and Figure 5.4.3(b) can be used.

5.4.3   From TV/FM Into SCPC/PSK

This should be in practical term, the case of Section 5.4, Item (c). As mentioned in preceding sections, the power spectrum of the TV/FM signal is very variable (non-stationary) and hard to predict in a short time. However, it has been reported in Reference [22] that the shape of the power spectrum is Gaussian in a larger time average. In this case, the result of Equation 5.4.1.3 can be applied. One thing which asks for some precaution is that a problem similar to that in Section 5.2.2 occurs in this case. When the frame rate energy dispersal is used and the TV modulation becomes weak, a TV/FM carrier with a large impulse may hit the SCPC/PSK signal whose error probabilities deteriorate very much during the

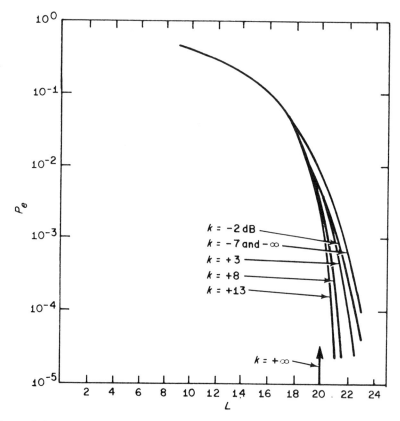

Figure 5.4.5(d)   Error Probabilities of 16-Phase PSK in the Presence of Gaussian Noise and Four Cochannel Interferences ($H = 4$, 16_ϕ)

impulse interference. If the line rate energy dispersal is used, this effect is very much reduced as explained in Section 5.2.2.

5.4.4   From SCPC/PSK Into SCPC/PSK

There are two kinds of cases, i.e., the cochannel interference which does not receive the distortion due to the signal filter and the case in which the interference PSK signal is distorted, since the carrier frequency of the interference is located at the edge of the signal filter passband.

For the former case, the analysis shown in Section 5.4 can be used, where there is only one cochannel interference, and Figure 5.4.3(a) can be used. For the latter case, some rigorous approach can be applied to the error probability degradation of the SCPC/PSK signal by computer simulations but the following integrated power is evaluated and considered to be the thermal noise in most practical cases, i.e.,

$$I = \int_{-\infty}^{\infty} C_I T_I \left[\frac{\sin\{\pi T_I(f - f_{0I})\}}{\{\pi T_I(f - f_{0I})\}} \right]^2 |Y_I(f - f_{0I})|^2$$

$$\cdot |Y_s(f - f_{0s})|^2 \, df$$

$$= C_I T_I \int_{-\infty}^{\infty} \left[\frac{\sin\{\pi T_I(f - f_{0I} + f_{0s})\}}{\pi T_I(f - f_{0I} + f_{0s})} \right]^2$$

$$\cdot |Y_I(f - f_{0I} + f_{0s})|^2 \, |Y_s(f)|^2 \, df \qquad (5.4.4.1)$$

where $Y_I(f)$ and $Y_s(f)$ are respectively the interference and signal IF filter (and I.F.) filters (the center frequencies of these filter transfer functions are shifted to zero). The evaluation of Equation 5.4.4.1 is usually enough for a rough approximation.

5.4.5 From Continuous Mode PSK Into SCPC/PSK

This case corresponds to Item (c), Section 5.4. Since the symbol rates of the continuous mode PSK are usually much larger than the symbol rate of the SCPC/PSK, usually around 32 K bauds, the interference power I is given by Equation 5.4.4.1 but with the following approximation

$$I \simeq C_I T_I B_s \left[\frac{\sin\{\pi T_I(f_{0I} - f_{0s})\}}{\pi T_I(f_{0I} - f_{0s})} \right]^2 |Y_I(f_{0I} - f_{0s})|^2. \qquad (5.4.5.1)$$

Although the power of I is not that of a Gaussian process, it is considered so in the case of an approximation, which usually gives a pessimistic result. The exact evaluation of the error probability degradation is very difficult to assess in this case.

5.4.6 From TDMA/PSK Into SCPC/PSK

In a way similar to the analysis of Section 5.1.6, the TDMA/PSK interference on and off effect due to the burst mode clearly exists in most cases, since the width of the impulse response $h(t)$ (Figure 5.1.6.2) is $(38 \times 10^3)^{-1}$, while the TDMA burst width (Figure 5.1.6.1) is longer than this value in most cases. For the time period in which the TDMA/PSK interference effects exist, Item (c) of Section 5.4 can be applied. However, as a power approximation, the result of Equation 5.4.5.1 can be used, i.e.,

$$I = C_I T_I B_s \left[\frac{\sin\{\pi T_I(f_{0I} - f_{0s})\}}{\{\pi T_I(f_{0I} - f_{0s})\}} \right]^2. \qquad (5.4.6.1)$$

Assuming that the power I gives a Gaussian effect, the error probability of the SCPC/PSK is given by

$$P_e \simeq P_B \, P_{eg}(I) \tag{5.4.6.2}$$

where $P_{eg}(I)$ is the probability of the SCPC/PSK signal error due to the Gaussian noise whose power is I.

5.5 INTERFERENCE EFFECTS ON CONTINUOUS MODE PSK SIGNALS

This case analysis depends on Items (a), (b) and (c) of Section 5.4 according to the characteristics of the interferences.

In this section, only the downlink noise case is discussed, where the interferences are added linearly to the signal. The uplink interference addition case will be analyzed in Section 5.6.

5.5.1 From FDM/FM Into Continuous Mode PSK

There are three cases (a), (b) and (c) in this case (Section 5.4). For case (a), the analysis shown in Section 5.4 can be used. For case (b), the reason why the Gaussian approximation is valid will be analyzed in Section 5.5.2. For case (c), the result of Equation 5.4.1.2, i.e.,

$$I = C_I e^{-R_{\phi_I}(0)} \, |Y_s(f_{0I} - f_{0s})|^2$$

$$+ \int_{-\infty}^{\infty} W_{ccI}(f - f_{0I} + f_{0s}) |Y_s(f)|^2 df \tag{5.5.1.1}$$

where $R_{\phi_I}(0)$ and $W_{ccI}(f)$ can be obtained by the approaches found in Section 5.3 of Volume I.

5.5.2 From SCPC/FM Into Continuous Mode PSK

As explained in Section 5.4 of Volume I, the power spectrum of the SCPC/FM is confined within ± 4 KHz around carrier frequency (this is only roughly true in practice). Also, the SCPC/FM signals exist as a group in most cases and a number of SCPC/FM interferences fall in the passband of the continuous mode PSK signal (if there is a small number of SCPC signals, the total power of the interference is very small and can be ignored).

Represent the cochannel interference by

$$e_I(t) = \sum_{\ell=1}^{H} B_\ell \sin(\omega_\ell t + \phi_\ell + \lambda_\ell). \tag{5.5.2.1}$$

In order to obtain the probability density function of e_I, let us derive first the characteristic function of e_I.

$$C_I(u) = E\{e^{jue_I}\}$$

$$= \prod_{\ell=1}^{H} E\{e^{juB_\ell \sin(\omega_\ell t + \phi_\ell + \lambda_\ell)}\}$$

$$= \prod_{\ell=1}^{H} J_0(B_\ell u). \qquad (5.5.2.2)$$

For analytical simplicity, assume that all B_ℓ's are equal. Then,

$$C_I(u) = [J_0(Bu)]^H \qquad (5.5.2.3)$$

where

$$B_1 = B_2 = \cdots = B_H = B. \qquad (5.5.2.4)$$

In this case, the total power of the interference is

$$P_I = \frac{1}{2} \sum_{\ell=1}^{H} B_\ell^2 = \frac{H}{2} B^2 \qquad (5.5.2.5)$$

i.e.,

$$B = \sqrt{\frac{2P_I}{H}}. \qquad (5.5.2.6)$$

Thus,

$$C_I(u) = \prod_{\ell=1}^{H} \left[J_0\left(\sqrt{\frac{2P_I}{H}}\, u \right) \right]^H. \qquad (5.5.2.7)$$

Here,

$$\lim_{H \to \infty} \prod_{\ell=1}^{H} \left[J_0\left(\sqrt{\frac{2P_I}{H}}\, u \right) \right]^H = e^{-\frac{u^2}{2P_I}}. \qquad (5.5.2.8)$$

From this result, it is clear that the probability density function of C_I can be approximated as a Gaussian process for many values of H, since the result of Equation 5.5.2.8 is the characteristic function of a Gaussian process whose power is P_I. From a practical point of view, as seen from Figures 5.4.3–5.4.5, if there are more than five cochannel interferences, the approximation of Equation 5.5.2.8 is valid.

5.5.3 From TV/FM Into Continuous Mode PSK

Depending on the symbol rate of this signal and on the TV/FM bandwidth, the analytical approach is different for items (a) and (c) of Section 5.4.

When the TV signal baseband modulation is weak and the energy dispersal is on, the result of Section 5.2.2 can be similarly applied to this case. In this case, since the filter bandwidth of the continuous mode PSK signal is much larger than the line rates, the pulse of the TV/FM interference hitting this signal occurs both in frame and line rate energy dispersal cases of the TV/FM interference. In such a case, the interference effect exists only during the time when the instantaneous frequency of the TV/FM interference stays in the PSK signal filter passband, and, otherwise, it disappears. In some cases, many continuous mode PSK signals share a transponder and only two TV/FM signals at most usually share a transponder. During the time period when the TV/FM interference hits the signal, a large effect may occur.

5.5.4   From SCPC/PSK Into Continuous Mode PSK

The symbol rates which decide the bandwidth of the PSK signals are much larger in the continuous mode PSK signals than in the SCPC/PSK signals in most cases and many SCPC/PSK interferences fall in the passband of the continuous mode PSK signal (if there are few SCPC/PSK interferences, the total power is very small and can be ignored). Therefore, according to the theory shown in Equation 5.5.2.8, the effects of all the SCPC/PSK signals can be considered as a thermal noise.

5.5.5   From Continuous Mode PSK Into Continuous Mode PSK

Since the symbol rates of these signals cover a wide range (e.g., from 200 K bauds to 60 M bauds), therefore, all kinds of cases may occur, for Items (a), (b) and (c) in Section 5.4. For case (a), the theory and results developed in Section 5.4 can be used. For case (b), the result of Equation 5.5.2.8 can be applied. For case (c), Equation 5.4.4.1 can be used to evaluate the interference power falling in the passband of the signal.

5.5.6   From TDMA/PSK Into Continuous Mode PSK

There are three cases to be considered, since the symbol rate of this signal is very variable, for Items (a), (b) and (c) of Section 5.4 for which the analysis of Section 5.4, and of Equations 5.5.2.8 and 5.4.4.1 respectively can be applied. The only precautions to consider come from the fact that the time period when the TDMA interferences occur (due to the burst mode of the TDMA) should be considered for case (a) (as in Equation 5.4.6.2, although I is no longer Gaussian) and factor P_s (Equation 5.1.6.8) should be multiplied in Equation 5.4.4.1 for cases (c) and (b).

5.6   INTERFERENCE ON TDMA/PSK

5.6.1   From FDM/FM Into TDMA/PSK

Since the power spectrum of the FDM/FM signal is narrowly distributed and the symbol rate of the TDMA/PSK signal (the bandwidth of the PSK signal) is higher than the bandwidth of the FDM/FM signal in most cases, cases (a) and (b) of Section 5.4 are applicable in this case, i.e., the analyses of Section 5.4 and of Equation 5.5.2.7 respectively can be used.

5.6.2 From SCPC/FM Into TDMA/PSK

In most practical cases, the bandwidth of the SCPC/FM is much smaller than the symbol rate of the TDMA/PSK signal and, since many SCPC/FM interferences usually fall in the passband of the TDM/PSK signal (if, anyway, there are few SCPC/FM signals, then the total power of the SCPC/FM interferences is negligible for the TDMA/PSK signal), case (b) of Section 5.4 can be applied.

5.6.3 From TV/FM Into TDMA/PSK

Since the TV/FM signal usually occupies a bandwidth of 18 MHz or 36 MHz depending on the e.i.r.p. values of the satellites, cases (a) and (c), for which the analysis of Section 5.4 and the result of Section 5.5 of Volume I respectively can be used to obtain the power falling in the TDMA/PSK passband, are applicable here.

If the TV/FM baseband modulation is weak and energy dispersals are used (frame or line rate energy dispersals), the pulsive interference effects of the TV/FM signal explained in Section 5.2.2 occurs. During the period of the pulsive interference appearance, the effects of the TV/FM interference become almost the same as those of case (a) of Section 5.4.

5.6.4 From SCPC/PSK Into TDMA PSK

For the same reason as that explained in Section 5.6.2, the Gaussian assumption for the SCPC/PSK interferences is valid as shown in Equation 5.5.2.7.

5.6.5 From Continuous Mode PSK Into TDMA/PSK

The symbol rates of continuous mode PSK signals are usually lower than those of TDMA/PSK signals. Therefore, case (a) of Section 5.4 is applicable, i.e., the analysis of the same section can be used. As mentioned before, this analysis can only be used for the downlink interferences which are linearly superposed on the TDMA/PSK signal.

The following analysis shows the uplink case interference effects of the co-channel PSK signals which pass through the nonlinear device (TWTA or SSPA) operating in the saturating power area. This analysis can also be applied to the case of Section 5.6.6 ("From TDMA/PSK Into TDMA/PSK").

Radio spectrum limitations have necessitated the consideration and implementation of frequency-reuse techniques in satellite communication systems. For example, the INTELSAT V system employs a four-fold frequency reuse; in the INTELSAT VI era, frequencies may be reused up to six times. With this frequency reuse, an undesired byproduct has been increased, co-channel interference

(CCI). In fact, with the larger satellite G/T and e.i.r.p., now available through more powerful TWT amplifiers and antenna spot beams, typical link budgets for fully expanded systems demonstrate that co-channel interference can easily be the dominant degrading factor, more important than thermal noise.

At the same time, there have been only limited available theoretical tools or measurement results for co-channel interference effects in a nonlinear satellite system. Thus, in system calculations, the interference has frequently been assumed to be identical in effect to that of an equivalent power Gaussian noise source. For a linear channel, it is widely known [77] that this supposition provides a pessimistic estimate for the degradation to a digital PSK system. For the nonlinear channel, it will be shown that, as in the linear case, if the number of interferers is not too great ($\simeq 6$) the non-Gaussian characteristics of the interference can be significant. Also, it might well be assumed that some amount of small-signal suppression should be experienced for the uplink interferers due to the satellite nonlinear transponder. It will be seen that the situation is more complicated than this. Although uplink suppression is indeed present, practical channel filtering (to minimize adjacent channel interference) may reduce the observed effect on the BER to an almost insignificant level.

The problem addressed here then is the effect of a number of co-channel interferers upon the BER of a QPSK system having a nonlinear transponder. As shown in Figure 5.6.5.1, the modulated QPSK signal is bandlimited by a transmit filter which may be narrow enough ($BT \simeq 1 - 1.5$) (B is the 3 dB filter bandwidth, T is the modulation symbol duration) to produce appreciable intersymbol interference (ISI). Because it is relatively wide, the satellite input filter can usually be considered as part of the overall filter function. The satellite contains a TWTA operating at or near saturation with specified AM-AM and AM-PM characteristics. The satellite output filter and receiving filter may likewise usually be considered as one filter with a bandwidth possibly narrow enough to cause additional ISI. Co-channel interferers are additive on both the up- and downlinks and are assumed to be angle-modulated, although, particularly in the QPSK case, channel filtering will produce some AM. Both uplink and downlink Gaussian noises are included but it will be assumed, in the theoretical analysis, that the downlink noise is at least 2 dB greater than that on the uplink (the reason for this assumption is discussed in the theoretical development). Thus, in this case, although uplink noise (and interferers) will more likely make errors by moving the signal sample points closer to the decision thresholds, the proximate cause for detected errors is downlink noise.

As an example of the way in which interference accesses arise, Figure 5.6.5.2 outlines the situation for the INTELSAT V environment. For the six accesses shown, only three originate independently but, since the transponder translation oscillators are not mutually coherent, they are all assumed to be independent. Two of the interferers arise from the co-coverage cross-polarized signal which has both an up- and downlink access. The others are caused by the opposite

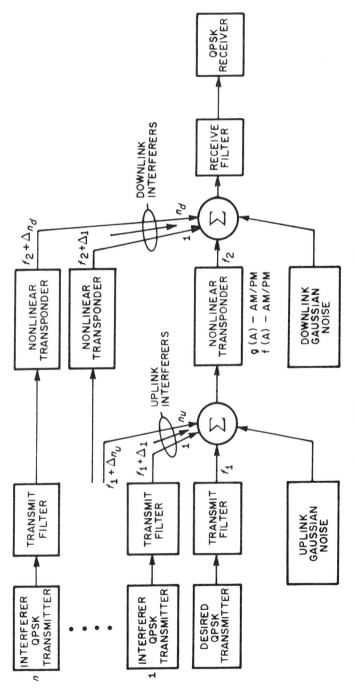

Figure 5.6.5.1 Cochannel Interference Model

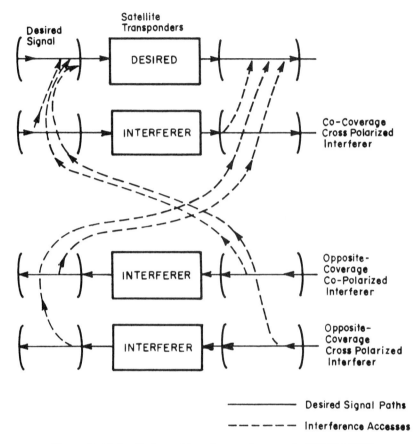

Figure 5.6.5.2 Cochannel Interference Accesses in INTELSAT V

coverage transmission signals, both co- and cross-polarized, and on both the up- and downlink.

An exact theoretical analysis of the system shown in Figure 5.6.5.1 has not been attempted and, instead, we have addressed a simpler system which does not have ISI. Even this more restictive system has not been previously analyzed, and thus the results presented are new. One facet of the results which has turned out to be of considerable interest is the (not unexpected) presence of a suppression of uplink interference. When digital computer simulations were run for the system without the up- and downlink filters, the suppression effects were evidenced and concurred with theory. However, as these filters were inserted and their band- width sufficiently narrowed to produce significant ISI, the suppression effects on the BER were reduced. What has been demonstrated is that, while the suppres- sion effect on uplink interferers can be small in a practical system, the non-

Gaussian characteristics persist. Additionally, as will be discussed, the manner in which the carrier-to-interference-power ration C/I is specified becomes important, whether or not C and/or I are modulated or unmodulated.

The dual approach to this problem is reflected in the organization of the following work. First, a theoretical analysis of the system will be presented which, as just discussed, falls somewhat short of the complete requirement since no ISI is included. We then present the results of digital computer simulations and show they are in accord with the theoretical ones when no filters are present. Further simulations are discussed in which the effects of ISI are included. The principal limitation of the simulation approach has been that when filters are added, it is difficult from a practical point of view to incorporate more than about two interferers.

In this section, an expression will be derived for the probability of bit error for a QPSK satellite system with up- and downlink co-channel interferers. The system model is shown in Figure 5.6.5.1 with the exception that no transmit or receive filters will be included and thus, there is no intersymbol interference.

Derivation of Probability of Bit Error

For a single carrier of amplitude ρ, the input to a nonlinear transponder is

$$e_i(t) = \rho e^{j(\omega_0 t + \lambda)} \tag{5.6.5.1}$$

and the output signal may be written (see Chapter 3 of Volume II) as

$$e_0(t) = g(\rho) e^{jf(\rho)} \cdot e^{j(\omega_0 t + \lambda)} \tag{5.6.5.2}$$

where $g(\rho)$ represents the AM-AM transfer characteristics and $f(\rho)$ the AM-PM dependence (this case has been referred to as "memoryless"). Here $\omega_0 = 2\pi f_0$ is the carrier frequency and ρ and λ can be time dependent. The functions g and f are assumed not to depend on frequency. In this case, the complex input signal with N_u and uplink interferers is

$$e_i(t) = A e^{j(\omega_0 t + \theta)} + N_u(t) e^{j\omega_0 t} + \sum_{k=1}^{n_u} B_k e^{j(\omega_0 + \Delta\omega_k)t + j\phi_k}$$

$$= \rho e^{j(\omega_0 t + \lambda)} \tag{5.6.5.3}$$

with A as the amplitude of the desired signal, B_k the co-channel interferer amplitudes, and the uplink noise with independent quadrature components

$$N_u(t) = N_{cu}(t) + jN_{su}(t). \tag{5.6.5.4}$$

The individual interferers are taken to be incoherent with respect to the desired signal, with the k-th interferer offset by $\Delta\omega_k$. Then defining

$$N_{cu_1}(t) = N_{cu}(t) + \sum_k B_k \cos(\Delta\omega_k t + \phi_k)$$

$$N_{su_1}(t) = N_{su}(t) + \sum_k B_k \sin(\Delta\omega_k t + \phi_k)$$

$$N_{u_1}(t) = N_{cu_1}(t) + jN_{su_1}(t) \tag{5.6.5.5}$$

the output signal is given approximately by (including only the linear term in a Taylor expansion)

$$e_0(t) \; \mathrm{a}\simeq g(A)e^{jf(A)}e^{j(\omega_0 t + \theta)}$$

$$+ j\frac{g(A)}{A}e^{jf(A)}[\mathrm{Im}\{N_{u1}e^{-j\theta}\}]e^{j(\omega_0 t + \theta)}$$

$$+ \frac{d}{dA}\{g(A)e^{jf(A)}\}[\mathrm{Re}\{N_{u1}e^{-j\theta}\}]e^{j(\omega_0 t + \theta)} \tag{5.6.5.6}$$

where Re $\{\cdot\}$ and Im $\{\cdot\}$ represent the real and imaginary parts of their arguments (this expansion is also similar to that of Equation 2.1.5.31). Retaining the linear term only implies that N_u and $\sum_{k=0}^{n_u} B_k$ are not too large with respect to A. A comparison with simulation results will show that this approximation is justified in most practical applications. We are thus assuming that errors are caused predominantly by noise on the downlink. If the downlink C/N is a few decibels worse than the uplink, as is often the case in practice, a study of typical QPSK bit error rate curves will quickly convince one that the contribution of the uplink noise to the overall error probability is negligible. Both $g(A)'$ and $f(A)'$ are given in linear units of volts/volts and radians/volts. If instead, $G(x_A)'$ and $F(x_A)'$ corresponding to $g(A)'$ and $f(A)'$, are given respectively in terms of decibels/ decibels and radians/decibels (as in the usual presentation of the AM-AM and AM-PM characteristics of a TWT), then it is easy to show that

$$G(x_A)' = \frac{Ag(A)'}{g(A)}$$

$$F(x_A)' = \frac{Af(A)'}{\alpha} \tag{5.6.5.7}^\dagger$$

with $\alpha = 20/\ln 10$. Then, omitting a common multiplicative factor[†]$ge^{j(\omega_0 t + f)}/$ A, the output becomes

$$e_0(t) = Ae^{j\theta} \simeq j[\mathrm{Im}\{N_{u_1}e^{-j\theta}\}]e^{j\theta} + [G' + j\alpha F']$$

$$\cdot [\mathrm{Re}\{N_{u_1}e^{-j\theta}\}]e^{j\theta}$$

$$= Ae^{j\theta} + N_{u_1} + [(G' - 1) + j\alpha F']$$

$$\cdot [\mathrm{Re}\{N_{u_1}e^{-j\theta}\}]e^{j\theta}. \tag{5.6.5.8}$$

[†]See Equation 2.1.3.5 for this relation.

[‡]In this no-filter ideal case, this omission does not affect the results. If filtering were present it could not be neglected.

It should be noted that the individual terms can be identified as

$$(G' - 1)\,\text{Re}\{\cdot\}: \qquad \text{component produced by AM-AM distortion}$$

$$j\alpha F'\,\text{Re}\{\cdot\}: \qquad \text{component produced by AM-PM distortion, which is orthogonal to the signal vector.}$$

Assuming n_u as uplink interferers, n_d downlink interferers, and $n = n_u + n_d$ as total interferers, the following is defined for the sake of convenience

$$\eta_{cu} = -N_{cu}\sin\theta + N_{su}\cos\theta$$

$$\eta_{su} = N_{cu}\cos\theta + N_{su}\sin\theta$$

$$\xi_k = \begin{cases} \Delta\omega_k t + \phi_k - \theta, & 1 \le k \le n_u \ (\text{uplink}) \\ \Delta\omega_k t + \phi_k, & n_u < k \le n \ (\text{downlink}) \end{cases}$$

$$N_d = N_{cd} + jN_{sd} \qquad (5.6.5.9)$$

where the downlink noise N_d is resolved into quadrature components. Adding downlink noise and interferers, the real part of the signal becomes, from Equation 5.6.5.8

$$\text{Re}\{e_0\} = A\cos\theta + \eta_c + N_{cd} + \alpha_\xi \qquad (5.6.5.10)$$

where

$$\eta_c = -\eta_{cu}\sin\theta + \eta_{su}(G'\cos\theta - \alpha F'\sin\theta)$$

$$\alpha_\xi = \sum_{k=1}^{n_u} B_k\,(\sin^2\theta + (G'\cos\theta - \alpha F'\sin\theta)^2)^{\frac{1}{2}}\sin\xi_k'$$

$$\qquad + \sum_{k=n_u+1}^{n} B_k\cos\xi_k \qquad (5.6.5.11)$$

and

$$\xi_k' = \xi_k + \tan^{-1}\left(\frac{G'\cos\theta - \alpha F'\sin\theta}{-\sin\theta}\right). \qquad (5.6.5.12)$$

Likewise, the imaginary part of e_0 becomes

$$\text{Im}\{e_0\} = A\sin\theta + \eta_s + N_{sd} + b_\xi \qquad (5.6.5.13)$$

where

$$\eta_s = \eta_{cu}\cos\theta + \eta_{su}(G'\sin\theta + \alpha F'\cos\theta)$$

$$b_\xi = \sum_{k=1}^{n_u} B_k (\cos^2 \theta + (G' \sin \theta + \alpha F' \cos \theta)^2)^{1/2} \sin \xi_k''$$

$$+ \sum_{k=n_u+1}^{n} B_k \sin \xi_k$$

and

$$\xi_k'' = \xi_k + \tan^{-1} \left(\frac{G' \sin \theta + \alpha F' \cos \theta}{\cos \theta} \right). \qquad (5.6.5.14)$$

The downlink noise can be written as

$$\overline{N_{cd}^2} = \overline{N_{sd}^2} = \sigma_d^2. \qquad (5.6.5.15)$$

Neglecting the signal space region where in-phase and quadrature components are both negative simultaneously, the probability of symbol error is

$$P_{es} \approx E \left\{ Q \left(\frac{A \cos \theta + \eta_c + \alpha_\xi}{\sigma_d} \right) + Q \left(\frac{A \sin \theta + \eta_s + b_\xi}{\sigma_d} \right) \right\}$$

$$\equiv \underset{\eta_c, a_\xi}{E} \{I_1\} + \underset{\eta_s, b_\xi}{E} \{I_2\}$$

$$\equiv P_{es,r} + P_{es,i} = 2P_e \qquad (5.6.5.16)$$

with obvious identifications for the $I_{1,2}$ and $P_{es,r}$, $P_{es,i}$ terms. Also $E\{\cdot\}$ is the expectation operator and $Q(x)$ is defined as

$$Q(x) = \frac{1}{\sqrt{2\pi}} \int_x^\infty e^{-t^2/2} \, dt = \frac{1}{2} \operatorname{erfc} \left(\frac{x}{\sqrt{2}} \right). \qquad (5.6.5.17)^\dagger$$

The bit error rate is taken as one half of the symbol error rate. For the BER region $<10^{-3}$, the approximation made below in Equation 5.6.5.14 is a good one.

Focusing on the first term in Equation 5.6.5.16, arising from the real part of e_0, it is straightforward to show, after some manipulation and using the characteristic function method, that the result after averaging over η_c is

$$\underset{\eta_c, a_\xi}{E} \{I_1\} = \underset{a_\xi}{E} \left\{ \frac{1}{\sqrt{2\pi}} \int_r^\infty e^{-1/2(z+x)^2} \, dz \right\} \qquad (5.6.5.18)$$

where

$$r = \left(2 \left(\frac{C}{N} \right)_{tr} \right)^{1/2} \cos \theta$$

$$x = \left(2\left(\frac{C}{N}\right)_{tr}\right)^{1/2} \frac{a_\xi}{A} \tag{5.6.5.19}$$

and

$$\left(\frac{C}{N}\right)_{tr} = \frac{1}{\left(\frac{C}{N}\right)_d^{-1} + \left(\frac{C'}{N}\right)_u^{-1}}$$

$$\left(\frac{C}{N}\right)_d = \frac{A^2}{2\sigma_d^2}$$

$$\left(\frac{C}{N}\right)_u = \frac{A^2}{2\sigma_u^2}$$

$$\left(\frac{C'}{N}\right)_u = \left(\frac{C}{N}\right)_u (\sin^2 \theta + (G' \cos \theta - \alpha F' \sin \theta)^{-1/2} \tag{5.6.5.20}$$

with

$$\sigma_u^2 = \overline{N_u^2}$$

$$C' = C (\sin^2 \theta + (G' \cos \theta - \alpha F' \sin \theta)^2)^{-1/2}. \tag{5.6.5.21}$$

Then, to average over a_ξ we have first from Equation 5.6.5.11

$$\left(2\left(\frac{C}{N}\right)_{tr}\right)^{1/2} \frac{a_\xi}{A} = \sum_{k=1}^{n} b_{kr} \sin \zeta_k \tag{5.6.5.22}$$

where

$$b_{kr} = \begin{cases} \dfrac{B_k}{A} (\sin^2 \theta + (G' \cos \theta - \alpha F' \sin \theta)^2)^{1/2} \\[2mm] \quad \cdot \left(2\left(\dfrac{C}{N}\right)_{tr}\right)^{1/2} & 1 \le k \le n_u \\[4mm] \dfrac{B_k}{A} \left(2\left(\dfrac{C}{N}\right)_{tr}\right)^{1/2} & n_u < k \le n \end{cases} \tag{5.6.5.23}$$

and

$$\zeta_k = \begin{cases} \xi_k' & 1 \le k \le n_u \\[2mm] \xi_k + \dfrac{\pi}{2} & n_u < k \le n. \end{cases} \tag{5.6.5.24}$$

The characteristic function of α is

$$E\{e^{jux}\} = \prod_{k=1}^{M} J_0(b_{kv}, u) \qquad (5.6.5.25)$$

with J_0 as a Bessel function of zero-th order. Conversely,

$$p(x) = \frac{1}{2\pi} \int_{-\infty}^{\infty} e^{-jux} \prod_{k=1}^{M} J_0(b_k, u) \, du. \qquad (5.6.5.26)$$

Thus, the average becomes

$$P_{es,r} = \frac{1}{\sqrt{2\pi}} \int_r^{\infty} dz \int_{-\infty}^{\infty} e^{-\frac{1}{2}(z+x)^2} \frac{1}{2\pi} \int_{-\infty}^{\infty} e^{-jux} \prod_{k=1}^{n} J_0(b_k u) \, du \, dx$$

$$= \frac{1}{2\pi} \int_r^{\infty} dz \int_{-\infty}^{\infty} e^{-\frac{u^2}{2}} \prod_{k=1}^{n} J_0(b_k u) e^{juz} \, du. \qquad (5.6.5.27)$$

The product of Bessel functions may be written as

$$\prod_{k=1}^{n} J_0(b_k u) = \sum_{m=0}^{\infty} C_{2m,r} u^{2m} \qquad (5.6.5.28)$$

with a recurrence relation for the coefficients derived in Section 5.4. Then,

$$P_{es,r} = \frac{1}{\sqrt{2\pi}} \int_r^{\infty} dz \sum_{m=0}^{\infty} C_{2m,r} \int_{-\infty}^{\infty} e^{-\frac{u^2}{2}} u^{2m} e^{juz} \, du. \qquad (5.6.5.29)$$

The integral over u is closely allied to the integral form of the Hermite polynomials He, and if Φ is defined as

$$\Phi_{2n}(x) = \frac{1}{\sqrt{2\pi}} He_{2n}(x) e^{-\frac{x^2}{2}} \qquad (5.6.5.30)$$

then,

$$P_{es,r} = \sum_{m=0}^{\infty} C_{2m,r}(-1)^m \int_r^{\infty} \Phi_{2m}(y) \, dy$$

$$= Q(r) + \sum_{m=1}^{\infty} C_{2m,r}(-1)^m \Phi_{2m-1}(r). \qquad (5.6.5.31)$$

It is noted that the co-channel interference dependence is contained in the coefficients $C_{2m,r}$.

In an analogous way, the average of I_2 can be derived:

$$P_{es,i} = Q(s) + \sum_{m=1}^{\infty} C_{2m,r}(-1)^m \Phi_{2m-1}(s) \qquad (5.6.5.32)$$

where

$$s = \left(2\left(\frac{C}{N}\right)_{ti}\right)^{1/2} \sin \theta,$$

$$\left(\frac{C}{N}\right)_{ti} = \frac{1}{\left(\frac{C}{N}\right)_d^{-1} + \left(\frac{C''}{N}\right)_u^{-1}} \qquad (5.6.5.33)$$

with

$$C'' = C (\cos^2 \theta + (G' \sin \theta + \alpha F' \cos \theta)^2)^{-1/2}. \qquad (5.6.5.34)$$

The coefficients $C_{2m,i}$ are also given by the approach in Section 5.4. The required expression for the BER has been derived.

Although this development is adequate in many cases, a more rapid convergence of the alternating series may be forced by a slight modification [41]. Defining, for the interference power,

$$I_v = \frac{1}{2} \sum_{k=1}^{n} b_{kr}^2 \qquad (5.6.5.35)$$

and taking Δ as a real number between zero and one, we can rewrite Equation 5.6.5.26 as

$$P_{es,r} = \frac{1}{2\pi} \int_r^\infty dz \int_{-\infty}^\infty e^{-\frac{1}{2}\{1 + \Delta I_r\}u^2}$$

$$\cdot \left[e^{\frac{\Delta I_r u^2}{2}} \prod_{k=1}^{M} J_0(b_k, u) \right] e^{juz} \, du. \qquad (5.6.5.36)$$

The expression for $P_{es,i}$ is similarly modified. The parameter Δ is empirically adjusted to provide a rapid convergence but, in general is taken to be small or zero if C/I is small and/or if only a small number of interferers are present, and, is taken to be larger, approaching 1, for cases in which the interference is near Gaussian. The inclusion of Δ will affect the details of the series expansion but does not alter the basic development. It is seen that the arguments of the Q and ϕ functions are modified by the multiplicative factor $(1 + \Delta I_r)^{-1/2}$.

Numerical Results

A computer program was developed and utilized to perform the extensive series calculations required to obtain numerical results. Here, a few specific examples will be presented.

In one case, the situation can be examined wherein all the co-channel interferers are on the downlink. In this case, the interference does not experience any nonlinearity and the previously derived results for a linear channel apply (see Section 5.4).

A particular case is shown in Figure 5.6.5.3 for C/I total $= 15$ dB with the BER as a function of the $(C/N)_d$ for the cases of 1, 3 and 6 (equal power) interferers and also for the case of the interference considered as additive Gaussian noise, i.e., $n = \infty$. The performance, in the case there is no interferer, is also shown. The uplink thermal noise was made negligible in comparison with that on the downlink by setting $(C/N)_u = 40$ dB.

Figure 5.6.5.4 provides similar results for the case where all interferers are placed on the uplink. The transponder operating point was 2 dB input backoff

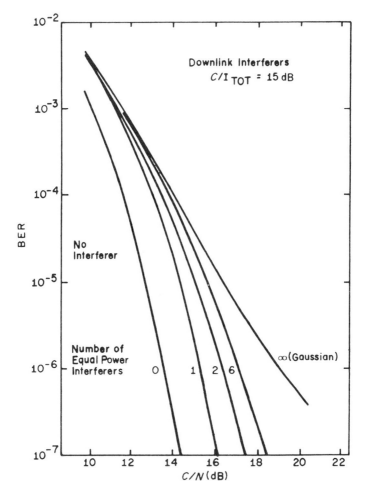

Figure 5.6.5.3   BER as a Function of C/N for Downlink Interferers with
                      C/I $=$ 15 dB

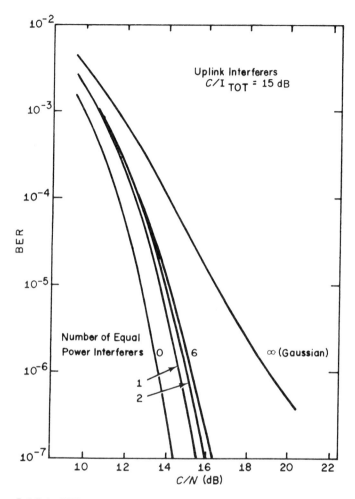

Figure 5.6.5.4 BER as a Function of C/N for Uplink Interferers with C/I = 15 dB

(IBO) with values of G' and F' representative of an INTELSAT-IV nonlinearity. The results are not very sensitive to reasonably small variations in G' and F'.

It is quickly apparent from these two sets of results that the influence of uplink interference is much less than downlink interference. This follows from the not unexpected small signal suppression which occurs for the uplink interferers. A closer study reveals this suppression to be about 2.9 dB. That is, if everything else remains fixed, a C/I total of x dB on the uplink (and no downlink interferers) will result in the same performance as when the C/I total equals $x + 2.9$ dB on the downlink (with no uplink interferers). Using the development of Section 3.2.11, the magnitude of this suppression could in fact be predicted and is suppression $= -10 \log_{10} (\sin^2 \theta + (G' \cos \theta - \alpha F' \sin \theta)^2)$ (5.6.5.37)

for the 2 dB IBO, $G' = 0.19$, and $F' = 0.0087$.

When only one interferer is present, the performance is much different from what would be predicted using the assumption under which the interference is replaced by an equivalent power Gaussian noise source. Even with six interferers, the departure from the Gaussian approximation can be significant, especially when the ratio I/N is large.

It should be noted that the results in Figures 5.6.5.3 and 5.6.5.4 are based on $\theta = 45°$, that is, on an ideal QPSK. In the practical case, particularly with filtering, there is a scattering of points in signal space at the sampling instant. This scattering will cause an effective degradation in the amplitude of the carrier vector (from the unmodulated value). We have called this degradation, in decibels, D. In the preceeding figures no degradation was assumed, that is, D = 0 dB. A representation of these two parameters in signal space is shown in Figure 5.6.5.5. In the real situation, the actual value of C/I is replaced by a lower (worse) "effective" C/I which is degraded by approximately D dB. Thus, if D is large, and indicative of considerable ISI, relatively large values of an actual C/I may be effectively reduced so that the observed system performance is at considerable variance with the Gaussian approximation. That is to say, for example, that for a C/I_{tot} of 18 dB from six equal power downlink interferers, the Gaussian approximation indicates only an approximate 0.3 dB worse C/N performance at a BER of 10^{-6} than when the interference is considered as peak-limited. However, if D is large, say 3 dB, the effective level of the C/I becomes

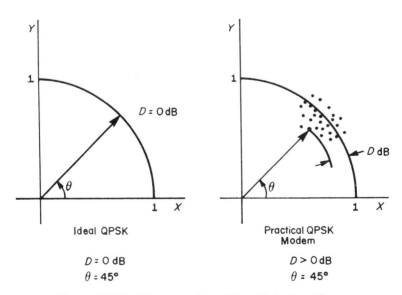

Figure 5.6.5.5   Representation of D and θ in Signal Space

about 15 dB at which point the difference in C/N performance is significant, about 2 dB.

Comparison With Simulation

On a limited basis, the results of the foregoing development have been compared with digital computer time domain simulations of the same system configurations. Figure 5.6.5.6 shows the results of several such simulations for a single interferer at a C/I of 15 dB. The interferer was alternately placed on the up- and downlink. In the uplink case, the interferer passed through the transponder which is common to the desired signal. For the downlink case, it passed through an independent

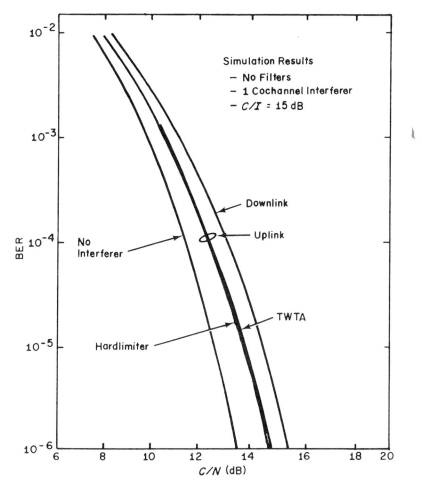

Figure 5.6.5.6   Simulation Results at C/I = 15 dB

nonlinear transponder. In either case, a frequency offset between the two signals was employed to avoid coherent effects. Two types of satellite nonlinearities were modeled, a hardlimiter without AM-PM and a softlimiter with AM-AM and AM-PM characteristics similar to the INTELSAT IV at a 2 dB IBO. Only a small difference is evidenced between the two types of nonlinearities for an uplink interferer and essentially no difference when the interference is on the downlink.

In these simulations, no filters were employed and thus, in the case when there is no interferer and no nonlinearity, the performance matches that of the ideal QPSK. When an interferer and a nonlinearity are present, a comparison can be made with the theoretical results (Figures 5.6.5.3–5.6.5.4). At a 15 dB C/I, the congruence is excellent, differing by less than 0.1 dB over the practical range of BER.

In the theoretical development, only the linear term was retained in the expansion for the uplink interferers which led to Equation 5.6.5.6. Using the simulation results, it is relatively easy to assess empirically at what point this approximation breaks down. Figures 5.6.5.7 and 5.6.5.8 show the comparison

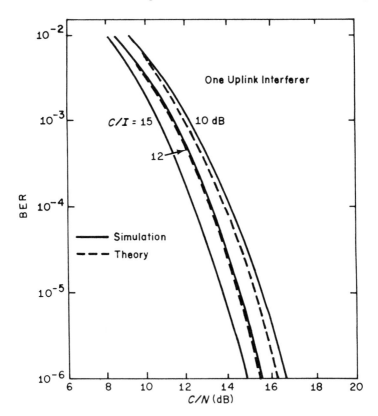

Figure 5.6.5.7 Comparison of Simulation and Theory for One Uplink Interferer

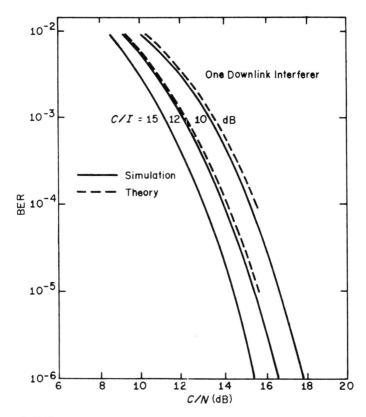

Figure 5.6.5.8 Comparison of Simulation and Theory for One Downlink Interferer

of theoretical and simulation results at $C/I_{tot} = 15, 12, 10$ dB for the up- and downlink. At $C/I = 15$ dB, the agreement, as pointed out above, is virtually perfect. At 12 dB, the downlink shows an approximate 0.2 dB difference while the uplink is still in good agreement. The uplink results show better congruence probably because of suppression effects on the interferer. At 10 dB, there is about a 0.2 dB difference between the two approaches, for both the up- and downlink results show only fair convergence. At this low value of C/I, there is probably some error in the simulation results which showed increased sensitivity to the form of the modulating sequence. It appears then that the theoretical approach provides accurate results to the region of $C/I = 12$ dB.

These comparisons have been done for the case where there is one interferer. With many interferers, it must be considered that the peak uplink interference effect is larger than the average by a factor $10 \log n_u$ (dB), n_u being the number of (equal power) uplink interferers. Of course, the peak interference occurs only rarely, particularly as the value of n becomes large, but for a large value of n, this peak-to-average factor must be considered in accessing the point at which the expansion of Equation 5.6.5.6 is no longer valid.

Simulation Results Including Intersymbol Interference

As just considered, the theoretical results are in good agreement with those of digital simulation in most cases of interest as long as no transmit or receive filters are present. When filters are added, the presence of intersymbol interference significantly affects the simulation results so that good agreement is no longer evidenced.

Most computer simulations were run using a single interferer and ideal filters; more elaborate interference configurations are not presently available. With tight filtering (i.e., small BT products), particularly, the results were fairly sensitive to several factors: 1) carrier frequency coherence between desired and interfering signals, 2) modulating sequence, and 3) synchronization and offsets in symbol timing between desiring and interfering signals.

The effect of transmit and receive filters is shown in Figure 5.6.5.9. Except as indicated, the satellite nonlinearity was a hardlimiter function and the filters were ideal cutoff with BT products equal to 1.15. Except for the case where there is no interferer, C/I was set to 15 dB and the interferer was modulated at the same data rate as the desired signal. When only a receive filter is present, more degradation is apparent than when only a transmit filter is used. With both a transmit and receive filter, the performance is most degraded. In each case, an uplink interferer causes less degradation than a downlink one. However, the amount of uplink suppression effect is smaller than the no-filter, no-intersymbol interference case discussed in the preceding Section.

In Figure 5.6.5.10, the case of both transmit and receive filtering is shown again but with a slightly wider receive BT product of 1.23. These results represent an average over modulating sequences and symbol offsets. This case will be discussed in more detail in the next Section. Here, it suffices to say that when the interferer is unmodulated, the degree of uplink suppression effect appears to be relatively small. When the interferer is modulated, the amount of suppression appears again to be significant, about the same as for the no-filter case.

Definition C/I and the Effect of Modulation

In studying the effects of co-channel interference upon a QPSK signal, it has been noted that the specification of C/I could be ambiguous and could lead to different interpretations of the results. The potential problem exists since both C and I could be specified as either modulated or unmodulated power. When the signals are not filtered or filtered just a little, there is little difference between modulated and unmodulated power. In practical cases, this could correspond to an interferer being an FDMA/FM signal. However, since rather severe bandwidth limiting is required in the TDMA/QPSK case, to avoid adjacent channel interference, appreciable reductions in power may result when modulation is applied. When C is a QPSK signal and I is an FM one, $C_{mod} < C_{unmod}$ and $I_{mod} \simeq I_{unmod}$.

Then,

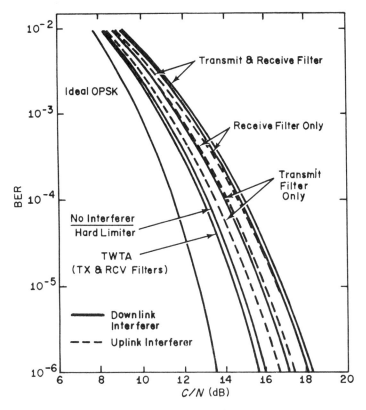

Figure 5.6.5.9 Simulation Results Including Transmit and Receive Filters

$$\frac{C_{\text{mod}}}{I_{\text{unmod}}} \simeq \frac{C_{\text{mod}}}{I_{\text{mod}}} < \frac{C_{\text{unmod}}}{I_{\text{unmod}}} \simeq \frac{C_{\text{unmod}}}{I_{\text{mod}}} , \qquad \begin{array}{c} C - \text{QPSK} \\ I - \text{FM.} \end{array} \qquad (5.6.5.38)$$

When both C and I are QPSK signals, the $C_{\text{mod}} < C_{\text{unmod}}$ and $I_{\text{mod}} < I_{\text{unmod}}$ and thus,

$$\frac{C_{\text{mod}}}{I_{\text{unmod}}} < \frac{C_{\text{mod}}}{I_{\text{mod}}} \simeq \frac{C_{\text{unmod}}}{I_{\text{unmod}}} < \frac{C_{\text{unmod}}}{I_{\text{mod}}} , \qquad \begin{array}{c} C - \text{QPSK} \\ I - \text{QPSK.} \end{array} \qquad (5.6.5.39)$$

In the theoretical results presented in this Section, this distinction between modulated and unmodulated C and I was not important since the tacit assumption was that no filters existed and the modulated powers equaled the unmodulated powers. It is clear, however, that when the results are applied in a practical situation, then both C and I should be interpreted as a total power that is either modulated or unmodulated depending on what is the case.

In the simulation results, both C and I are taken to be unmodulated power in the initial specification of the computer runs. If, in fact, C or I is modulated

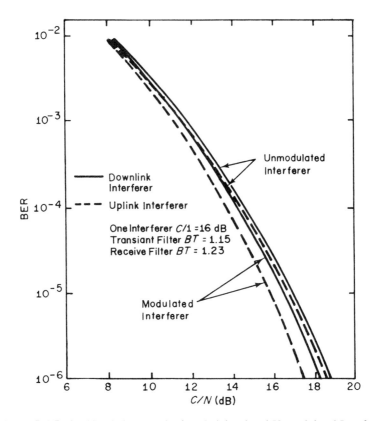

Figure 5.6.5.10 Simulation Results for Modulated and Unmodulated Interferer

and filtering is present, then C or I will be reduced. An example of this effect is shown in Figure 5.6.5.10 for an up- and downlink interferer both modulated and unmodulated. C is modulated in each case and the filtering BT products are fairly small, 1.15 at the transmitter and 1.23 at the receiver. The results for I_{unmod} fail to exhibit significant uplink suppression. When I is modulated, however, there is a significant reduction in the interference effect. There appear to be at least two reasons for this. First, the average power of I may be significantly reduced by the filtering of the modulated spectrum. Also, the instantaneous power of the (unsynchronized) interferer at the sampling instant (in the desired signal) may be greatly reduced due to filtering induced envelope fluctuations. It is seen that with I modulated, there is a recurrence of an uplink suppression effect which again is probably tied to the envelope fluctuations which occur when I is modulated.

An understanding of the effects of modulation on co-channel interference is important in the determination of link budgets. The ratio of C/I is normally specified in system studies with both C and I unmodulated. For the sake of convenience, C/N is also usually given for C unmodulated. In the real situation, C and I are usually modulated power levels. Thus, available results must be studied to determine whether in light of Equations 5.6.5.38 and 5.6.5.39, a correction factor should be applied to a particular C/I.

Conclusions

Several results relevant to the co-channel interference environment found in current and future satellite systems have been presented. Existing theory was extended to treat the effect on the QPSK BER of an arbitrary number of up- and downlink angle modulated interferers with a nonlinear satellite transponder. The theoretical results were compared with results of a digital computer simulation program and good agreement was demonstrated. It was shown, however, that the presence of tight filtering in practical systems could reduce or eliminate one feature of the co-channel interference, namely, the uplink suppression effect. Nevertheless the non-Gaussian nature of the interference was shown to be often still significant.

5.6.6 From TDMA/PSK Into TDMA/PSK

In this case, cases (a), (b) and (c) of Section 5.4 can occur. For cases (b) and (c), the approaches explained in Section 5.5.6 can be used. For case (a), the analysis shown in Section 5.6.5 can be used.

The difference is that the interference appears only when the interference TDMA/PSK signal exists in the burst mode.

5.7 EXERCISES

1. Prove the result of the second term of Equation 5.1.5.1.

2. Draw the curve calculating Equation 5.2.2.2 for $f_e = 30$ Hz, $f_d = 1 \times 10^6$ Hz.

3. Derive Equations 5.4.17 and 5.4.18 yourself.

4. Derive Equation 5.4.19.

5. Derive Equation 5.6.5.6.

6. Find a case from Equations 5.1.1 and 5.1.18 where the interference power falling on the top frequency channel is not the largest. In most cases, the interference power falling on the top frequency channel is the largest in comparison with the other frequency channels.

7. In TV/FM and FDM/FM modulations, the energy dispersal modulation sometimes dominates because of a small baseband modulation power. In cases of interferences from the energy dispersed FM signals with small

baseband signal modulation into SCPC/FM and SCPC/PSK signals, prove why the line rate (approximately 15 KHz) energy dispersal modulation is better than that of the frame rate (approximately 30 Hz). See Section 5.2.2.

8. In Figures 5.4.3, 5.4.4, and 5.4.5, study how the effects of interferences become closer to those of the cases where the interference statistics are approximated by Gaussian process, when the number of interferences becomes larger.

9. Think of the reason why the cochannel interferences analyzed in Sections 5.4 and 5.6.5 have smaller effects on error probabilities than the Gaussian noises which have the same power.

10. Think of the difference of interference effects on FM and PSK signals and why these two cases are different.

REFERENCES

[1] G. N. Watson, *The Theory of Bessel Functions*, Cambridge, England: Cambridge University Press, 1958.

[2] Edited by M. Abramowitz and I. A. Stegun, *Handbook of Mathematical Functions*, New York: Dover Publications, 1970.

[3] M. Schwartz, W. R. Bennett, and S. Stein, *Communication Systems and Techniques*, New York: McGraw-Hill, 1966.

[4] P. R. Harmos, *Measure Theory*, New York: Van Nostrand, 1974.

[5] Members of the Technical Staff, *Transmission Systems for Communications*, Rev. 4th Ed. Winston-Salem, N.C.: Springer-Verlag, 1971.

[6] B. D. Holbrook and J. T. Dixon, "Load Rating Theory for Multichannel Amplifiers," *Bell Syst. Tech. J.*, Vol. 18, October 1939.

[7] W. R. Bennett, "Spectra of Quantized Signals," *Bell Syst. Tech. J.*, Vol. 27, April 1948, pp. 446–472.

[8] R. W. Hamming, "Error Detecting and Error Correcting Codes, *Bell Syst. Tech. J.*, Vol. 29, 1950, pp. 147–160.

[9] F. Gray, "Pulse Code Communications," U.S. Patent 2632058, March 17, 1953.

[10] J. M. Sipress, "A New Class of Selected Tenary Pulse Transmission Plans for Digital Transmission Lines," *IEEE Trans. Commun. Tech.*, Vol. COM-13, No. 3, September 1965, pp. 366-372.

[11] W. R. Bennett and J. R. Davey, *Data Transmission*, New York: McGraw-Hill, 1965.

[12] B. R. Saltzberg, "Intersymbol Interference Error Bounds with Application to Ideal Bandlimited Signaling," *IEEE Trans. Inform. Theory*, Vol. IT-14, July 1968, pp. 563–568.

[13] R. Lugannani, "Intersymbol Interference and Probability of Error in Digital Systems," *IEEE Trans. Inform. Theory*, Vol. IT-15, November 1969, pp. 682–688.

[14] F. E. Glave, "An Upper Bound on the Probability of Error Due to Intersymbol Interference for Correlated Digital Systems," *IEEE Trans. Inform. Theory*, Vol. IT-18, May 1972, pp. 356–362.

[15] O. Shimbo and I. Celebiler, "The Probability of Error Due to Intersymbol Interference and Gaussian Noise in Digital Communication Systems," *IEEE Trans. Commun.*, Vol. COM-19, April 1971, pp. 113–119.

[16] E. Y. Ho and Y. S. Yeh, "A New Approach for Evaluating the Error Probability in the Presence of Intersymbol Interference and Additive Gaus-

sian Noise,'' *Bell Syst. Tech. J.*, Vol. 49, November 1970, pp. 2249–2265.

[17] J. P. A. Albuquerque, R. Mukunda, and O. Shimbo, "On the Choice of an Efficient TV Energy Dispersal Wave Form for Interference Reduction," *IEEE Trans. Commun.*, Vol. COM-34, No. 9, September 1986, pp. 965–969.

[18] Z. Kiyasu, "Power Spectrum of Frequency Modulated Signals," *Journal of Electrical Communication Engineers of Japan*, November 1951.

[19] S. J. Campanella, H. G. Suyderhoud, and M. Wachs, "Frequency Modulation and Variable-Slope Delta Modulation in SCPC Satellite Transmission," *IEEE*, Satellite Communication Special Issue, March 1977, pp. 419–434.

[20] R. Sampaio-Neto and J. P. A. Albuquerque, "Intermodulation Effects in the Transmission of Voice-Activated SCPC/FM Carriers Through a Nonlinear Repeater," *IEEE Trans. Commun.*, Vol. COM-29, No. 10, October 1981, pp. 1537–1547.

[21] L. E. Franks, "A Model for the Random Video Process, *Bell Syst. Tech. J.*, Vol. 45, No. 4, April 1966, pp. 609–630.

[22] A. A. Ali, "FM Spectrum of Video Signals," *Proc. IEEE*, Vol. 70, No. 3, March 1982, pp. 306–307.

[23] INTELSAT, BG/T Temp. 39-XXE, 30 November 1981, Carrier Interleaving Requirements for INTELSAT V and V-A Leased Transponders.

[24] O. Shimbo, "General Formula for Power Spectra of Digital FM Signals," *Proc. IEE*, Vol. 113, No. 11, November 1966, pp. 1783–1788.

[25] W. R. Bennett and S. O. Rice, "Spectral Density and Auto-Correlation Functions Associated with Binary Frequency-Shift Keying," *Bell Syst. Tech. J.*, Vol. 42, 1963, pp. 2355–2385.

[26] J. Saltz, "Spectral Density Function of Multilevel Continuous-Phase f.m.," *IEEE Trans.*, Vol. IT-11, 1966, pp. 429–433.

[27] G. Robinson, O. Shimbo, and R. Fang, "PSK Signal Power Spectrum Spread Produced by Memoryless Nonlinear TWTs," *COMSAT Tech. Rev.*, Vol. 3, No. 2, Fall 1973, pp. 227–256.

[28] O. Shimbo and C. Loo, "Digital Computation of FM Distortion Due to Bandpass Filters," *IEEE Trans. Commun.*, Vol. COM-17, No. 5, October 1969, pp. 571–574.

[29] E. Bedrosian and S. O. Rice, "Distortion and Crosstalk in Linearly Filtered, Angle Modulated Signals," *Proc. IEEE*, Vol. 56, No. 1, 1968, pp. 2–13.

[30] W. R. Bennett, H. E. Curtis, and S. O. Rice, "Interchannel Interference in FM and PM systems Under Noise Loading Conditions," *Bell Syst. Tech. J.*, Vol. 34, 1955, pp. 601–636.

[31] J. H. Roberts, E. Bedrosian, and S. O. Rice, "FM Distortion: A Comparison of Theory and Measurement," *Proc. IEEE*, Vol. 57, No. 4, 1969, pp. 728–732.

[32] CCIR, Recommendations 464-1 (1970–1982), (Study Program 20/4), Pre-Emphasis Characteristics for Frequency-Modulation Systems for Frequency-Division Multiplex Telephony in the Fixed-Satellite Service.

[33] CCIR, Recommendation 405-1 (1959–1963–1970), (Question 3/9), Pre-Emphasis Characteristics for Frequency Modulation Radio-Relay Systems for Television.

[34] O. Shimbo, "Threshold Characteristics of FM Signals Demodulated by an FM Discriminator," *IEEE Trans.*, Vol. IT-15, 1969, pp. 540–549.

[35] M. C. Wang, in J. L. Lawson and G. E. Uhlenbeck (Ed.), *Threshold Signals*, New York: McGraw-Hill, 1950.

[36] N. M. Blachman and J. H. Roberts, "FM Click Rates: A Simple Derivation," *Electron. Lett.*, Vol. 10, No. 15, 1974, pp. 305–307.

[37] S. O. Rice, "Noise in FM Receivers," in M. Rosenblatt (Ed.), *Proc. Symposium on Time-Series Analysis*, New York: John Wiley, 1963, pp. 395–422.

[38] S. Morita and Y. Ito, "A High Sensitivity Receiver for the Frequency Modulated Waves," *J. Inst. Elec. Commun. Engrg.* (Japan), Vol. 42, August 1959, p. 738.

[39] L. H. Enloe, "Decreasing the Threshold in FM by Frequency Feedback," *Proc. IRE*, Vol. 50, January 1962, pp. 18–30.

[40] J. G. Chaffee, "The Application of Negative Feedback to Frequency-Modulation Systems," *Bell Syst. Tech. J.*, Vol. 18, July 1939, p. 404.

[41] O. Shimbo, R. J. Fang, and M. I. Celebiler, "Performance of M-ary PSK Systems in Gaussian Noise and Intersymbol Interference," *IEEE Trans. Inform. Theory*, Vol. IT-19, January 1973, pp. 44–58.

[42] O. Shimbo, M. I. Celebiler, and R. Fang, "Performance Analysis of DPSK Systems in Both Thermal Noise and Intersymbol Interference," *IEEE Trans. Commun. Tech.*, Vol. COM-19, December 1971, pp. 1179–1188.

[43] R. Fang and O. Shimbo, "Unified Analysis of a Class of Digital Systems in Additive Noise and Interferences," *IEEE Trans. Commun.*, Vol. COM-21, No. 10, October 1973.

[44] S. Benedetto, E. Biglieri, and R. Daffara, "Modeling and Performance Evaluation of Nonlinear Satellite Links—A Volterra Series Approach," *IEEE Trans. Aerosp. Electron. Syst.*, Vol. AES-15, No. 4, July 1979, pp. 494–507.

[45] INTELSAT Studies Contract to COMSAT, Contract INTEL-317, Subtask TSC-317-85-325, February 1986, "Effects of Spacecraft Phase Noise on Low Data Rates Links for the INTELSAT Space Segment."

[46] J. Saltz, J. R. Sheehan, and D. J. Paris, "Data Transmission by Combined AM and PM," *Bell Syst. Tech. J.*, Vol. 50, September 1971, pp. 2399–2419.

[47] C. M. Thomas, M. Y. Weidner, and S. H. Durrani, "Digital Amplitude-Phase Keying with M-ary Alphabets," *IEEE Trans. Commun. Tech.*,

Vol. COM-22, No. 2, February 1974.

[48] J. C. Hancock and R. W. Lucky, "Performance of Combined Amplitude and Phase-Modulated Communication Systems," *IRE Trans. Commun. Syst.*, Vol. CS-8, December 1960, pp. 232–237.

[49] G. R. Welti, "Pulse Amplitude-and-Phase Modulation," *Proc. Second Int. Conf. on Digital Satelite Communications*, Paris, November 1972, pp. 208–217.

[50] G. R. Welti, "Application of Hybrid Modulation to FDMA Telephony via Satellite," *COMSAT Tech. Rev.*, Vol. 3, No. 2, Fall 1973, pp. 419–430.

[51] C. M. Thomas, D. L. May, and G. R. Welti, "Hybrid Amplitude and Phase Modulation," *IEEE Trans. Commun. Tech.*, Vol. COM-23, No. 6, June 1975, pp. 634–645.

[52] E. Bedrosian and S. O. Rice, "The Output Properties of Volterra Systems (Nonlinear Systems with Memory) Driven by Harmonic and Gaussian Input," *Proc. IEEE*, Vol. 59, No. 12, December 1971, pp. 1688–1707.

[53] R. J. Westcott, "Investigation of Multiple FM/FDM Carriers Through Satellite TWT Operating Saturation, *Proc. IEE*, Vol. 114, No. 6, June 1967, p. 726.

[54] K. Y. Eng and On-Ching Yue, *IEEE Trans. Aerosp. Electron. Syst.*, Vol. AES-17, No. 3, May 1981, pp. 438–445.

[55] J. C. Fuenzalida, O. Shimbo, and W. L. Cook, "Time Domain Analysis of Intermodulation Effects Caused by Nonlinear Amplifiers," *COMSAT Tech. Rev.*, Vol. 3, No. 1, Spring 1973, pp. 89–143.

[56] R. Fletcher and M. J. D. Powell, "A Rapidly Convergent Descent Method for Minimization," *The Computer Journal*, Vol. 6, 1963–1964, pp. 163–168.

[57] O. Shimbo and L. Nguyen, "Intelligible Crosstalk Between Two FDM/FM Carriers Accessing Double Cascaded Nonlinear Amplifiers," *IEEE Trans. Commun.*, Vol. COM-30, No. 8, August 1982, pp. 1993–2000.

[58] B. A. Pontana and O. Shimbo, "TDMA Modulation Transfer Noise on FM Signals Sharing a Common TWT," in *Proc. 3rd Int. Conf. on Digital Satellite Communications*, November 11–13, 1975, Kyoto, Japan, pp. 73–80.

[59] N. A. Mathews, "Time Domain Analysis of Distortion and Crosstalk in Dual TV/FM Transmission Through a Single Satellite Transponder—Computation of Crosstalk Interference," unpublished, December 1983, INTELSAT.

[60] P. Y. Chang and O. Shimbo, "Input Power Assignment of Multi-Carrier System from Given Output Power Levels," *IEEE Trans. Commun.*, Vol. COM-27, No. 10, October 1979, pp. 1577–1584.

[61] O. Shimbo, "Effects of Intermodulation, AM/PM Conversion, and Addition Noise in Multi-Carrier TWT Systems," *Proc. IEEE*, Vol. 59, No. 2, February 1971, pp. 230–238.

[62] P. Y. Chang and O. Shimbo, "Effects of one Large Signal on Small Signals in a Memoryless Nonlinear Bandpass Amplifier," *IEEE Trans. Commun.*, Vol. COM-28, May 1980, pp. 739–743.

[63] R. C. Chapman and J. B. Millard, "Intelligible Crosstalk Between Frequency Modulated Carriers Through AM-PM Conversion," *IEEE Trans. Commun. Syst.*, Vol. CS-12, pp. 160–166.

[64 J. Bryson, "Intelligible Crosstalk in Multiple-Carrier FM Systems with Amplitude Limiting and AM-PM Conversion," *IEEE Trans. Commun. Tech.*, Vol. COM-19, June 1971, pp. 366–368.

[65] G. R. Stette, "Intelligible Crosstalk in Nonlinear Amplifiers: Calculation of AM-PM Transfer," *IEEE Trans. Commun.*, Vol. COM-23, No. 2, February 1975, pp. 265–269.

[66] O. Shimbo and B. A. Pontano, "A General Theory for Intelligible Crosstalk between Frequency-Division Multiplexed Angle-Modulated Carriers," *IEEE Trans. Commun.*, Vol. COM-24, No. 9, September 1976, pp. 999–108.

[67] O. Shimbo and L. N. Nguyen, "Intelligible Crosstalk Between Two FDM/FM Carriers Accessing Double Cascaded Nonlinear Amplifiers," *IEEE Trans. Commun.*, Vol. COM-30, No. 8, August 1982, pp. 1993–2000.

[68] U.S.A. Patent, O. Shimbo and L. N. Nguyen, Patent No. 4,500,984, February 19, 1985.

[69] D. Chakraborty, J. Ehrmann, and E. W. McCune, "Wideband Klystron High-Power Amplifiers for FDM/FM/FDMA Applications," *COMSAT Tech. Rev.*, Vol. 14, No. 1, Spring 1984, pp. 53–82.

[70] J. P. A. Albuquerque, O. Shimbo, and L. N. Nguyen, "Modulation Transfer Noise Effects from a Continuous Digital Carrier to FDM/FM Carriers in Memoryless Nonlinear Devices," *IEEE Trans. Commun.*, Vol. COM-32, No. 4, April 1984, pp. 337–345.

[71] J. P. A. Albuquerque, O. Shimbo, and L. N. Nguyen, "A Power Series Expansion Approach to Evaluate Modulation Transfer Effects from Digital Carriers to FDM/FM Carriers in Memoryless Nonlinear Devices," *IEEE Trans. Commun.*, Vol. COM-32, No. 4, April 1984, pp. 346–353.

[72] J. P. A. Albuquerque, O. Shimbo, and L. N. Nguyen, "Modulation Transfer and Other Impairments in Multi-Carrier QPSK Transmission Through a Memoryless Device," in *Proc. IEEE Int. Conf. on Communications*, May 14–17, 1984, Amsterdam, Netherlands, pp. 330–335.

[73] J. P. A. Albuquerque, O. Shimbo, and L. N. Nguyen, "Modulation Transfer Noise Effects from TDMA Carriers to FDM/FM Carriers in Memoryless Nonlinear Devices," *IEEE Trans. Commun.*, Vol. COM-32, No. 11, November 1984, pp. 1191–1195.

[74] M. P. Stojkovic and Z. K. Stojanovic, "Error Probability Variation Due to the Nonlinearity of the TDMA/PSK Multicarrier System Caused by On-Off Bursting," *IEEE Trans. Commun.*, Vol. COM-32, No. 11, November 1984, pp. 1196–1200.

[75] R. J. F. Fang, "Modulation Transfer from TDMA On-Off Bursting to FM Carriers in Memoryless Nonlinear Devices: Part 1—Power Spectra," *IEEE Trans. Commun.*, Vol. COM-27, No. I, January 1979, pp. 94–100.

[76] R. J. F. Fang, "Modulation Transfer from TDMA On-Off Bursting to FM Carriers in Memoryless Nonlinear Devices: Part II—Baseband Performance," *IEEE Trans. Commun.*, Vol. COM-26, No. 4, April 1978, pp. 439–449.

[77] O. Shimbo and R. Fang, "Effects of Cochannel Interference and Gaussian Noise in M-ary PSK Systems," *COMSAT Tech. Rev.*, Vol. 3, No. 1, Spring 1973, pp. 183–207.

[78] D. J. Kennedy and O. Shimbo, "Cochannel Interference in Nonlinear QPSK Satellite Systems," *IEEE Trans. Commun.*, Vol. COM-29, No. 5, May 1981, pp. 582–592.

[79] E. K. Koh and O. Shimbo, "Computation of Interference into Angle-Modulated Systems Carrying Multichannel Telephone Signals," *IEEE Trans. Commun.*, Vol. COM-24, February 1976, pp. 259–263.

[80] B. A. Pontano, J. C. Fuenzalida, and N. K. M. Chitre, "Interference into Angle-Modulated Systems Carrying Multichannel Telephony Signals," *IEEE Trans. Commun.*, Vol. COM-21, June 1973, pp. 714–727.

[81] A. S. Rosenbaum, "PSK Error Performance in Gaussian Noise and Interference," *Bell Syst. Tech. J.*, Vol. 48, No. 2, February 1969, pp. 413–442.

[82] V. K. Prabhu, "Error Rate Consideration for Coherent Phase-Shift Keyed Systems with Co-Channel Interference," *Bell Syst., Tech. J.*, Vol. 48, No. 3, March 1969, pp. 743–767.

[83] S. Benedetto, E. Biglieri, and V. Castellani, "Combined Effects of Intersymbol, Interchannel, and Co-Channel Interference in M-ary CPSK Systems," *IEEE Trans. Commun.*, Vol. COM-21, September 1973, pp. 997–1008.

[84] A. S. Rosenbaum, "Binaray PSK Error Probabilities with Multiple Co-channel Interferences," *IEEE Trans. Commun. Tech.*, Vol. COM-18, June 1970, pp. 241–253.

[85] M. Stojkovic, Unpublished Report in INTELSAT, "Effects of Distorted Interferences on PSK Signals."

[86] N. M. Blachman, "Bandpass Nonlinearities," *IEEE Trans. Inform. Theory*, Vol. IT-10, April 1964, pp. 162–165.

[87] V. K. Prabu, "Performance of Coherent Phase-Shift-Keyed Systems with Intersymbol Interference," *IEEE Trans. Inform. Theory*, Vol. IT-17, July 1971, pp. 418–431.

[88] N. M. Blachman, "FM Reception and the Zeros of Narrow-Band Gaussian Noise," *IEEE Trans. Inform. Theory*, Vol. IT-10, July 1964, pp. 235–241.

INDEX